{ c a p t u r e d } by history

Books by John Toland

Nonfiction
Ships in the Sky
Battle: The Story of the Bulge
But Not in Shame: The Six Months After Pearl Harbor
The Dillinger Days
The Flying Tigers
The Last 100 Days
The Rising Sun: The Decline and Fall of the Japanese Empire 1936–1945
Adolf Hitler
Hitler: A Pictorial Biography
No Man's Land
Infamy: Pearl Harbor and Its Aftermath
In Mortal Combat: Korea, 1950–1953

Fiction
Gods of War
Occupation

John Toland

{ c a p t u r e d } by history

One Man's Vision of Our Tumultuous Century

St. Martin's Press ❧ New York

Production Editor: David Stanford Burr

Design: Songhee Kim

Library of Congress Cataloging-in-Publication Data

Toland, John.
  Captured by history : one man's vision of our tumultuous century / John Toland.
      p. cm.
    ISBN 0-312-15490-9
    1. Toland, John. 2. Historians—United States—Biography.
  I. Title.
  D15.T59A3   1997
  973'.07202—dc21
    [B]   97-1619
                                                                  CIP

First Edition: July 1997

10 9 8 7 6 5 4 3 2 1

To my wife, Toshiko

Contents

Contents

Volume II: Living History

Volume III: Adolf Hitler

Acknowledgments

This book could not have been written without the cooperation of a number of people in Europe, Asia, and North America, particularly those who had lived in Japan and Hitler's Germany as well as many in the United States and those in Eastern Europe who were still living behind the Iron Curtain at the time much of the research was done many years ago. I am also grateful to the National Archives, the Franklin D. Roosevelt Library, and the Library of Congress, recipients of my documents, letters, and tapes of interviews with those who were close to Hitler and in his inner circles as well as all material on Japan, China, Korea, and Southeast Asia, and the Philippines. These tapes are made available to all researchers once an interviewee is dead.

I would also like to thank five people who made outstanding contributions to this book: my chief assistant and interpreter, my wife, Toshiko; my agent, Carl Brandt; my Williams classmate Fred Stocking, who has been helping me since my first book; James Wade, who worked with me in combining and cutting several volumes; and Robert Weil of St. Martin's Press, who persuaded me to change the first draft drastically. I also am indebted to Randolph and Elizabeth Summ for use of their fax.

Prologue

I was what the world would term a failure until I was forty-two years old. I did not regard myself as a failure; I learned from every mistake as best I could. My wife, Toshiko, once told me that what others call failure is merely a stepping-stone. I am now eighty-four years old; I look back on my life and see that everything that happened to me in its first half was somehow part of the preparation for what I would do with its second half. As Shakespeare reminds us, "There's a divinity that shapes our ends, rough-hew them how we will."

I became an historian not by accident, not by design, but by fate. Sometimes I think I had very little to do with what happened in my life—because at every crucial stage in it people opened doors for me, doors of discovery. I was not trained as an historian; I have no academic credentials as an historian. So I must let my work speak for me. I wanted, with all my heart and mind, to be a playwright for the first twenty-five years of my adult life. I also held down a great and not particularly distinguished variety of jobs. In the thirties I rode the freights, just another bindle stiff (albeit one with a Williams College sticker on his suitcase). I found that I was good at making money but never became a businessman—money was always a means (to put myself through college, to buy time to write plays, to support a family). It was never an end.

Physically I am not imposing; short, not strong or muscular, and an observer rather than a participant, a man who never was involved in combat on the streets or in wars. Neither am I intimidating in manner. Perhaps that is why people initially talk to me—because I am not threatening. It is extraordinary how many people will help you if you demonstrate in your words and deeds that you seek nothing from them—not money, not advantage, not power or influence derived at their expense. I have always been a listener, someone who loved to hear the narratives of lives from those who lived them. That, more than anything else, sealed my fate. I met and interviewed thousands of people who told me their stories—because they sensed, somehow, that I wanted to listen and genuinely enjoyed meeting them. That many of those I met had done terrible things was not my concern. I had not been sent to judge them—only to listen to what they had to say about the roles they played in the turbulent history of the twentieth century.

Very early in life I learned to put aside any preconceptions I had about anyone. The plea of André Gide, "Please do not understand me too quickly," encapsulates the way I approach anyone. I learned this, as the reader will see, from one of my first mentors, Porter Emerson Browne, a brilliant playwright who took to alcohol after the death of his beloved wife. My father brought him home to dry him out and he stayed for several years, and thus became a central influence in my life. Earlier, when I was eight, he had taken me to the workroom in his mansion and showed me a miniature theater he had. He could move the characters around on the stage. He told me, "I look down on these characters in the drama and I let them do what they have to do. I got this from the Greeks—I am the god in the machine of plot—but the characters are independent of me. I sit down and let them say what they are compelled to say." It was Porter who taught me to eliminate myself, to take my opinions and judgments out of the equation.

I applied this principle to writing history. I learned that you had to go out and meet the people who had played roles, great and small, in history and not just read about them in documents. I could not have written about Adolf Hitler without meeting over a hundred people who knew him, who saw him in all his different, mostly quite frightening, aspects. At the time I wrote my biography of Hitler, I probably knew more people who knew him than any other historian. They would talk to me because, quite simply, I was prepared to listen to them.

Of course, I compared one person's version of a particular event with another observer's version. For example, I spent hours with Otto Skorzeny and Albert Speer—Speer would ask me, "What did Skorzeny say about this?" and Skorzeny would ask me, "And what was Speer's version of this story?" Each disliked the other—to put it mildly. Both men knew I was cross-checking; they knew I was talking to everyone I could, even those who would contest their versions of events or possibly attack them. And they didn't mind. I gave each person I interviewed, for all of my books, my word of honor that nothing I wrote about them, particularly when I was quoting them, would be published without my giving them an opportunity to read it first, and if anyone objected to anything I had written, I would cut it out of the book. I did not promise I would do anything more than that.

If I had clear evidence that I was being given an untruthful or malicious account of any event, I simply would not use it. I also discarded self-serving and untruthful stories when cross-checking proved them to be misrepresentations or at least not the whole truth. I have to tip my hat to Albert Speer—he was the most accomplished fabricator of the lot and had a genius for mixing truth and fiction. He fooled me several times. But Skorzeny never once lied to me. Such are the pitfalls that historians encounter. One must expect them, guard against them—and accept the fact that if you are attempting to break new ground in history you will make mistakes. The important thing is to correct the record when you become aware that you have been misled. But I also vowed to myself that if I had made a clear error, and distorted what someone I interviewed said, I would correct it.

But otherwise I wrote about what I had heard and seen. Those interviewed might not have liked seeing what their remarks looked like in typescript but at least they had the chance to make a correction for the record. I told them that they could delete anything they told me—but I never lost a good story. Not many historians work the way I do—and I have been criticized for being "uncritical" and "easily taken in." Like Ambrose Bierce, I attempt to see things as they are, not as they ought to be. I hope this book will show the reader that I was neither naive nor, in some subtle way, pursuing any agenda.

This memoir focuses on a selection of people from the thousands I interviewed for my fourteen histories, individuals who remain embedded in my memory because, for good or ill, they were my most eloquent witnesses to the history of this century. In order to present them in a context that brings them alive, I have retold and added to their stories recorded in my books. For those not familiar with the events and personalities in the periods of history I cover, I hope these brief versions provide intriguing snapshots of our era—and encourage them to read more.

In addition to the warriors, criminals, heroes, and villains I have met I include people I encountered in Depression America during four long summers I spent riding the freights and hitchhiking across this huge country. Of course that entailed spending some interesting times in various jails and prisons—the price of the ticket, one might say, for such travel. But the central theme of this book is what an adventure it was to seek out those, in major and minor roles, who made history, and how I found them and persuaded them to tell their stories.

These people were my witnesses; I never broke my word to them, but I made it clear that I intended to speak to everyone I could and that the conflicting versions of accounts of any one event would be allowed to stay in conflict. The reader and history itself could judge them—but I would not.

Above all, I saw history as a play, with narrative structure and drama. If it is not that, then it is not fully human. God, someone said, made man because He likes interesting stories. We humans tell the stories; God alone is as objective as some historians would like to be.

I made many foolish mistakes in my life, so I don't feel I can be judgmental about others. When I interviewed people who had played a part in the period of history that concerned me, what I wanted to know was what they were like, what they did and what they thought. Moral evaluation of their conduct was not my concern.

I have been criticized because I did not make extensive comments on the moral significance of what others told me about their actions and beliefs. My job, I felt, was to get to know them as individuals and then to understand why they did what they did, why they believed what they believed.

In a sense, this book is an extended interview of John Toland by John Toland. Montaigne said that he did not know what he knew until he wrote it down on paper. I have undertaken this memoir as part of an attempt to understand what made me tell the stories of those who had been caught up in the remorseless grip of history. The playwright in me yielded to the historian; I could not impose "dramatic" constructions on either their characters or their fates. I could only watch them enact their lives, and, by setting forth what I learned from each of these actors in the drama of history, try to transcribe the scripts that had been written long before I looked down into the theater like the god in the machine and watched the play unfold.

John Toland
Danbury, Connecticut
October 1996

Volume I

Growing Pains

[Part One]

In the Beginning (to 1923)

{1}

I Arrive

I have heard the story of my birth so many times that I feel I was present as a spectator. It was a hot Saturday—the 29th of June, 1912, a few weeks after the sinking of the *Titanic*—and my parents were aboard my father's houseboat. That afternoon my mother, Helen Chandler Snow, felt that I might be coming and asked my father, Ralph, to please return to the dock. The Mississippi was unruly near La Crosse, Wisconsin, and the houseboat was difficult to handle. But my father could perform any physical task, being six feet tall, a prominent local athlete, and Irish. After docking, they hurried to their red brick house on Vine Street, where my maternal grandmother Belle (actually Lell) Snow and a Christian Science nurse, Mrs. Annie Slinn, were nervously waiting.

Mrs. Slinn told my mother she should not eat too heartily at dinner. Afterward the two older women went upstairs to prepare things while my mother went to the backyard to tell Ralph. "You know, honey, things are going to happen tonight," she said. It was still hot.

"I'm sure of it," he said.

The MacDonalds from across the street approached and invited them to a party that evening. "That's wonderful, Don," said my mother. "Thank you, but I'm going to have a party of my own."

My mother went upstairs and started helping the others gather clothing and towels, but her mother scolded her and she was put to bed. At 10:00 P.M. I was born. My father was at the foot of the bed next to my grandmother, whom everyone in the family called Dammy. They could see my face turning dark blue. The umbilical cord was wrapped around my neck. Grandma never saw anyone act as quickly as Annie Slinn. Her hands flew as she disengaged the cord and snipped it. Then she held me by my feet with one hand and slapped my rear so vigorously that Dammy called out, "Oh, Mrs. Slinn, not so hard!" But the nurse kept pounding until she heard a squeal. She then handed me to my grandmother, who had four daughters. But the sight of a boy was so unsettling she could only say, "What'll I do with him?"

"You might wrap this towel around him," suggested my father. Then, when all was calm, he went downstairs and played Chopin softly on the piano, accompanied on the violin by his older brother, Leigh. It was the most beautiful and soothing music my mother had ever heard.

My parents agreed to call me John after my renowned great-uncle Colonel John Toland, a cavalry officer in the Union Army. My middle name, Willard, came from my mother's father, Willard Snow. My other grandfather, Frank Joseph Toland, had died two years earlier; but his widow, Margaret Leigh, a beautiful and talented singer, was still in La Crosse—at a mental institution.

On the third day of my life a stocky nurse from the asylum brought Margaret to Vine Street. How stunning she looked, thought my mother, as Margaret sailed into the room like an opera star, wearing a huge hat. She was delighted to see the baby and expressed such happiness that she seemed perfectly normal. After some time the attendant started toward Margaret. Seeing she was about to be taken back to the institution, Margaret took me, then drew out a long hat pin and put it to my throat. "If you make me go back to that place, Ralph," she exclaimed, "I'll kill him."

My father seized her and tried to shake the pin from her hand, but she doggedly held on to it. The pin was waving around dangerously, and my mother grabbed me. My father finally flung his mother to the floor, but she kept struggling, lashing out with her feet, her eyes gleaming. Never had she looked so beautiful, my mother thought incongruously. Finally my father had his mother under control. She couldn't move. As the attendant leaned over to pick her up, she looked up pleadingly and touched my mother's dress. "Helen," she said, "you can understand as a mother. Plead with the boys to let me stay! You understand," she kept repeating. "Please help me, Helen! Please, Helen!"

Few of my immediate ancestors could be described as dull. My paternal great-grandfather, a native of Kentucky who moved to St. Louis, was not born a Toland. He was Dr. Cyrus C. Fitch until he married Rebecca Toland in 1848 and immediately took her name, for reasons which I have heard were "professional," perhaps indicating a need to cover up some scandal. I was named after one of his sons, Colonel John Toland, the cavalry officer in the Union Army. A dentist by profession, the colonel conducted one of the most daring raids in the war in 1863, driving more than twenty miles behind Confederate lines. He brought almost all of his troops safely back, but on the last day was shot and killed by someone in a church belfry. He was posthumously promoted to brevet general, and during World War II an army camp in Ohio was named in his honor.

Another son, Frank Joseph Toland, was my grandfather. He called himself "the World's Greatest Handwriting Expert" and established a dozen successful business schools in the Midwest. He fell in love with a boisterous and gorgeous girl of sixteen, Margaret Leigh, a descendant of an Irish nobleman, and "married" her in 1879—fourteen years prior to the date on the marriage license in my possession. This suggests that both my uncle Leigh and my father may have been bastards. As a boy I often heard them angrily calling each other bastards, but this was undoubtedly no more than a Toland manner of speech.

My uncle Leigh, eight years older than my father, wrote a long account of his early years in Ohio when his father traveled with his little family from town to town, stopping at hotels, in order to teach penmanship. Leigh recalled, "Occasionally a rowdy or two tried to have fun at the little class's expense. The Dad asked no help, he just went out and socked the first smart aleck he could get to; that ended the fracas almost always. I never heard of or remember that he had to take more than fifteen seconds to whip the average man. He was fast and his physical courage was boundless . . . though he was an artist at heart."

The closeness of the three members of this small family in those days undoubtedly caused both parents to shower all their love on the firstborn, Leigh. In later years my father, Ralph, and the youngest brother, Putch, got only the leavings. It was Leigh who always got the most of everything, in the spirit of the outworn Irish rule of primogeniture.

Leigh as a boy was never allowed to forget his father's Irish temper. "Some man about town made derogatory remarks about the little mother," he wrote. "In the small towns no handsome, well-dressed woman was free, evidently, from such remarks. In any event the Dad was particularly incensed, so he took his shotgun and the Mother to call on the gentleman, who signed a statement admitting himself a liar, and apologizing."

My grandfather Frank was convinced that the well-known Irish author John Toland was his great-grandfather. The *Encyclopædia Britannica* describes him as a "controversial freethinker whose Rationalist philosophy and political writings forced church historians to consider seriously questions concerning the biblical canon." Born in North Ireland in 1670, he converted to Anglicanism in his teens and studied in Glasgow, Edinburgh, and Oxford universities. His first book, *Christianity Not Mysterious,* caused such offense that he was forced to flee England. He wrote a number of controversial books and articles, including diatribes against the oppression of Jews and Negroes.

Frank Toland left behind a mass of material on the famous John Toland, including a statement by an Irish priest who one day met him on the highway when he was a boy and reported to his superiors that "the lad spoke with the voice of the devil." The same charge has been made by some of my critics. I cannot share the delusion that he was my great-great-great-grandfather, but there is no doubt that his unorthodox ideas had some impact on me.

I never saw my grandfather Frank, but I have a picture showing him on a horse in cowboy attire. In imitation of his close friend the famous gun-slinger Doc Powell, he is wearing the sort of flowing mustache and goatee that Buffalo Bill made popular. My father told me that Frank often went to the Wisconsin Business University in this outfit. He must have caused quite a stir. When my father was two, Frank had stuck his cowboy hat on him and photographed him for history. When I was almost two, my father put the same hat on me for the same purpose.

In his photo my father is as dashing as his father. I, with my curls, just look cute. As I grew up I realized that I was not like my father. I was not at all athletic or physically well coordinated; I was just a kid who couldn't pitch a curve or kick a football more than twenty-five yards. By the time I was in junior high school I realized that I wasn't a typical Toland.

The most memorable ancestor on my mother's side was my great-grandmother Clarabelle Chandler, a dynamic and fearless woman who turned out to be a major influence in my life. I never knew anything about her until I hitchhiked across the country and stopped at Danville, Illinois, to see my mother's sister, Jeanette Ludwick. In my grandmother Dammy's room I noticed an oil portrait of Clarabelle; Dammy told me that when her father died, Clarabelle, by sheer grit, had left her home in the South and taken her eight children to the North before the Civil War. She brought them up by herself under the most difficult circumstances imaginable.

Clarabelle (*née* Grigsby) had been born in the Midwest but married a Virginia plantation owner, Claiborne Chandler, a man who had been shang-haied in his early teens and was the first on either side of my family to visit China. Years after his marriage and the birth of eight children, his adventures in the Far East tempted him to explore California and the West Coast. He bought considerable property in Seattle, got sick, was bilked by a business partner, and died not long after his return to his Virginia plantation.

The portrait of Clarabelle Chandler depicted her as a typically beautiful Southern belle. In reality, Dammy told me, she was always a hard-working Grigsby from Missouri. She was meticulous, for example, in her care of the plantation slaves. The third of her six daughters, Lell—my grandmother Dammy—never tired of telling me about her mother. "Clarabelle had a great love for the slaves and on certain days would make an inspection tour of their quarters. She'd go through just like a whirlwind. She tore the beds apart. She inspected their food and clothing. 'This is not right,' she would scold. 'Your children have to be brought up properly. They have to have the proper food. They have to be clean.' " Clarabelle, she added, was always into something. "She won many horse races. She was a great horsewoman, and I often saw her mounting her horse for the race. I never saw anything quite as lovely. Sidesaddle, with everything just so. Her gloves had to be right, and she wore this high hat. But when she went to the slave quarters she wore a divided skirt and rode like a man."

Clarabelle also brought the spirit of a pioneer with her from Missouri. After her husband died almost penniless, she decided to take her children north for a better education. She sold all but a dozen of her slaves for a dollar apiece to friends who promised to treat them well, then took her brood of six daughters and two sons to Wisconsin, along with the dozen servants who refused to leave her. "You can go with me," Clarabelle had said, "if I pay you. Because you're no longer slaves. I freed you. I will not let you come with me unless you take money for your work." And so Clarabelle Chandler, her children, and a dozen of the former slaves, all of whom took the name Chandler, moved to the outskirts of Boscobel, a small Wisconsin town, in 1858. There she bought a farm with the little money salvaged from the plantation and put everyone to work planting and harvesting.

Clarabelle became my ideal. I wanted to be like her. She had courage and common sense. She could improvise, yet lived a life of regularity. By the time I was in college I had planned every day before it started. How it irritated my father when I came home on holidays and still planned each hour of every day. But Clarabelle would have understood.

Although many of her neighbors were harassed by Indians, and some even murdered, Clarabelle maintained peaceful relations with them. "Don't ever fight anyone with their weapons," she told her children and the black workers, "no matter how bad they are. Fight them in your way." And Clarabelle's way was to invite the Indians into her house, where she, clad in her Southern finery, served them brownies and cider. The children would be hiding in a secret place behind the wall, but could see through peepholes what was going on in their living room. It was Lell's duty to prevent their little dog, Rags, who apparently hated Indians, from barking; she would stuff a towel in his mouth.

Two years after their arrival in Boscobel, the Civil War broke out. This grieved everyone in Clarabelle's extended family, because they loved both North and South. My grandmother remembered the day her two brothers confronted their mother while she was knitting in the living room. They kneeled in front of her, and one said, "Mama, we've had to make a decision. We must fight in this war, and we had to make a terrible choice."

"Which side?" asked Clarabelle.

"The North."

Lell would never forget how their mother placed a hand on each boys' heads and said, "My dears, you have made the right choice."

"Mama," said Lell once the boys had left, "what would you have said if they had decided to fight for the South?"

"My dear girl, I would have said the same thing."

Years later a young man of Scottish descent from Boston, Willard Snow, heard that there was a beautiful girl called "the Belle of Boscobel" teaching in that little town. Willard's father had made considerable money in copper but, after a hint of scandal, had turned to timber in Wisconsin. Willard was now working in one of his father's logging camps not too far from Boscobel. He was a big man, but gentle, and disliked every moment he spent in the camp. "I couldn't stand to be in a business," he once told me, "where I had to watch beautiful trees, that took many years to grow, cut down wholesale. That's destroying life. I just couldn't stay in a business like that."

Willard came to Boscobel and met the "Belle," who would become my maternal grandmother. During the courtship Willard once stepped in a bear trap and later almost suffocated after stumbling into a huge pile of sawdust. When the workers finally dug him out, he was laughing. While telling this to me, he was still laughing. What Toland could laugh at himself? I thought. And what Toland (except myself, of course) could be so clumsy? Was it any wonder that I felt closer to him than to anyone on my father's side of the family?

Willard quit the lumbering business, got a job as an insurance investigator, and married Lell. They moved to Sioux Falls, South Dakota, and had four daughters in this order: Floss, Jeanette, Grace, and my mother, Helen. Only Helen had children—Virginia in 1910 and me two years later.

When Helen's sister Jeanette saw me for the first time, she remarked that I had the Grigsby eyes. "Yes," said Floss, "but I hope he also has the Grigsby grit and brains!"

Clarabelle's younger brother, Melvin Grigsby, had enlisted in the Union Army when he was sixteen. After almost two years of service he had been captured and imprisoned at Andersonville. His book *The Smoked Yank* (a copy of the 1888 edition is in the Library of Congress) relates in absorbing detail the horrors of that camp. Later he became the commander of a voluntary cavalry regiment known as Grigsby's Cowboys, or the Rough Riders. According to family records and letters, it was he who invited Teddy Roosevelt, a hunting buddy, to join him on the charge up San Juan Hill in the Spanish-American War of 1898. This exploit helped Teddy, a Republican, to win the presidency in 1900.

After Roosevelt was elected he came to Sioux Falls to thank Uncle Melvin. It was a great occasion for the city. On Sunday my grandfather Willard Snow escorted the president to a small Dutch Reformed church. The place was jammed. As the services were about to commence, the floor collapsed, and half the congregation, including Roosevelt, plunged into the basement. Dadda peered down. "Will you take the hand of a good Democrat, Mr. President?" he asked with a big smile. Roosevelt good-naturedly grasped Willard's hand and was hoisted up.

After a formal dinner in his honor, Roosevelt asked if he could try out Melvin Grigsby's mare. Half an hour later he returned, entering the court-yard at a gallop, then jerking the mare to a sudden stop. Grigsby was furious, and my mother would never forget his red face. "Get off!" he shouted. "You'll never ride a horse of mine again! Any man who rides like that should be flogged!"

The president humbly dismounted, and just before he left Sioux Falls he offered Grigsby the position of attorney general in Alaska. Melvin went north with his son but returned alone a week or so later. "It was a cold gift!" he remarked. He had turned over the job of attorney general to his son, without consulting Washington.

Uncle Melvin remained vigorous until the last day of his life. In his eighties he journeyed alone to Chicago and was attacked one evening by two young men. A newspaper reported, "Colonel Melvin Grigsby, former com-mander of the South Dakota Rough Riders, was assaulted by two footpads last night. He routed them with his cane."

Clarabelle's sister, for some reason always called Matt, also brought us no-toriety. She was engaged to an older man from a prominent family who built her a magnificent house in St. Louis. They were in love, but just before their marriage his family insisted that he wed a wealthy girl. After his marriage, while Matt was pining away in her huge empty house, her lover returned. "You can't go on like this all your life," he said. "We can still live together."

As my mother explained to me many years later, only after this particular family skeleton had been revealed to me by her sister Floss, "One thing led to another and she turned the house into . . ."

"A house of prostitution?" I guessed.

"Oh, yes, it did evolve into that kind of house. But," she continued brightly, "it was the best house in St. Louis!" She added that the Snow family was, of course, crushed and refused to associate with Matt.

"Well, *we* will!" said Willard, and insisted that my grandmother's sister Matt be invited to Sioux Falls.

Matt was delighted. "How we loved her!" recalled my mother, who had been about fifteen at the time. "Oh, Matt was such a dear! And when she saw what I was doing with my art, she told my mother, 'Lell, Helen should be trained.' And my mother said, 'There's no one out here and we can't afford to send her away.' But Matt replied, 'Well, I've investigated, and there's a teacher out at All Saints College. She's not as good as they are in the East, but she's better than nothing.' And my mother said, 'I don't know if we can afford that.' 'Well,' said Matt, 'I can!' And so she sent me the money every week to go on. 'Helen's going to be something,' she wrote, 'and I know it!' But the money stopped after about six weeks, and we never heard from her again. That was the last heard from Aunt Matt."

Because of Willard's modest salary, the Snows lived in what he called, from his proper Bostonian perspective, "threadbare respectability," but Willard was highly respected by his wealthy friends, and it was through his influence and industry that a swimming pool was built for the children at the Flandreau Indian reservation near Sioux Falls. Willard often took the two youngest daughters, Grace and Helen, to the reservation pool to meet the children. Other white children would throw pennies into the pool for Indian children to dive for, but Willard told Grace and Helen they could not do so. "That's making you better, and that's not right. If the other children want to throw pennies, that's all right. But don't let me catch you doing it. The Indians are not inferior."

Helen confessed to me that she used to be jealous of young Indian children. "I can just see them hanging on to Dadda's legs, and he had to drag them along. They loved him and were afraid they'd lose him."

Although my mother's name was Helen, as the baby of the family she was given the affectionate nickname Collie. She was a sweet, good-tempered girl, loved by all. Soon after her twelfth birthday she was wooed by a good-looking youngster, Billy Pattee, whose father owned five banks in Iowa. They had met at Lake Okoboji, a resort area in Iowa. When they were fifteen, Billy taught her to sail on the lake in his boat, the *Fair Maid,* which he had named after her. Both families assumed they would get married. Then Ralph Toland came from La Crosse to Sioux Falls with his father, Frank Toland, to establish another business university. From the day Frank arrived in town, he made a poor impression on Willard Snow, who had heard from a friend that a sporty stranger had strutted into the bar at the Cataract Hotel wearing a beautiful fur coat, diamond rings, and a large diamond pin. He slapped his gold-headed cane on the bar and said, "I can lick any son of a bitch in this room!" and then added, "Drinks for everyone on me!" The next day, Willard, by chance, saw Frank Toland leaning on the front desk of the Cataract in a manner that Willard found offensive. "A gentleman," he said to his wife, "doesn't do that."

A few weeks later, Clifford Peck, one of Ralph's newfound friends, offered to take him along to a swanky dance, the Patriarchs' Ball. "Have you any evening clothes?" Ralph did. And that night he was introduced to Helen Snow. He was tall (her current boyfriend, Billy Pattee, was short) and handsome despite a broken nose, which certainly made him look different. I later learned that this had come in a fistfight at parochial school. His father had refused to have the nose set because it was, in his words, "a badge of manhood."

"I kind of liked him," my mother recalled. "And he was a pursuer. A terrific pursuer." But by chance Minnie Boyce, a cousin from Fargo, was visiting the Snows, and she fell instantly in love with Ralph. He would come to the Snow home three or four times a week, always bringing flowers and candy, not only for Helen but for the smitten Minnie and Mrs. Snow. He soon became a favorite with all the females. Willard was thus forced to be a bit more friendly, but did not trust him.

Helen knew Ralph was living in a dismal rooming house and asked Lell if they could invite him to Thanksgiving dinner. She knew it was wrong, since she had already invited Billy Pattee, but she couldn't resist the temptation.

"Oh, of course!" exclaimed cousin Minnie, and Lell gave her permission.

By then Helen was feeling guilty, but Lell could see no wrong in it. After all, Ralph was all alone and Billy had a lovely home and plenty of money. Besides, Billy was a fair-minded young man. But Helen knew it was wrong, since she was almost sure Billy was soon going to give her an engagement ring. She wrote to tell him that Ralph was also coming. He replied that he would not join them. "That was the end," recalled my mother. "I never saw him again. It just cut him to pieces to think that someone else was more important. I still feel guilty." When my mother told me this, her face and voice betrayed a certain wistfulness. Her life with Billy would have been so different.

In 1909, Ralph Toland asked Helen to marry him. She said it was too quick. A few months later he asked again and got the same answer. The third time she accepted, but Ralph never forgot—possibly because there had been a pattern of rejection in his life—that he had been twice refused. His parents' first child, Ralph Joseph, had died soon after birth. This intensified the affection they lavished on their next child, a boy named Leigh. Then came my father, Ralph Joseph, named in memory of the baby who had died.

Ralph told Helen, "I never had a name of my own." He had adored his mother but was allowed to have her entirely to himself on only one day of each year—his birthday. The rest of the year his older brother, Leigh, was the beloved child.

When Ralph was in the sixth grade at parochial school, a nun rapped him vigorously on the hand with a metal ruler. Ralph, who hated his middle name, Joseph, and dropped it, stopped going to school. His parents, who paid so little real attention to him, kept receiving report cards which Ralph concocted. From that point on, Ralph was self-educated. The nearest he ever got to his parents was to sneak a ride on the back of their carriage. His first touch of genuine family life came at the Snow home. Once Helen accepted his proposal, all except Willard Snow were delighted.

Willard could see in Ralph some problems that his charm hid from the mother and daughters. He was not flamboyant and boastful like his father, and he acted like a gentleman in public, but it was obvious that he had an Irish temper to go along with his remarkable musical talent. Once my mother had said yes, however, Willard accepted Ralph wholeheartedly and tried to repress his doubts. Willard was a big man in every sense, but when he walked into a room he was not the focus of attention, as Ralph was. To me Dadda (as I always called Willard) was not threatening, only reassuring. He never argued, even about politics, and he never made an enemy.

Ralph regarded his father-in-law as a superconservative, but he was just the opposite. Years later I found Dadda's "traveling" notebook; it was filled with socialist comments and his dreams of a world without prejudice and with equality for all. Willard believed in the solid virtues, but whenever a young man got into trouble in Sioux Falls, Willard was on hand to help him get out of the mess as long as he promised to "do the right thing." Ralph used to belittle Dadda good-naturedly for this "social work," but when I hitchhiked to Sioux Falls years later, several men told me that Willard Snow had turned their lives around.

I adored him. He would send me letters addressed to "J. Willard Toland," and if he had been alive when my first book was published I would have called myself J. Willard Toland. I never realized until years later that my uneasy relationship with my father may have resulted from my love and admiration of Dadda. My sister and I were brought up to believe that the Tolands were superior to the Snows because the Tolands were colorful and fun whereas the Snows were dowdy and uninteresting. My father could not conceal how ashamed he was of my being small, having girlish hands, and being poor at athletics. Although my father constantly chided me for walking slightly pigeon-toed, Dadda assured me I was walking "Indian file," and this was more practical in climbing hills. My father's focus on my shortcomings was one reason I had always felt that I more truly belonged to Dadda than to him.

I now know that my failure to please my father must have made me resent him. I also know now that he could not have changed the way he felt about me. He spent many days teaching me and the neighborhood kids in Norwalk how to play baseball, and I felt jealous of those who were good at it. He never criticized me, but how often I wished he would say to me, "Good going, kid!" as he did to the Italian boys with athletic talent! When my father walked into a room he was obviously the best man, even though he had little money. I revered him but I knew I wasn't *his* boy. But when Dadda took me and a group of kids to get ice cream, everybody loved him, yet I was not jealous. I knew I was *his* boy.

I realize now that the barrier between my father and me was as much my fault as his—perhaps more, since I was so resentful. If I had not continually retreated into my protective shell, I might have become *his* boy, because he was basically a warm and loving person. But then I wouldn't have revered him; I would have loved him as I loved Dadda. The last time I saw my father, on my fourth summer of riding freight trains across the country, this truth finally struck me, and we had two weeks of understanding and healing. I had not realized, until too late, that I was a Snow, not a Toland. Although I worshiped my father as a hero, my temperament had been shaped by Dadda and Clarabelle.

Ralph insisted on bringing Helen back to La Crosse to meet his family before the wedding. Never had Helen seen such a beautiful woman as my father's mother, Margaret. "She had glorious eyes, the most beautiful color! Violet! Her features were lovely—and her skin!"

From the outside, the Toland residence at 1402 King Street looked like no other house in the area, because of its stately porte cochere at the side and its impressive frontage. The Wisconsin Business University—founded by Frank Toland—had paid for this beautiful house. Grandfather Frank had also turned the inside into a magnificent stage for the highly theatrical temperaments of its inhabitants. Never had Helen seen such a combination of singular beauty and flamboyance. The mahogany and walnut paneling throughout the house must have cost a fortune, yet the opulence was restrained by good taste. Beneath the surface bravado of Frank Toland, she decided, must lie a sensitive and thoughtful human being.

Helen was the first down for dinner, and she wondered where the others were. Then they began, one at a time, to descend the staircase that led directly into the living room. First Frank, not large but imposing in his dinner jacket as if he, like Margaret, had come from nobility. Then Leigh, named after an apocryphal ancestor Lord Leigh, slight but truly elegant, carrying a violin. He walked up to the Steinway grand piano, hopped like a dancer onto a chair, and then regally stepped higher onto the top of the piano itself, where he played brilliant cadenzas that he had obviously rehearsed for weeks.

Then came my father. Halfway down he began singing, with Leigh accompanying him. He was a baritone. Never had my mother heard such a voice. It was operatic, and it made her tingle. Once the song was over, there was a pause; then Margaret, like a queen, slowly descended. She had pillaged the attic for her finery and wore a beautiful satin dress, a cape, and a magnificent hat with plumes. She stopped about five steps above the landing and slowly surveyed the audience. Ralph stepped to the piano and, with a flourish, struck a sort of fanfare on the piano. Leigh descended majestically and stood next to him, joining in with his violin. Then Margaret, a diva properly introduced, began her aria. My mother was entranced by Margaret's voice. All this was better than any show on earth, but she wondered what her folks would have thought. Dammy, of course, would have loved it, but Dadda might have been a bit put off.

When the aria was over, Ralph walked to the landing and gallantly escorted his mother to the bottom. He then rushed to the piano and played chords while his mother began bowing graciously. "She bowed almost in two, then said to us, 'My corset was ready to bust on my last bend,' before bursting into laughter."

That was Helen Chandler Snow's introduction to an Irish family of dubious nobility.

The Snows had originally been Congregationalists, but they had become Christian Scientists after a healing of Willard's mother, who lived in Fargo, North Dakota. Helen had been invited to sing in the Episcopal choir by the Booth girls, who were soloists. Lell urged her to accept, since this would mean she could go to the elegant parties held for young people. Her only advice was "Just don't sing loud and shrill."

Lell also decided that my mother should be married in the Episcopal church, but she was turned down by the Episcopalians. "We're Christian Scientists," Lell protested, "and there's no one in our church who can perform a legal ceremony."

She was again refused. It was ten days before the wedding, but Helen was not nervous. "I didn't know enough," she later told me. "And Ralph wasn't worried. If we couldn't do anything else, he'd take me down to the court-house." A few days later, the Episcopal rector telephoned Lell. "Mrs. Snow, a friend told me it was my duty to perform the wedding." The ceremony could not be in the church, but he would be happy to marry Helen and Ralph in the Snow home.

Helen's sister Jeanette and her husband, George Ludwick, an architect, came to Sioux Falls from Illinois, arriving on the day of the wedding, October 2, 1909. Floss and her husband, Jack Henjum, known as a man who could sell anything, came from distant California. Willard was his beaming self, acting as if he had never had doubts about Ralph. The sole Toland present was my father; his father didn't bother to attend. "I'm all alone," he sadly confided to Floss, who adored him.

"Never mind," she said. "You were never with more friends."

{2}

A Boy's Life

In the first three years of his marriage, Ralph Toland was a perfect father. We lived in La Crosse, first in the house in which I was born in 1912. My mother has told me how my father insisted on sleeping in the large playroom with Virginia, my older sister, in a little bed on one side and me on the other side. When I woke up in the middle of the night for a meal, Ralph would pick me up and take me to his and my mother's room for her to nurse me. Once the meal was over he took me back so my mother could get more rest.

I have also been told that from the time I was able to crawl I was a problem. And as I look back I can see that my behavior as a small child set a pattern for the rest of my life. I was a miniature Marco Polo, always exploring new worlds. When I was not quite two I toddled outdoors during a warm spring rain and made my way to the drainpipe. News of my absence went through the house, and my mother ran out with Dora, the nurse girl. There I was, stooping over to let the water pour over my bare bottom. I looked up at my mother and laughed delightedly.

I took my afternoon naps on the upstairs porch, and one day I managed to scramble out of my crib and creep onto an adjoining roof. I sat on the very edge and—they tell me—began to coo. My uncle Hewitt, better known as Putch, was only fourteen, and every time he ventured onto the roof to save me, he slipped. (Putch got his unusual nickname because his mother kept calling him "Pretty Boy" and his attempt to say this turned into "Putchy Boy." His legal name, Hewitt, was practically forgotten.) Apparently I thought he was trying to entertain me, and I was delighted with his performance. I moved even closer to the edge. Then my father appeared and grabbed me by the neck just before I would have fallen. "He had wonderful hands," my mother recalled, "beautiful hands. Ralph was strong, he had courage, and he always knew just what to do. I grabbed you from him and held you for an hour."

The summer of 1915, when I was just three, the family took a cottage on a nearby lake. While Putch was getting dressed for a dance, he saw me striding right into the lake. I kept on walking until I disappeared. He scrambled out the window onto a porch roof, leaped down, and pulled me out of the water. Putch then looked down and realized that he had no pants on. Enraged, he dropped me and dashed into the cottage—certain that his girlfriend, in the next cottage, had seen him.

A week later I was an accessory in a crime that brought my first spanking. My sister, Virginia, two years older and much bigger and stronger, persuaded me to help her play a trick on the crabby lady next door, who was always scolding us. We stuffed all the clean clothes from the woman's clotheslines down her privy.

Discovering what we had done, Helen removed the filthy clothes and washed them by hand, stopping every few minutes, as she wept, to spank us. When my father showed up, my mother, who had never before physically chastised either of us, now demanded even more. Ralph did give Virginia a few restrained spanks, but he took me behind our privy and told me, "Cry out when I slap my knee!" I'll never forget my father pretending to punish us. How I loved him at that moment.

My fifth birthday, in June 1917, was celebrated in Watertown, South Dakota, where we had moved from La Crosse in 1916. My father had opened a new business school there, a way of ending the constant arguments with his father at the Wisconsin Business University in La Crosse. Up to that time my mother had insisted on letting my curly hair grow long and dressing me up as Little Lord Fauntleroy. I grew to hate this, and my father didn't like it either. On the Fourth of July he declared he was going to show his son the town. We walked down the wooden sidewalks and found the barbershop open. My father took me in, and I was given a thrill I have never forgotten. The sound of clipping and the falling of curls to the floor brought sheer ecstasy. I knew it was the end of Lord Fauntleroy, and on our walk back home my head felt wonderful. But my mother burst into tears. "My baby's gone!" she wailed. And my father hadn't even saved the precious curls!

Later that year we moved back to La Crosse. Then something happened that probably led to the end of my father's singing career. He and his brother, Leigh, were walking home after docking their houseboat when a large man, the town bully, shouted an insult. My father ignored the remark and kept walking. The bully started toward him, Leigh shouted a warning, and my father turned just in time to be floored. He got up, and a ferocious battle began between my father and the bully as well as the man's brother. Leigh thought it would never end. My father finally walked away after the fight with two black eyes and his nose broken for the second time.

My mother was shocked at the horrible sight. "Didn't Leigh help you?"

"No," he replied, then added, "He might have gotten in my way." The broken nose was never straightened, and for the rest of his life Ralph had to wear a truss.

As I grew older the fight became a classic family event and my father became a great hero to me. The blood and pain faded from my memory. I knew he had to wear a "truss," but it was just a word. Then one day I saw it hanging down from his bedpost like an ugly snake, a disgusting and threatening object.

I hurried to my room and looked up "truss" in the dictionary: "an apparatus for maintaining a hernia in a reduced state." Since it was against the principles of Christian Science to discuss the body, I looked up "hernia": "the protrusion of an organ or tissue through an opening in its surrounding walls, esp. in the abdominal region." I looked up "abdomen": "that part of the mammal between the thorax and the pelvis." I kept going until I decided it must be down in the crotch in a very personal place! My God! My poor father had been wearing this evil device every day for years and years! I think I cried, but I'm not sure. But I do know that from that moment I felt sorry for my father and I wished I could do something to make him proud of me.

My fondest memory of 1917 was meeting the sons of the most famous man in La Crosse, Doc Powell, the noted gunfighter known as White Beaver. He was a close friend of Calamity Jane, Bill Cody, and other renowned Western characters. Doc, son of a doctor, had returned to La Crosse to become mayor. He had two sons, Pog (Pollywog) and Tad (Tadpole). Pog greatly admired Ralph, mostly because my father was the best baseball player on the town's semipro team. A Chicago Cubs scout once offered Ralph a tryout after watching him strike out some twenty men in one game, but Ralph refused, explaining that he was going to be a professional singer.

Pog visited us almost every day, and I always greeted him raucously and demanded that we play "war." Pog would sit in an easy chair while I lunged at him from all sides until he was exhausted. During one of these war games, Helen's sister Grace arrived for a visit. She fell in love with Pog, and before long they were married in Sioux Falls. Ralph was the best man, Virginia was the flower girl, and I had the embarrassing chore of carrying the wedding ring, which had been placed around the pistil of a huge lily. Fortunately none of those present were students of Freud.

Movies fascinated me from an early age. What I watched on the big screen seemed to be really happening and could make me laugh or cry. Every Saturday afternoon, Virginia and I would attend a special showing of serials at the movie theater in the Wisconsin Business University building. I could thrill at the narrow escapes. The movies became another form of my life, and while I was in the theater I *believed*. Perhaps I was later impelled to write so I could be living another life that was more interesting than my own.

I soon lost my taste for serials. The other theaters featured films such as D. W. Griffith's *Intolerance*. I became so engrossed watching the four separate stories ranging from modern days to old Babylon that I watched several consecutive performances—until I was finally discovered by the police, who had been aroused by a frantic telephone call from my mother. I was chiefly fascinated by the movie's shift from ancient days to present times. This made the mysterious past come alive, with its tremendous crowds and formidable buildings. I was living *in* the past.

By the end of 1917, my thoughts were concentrated on the Great War in Europe. I nagged my mother until she made both navy and army uniforms for me to wear. I also had an army helmet, purchased by my father in Chicago, and a collection of shell casings and other battlefield memorabilia sent by the doughboys in France whom I had met during a vacation in the summer of 1917.

Putch was eager to get into the fray, and on his eighteenth birthday he was accepted in the navy. My father wanted to enlist in the army. "I'm fit and the right age, but the government won't accept me because I'm married and have two children," he told my mother. He went to Leigh. "It's our duty. I'll do the fighting, and if anything happens to me, you must promise to take care of Helen and the children all their lives."

"I will not," Leigh replied. He was never a big one for "duty."

So my father stayed home and almost died in the influenza epidemic of 1918—which killed more Americans than the Germans did. Allied victories in the summer and fall caused great excitement throughout the nation, and ecstasy came on November 7, a beautiful Indian-summer day. In New York there was a din of sirens, factory and ship whistles, automobile horns, and church bells when it was announced that hostilities had ceased.

There were celebrations all over America, in small towns and villages as well as in the great cities. In La Crosse, a town with a pronounced German flavor thanks to the 1848 generation of immigrants, it was a hard thing to be a German-American. German-Americans had to be excessively patriotic. My father took Virginia and me downtown that evening to witness a scene of unbridled joy. We went to the newspaper office, where a straw effigy of Kaiser Bill, whom I hated, was hanging. A man set it on fire, and we all cheered. I wanted to put on my army uniform, but my father made us go to bed. It was a sight to remember, even though it was only the false armistice. The real one came four days later, but it didn't mean much to me, since I had already seen Kaiser Bill burned and knew it was over, over there.

[3]

Eastward, Ho!

By early 1919, when I was still six, my father was eager to leave La Crosse. He regarded his work with Leigh in the family business school as a dead end, and he yearned to go east and continue his singing career. "I'm going to train my voice," he told Helen. "The school can go to hell for all I care!"

Entranced by an article in *The Saturday Evening Post* about a Promised Land in Connecticut near New Canaan where a group of Midwestern artists and musicians had established an artists' colony, my parents spent hours dreaming and talking about this haven, referring to it as the Valley of the Moon. Within a few months our furniture had been shipped to New Canaan and we were on a train to New York City.

I was totally prepared for this new world. La Crosse had become too confining for the Toland family, including my uncle Putch, who had begged Ralph to take him along. Helen was the only real mother he had ever known. "You've *got* to take me!" he said. Uncle Putch was taller and heavier than Ralph, but was pigeon-toed and had none of Ralph's athletic ability. He reminded my mother of a tame, clumsy bear who had lost its mother, and she had urged my father to let him join us. And since he was a talented pianist, he could accompany my father at recitals.

We made our base camp in a few cramped rooms in a boardinghouse near New Canaan while my parents searched in vain for a house they could afford. Eventually they turned to a real estate agent in Norwalk, Sam Keeler. Upon learning that my father was a singer and we were Christian Scientists, he said, "I'm not going to let you folks go. I want you to find a place in Norwalk." He knew that the Science church there needed a soloist. Because we had very little money, the only place he could find us was a farm between Norwalk and Westport.

Before long Ralph was commuting to New York several times a week for singing lessons with a well-known Italian teacher, trying to sell pianos, giving recitals—and running our farm.

Soon after we moved into our new house, Mother took Virginia and me down the road to a one-room schoolhouse. There was one teacher, a pleasant young woman who handled all six grades. I was put in the first grade and Virginia in the third. But after a week the teacher sadly announced that the school was being closed because there were only half a dozen of us, and we were transferred to the Bedford Elementary School in Westport.

The best part of this arrangement was riding the bus. School itself was overwhelming. The boys were all bigger and the girls aloof.

I was learning things on the farm that were not taught to me at school. Across the road from our house lived the actor Harrison Hunter, who was playing the title role in a Broadway hit, *The Bat.* Spending the summer with the Hunters was his niece, Carolyn, who was one year older than I was. She liked to play with me and two farm boys who lived down the road, across from the Nell York mansion.

Nell was the most beautiful woman I'd ever seen. All of us worshiped her. According to Mr. Hunter, she had been in the Ziegfeld Follies. We all played around the York swimming pool, which lay far down the hill next to our farm. The pool was overgrown with weeds, and we used it for races with our homemade boats, which we pushed with long sticks. One day we were startled to find Nell York watching us. We were too paralyzed with fear to leave, but she smiled and said we were welcome to use her pool. She also invited us into her huge kitchen, which was furnished with every imaginable device, even a huge object where she kept perishables. I thought it was an icebox, but Nell explained that it ran by electricity. Nell treated us to cookies and milk. I couldn't keep my eyes off the refrigerator—I'd never seen one before.

When I returned home that day to announce the good news about Nell's cordial welcome, my father burst out laughing. That wasn't Nell York's mansion at all. It was owned by a wealthy New Yorker who only came down on weekends. It was left unexplained that Nell was his mistress. We children could only suppose that he, too, liked her cookies and milk. When my mother meekly suggested that it might be a good idea if I didn't go up to the mansion anymore, my father again laughed. "John's too young to be corrupted, and she sounds like a good sort." I had no idea what they were talking about; but even when I found out, years later, I retained my vision of a lovely and kind woman.

About the only chore on the farm I really liked was hunting for warm chicken and duck eggs each morning. Chickens almost always laid their eggs in nests, but the imaginative ducks kept me searching all over the barn, even up in the hayloft. Finding an egg up there was a major triumph. By far the worst jobs were cleaning the chicken coop and weeding the potato patch. Daisy the cow was good company, however; everyone loved her. She was amazingly patient, even when I fumbled around at her teats in an effort to milk her. She forgave me; but my father, who could not understand why I was so inept, did not.

I loved all seasons, particularly winter. I would get up before breakfast, hunt the eggs, and then go clumping through snow up to my hips. Well, it was probably a foot deep but seemed a lot deeper.

My chief companion, or rather master, was Virginia. Living in the country would have been lonely without her, especially on nights when the folks were off at one of my father's recitals. I was never really afraid to be alone in the house with her, for I knew she could handle any burglar dumb enough to break in. And during the long empty hours after school she always managed to do something that amused me. One Sunday a rich boy from the Christian Science church came to the noonday dinner with us. Afterward the three of us went to Nell York's pond, where Virginia showed off, stick-pushing her boat with élan. She got so ambitious she fell in, still in her Sunday dress. My father heard the splash and rushed across the stone wall that divided our property. Unperturbed, she was just getting out of the pond. Regally she said, "I did it on purpose," and resumed pushing her boat with the long stick. Most girls would have cried, but not my big sister.

On Sundays, first we had to go to Sunday school on the second floor of the church while my father sang below. Afterward we all drove home in our newly acquired Model T Ford for Sunday dinner. This meal always featured chicken, which I loved—although I detested the way the chicken got from the coop to the table, a feature of farm life that genuinely repelled me.

After dinner we often attended a concert or an art exhibition at the Silvermine Guild. This was an association of artists, sculptors, playwrights, authors, musicians, and composers in a little community near Norwalk. Every other Sunday there would be an exhibition, lecture, or concert. My father was a highly respected member and was often asked to sing. I had to listen to music at home almost incessantly, and this never bothered me, but seeing my father in public always made me nervous. I was afraid he'd miss a note, or step onstage with his fly open.

Music came to be part of my everyday experience, because my father would go over and over difficult passages whenever he could steal an hour from his piano-selling and farming. I was not aware of it but, despite my distaste for music, I had become accustomed to it. The songs that my father constantly rehearsed were permanently implanted in my memory. I have never been able to wipe out certain phrases from the *Messiah:* "Why do the nations so furiously rage together? Why do the people imagine a vain thing?" When I was a small boy these words meant nothing to me, but they had been indelibly inscribed in my brain. I can hear them this moment.

One day when my parents were in the Norwalk Bank, the cashier nodded at two men who were entering and whispered, "That's the famous playwright Porter Emerson Browne. He wrote the big hit running on Broadway, *The Bad Man.*"

My father was delighted at this opportunity to meet the playwright. He approached the first man—tall, good-looking, and well-dressed. "Glad to meet you, Mr. Browne!" he said with great cordiality.

"I am Mr. Browne's chauffeur." Behind him was a small, pudgy man wearing overalls—the actual Mr. Browne, who admired my father on first sight.

Later Mr. and Mrs. Browne attended my father's first recital at Hillside, a fashionable girls' school in Norwalk, where their daughter, Prudence, was a student. The recital was a great success, and Browne was so pleased that he invited us all to dinner at his huge house. After the meal he invited my father to sing. Ordinarily my father would have refused, but that night he obliged with several Russian songs. Browne congratulated him as well as Putch, who had accompanied him, and then asked my mother what she did.

"I like to paint," she said.

"And you, Virginia?"

"I'm a dancer."

"And you, John?"

Like any eight-year-old, I had no idea of what to say, and finally, in my embarrassment, I blurted out, "I'm their manager."

Porter Browne was so amused that he took me by the arm. "I want to show you how I write plays," he said, and he led me to a small room where there was a table next to a typewriter. On the table half a dozen small figures were standing on a miniature stage. Browne looked down at his characters. "I just watch them and let them do everything they have to do." I was entranced. "Then I type down what they say."

It was the first time anyone had really taken me seriously. I don't think you ever forget such moments. He instantly became my role model; hero worship of this kind is natural when you're impressionable.

———

My parents decided that Virginia needed a better education than the one she was getting at Bedford School, so Putch drove Helen to Norwalk to see the Hillside School principal, a dignified and attractive woman, Miss Brendlinger. My mother suggested that my father give two free recitals a year as a way to pay for Virginia's tuition. Miss Brendlinger consented, having heard of my father, who was now the regular soloist at the local Christian Science church. I too rejoiced at the farm that night—until I discovered that I had been included in the deal. I was about to become the only boy in an exclusive girls' school!

I found myself in a boy's hell. Immediately adjoining Hillside was the Jefferson Elementary School. At noon I would take my lunchbox to the stone wall dividing the two schools and watch the boys streaming past on their way home for lunch. During the afternoon whenever possible I would again sneak off to the wall and watch the boys enjoying their recess games, little realizing that they were well aware of my presence and that in a year and a half I would be among them.

Finally, in the summer of 1921, what I longed for came about. By then our parents were also fed up with the farm. They decided to move into Norwalk if a suitable house could be found, one that required only a small down payment. Again Mr. Keeler came to the rescue, helping us secure a modest but pleasant two-story house at 7 Lynes Place.

A few weeks after we moved I was at last allowed to enter the third grade at Jefferson School on the Tuesday after Labor Day. Now I knew how a man released from a long term in prison must feel. It was the most glorious day of my life. No longer would I be swallowed up in a mob of chattering girls.

My heart thumped as I entered the third-grade classroom. Miss Fagan, a pretty young Irish woman, asked me to stand while I was introduced to the class. I didn't know what to do with my hands, so I finally clenched my fists and held them tight to the sides of my legs. I could see several girls glancing sideways at me, but the boys did not seem at all interested.

When I went outside for my first recess period, the boys in my class started jeering, "Sissy! Sissy!" Boys from the upper classes then joined in, chanting, "*He* went to Hillside! *He* went to Hillside! *Toenails* went to Hillside!"

I was petrified and wondered what "Toenails" meant. Then several of the boys tried to grab me. I darted away and got into the boys' toilet, where I was backed up against one of the urinals, facing a charging swarm of fellows all bigger than myself. There was no escape.

Then a low authoritative voice proclaimed, *"Don't anybody touch that little kid!"*

It was a big boy named Joe Toomey, a son of Turkish immigrants. He took my elbow and led me outside. Nothing happened when I was released for lunch, and nothing happened at the afternoon recess. I found myself suddenly accepted, for Joe Toomey had spoken. On the way home I asked Joe why they called me Toenails. "That's nothing. They're just making fun of your name, 'To-land.' They'll get tired of it."

I loved every day of public school and soon became Miss Fagan's prize pupil. What I had been forced to learn at Hillside put me ahead of the others. My mother had been right. I idolized Miss Fagan and felt a friendship for Joe Toomey I'd never experienced before. I spent many afternoons after school with Joe at a little house on the Norwalk River, where we played with a colored boy—the genteel term in those days—of my age named Calvin. After a month I asked Joe and Calvin to play in our backyard, where my father had hung a trapeze on the apple tree. One of the neighbors complained to my father that his son was playing with a colored boy. He summoned me. "I hear you're playing with a little colored boy."

"Yes, Daddy. His name is Calvin. Why?"

"Can he sing?"

I was puzzled.

"Can he sing?" he repeated, and then blasted out a string of vivid expletives aimed at our nosy and racist neighbors. "Oh hell, play with him all you want," he muttered as he walked off. It was many years before I realized what my father meant: that a person should by judged by what he could do, not who he was.

That summer of 1922, Calvin fell into the Norwalk River and drowned. This was my first taste of death. I remember feeling both terrified and confused. At Christian Science Sunday school I had been told there was no death, but I had seen my friend lying in a little coffin and not looking at all like the real Calvin. I only knew that Calvin was gone and would never come back.

The next year my teacher, Miss Donovan, brought me some fourth-grade fame by calling me a "whiz at long division." She was always praising someone—unlike the sixth-grade teacher, Mrs. Ryder, who was notorious for torturing her boy pupils. Miss Donovan, like Miss Fagan, was Irish. But she was larger, her hair was darker, she seemed to burst with enthusiasm, and she always saw the positive side of things. Yet she brought me face to face with a difficult problem when she asked us all to buy War Stamps so Uncle Sam could pay for the war. We all received cards on which to paste the stamps. The first one to fill the card would be a hero.

I didn't have any money, and as I watched the others filling up their cards,

Eastward, Ho!   [29]

I resolved to do something to help my country. I stole twenty-five dollars from an envelope marked "House Money" in my mother's dresser. Miss Donovan was delighted when I filled up my card and handed it to her. She asked the others to clap, and I felt wonderful—until I got home and found my mother in tears. She had lost all the house money, she said, and there was nothing for food. My father would be furious!

There was no alternative. I confessed. Instead of scolding me, my mother put on her hat and took my hand, and we headed for Jefferson School with the stamps. Miss Donovan was still there, and when she heard the story she returned the twenty-five dollars. I was crushed with humiliation; I was no longer a hero. I had to force myself the next day to return to school, where I knew Miss Donovan would brand me as a thief. But she treated me as if nothing had happened.

By now, my father, having finished his singing lessons in New York and abandoned his effort to sell pianos, was trying to peddle a set of books called *Modern Eloquence* and was giving more recitals. Otherwise the only money coming in was from his job as church soloist. But I did not feel in any way deprived. Besides, life at home was never dull.

Although Virginia often got me into trouble, sometimes she got me out of it. For example, there was one boy who decided to make my life miserable; he finally beat me up.

When I arrived home after the fracas, disheveled and with a bleeding nose, Virginia was furious. She grabbed my hand, dragged me to the boy's home, and called him out, and when he emerged, leaped on him, knocking him to the ground. Then she started to flail him with her fists. He could only try to defend himself, for he would not hit a girl. Finally Virginia stopped. "If you ever hit my brother again," she said, "I'll kill you."

Virginia was an accomplished thief, and she taught me how to swipe small items from Ali Hassan's grocery store on West Avenue. To acquire a copy of my favorite magazine, *Wings,* she demonstrated how I could put my large notebook on a copy and then pick up both notebook and magazine. When she boasted that she could steal anything, I bet her she couldn't swipe a catcher's mask—whereupon she stuck one under her shirt and shuffled safely out of the store. This occurred after I had confessed to taking my mother's housekeeping money to buy stamps for Uncle Sam and had vowed never to steal again. So I felt it was necessary to return that catcher's mask. I carried it in a paper bag, and Ali approached as I was replacing it. "I've been looking all over for that," he said. I waited for him to shout "Thief!" at me. Instead he merely said, "Thanks, John," and walked off, leaving me to wonder if he knew about the other thefts.

The summer after fourth grade, in 1923, was special because Uncle George, the architect, sent money to take my mother and me to Danville, Illinois, for a week and then on to Minneapolis to spend the rest of the summer with Mother's parents at their cottage on Lake Harriet. I think the next two months were the most exciting of my boyhood life. Grandfather Willard, whom we called Dadda, spent nearly every day with me.

Within a week I knew every boy on Lake Harriet because of Dadda, who took all children in sight to a little store for ice cream cones and often escorted a gang of us to a fun place on the lake. When we arrived I had been afraid of the water because of my near-drowning in the Mississippi and I couldn't swim, but Dadda taught me how to overcome my fear and become a fairly competent swimmer. I even won a swimming contest. In a real sense, this changed my life. At last I had done something to make my father proud of me! But I had derived my self-confidence from Dadda: my father and I could not create such a bond.

My grandmother—Dammy—was not used to little boys and had a difficult time accepting the scrapes and adventures boys get into. And she couldn't tolerate my wandering off at night to look into the interiors of other people's homes to see how they lived. She also could not understand why anybody, much less her grandson, would want to keep a frog in his pocket.

That fall, my father did spend more time with me, especially on Saturdays and Sundays, when we would often meet some boys from the Italian neighborhood and play football, with my father as coach for both sides. Alas, I was his worst pupil, since I had small hands and little strength, and I felt my father was secretly ashamed of me.

Since our move from the farm to Lynes Place in Norwalk, I had fallen in love with reading. I had started with *Mother West Wind,* gone on to *Uncle Wiggly,* then *the Bobbsey Twins, Tom Swift,* and *Boy Allies* series. Then I had discovered treasures among Ralph's books. My two favorites were *Bill Nye's History of the United States* and *Brann, the Iconoclast.* The first was a satire on sentimentalized American history. One page, for example, would be labeled "Indian Maiden of Fancy" and depict a beautiful squaw; the opposite page would be called "Indian Maiden of Fact" and show a wrinkled hag. I didn't understand most of *Brann,* but I was entranced with the word "Iconoclast," which I discovered meant "one who attacks cherished beliefs as based on error or superstition." Yes!—*that* was exactly what I wanted to be—an Iconoclast!

I also read many novels by Horatio Alger. I devoured them. Alger's hero was always poor (as I was), ambitious (as I was), faced with tremendous barriers to success (as I was); and always succeeded (as I was going to do). I would succeed against all odds—and all by myself! Of course, I would be an Iconoclast as well!

[Part Two]

A Raw Youth (1 9 2 4 – 1 9 3 6)

{4}

Growing Up

I was now growing into my new life. Ten years old seemed very grown up to me in 1922. A sign of my more mature status at 7 Lynes Place in Norwalk was the bathtub. No longer would Virginia and I have to jam ourselves into a small tin tub.

Our move also meant that my father could spend more time with me. He built me a kite and showed me how to fly it in the Morgan estate. He bought me a pair of boxing gloves and tried to teach me the manly art. The gloves hid the smallness of my hands and the punching didn't hurt, but as usual I was inept. He also took me down to the *Norwalk Hour* whenever there was a big prizefight so we could listen to a reporter leaning out of the second-story window and shouting down round-by-round news to the crowd below. Naturally I was always for Jack Dempsey, because he was Irish. In the several Delaney-Berlenbach bouts we were both, of course, for Delaney. I will never forget the World Series of 1923, when my hero, Babe Ruth, and the Yankees finally won after losing the previous two series. At last I had beaten my father, who was a boastful fan of the New York Giants. But that same year we were united Irishmen when Jack Dempsey defeated Firpo, even after the huge Argentinian savagely knocked him out of the ring. Our hero gallantly scrambled back and knocked out his opponent. In the early 1920s we listened to fights and World Series games at our neighbor's house over a radio, an instrument that changed the world for me. With the help of Putch I was the first kid in town to make a crystal set, and I then helped Putch construct a set with tubes. It had earphones, and I tried for hours to get stations outside of New York City. I still remember the thrill of writing in my record book: "Today got KDKA Pittsburgh!" I was at last getting out into the big wide world.

Radio also offered my father a big opportunity. Emily Roosevelt, of Theodore's branch of the family, a very rich woman who had a voice like a frog and sang duets with Father, set up an interview with a New York station, possibly WEAF, that was looking for a musical director. My parents and I drove to New York in our Model T; halfway there, on schedule, I had to get out and throw up. In the city my parents went into a big building, and I stayed in the car and constructed financial castles in the sky. An hour later the two reappeared, looking very sober. Once in the car, Father swore for some time and then said, "Why did I have to open my goddam big mouth!" I learned that the head of the station, at first much impressed with my father, had started to talk about his own ideas for using bits and pieces from classical music for advertisements. "Like hell you say!" burst out my father. "How the bejesus can you use Beethoven to sell soap?"

As a boy I could not help deeply resenting my father's attitude toward my grandfather. When Dadda came east to see us, my father could not hide his disdain. He would make fun of Dadda's ability to make friends with everyone from the mayor to the iceman. In the first week Dadda got to meet more people than all the rest of us ever got to know. I would walk downtown with him every morning. Dadda simply exuded easy good fellowship, which, for some reason, irritated my father. I tried to explain that Dadda was genuinely interested in the woes and triumphs of his new friends. He was not, as my father charged, a "windbag," since most of the time he was listening. As I look back I think this trait, which I admired, was crucial in my own later success in gathering material for my books, since I could see that in Dadda's two weeks he had learned more about Norwalk and those who lived there than my father could gather in a lifetime. Dadda taught me how to listen.

On June 29, 1924, I became twelve. As I look back I see that this was the second great day in my rocky road to manhood, the first being my initial haircut. Now I was old enough to graduate from knickers to long pants. A photograph taken on this day is pitiful. My pants were too long and bulky, and I had an uneasy smile, as if I were wearing my father's trousers. Perhaps deep down I realized I was not ready for them. Obviously my self-confidence was not helped when Virginia kept chanting, "Little boy thinks he's a little man!" Of equal importance was the permission to buy a .22 rifle to replace the BB gun I had long outgrown. I had started to sell copies of the *Literary Digest* in order to make money for contingencies such as this. I had only a dozen regular customers, so I tried to sell a song Putch had written, "Let's Give the Boys a Bonus." As a veteran, he was indignant when he learned that he and the others who had served were not to receive a bonus, and masses of vets without jobs were planning to march on Washington in bitter protest. I managed to sell three copies—which was more than anyone else had done. Even the sales pitch that 10 percent was to go to the American Legion cut no ice. Then I hit on the idea of peddling small garden spades for ladies. They too were a hard sell, and by the time I finally had enough to buy the gun I swore I would never again knock on a door.

I gradually increased the number of my *Literary Digest* customers to twenty, and I was spurred to even greater financial triumphs when I read an ad in *Wings:* "BOYS! Get a motion-picture machine and give shows. MAKE BIG MONEY!" Great idea! But first I had to earn enough to buy the projector. I then remembered how often Helen complained about the difficulty of buying bluing, the stuff used to make laundry look whiter and brighter. Even the new store, a Piggly Wiggly, always seemed to be out of it. So I wrote to the manufacturer, saying that I was a salesman and wanted to buy fifty packages wholesale. Although whoever read the letter must have guessed from my wording and handwriting that I was only a boy, he or she apparently liked my spirit and sent me the bluing. I got rid of the fifty packages in one week by pestering all the neighbors within half a mile, along with special friends of the family. In several weeks I had accumulated enough money and sent for the motion-picture machine.

Its arrival was a high point of my young life. Here was the future. I unpacked it cautiously and, with my father's help, set it up in the basement, along with a screen made out of a sheet. The shipment included three reels of westerns and two reels of comedy. I felt like a great hero, Columbus or somebody, as I started grinding the first western. The images flickering on the sheet were magical. I put up signs on nearby telephone poles advertising "MOVIE SHOW. *Saturday. Westerns and Comedies! Only 3 cents!* TOLANDS' BASE-MENT, 7 Lynes Place, 2 P.M."

Some twenty children piled into our basement on a rainy afternoon for the premiere. The first western was a great success. But the second suddenly fluttered. The film was broken. My heart sank. Then my father appeared and expertly repaired the film. This is why I silently worshiped my father. He could do *anything!*

My relationship with Virginia was still good. I did not forget how she had knocked down my nemesis. But in the fall of 1923 she did something that made me ashamed. She was in the finals of the tennis championship at Hillside and we were all on hand for the big event. The first set was exciting. It was close, but Virginia's opponent won. Then, at the start of the second set, Virginia fell, clutching her leg. My father rushed out to pick her up and carry her off as she grimaced with pain. But when I saw her face I knew she was faking. I knew that she *had* to be the best and the brightest all the time.

I couldn't understand. If I ever became so much as a runner-up, I'd have been delighted. I now knew something about her that my parents did not: she wasn't straight. But I kept this discovery to myself; they would not have understood.

The high point of my father's musical career came when the People's Chorus, run by a wealthy local woman persuaded the Metropolitan Opera Company to do a concert version of *Faust* backed by the chorus. A famous tenor had the lead, with Marie Sundalius as Marguerite, and Wilfred Pelletier was the conductor. My father would be Mephistopheles. It was to be the greatest musical event ever held in the area and would take place at the Regent Theater.

My mother attended both rehearsals at the Regent. At the first one Mr. Pelletier was aghast to discover that Ralph had learned the Italian version, as earlier instructed. The other three soloists were doing the French version.

"Don't be in an uproar," said my imperturbable father, who only lost his head when everybody else was calm. "I'll learn the French tonight." Although he didn't speak any foreign language, he could sing like a native in Russian, Italian, French, or German after hours of recording numbers on wax disks, then listening intently, and finally comparing his renditions with those of foreign baritones. He was a perfectionist.

Alas, my father lost his temper a week later at a Met audition set up by Pelletier. Other singers, who did everything possible to block new talent, made noises offstage in an obvious attempt to annoy him. The climax came, according to my mother, when his accompanist made so many mistakes that my father angrily invited him to "step outside." The pianist wisely declined. It was another example of my father's inability to cope with the mean politics of the musical world. On the sad trip home, Ralph claimed he wasn't too disappointed, because he didn't like opera. The great Russian bass Chaliapin, he claimed, was the only one who acted opera the right way. I heard both sing the same songs many times; my father's voice was somewhat like Chaliapin's but not as deep or big.

When my father learned that Chaliapin was giving a concert in New York, the family funds were raided and he got box seats. Later my mother told me that he sat through the performance completely enraptured but silent. During the encores, however, my father stood up and let loose with his two-handed whistle, which startled everyone, including Chaliapin, who glared up at him, since in Europe a whistle was an insult; but when my father shouted out in Russian one of his favorite songs, the great singer smiled, waved, and proceeded to the piano, which he pounded with his left hand while he sang. My mother told me she had never heard anything like it, and my father was actually shining with delight.

Although we had little money, we were respected in town. My father was accepted as a peer by the large and fascinating conglomeration of artists in Silvermine. These artists understood his flamboyant, tempestuous nature; and though they could never pay except with buffet suppers, performances of their own, and genuine enthusiasm, they kept the flame of my father's artistry burning through fifteen years of poverty.

It looked as if there would be no money for coal one winter. But the powers that be decided to tear up the old wooden blocks on West Avenue, which was a part of the Boston Post Road, in order to pave it properly. The wooden blocks, which had been soaked with oil for many years, were piled up on the side of the street. I saw a man stacking the blocks into his cart and asked him why. "To burn, sonny," he said.

I raced home, grabbed my cart, and for the rest of the day brought load after load to our empty coal bin. And for the next week I roamed up and down West Avenue collecting blocks until our bin was filled. My parents were deeply grateful—though it later cost my mother a lot of work cleaning the lace window curtains, which had become black with soot.

In the fall of 1925, Virginia and I were taken to our first Broadway show. It was the *Music Box Revue,* and it featured an act by the duo Columbus and Snow. To the consternation of his family, Helen's cousin Nelson Snow had become a dancer—though now that he had become well known, the family was proud. While I enjoyed watching Nelson in a magnificent underwater scene in which he and Charlie Columbus threw a girl around as if she were a basketball, my favorite act was a comedy monologue by Robert Benchley, who pretended he was making a report on a club's activities. I had never heard anything so funny. This man, with no props, could have kept the audience enthralled all day. I was excited all through our ride back to Norwalk. Yes! Someday I would write stuff like that!

By then I was at the Center Junior High School, and during study periods I began writing an endless narrative that I tried to make both comical and exciting. I realize now that my teachers in eighth and ninth grades were aware that I was writing stories in study period and were helping me with their silence.

Putch insisted on rushing back to La Crosse. His recent love letters had blossomed and he was now determined to get married. But he didn't have the train fare. My father was broke too, and mother had spent all the money she had made from painting flowers on ivory toilet articles. I was the only one left, and Putch knew I had been saving money to repair the bicycle I'd smashed trying to ride it down Hospital Hill backward. I loved Putch. He was like a big brother and would do anything for me. So I simply gave him the money for his train fare.

After Putch left, my mother, in embarrassment, asked me to go with her when she went to borrow some money from a wealthy factory owner who belonged to our church. Ralph was now trying to sell something else without much success, and Helen had to have fifty dollars for groceries and supplies to last until he received his monthly check as church soloist. We drove in the Model T to a small factory across the street from Center School. As I started to get out of the car, Helen told me to stay behind. She would be all right, she said. Mr. Schwartz was a fine man.

The fifteen-minute wait seemed endless. When she finally returned I could see that she was holding back her tears. That must mean, I thought, that Mr. Schwartz had refused her request. How awful she must feel! She got into the car and I got out to crank it. My father always succeeded after one deft spin, but it always took me a half-dozen tries. Each time I was terrified that the handle would jerk back and break my arm, something that had happened to the football captain of Norwalk High School. My seventh try worked, and I tried to console my mother for not getting the money. But she handed me fifty dollars. Then I realized that she was crying because she was humiliated. "He was so kind," she said in a choked voice. "So kind . . ." The tears flowed. Then she set her face and we drove off.

Why had Ralph allowed *her* to beg money? It wasn't right! It wasn't manly! I didn't say anything, but I wasn't able to look him in the face at dinner. That night I didn't say anything to him about Mr. Schwartz. But many years later my mother revealed that from that day my father avoided Mr. Schwartz at church. He also must have felt the shame of having allowed my mother to endure this humiliation. I think this moment marked the end of my childhood. I resolved to do everything in my power to prevent anything like this from ever happening to my mother again.

[5]

The Play's the Thing

During my second year at Center Junior High, in 1927, an event occurred that proved to be crucially important in my life: our friend the playwright Porter Emerson Browne came to live with us. After his beloved wife died he had begun to drink so heavily that he was unable to write. When my father discovered how bad his state had become, he peremptorily ordered Porter to move into our house. Who better to dry out an alcoholic than an Irishman? My father laid down the rules. Porter must promise not to touch a drop of anything, including the beer my father was brewing in the cellar in defiance of the law. "Don't you dare touch one of those bottles! They can explode in your face!"

Because Porter worshiped my father, he would have promised anything. Yes, he would go to church every Sunday and even on Wednesday evenings. Yes, he would try to write. Yes, he would keep clean. Within a week he was spending a large part of the day telling me about his experiences: doing research in Mexico and China; writing speeches for President Teddy Roosevelt; achieving his first Broadway success, *A Fool There Was,* and hearing that magic call at the curtain: "Author! Author!" He also taught me how to deal from the bottom of a deck of cards—"just in case you get in a game with crooks."

I begged Porter to teach me how to write plays. That would be the goal of my life. He agreed, and for the next year he expounded the techniques of a playwright. He began by reminding me of the time seven years before when he had taken me upstairs to his studio. "Remember how I looked down on that little stage and said you must let the characters do what they have to do? You must make your play come alive and be true to life." His most famous play, *The Bad Man,* had been a great success because it was based on a character who was a Mexican revolutionary, and Porter had ridden with the model, Pancho Villa, for two years as his secretary.

I gawked at this, for I'd heard of Villa as a terrible murderer. "All Americans," said Browne, "assume Villa was a villain. The truth is that he was a patriotic Mexican. So I wrote a comedy and made people laugh when I showed that the so-called bad guy was actually a good guy."

I had just turned fifteen, but Porter treated me as an adult while teaching me the principles of a well-made play: exposition, plot structure, characterization, and the obligatory scene that sums it all up. Then he told me it was time to get some practical training. He took me to an afternoon showing of a movie at the Regent Theater. In the middle of it he tugged at my sleeve. "Let's go." I was puzzled. Once we were outside he explained that we would go home and write the last half ourselves, then return two days later to see how the movie actually came out.

We did this half a dozen times, and on each occasion our version was better than the movie version—and he would explain why. One movie, for example, ended with the hero pulling out a gun and shooting his wife. "Obscene!" Porter exclaimed, to the shock of nearby adults. "The gun wasn't planted. It came as a surprise to the audience. It should have been planted in the first reel! Whatever comes at the end of the play—a gun, a character flaw, virtue—*must* be planted in the first act."

This teaching continued, punctuated by cardplaying, odds and ends of practical advice, jokes, and good companionship. One day while we were playing cards, Porter, in cogitation, began absentmindedly twirling his false teeth with his tongue. Helen entered the room. She gasped at the sight. Porter popped his teeth back into place and apologized.

By now Porter was my great hero, even with false teeth. I wanted to be exactly like him without having the least idea what such a desire entailed. A test of this ambition came a few weeks later. It was a Sunday morning and my father was getting into his formal church outfit when we heard downstairs a muffled bang, followed by a series of bangs. "Je-sus Co-rist!" exclaimed Ralph. "Porter's got at the green beer!"

We all raced to the dining room just as a most bedraggled Porter appeared at the cellar door. He was drenched with beer and smelled horrible. "Goddam you, Porter, I told you it would explode!"

Porter bowed his head in shame. "So I found," he said after groping for a proper response. By then my father was almost as amused as he was angry. "If you think you're going to get out of going to church, you're wrong! Now get the bejesus upstairs so we can clean you up!"

My parents and Porter disappeared into the bathroom while Virginia and I eavesdropped outside. During the pain and indignity of being bathed and scrubbed by his host and hostess, he never uttered a peep. Our mother murmured soothing words while our father alternated between blasphemous shouting and explosions of laughter. Finally Porter emerged in a pair of my father's long johns. They were a foot too long and the waist was so tight that Porter could hardly breathe. He was marched to my father's room and the door closed while my mother, in her room, hastily worked on a pair of my father's trousers. She shortened the legs with safety pins and Porter was brought to try them on. There stood Porter, a pitiful sight with a woebegone face—yet I would have died for him. He was still my hero and benefactor.

"He'll never button them," said my mother. But in a few seconds she solved the problem, stitching in a wide piece of dark cloth over the gaping open fly. Fortunately Porter had not worn his lone jacket into the basement.

Although it was only two blocks to the church, my mother insisted we go in the Model T. My father laughed all the way home. "The next time you go visiting, Porter, for Christ's sake take along an extra pair of pants."

My mother's only comment was, "Ralph, I don't think you ever sang so beautifully."

"No man sings 'beautifully,' " he retorted, but it was evident he was pleased.

I was finding high school much more challenging than Center, where I had won the two-and-a-half-dollar gold piece for the highest grades. But I knew that the girl winner, Emily Daggy, the daughter of a well-known painter, was smarter than I. She was far, far beyond me. Perhaps the greatest change was the faculty. For the first time I had two male teachers. By now my reading interests had drastically changed. Although I hated every page of *Silas Marner,* I enjoyed most of the books we were forced to read in English class and I still read voraciously on my own. For a while my favorite books were a romanticized series on the lives of artists and writers in Paris. Then I came across a volume in the local library entitled *A Raw Youth.* It was by Dostoevsky, a name I could neither spell nor pronounce; and although the language was much more difficult to understand, I soon became so engrossed in this strange, realistic tale of a sensitive boy that I began to imagine *I* was the raw youth.

I remember wishing that Ralph and I could emulate the crucial scene, told in the first person by the father, when the barrier between father and son finally breaks down. Again and again I turned to that scene and read the final words when Arkady met his father on the canal bank to say goodbye:

> "Will you never give me a real warm kiss, as a child kisses its
> father?" Arkady said, with a strange quiver in his voice. I
> kissed him fervently. "Dear boy . . . may you be always as pure

in heart as you are now." I had never kissed him before in my
life. I never could have conceived that he would like me to.

I too had never kissed my father, and it would have been impossible in
our family. Kissing was for women. But Russians were not like Americans;
it was all right for them. What I most longed for was an end of the barrier
between my father and myself, as well as an end of my own strange feelings
of simultaneous love and dislike. If we could only just talk openly like
Arkady and his father!

I also loved the descriptions of St. Petersburg; they were so vivid that I
felt I was living there. But what I found most compelling was the "idea" of
the hero, Arkady. Like me, he had taken a number of vows to do or not do
things, and he was driven by an "idea" that enriched his barren life. "My
idea," he confided to the reader, "is to become as rich as Rothschild—not
simply rich, but as rich as Rothschild. What objects I have in view, what
for and why—all that shall come later. First I will simply show that attain-
ment of my object is a mathematical certainty. It is a very simple matter;
the whole secret lies in two words, *obstinacy* and *persistence.*" I had underlined
those key words—the two words that I believed would automatically make
me a great playwright.

But first I had to make some money so I could *become* a playwright. I
needed an education in the best school and college in America, and although
I was the top male student in my class, I knew I'd never make it if I went
directly from Norwalk High School to a college. Having heard from a friend
of the family that Phillips Exeter Academy in New Hampshire was the best
preparation for college, I made another vow: I'd go *there.* But I needed money.

When Virginia graduated from Hillside, our parents borrowed money from
our relatives the Ludwicks to send her to the Albertina Rasch Dance Studio
in New York, where she did so well that she was put into one of the Rasch
professional groups. The family went to see her in *Lovely Lady* at a Hartford
theater. When that run was over she brought home two stars of the show, a
well-known dance team. I was delighted. She had achieved her goal and was
sending money home.

Determined to earn more myself in the coming summer, I became water
boy for a contractor, Charlie Myers, who was a member of the Christian
Science church. He was constructing a grammar school in Wilton. I will
never forget the agony of my first day. My main job was to help carry lumber,
and by midafternoon my small hands were bloody. I began to cry, but only
my partner noticed—and lent me his gloves. The next day's job was carrying

sacks of cement. I staggered off with the first one, which felt as if it weighed a hundred pounds. The man who had lent me the gloves then took me aside. "Carry it over your shoulder, kid." I did, and found I could keep going all morning.

Once the building started, I enjoyed my job as water boy, but as soon as the forms for the cement foundation had been erected I was given a job that only I could do. Since I was the smallest person on the site, I was lowered inside the forms to paint them with old crankcase oil so the cement wouldn't stick to the wood. It was a difficult and stifling job, and every half hour I'd be hauled up for some fresh air.

By the end of the first day I was accepted as one of the crew, despite some rough teasing at first. I quickly came to like and respect them all despite their foul language. Because almost all of our family friends were artists, musicians, writers, or successful businessmen, I had never experienced close contact with working-class men, and I soon found that I felt completely at home with them. They were rough but good-hearted, and in many ways brighter than my family's friends. They knew how to build a school.

I was in the advanced senior class of Norwalk High, and I graduated in February 1930. My only thought after graduation was Exeter. I had finally been accepted because of a glowing recommendation from an alumnus, Cliff Peck, one of my mother's best friends in Sioux Falls. But I had saved only about four hundred dollars, and it would take at least a thousand even if I got a cheap room and a job waiting on table.

I was sent a book the size of a small pad, *The E Book,* which told all about Exeter. I read it so often I almost memorized it. It began with a declaration that Exeter was democratic and everyone said "Hi!" to everyone else. It also told of the previous year's baseball game against Andover, the school's great rival, and described the key play in which a fielder dropped a fly ball that could have been caught by the "veriest tyro." Those two new words became engraved in my mind, and I was determined to use them eventually in my writing. But I have never gotten around to it until now.

By that time my father had stopped making wisecracks about preparatory school and confided to my mother that he had a great scheme to make a lot of money so I could attend Exeter. He would start a glee club. He went forward with his usual supreme confidence, and after much newspaper publicity and circularizing (he was an expert at putting out mimeographed circulars), he called for the first meeting of the glee club at the high school auditorium. We all caught his enthusiasm. At last we were going to be on that elusive street called Easy! Our Ship Was Coming In—after fifty false starts. We were approaching the Valley of the Moon. We all had different estimates of the membership of the chorus. Virginia thought the auditorium would be too small to hold the crowd; Ralph thought it would be about the right size, big enough for three hundred. Helen, always conservative, guessed 125, and I, always less sanguine than the others, was expecting a mere hundred.

Five people came. I was shattered, and left the auditorium—not because now I wouldn't get any money for Exeter, but because I was afraid of how the disappointment would strike my father. I waited outside, almost sick to my stomach, wondering what to say. At last he came down the steps of the high school with his faithful five. He was talking excitedly, magnetically, brilliantly. "The five of you," he said, "will be the nucleus for the largest, finest chorus ever assembled!" But once the four of us sat down in the kitchen for coffee and cookies, he said with an engaging grin, "Well, we had another 'small but appreciative audience' tonight."

I don't think I ever admired my father more than I did that night, for at a moment when the average person would have been crushed by defeat he still shone with optimistic, if foolhardy, courage. During the night I lay sleepless in my bed with visions of my father's future triumphs on the concert stage intoxicating me.

He soon got a job selling cars. I think they were Buicks. A week later I tried to drive one, and after twenty yards I smashed into a telephone pole. When Ralph came running out of the house, I thought he would at last strike me. To my amazement he didn't even raise his voice. "I'll tell them a customer did it," he said. I never felt closer to him, and for the first time even experienced a little guilt about leaving the family so I could go to prep school.

I still had to make at least six hundred dollars before September. I looked in vain for any kind of work, for the effects of the previous year's stock market crash were being felt. But Virginia came to my aid. Her new boyfriend, who wanted very much to marry her, got me a position at the Norwalk Tire and Rubber Company, where his father was one of the top officials.

By midsummer I had saved more than seven hundred dollars and written a number of short stories. While making my tour around the factory I would be thinking about a story in progress. One morning I thought I was stepping into the ground-floor elevator but it wasn't there; the warning gate had carelessly been left open. I fell into the pit. It was only a five-foot drop, but I was stunned. Then I heard the noise of the descending elevator, looked up, and saw the bottom of the elevator coming down to crush me. Ordinarily I was a slow mover, but this time I acted quickly and adroitly, leaping just in time into an indentation at one side. The man who had forgotten to close the warning gate looked at me with terror. His face was white. Yet I was calm.

I thought little about this until later, when our Hi-Y basketball coach picked me up and was driving me home. Then I suddenly realized what had happened and threw up. I knew that ordinarily I could not have jumped into that indentation without thinking. What had happened? I asked Coach. "That must have been adrenaline," he said. I had heard the word "adrenaline" but it meant nothing to me. "If you had stopped to think," he added, "you'd have been killed."

While writing this chapter I marveled for the first time at my many escapes from death—first from my grandmother's hat pin, once when I tod-dled along a trolley track, later when I crawled onto the porch roof, later still when I wandered into the lake, and finally when my uncle threw me into the Mississippi to teach me how to swim. Fortunately my sister saved me. In years to come I would get into even more serious trouble through my own rashness and then, miraculously, be rescued. I always assumed this was the luck of the Irish—which is probably just another term for fate.

6

"Exeter Fair, Mother Stern Yet Tender"

With a suitcase inherited from Uncle George and a huge old-fashioned Victrola horn, I boarded a train for Boston on a bright morning in early September 1930. I had already mailed the Victrola itself to my dormitory. When I finally arrived at Exeter, there, across from the Administration Building, was my goal, Abbot Hall—an impressive old structure that lay almost at the center of the campus.

My room was on the top floor, and I was exhausted by the time I got up there and pushed open the door. The room was small, and because of the roof slope I had to bend down to get into my part of the area. It was the cheapest room in the school—fifty dollars a year. Lying on a bed near the window was a young man who looked much older than I and was obviously very much at home. "You take the other bed," he said and introduced himself: Bill Barnes. He immediately explained that this was his second prep school; he had previously attended Loomis. He was a senior, and I was only an upper middler (a junior).

Bill, amused by the huge horn of the Victrola I'd brought from home, speculated that it had come over on the *Mayflower.* He then discovered that I had only classical records. This information may have been the reason for his casually remarking that he'd had the hardest head of anyone back at Loomis, and he could smash it through our closet door anytime he felt like it.

His manner abruptly changed, however, when I put the picture of a pretty girl in a scanty dance costume on my dresser. It was a professional shot of one of Virginia's friends, and my sister had signed it: "With all my love, Cynthia." I had never met her. Bill surveyed the photo and looked at me with sudden respect, and I knew I'd been accepted.

The next day I went to the bursar's office to pay for the first semester's room and tuition. The bursar's eyes bulged as he watched me extract my big roll of bills and methodically count out what I owed. Many years later he told me that he was astonished, particularly when he learned that I had earned much of that cash in a tire factory.

Exeter had just introduced the Harkness Plan, which meant that most of the classrooms contained a large oval table with seats for no more than a dozen pupils. I grew to like this system, because it helped us to really know our instructors as well as one another. At the end of the first marking period I received an A in Ancient History but was low or failing all my other courses. I was summoned to the office and told that I would be dismissed unless I drastically improved. Did I have any comment? In my enthusiasm I had signed up for an extra course, and I proposed dropping this. I also suggested reverting to beginning French. This worked. At the end of the next marking period I was on the honor roll and was awarded a scholarship.

Instead of going to Sunday chapel at Exeter, I chose to attend the services of the local Christian Science Society, held downtown on the second floor of an office building. Half of the members were local, the rest from the Academy. After the first service I noticed a very old woman, Alice Sullivan, who seemed to be partially blind, being escorted down the stairs by several students. They were taking her to her apartment on the top floor of a small house not far from the gymnasium. I joined them and was delighted to find that she was as merry as a cricket. She was the widow of a Civil War veteran and was living on his tiny pension. By the end of a month I had become a close friend of Aunt Alice, as everyone called her. She showed me her little apartment and demonstrated how competent she was at building a wood fire in the oven and preparing her own meals. She never complained. The grocery store made deliveries, and occasionally relatives in town would visit her. What I liked most about her was her independent spirit.

Most of the students went home for Thanksgiving, but I stayed at Exeter. That Sunday another boy and I were the only students at church, and I spent most of the day listening to Aunt Alice's stories about the hard but fascinating years following the Civil War. She also made the Gay Nineties come alive. During the first three weeks of December I saw her every day. I could tell that her sight was getting worse by the number of burns on her hands from lighting her two stoves, but she was as cheerful as ever. I told her about some of my problems, and her sympathetic counsel, salty Yankee wit, and fathomless faith in God were a great help. I marveled at how she could be so concerned about me when she herself had to clump through the snow in the dark to chop wood to heat her dingy little apartment.

Just before Christmas vacation, I went to say goodbye to Aunt Alice, since I would be in New York for ten days, and overheard her arguing with a visiting relative, who was worried about her and wanted her to go immediately to the old ladies' home. After the relative had gone I discovered by chance that her monthly government pension check for twenty-one dollars had not arrived. A friend and I pooled the tips we had received for waiting on table and left the money with her.

To the amazement of my friends at Exeter, I planned to hitchhike to New York, where my folks now lived, in the Murray Hill neighborhood. It would take me forever, I was warned, but I was in the city before 11:00 P.M. I had put an Exeter sticker on my suitcase and I was sure this had helped.

I knew the family now lived in a brownstone house on Thirty-first Street just east of Park Avenue. I took a subway to Thirty-third and Park, appalled to find hundreds of people sleeping on newspapers. This was the first sign of the Depression I had witnessed. It had made no impact on us, since we'd rarely had much money. Now most of the United States was experiencing what I had been familiar with all my life. The beaten looks on the faces of middle-aged men made me realize that our country was *really* in trouble. I had to be careful stepping over the sleepers, and I was impressed to see that those returning from the theater were also careful and sympathetic. New York was a good, safe, and even friendly city to live in back then. People were kinder to each other, because the Depression made us less selfish and more aware of what we all had in common. I walked to Thirty-first Street, startled to see that Park Avenue had suddenly become Fourth Avenue, and when I reached home, the first floor of the brownstone, I was greeted with kisses and scolding. Why was I so late? When I explained that I had hitchhiked, my mother was appalled and my father was angry. But Virginia laughed and said she wished she had been along.

During that vacation my relationship with Virginia deepened. She now laughed at what she called my "pixie sense of humor" and insisted that we go out to "look for parties." I had no idea what she meant, but soon found out. We headed north to a better neighborhood and soon heard the sounds of revelry in an apartment house. Virginia rang several bells on the right floor and then led me up to some party, where she was welcomed. In a few minutes she was the life of the party, while I did my best to be invisible. She tossed off the first drink and was funnier than before. I took one sip of my drink and almost choked, bringing myself into the spotlight, much to my embarrassment. After the third drink Virginia was still the center of attention, but I noticed that her speech had begun to slur and she was making caustic remarks. After the fourth drink she became argumentative, and the host told me to take my "damned sister to hell out of here!"

I had to use physical force to head her back home, and by the time we reached Thirty-first Street she was swearing at me in a loud voice. I shook her and told her to shut up or Father would raise hell. This quieted her.

A few nights later she again suggested we go looking for a party. I refused until she promised not to take more than two drinks, and we had a good time for the rest of the vacation. One night she took me to a speakeasy—a new experience for me. I found it interesting even though the smoke and alcohol stench nauseated me. So she led me to a nearby little nightclub where the music was not blaring. Within minutes she knew almost everyone and was dancing with various partners. I was not a very good dancer, despite Virginia's efforts to teach me. But an older woman invited me to dance, and I reluctantly complied. My partner was very patient and talked with a heavy accent that I found intriguing, and our dance was pleasant until she pushed her hips against me and, to my horror, I had an erection! How could I get back to the table without causing a sensation? But I did—and remained glued to my chair for the rest of the evening.

The most fun I had was seeing four of the best shows on Broadway. Virginia took me to a place under Gray's Drugstore near Broadway and Forty-third Street where cut-rate tickets could be bought minutes before curtain time. We never spent more than two dollars for seats in the second balcony.

I hitchhiked back to Exeter, arriving before dark, perplexed by my sister's behavior. I couldn't understand it. With one or two drinks she would be charming and exhilarating, but one drink later she would be another person—touchy, irritable, and challenging.

The next day I found Aunt Alice's apartment ice-cold. The wood bin was empty, and I could see the disorder of ill-prepared meals strewn all over the kitchen. She heard me and called me to come into the parlor. It was pitch dark, and I could hardly see her face as she sat in her little rocker. She was glad that I was back and chattered away cheerfully. She said I looked wonderful, but I knew she couldn't see a thing. She had been alone during the entire holiday. "The lights are out," I said in an offhand manner. She admitted that she had gone blind, but if she told her relatives they would send her to the old ladies' home. "Then I could never see you boys," she said. I told her that a friend and I would take turns building her fires every morning and helping her prepare meals. She smiled like a young girl. "I'll have two beaus," she said. "You'll be my eyes."

In February I received a surprise visit from my father, who was beaming. Once we reached my room he began pulling from his pockets rolls of money and dumping them onto my bed. He was now selling something called Pyroil, an additive to oil that gave it longer life. It had been invented by an old friend in La Crosse, and my father had been given all of New England as his territory. He was now getting commissions from dozens of salesmen. Never had I seen my father so full of life.

The following summer I worked in his office, which was only a block away on Fourth Avenue. He was not only New England manager for Pyroil but had organized Associated Artists, a group of more than a hundred talented musicians who had trouble finding paying engagements. He had already set up so many dates that he could afford to buy the front page of *Musical Courier,* featuring a large photo of himself surrounded by several of his best-known artists. In addition he made money from others in the building who had heard of his ability to write effective ads. He would charge fifty dollars for an ad that he dashed off in half an hour. But he told me not to deliver the finished copy for two days lest his customers think it was too easy.

The summer of 1931 rushed by and I found myself returning to school, loaded down with more than a hundred Exeter pennants and banners. When the parents of the new students arrived I was on hand, and before the end of the day I had sold every pennant and banner at a substantial profit.

My second year at Exeter was even more rewarding. I persuaded the new chemistry teacher from England, John Hogg, to hire me as cleanup assistant. Every afternoon I spent two hours rearranging instruments and wiping off every bottle in the large room. On the first day I spilled a few drops of hydrochloric acid on the back of my hand, and the scar remained for many years. This was my first and last accident in that lab. Mr. Hogg was a very reserved man, and I never felt at ease with him. Then one day in morning assembly, before the entire student body, he talked of his experiences as an infantryman in the Great War. Ordinarily I spent my time in assembly studying the gilded names of those Exonians killed in battle, always ending at the two who had died in the Civil War on the same day. But this morning I, along with everyone else in the room, was riveted by Mr. Hogg's calm recitation of the horrors of battle. He described seeing his best friend dead, sitting at the edge of the dugout as if he were alive, day after day, until finally no one even noticed him. Suddenly Mr. Hogg broke into tears. We students were horrified. I had never seen a full-grown man cry—and Mr. Hogg above all! The reserve between us began to disappear after that, and we became close friends.

Perhaps it was this experience that caused me to reread *A Raw Youth.* Incidents I had earlier skimmed over now came to life, and Arkady's quixotic behavior began to make sense. Grown-ups were just as confused as their children, and I began to understand the curious love-hate relationship between Arkady and his father in the scene where the youth finally met his legal father, the aged Makar, who had become a monk. It helped me understand my own father, who would, I hoped, in turn understand why I was going to devote my life to writing.

In the spring of 1932, the seniors' primary concern was getting into a good college, preferably one of the Big Three, and most of them were sweating out their college entrance exams. I had been selected as a member of Cum Laude, the preparatory school equivalent of Phi Beta Kappa, and didn't have to take the exams. The secret of my scholastic success lay in the Harkness Plan and the high quality of the faculty. Sitting around a table with a bright teacher and eleven bright comrades forced me to think fast and not open my mouth until I had something specific to say. We were also taught how to take notes, something I had rarely done in high school. If I had gone to college after high school I would have had to struggle to get passing grades. Now I was confident I could compete with the top students at Harvard.

As graduation neared I received offers of full scholarships from Princeton, Harvard, and Dartmouth. Then to my surprise I was invited to the home of the headmaster, Lewis Perry. In two years we had never exchanged a word, and I wondered what I had done. "Why don't you try my college, Williams?" he said. I knew little about Williams except that it was a dinky college in the hills of the northwest corner of Massachusetts. Mr. Perry said I could not only get a full-tuition scholarship but a guarantee of a job waiting on table. "I hear that you have probably made more money here than any other student," he added, looking at me as if to say, "I know all about you, son," and I wondered how he knew about my salesmanship of pennants and other items. "Williams is a rich man's college in many respects, and for an ambitious young man there are many more opportunities to make extra money than at Harvard or Yale." I accepted.

My immediate future was now determined, but I had one more task. Next year there would be nobody to light Aunt Alice's stoves and take care of her. I got the names and addresses of all the students who went to the Christian Science Society and asked their parents to contribute to a fund for sending Aunt Alice to the Christian Science Home near Concord, New Hampshire. I was putting up two hundred dollars from my savings, and I suggested that the parents do at least the same. All did so, some being very generous, and arrangements were made to send Aunt Alice and her pitiful belongings to the home. When we parted she promised to write every week "to my dear boy." She did, and it is one of my greatest regrets that those loving letters, almost indecipherable, were lost.

Upon arriving home three days before my twentieth birthday, I learned that we were going to spend the summer on Fire Island, a long, narrow sand strip off the coast of Long Island. At Babylon we boarded a ferry, the *Sea Queen,* which would take us to Ocean Beach, the largest town on the island. I watched the blur of the village slowly focus into individual structures as our ship drew closer. First appeared a disdainful-looking building (the yacht club) with many-colored pennants flapping lazily; then a more democratic structure (the Community Center) with a pier crowded with bathers; then a single row of two-story buildings (the business section); and finally the tiny cottages in precise military lines, shaded by occasional small pine trees and flanked by hardy shrubs trying to pull a living out of the sand.

From the upper deck I scanned the long spit of sand that stretched in both directions as far as I could see. I could just make out the ocean side of the island with its long, even rows of breakers pounding with slow, relentless monotony against the white beach. I tried to see this as a mighty conflict: the Sea attacking this weak but courageous Island, tearing at it with hungry waves and devouring it inch by inch. Now and then it triumphantly broke through to the calm, comforting Bay, only to have man rebuild the Island's defenses. What a terrific idea for a play! I visualized the quiet, peaceful Bay as a traitor to its fellow waters and an ally of the Island—calmly bringing reinforcements from the mainland and rarely boiling in anger. Not only were natural forces pitted against each other, but so were the inhabitants of this strange island.

That was the cast. Now all I needed was a situation. But my dream world was suddenly blasted to bits by the sharp, fishwife shriek of the *Sea Queen's* whistle as the village of Ocean Beach rushed toward us.

"I hope to God they at least have a movie theater!" said Virginia.

By the end of the first week at the resort my sister had become the most popular girl in Ocean Beach and I had found, after exploring every walk along the shore, a stretch of beach where I could swim out as far as I pleased without being whistled back by lifeguards. I had also fallen desperately in love with a girl with odd, almond-shaped eyes and high cheekbones that gave her a marvelous, almost Indian appearance. Her mouth was full and sensuous, and she had been nicknamed Exotic. When I finally got up nerve to approach her, I said, "I already know your name. It's Ex—"

"You were going to say Exotic. Go ahead. Some silly college boy gave me that nickname, and it's stuck. He was a fraternity man. Belonged to I Phelta Thigh." She burst into laughter.

Needing money to take out Exotic, I had already wangled a job selling oil, which the cottagers used for lamps and cooking. Every morning I filled up a large, cumbersome tank on wheels and pushed it from house to house. One of my first customers was the sister of Joe Laurie, a well-known vaudeville comedian; noticing me ogle a bookcase crammed with famous plays, she invited me to come over anytime and read them. She also promised to introduce me to such famous residents or visitors as Gertrude Lawrence, Fanny Brice, and Jimmy Durante.

Several times a week, Virginia insisted that we go wandering around after dark looking for parties. She had an instinct for finding the action, and soon learned that the most effective technique was to tag after Ricky, the local bootlegger, who delivered his goods on roller skates.

At first she stopped after two drinks, but on the next outing she started a heated argument which put an end to the party. She promised never to drink again, but two days later, when the toilet flush at our cottage didn't work, I found a half-full bottle of gin in the toilet tank, interfering with the ball-cock mechanism. I then heard Virginia arguing stridently with my mother.

"What the hell's the idea, Virginia?" I asked, holding up the bottle.

"What do you mean, *Virginia!*" she yelled, taking a staggering step toward me. "Aren't there other people in this cottage?" She drew herself up haughtily. "What makes you think it's mine?"

Virginia continued to insist that the bottle had appeared in the toilet tank through some mysterious agency that had nothing to do with her. In a mixture of rage and frustration I started to leave the cottage and accidentally slammed the screen door on her hand. She indicated that the pain was unbearable, but I had my suspicions; why had her hand been on the doorjamb in the first place?

While I can't vouch for her pain, her reactions were excessive. When she dramatically disappeared into the bedroom to nurse her wound, I stated flatly that I thought she was faking.

Later, when my father found me down on the beach, he bawled me out for suspecting Virginia of faking. "I was in a responsible position when I was your age—not having a good time going to school."

Good time! I thought. How would he know? He'd only gone through the fifth grade. "In case you've forgotten, I've been supporting myself ever since leaving Norwalk."

"Supporting, shit! Are you paying for this cottage or buying the food?"

I was indignant. I was indeed paying for much of the food that summer. "I didn't ask to come down here. I worked my way through Exeter."

"Do you want a medal for it?"

"It didn't cost you a damned cent!"

"You're too damn fresh sometimes. What you need is a little hot-ass!" He drew his hand back as if to strike me, but I wasn't at all afraid. My father had never hit me or even spanked me. He often lost his temper and broke furniture and dishes, but he never hit anyone in the family. He raised his voice angrily. "Yes, I said hot-ass!" He slammed his own thigh sharply and cried out in pain. "Holy jumping Jesus, I'm getting a damn sunburn!"

I took off my jacket and handed it to my father. "You need it more than I do."

He gratefully, carefully slipped into it. "I'm the biggest goddam fool on the beach!"

I suggested that we run home and get some olive oil for the sunburn. As we jogged off the beach I was glad that my father did not have a potbelly like most other guys' fathers. And a special advantage of having an Irish father was that the most bitter arguments soon ended with no rancor on either side. Now we were laughing, the ancient father-son antagonism lost for the moment in companionship.

By the end of the summer my passion for Exotic had undergone some changes. She would occasionally go to a Saturday-night dance at the Community Center and sometimes would let me kiss her. She said I was the most interesting boy she'd ever met and I shouldn't be in love with her because right at this moment I was more interesting than she would ever be in her whole life, and I would be even more interesting when I was older.

The end came after the Labor Day dance at the yacht club when a ten-piece band from Babylon was blasting out, "Yes, Sir, That's My Baby!" As I pushed the heavy-armed Exotic around the packed floor, I wondered how I could have been so impressed by the Yacht Club only two short months before.

It had all been a mirage. For I now "belonged." I was one of the tannest, the lifeguards were all my friends, and the girl I was dancing with had been the most sought-after girl of the season. Yet I had only one real desire, and that was to go home and go to bed. My mind was whirling with thoughts of going to Williams. This island life was already a life of an unreal past, and I eagerly looked forward to moving into a new world.

When the band began playing "Blasé," Exotic started singing the words in her off-key voice. "'Member the night we copied down all the words to this?"

Yes, I remembered. It had been the first time she'd ever let me kiss her. As we then headed for her cottage she called me "cute," and I wondered how I could leave without hurting her feelings. Once we arrived at Exotic's cottage she said, "I'll get into something more practical. We don't want to ruin a new dress, do we?" My wait on a lumpy couch was interminable. Different emotions tumbled around in my turbulent mind: fear, desire, repugnance, curiosity, depression, and excitement. But the strongest feeling was desire.

She whispered softly over my shoulder, "Hi, sweetie!" She had her mother's salt-encrusted beach robe around her. I wasn't sure what she had on underneath the robe. She was wiping off the last traces of makeup with a piece of toilet paper.

"This is better than Kleenex," she said in a matter-of-fact tone. Then she balled up the soiled toilet paper and threw the wad into a corner. This little act of untidiness offended me more than anything she had ever said or done before. "Now I'm all set, hon." She sat on the couch next to me and wound her arms around me. I started to say something. "Don't talk, sweetie, let's just have some fun." She put her moist lips on mine, and we embraced passionately. Then she took my left hand and put it under the bathrobe on her full breast. She was naked underneath the robe.

"Now," she whispered. As she pulled me over on her, the couch creaked. "This is no place for this kind of thing." She stood up, her bathrobe opening carelessly. "Come on in the bedroom." She took one of my hands and yanked me to my feet. "Don't be afraid, hon," she said softly in an almost maternal manner as she pressed her warm body to mine. "I've taken care of everything."

I said I felt sick.

She looked at me anxiously. "You want an aspirin first?"

"I think I'd better go home."

She put a cool hand on my forehead, and an odd thought crossed my mind: How could her body be so warm and her hand so cool?

"Gee, hon, you really do feel hot! I bet you got a temperature! You go home and take care of yourself. From now on you got to take good care of yourself—for me."

I wanted to thank her for being so understanding, but I was afraid to linger a moment longer. It wasn't that I was afraid of making love, I assured myself. I was afraid that if I didn't I'd be forced by honor to marry her because she loved me so much.

"It was a wonderful night, hon," she called softly after me. "Nighty-night, sweetie!"

[7]

Williams College, or Building Castles in the Air

It was truly the end of summer and the start of a new season by the time I boarded a train for Williamstown, Massachusetts, in early September 1932. I was thrilled to be taking another major step in life, and this time I carried only a suitcase and a massive typewriter—an unexpected gift from my father, who had bought it at an auction for very little. It was in excellent condition and boasted a long carriage for use in bookkeeping. My trunk, I was told, would arrive a day or so later because of the transfer to another train in North Adams.

I guessed that the others in my car were also bound for Williams. Like some of the wealthier guys at Exeter, they were better dressed than I and had an air of confidence and ease which I disliked but envied. At North Adams we all changed to another train, which soon stopped at a tiny station where all the young men raced for a door. With my suitcase and heavy typewriter, I was the last one off. I followed the others past an athletic field and reached the outskirts of the campus. I had been informed that my dormitory, Williams Annex, would be the first college building I would see, and if I missed it I would come upon the Haystack Monument, a memorial to a small group of young men who long ago had used a haystack as shelter during a thunderstorm and, while waiting, had vowed to devote their lives to serving God as missionaries in Asia.

The Annex was not imposing, and I was directed to a large room on the second floor, where a tall young man was unpacking. This was Fred Anderson, my roommate, who informed me that our dorm had once been the college infirmary and we occupied the old operating room. When Fred stared at the big typewriter I explained that I was a writer, and he expressed hope that the noise would not be too distracting. The two of us headed past other dormitories to the gym, where all freshmen would eat until pledged by the fraternities. All those rejected by fraternities would automatically become members of the Commons Club. Fred, like me, had been offered a job as a waiter, and we were soon weaving our way through the chaos to our assigned tables. At Exeter each waiter served two tables of eight, but here I only had one, and I soon discovered why. Most of the other waiters were inexperienced and carried their trays clumsily.

Most freshmen had half a dozen fraternity bids, but I had only two—even though I came from Exeter. I went to the rushing interviews only out of curiosity, for I had come with just enough money to pay for my room and twenty dollars for sundry expenses, confident that I would soon get part-time jobs.

I found the Commons Club to my liking. It was an interesting collection of some 125 "undesirables"—the Jews, the very bright who talked too much, graduates of public high schools, the terribly shy, and sundry nonconformists who obviously did not "belong." I felt right at home. I had asked to wait on the farthest table and soon became an object of wonder as I easily wove my way across the dining room, carrying my tray on my left hand. The sophomore waiter next to me, Bus Navins, soon gave me a nickname that lasted four years: Shifty. This name was a compliment, and I repaid Bus by showing him how to pile dirty dishes properly so that he had perfect control of the tray with his left hand. This also left his right arm free to clear away traffic and open the door to the kitchen, whereas those who used two hands had to turn and ass-bump their way in. Within a few weeks the majority of the waiters were using only one hand.

My two favorite instructors during my freshman year were Stanley Young in English Composition and Michele Vaccariello in French. I spent every Sunday afternoon at the home of Mr. and Mrs. Vaccariello, the "Vacs," along with a few other students who were interested in the arts. I was asked to read the one-act play I had just finished and was encouraged by the Vacs to start a three-acter. Stanley Young was also encouraging and revealed that he was writing a play about Shelley (or was it Keats?) which was being considered by a Broadway producer. Unfortunately he couldn't find a good typist for the final draft. On my own I asked a town resident, also a freshman, for a list of typists available in Williamstown. I interviewed several and picked the best. She turned out to be so good that I started a typing agency. A group of students who were flunking Young's course were also advised by him to tutor with me if they wanted to pass the first marking-period test. Mr. Young advised me to charge them twenty-five dollars apiece, to be paid only if they passed. All passed.

That fall of 1932 I got my first taste of politics. Up to then I had taken no interest in the presidential race. The student body had recently held a mock election, with Herbert Hoover scoring an overwhelming victory, and then

Governor Franklin Roosevelt was scheduled to come through town. The Democratic governor of Massachusetts, Joseph B. Ely, an alumnus of Williams, had urged Roosevelt to speak to the students from an open car. It stopped near the chapel, and I had been inveigled by an Irish fellow waiter to come out and see "the greatest man on earth." The two of us had pushed our way to the edge of the Roosevelt car, and I noticed the livid fury in Governor Ely's face when the students, almost to a man Republican, raucously booed and refused to let Roosevelt speak. Mrs. Roosevelt and another man in the car were also angry, and so was I, because I always favored the underdog. But Roosevelt only smiled good-naturedly as if to say, "Just what I expected from a country-club college."

I was so taken with Roosevelt that I followed the car eastward down the hill to see how he would be treated by a crowd of more than a hundred workers from a factory on the town's little river. As the car slowly passed, Roosevelt took off his soon-to-be famous fedora and smiled. It was a smile that seemed to embrace everyone personally. I will never forget the look of adoration on each worker's face, as well as the exuberant, heartfelt ovation that followed. The Irish fellow student was right, I felt. This *was* a great man!

In late April, Dorothy Canfield Fisher, a well-known novelist of the period who lived in Vermont, gave a lecture at Williams. I had read two of her novels, and I was particularly interested when she went into details about the craft of writing. She told how in her final draft she would "de-which" the manuscript and cut out adjectives and adverbs. Even some good writers like Tom Wolfe, she said, were addicted to "adjectivitis" and "adverbosity." Young writers, she advised, should begin their careers dedicated to leanness.

I was so excited that I wrote her a letter that night asking if I could come up to Arlington to talk with her about my career. Two days later she replied, "I'll be glad to see you about your plans," and gave me her phone number. I called at once and asked if I could come the following Sunday, when I could easily get a substitute waiter. She agreed, and said she believed a bus ran back and forth. But I hitchhiked as usual. Arriving at Arlington, I started walking north until I came to a postbox labeled "Fisher," where I turned up a steep hill to a modest house. Then began, as I wrote on my college calendar, "the greatest day of my life."

We talked at length of my determination to become a writer and about the stories and plays I had already written. She told me about her early days at college when she too had vowed to be a writer. Like Porter Emerson Browne, she treated me as an equal. After lunch we continued talking until it grew dark. As I was putting on my sheepskin coat I noticed a huge pile of paper on her desk, the galleys to a new novel, *Anthony Adverse.* I hefted it and groaned. "Who'll read this?" I asked. "Not very lean."

She laughed. "It's going to be a big best-seller." She and the other judges for the Book-of-the-Month Club had voted for it. "And it will sell *because* it's so huge. It also reads well."

In the weeks to follow she read some of my stories. The first she found "fresh and interesting and very pleasant." I was right in sticking to characters and situations and emotions "that are not far from your own experience." Further, "the naming of the bass viol 'Daisy' and the rest of the color of that instrument's role in the story was very amusing and done with the right sort of light touch."

Although I was spending at least two hours every night writing plays, I was getting A's and high B's, thanks to my training at Exeter. My weakest subject was physics, which was made palatable by a fellow student, Fred H. Stocking.

I was less inspired by the physics classroom than by my walk to the physics lab when I passed a gateway with the inscription "Climb High, Climb Far, Your Goal the Sky, Your Aim the Star."

After my first year at Williams, in June of 1933, I picked up Virginia in New York and went on to Fire Island, where we stayed in a different cottage on the next street. I got so bored with the cottage's name, Sea Spray, that I bought a large box of the latest laundry soap and superimposed SUPER SUDS on the cottage name plaque. I was also busy with a complete revision of a play I had written the previous summer, called *The Enchanted Island.* I dashed off a first draft, but it didn't read well. It was too pretentious, and I buried it at the bottom of my pile of manuscripts. I would later make another draft and try to bring life to that long strip of sand that made up Fire Island, a place which seemed to act as a catalyst, bringing out people's basic qualities with miraculous speed. It was almost as though each person had been put on a microscope slide in a drop of alcohol—neatly mounted and prepared for a researcher's analysis.

My father's relationship with my mother was much worse than it had been the previous summer. She was famous for her malapropisms, and formerly he had just laughed at them, but now he grimaced every time she referred to the "elbows" (instead of shoulders) of a road, or described something elite as very "upsy-tupsy." No longer would her term "hillybilly" bring a smile, or her calling a doubleheader a "two-headed ball game." When she remarked to a friend on the phone, "You must be a psychopath!" because the friend had been just about to call her, my father groaned with unforgiving embarrassment and irritation. Nor did he so much as grin if she announced, when his favorite spoon was missing, that "the Kremlins must have taken it."

Such remarks endeared her to me, but they now drove my father out of the room. I also felt outraged at my father and became more devoted to my mother than ever when it was revealed that my father had been unfaithful. One day my mother discovered a torn letter in the wastebasket. It was a love letter to my father from a woman in La Crosse. I found my mother staring at the pages, tears running down her cheeks. She managed to tell me what had happened.

Not knowing what to do in such a crisis, I put an arm around her. "May I read it?" I asked; and when I saw the opening words, "My dearest Sweetie Pie," I couldn't help laughing. Curiously this didn't offend my mother, nor did she object when I started reading aloud the rest of it. I finally had to stop. "God, this is great!" I said, and tears of laughter erupted. I silently read the next few lines. "It's getting even better, Mother! 'And as I opened your dear, thoughtful letter everything went black and I slid quietly under the breakfast table.'" I myself slid to the floor, roaring. "Wouldn't that make a great line in a play!"

My boisterous reaction didn't seem to bother my mother. She stopped crying, and she even smiled. That moment was a turning point. For some reason I knew that never again would I be persuaded to spend another summer at Fire Island. And I now felt so close to my mother that I started calling her Helen. Yet I never called my father Ralph.

When I returned to Williams in the fall of 1933 for my sophomore year, Stanley Young had left to put his play on Broadway, but I found another ally on the English faculty, old Albert ("Birdie") Licklider, who communicated to us a feeling for theater and made Shakespeare come alive. "Not more than a hundred years ago, when I first went to the theater," he began, and turned the classroom into a stage. "Of course you don't have to go outside of Williamstown to find a Romeo, but you do have to go outside of Williamstown to find a Juliet." Whereupon he turned himself into Juliet with the magic of his voice. Most of us were delighted. A few, however, expressed their distaste for such antics. "I know how you feel," Licklider once observed to us, "but I feel ten times worse."

He was a small, energetic man who reminded me of a bird—constantly on the move and keeping the air lively with quips and repartee. I wangled a visit to Birdie's untidy little room and told him of my ambition to be a playwright. Did I have anything to show for it? he asked. Yes. I handed him my latest play. After reading it he offered to give me Honors Work in playwriting (which meant that I would be the only member of the class) during my junior year provided I had high enough grades.

This presented a problem. Vac had already promised to give me Honors Work in French literature. Would I be allowed to take two Honors courses? When I brought this up, Vac replied that the answer was simple: all I had to do was get all A's in my sophomore year.

By then I had found another job, this one at the biology laboratory, which required only three hours a day. I was also getting so many orders for typing that I had to hire another typist, and at the Commons Club I was one of the two permanent waiters at the head table.

At the same time I was spending a good share of every evening working on my plays with the aid of background music from a more modern phonograph and records of Moussorgsky, Schubert, and Debussy. Although I was also reading Russian novels for pleasure, I spent most of my time with the plays of Ibsen and Shaw, and I wrote several letters to my father about my new heroes. The next time I arrived at our new home on West 143rd Street, the ground floor of a small dwelling next to a large apartment house near Riverside Drive, I was greeted with the manuscript of a play by my father, lifted more or less directly from Ibsen. I didn't have the heart to tell him how awful it was.

There was relative peace in our home during the first week of my vacation, but one night, during a heated family conversation on Franklin Roosevelt, Virginia made several trips to the bathroom, coming back each time a little more lively. After a fourth trip my father got suspicious and left, soon returning with a half-full bottle of gin he had found in the toilet tank, Virginia's traditional hiding place. He shook the bottle at Virginia, who haughtily denied ownership.

"Like hell you say! Why am I always the one suspected?"

"Who the hell else drinks in this family?" He shook her, and she angrily tore herself away. She began shouting and ripping off her clothes until she stood naked. "I'm getting out of this hellhole!" she screamed and darted toward the front door. At first my father was so stunned that he couldn't move. Then he started after her.

But I held him back. "Let her go, Daddy. She *wants* you to stop her."

He was horrified when Virginia flew outside.

"She'll be back," I added. "It's damned cold out there."

In a few seconds she was back in the house, shivering. My parents were too shocked to speak, but I couldn't help laughing. Virginia glared at me, then she too started to laugh. She grabbed some clothes and disappeared.

There was a prolonged silence until I finally remarked, "Anyway, we now have the bottle out *here*."

My mother was crying and my father was fuming, but when Virginia eventually returned, now cold sober, I said, as if nothing had happened, "How about some coffee?"

"Gawd!" she replied dramatically with a comically snobbish British accent. "I thawt yewd *nevah* ahsk mi!"

When I came back home in June 1934 after the end of my sophomore year, I found the little house on 143rd Street still a battleground. After one week I announced that I was hitchhiking to California for the summer. My mother insisted that I take along a pack of prestamped postcards addressed to her— "just to let us know where you are every so often." My father growled something about "goddam fools!" and Virginia kissed me with embarrassing energy.

Armed with a battered suitcase (donated by Uncle George) plastered over with Williams and Exeter labels and a ten-dollar bill sewed into the belt lining of my blue jeans, I headed west.

Three days later I arrived in La Crosse and slept in a real bed at Uncle Leigh's. This was my first visit to my hometown in years, but I still remembered the long bridge across the Mississippi and the apartment house next to the church where I had played war. I spent hours at the Wisconsin Business University gabbing with Uncle Leigh, who was so delighted to hear of my experiences on the road that he promised to let me have the painting of Colonel John Toland which hung behind his desk—"when I am no longer here."

He also promised to leave me all the colonel's papers, including the citation for his last action as commander of the expedition of July 13–25, 1863, from West Virginia to Wyethville, Virginia, by his 34th Regular Mounted Regiment.

Uncle Leigh added that the colonel had been shot by a minister from the vantage point of his belfry, and for that reason he, for one, would never again enter a church.

The trip from La Crosse to Sioux Falls took only a day and a half, and I slept in a bed at the Pecks'. They urged me to stay a week, but I was eager to move west. It was exciting to travel through the West for the first time; it was as new as Eden for me. I saw the places Pog Powell had described, where his father had bested Buffalo Bill and other Wild West greats in shooting contests. I visited Yellowstone Park and then headed for the coast, overwhelmed by the vast spaces and massive mountains. Nor was I disappointed as I started south through Oregon and California, until I came to Los Angeles—where civilization of a sort had replaced nature. My reward was to again meet my favorite aunt, Mother's oldest sister, Floss, with whom I had been corresponding regularly. She had always encouraged me to keep writing.

She had told me of her own struggle for survival in a world that did not appreciate eccentrics, yet she never complained. Her husband, Jack Henjum, had made a great deal of money but lost it all in such ventures as the construction of a large ice skating rink, of all things, in Los Angeles. He had left her nothing but bills, and she had survived by writing clever poems advertising the charms of Lake Arrowhead. She also had several rich friends who helped her. Aunt Floss's striking eccentricities drew me closer to her than to my own mother, who was herself an eccentric. I think she showed me the road to freedom.

After two wonderful weeks with Floss, I caught a ride with a couple who took me all the way to Missouri, and I arrived back in New York to find myself in the middle of a wrangle between my father and Virginia, a quarrel which raged for three days before I set out for Williamstown.

At the beginning of my junior year, both of my Honors professors, Vac and Birdie Licklider, encouraged me to attend the Yale Drama School after graduating from Williams. At the time it was run by George Pierce Baker, whose renowned workshop at Harvard had produced such famous playwrights as Philip Barry and Sidney Howard. Since there were no drama school scholarships available, I would have to make considerable money. So my former roommate Jim Wood and I applied as competitors for management of the newly organized Williams Christian Association Bookstore. This had been formed as a protest against the high prices at the two commercial bookstores in town. There would be four competitors, known as "compets," and only two winners, who would run the bookstore the following year—a sufficient reason for Jim and me to work more hours at the bookstore than the other two.

At the end of the spring term in 1935 it was announced that Jim and I had won the management of the WCA Bookstore. I was also selected to be headwaiter at the Commons Club, now renamed the Garfield Club in honor of the Williams president, who had been succeeded by Tyler Dennett, a winner of the Pulitzer Prize for his biography of John Hay. This meant that

I would get not only free meals but fifteen dollars a week. My future at the Yale Drama School was assured. I returned to New York with the good news, announcing that I was returning immediately to Williamstown, where I had been offered a ride to the Twin Cities by Professor Hoar, who was to spend the summer at the University of Minnesota.

The trip west, with Mrs. Hoar driving, was uneventful until we reached the outskirts of Three Rivers, Michigan, where a farm truck lurched from a side road and smashed into our car. Three days later, after the car was repaired, I went on with them to Minneapolis and St. Paul, then started hitching.

Two days later, in Kansas, I was stranded for two hours. Nearby a freight train had stopped for water, and I could hear shouts from men sitting on top of boxcars. They were beckoning me to join them. I hesitated. Then came two toots from the engine and it strained to get its load under way. I hurried over. A tall young man who had climbed down a side ladder held out his hand for my suitcase. I let it go, then slipped and fell. Urged on by shouts, I scrambled to my feet and jumped clumsily at the ladder of the next car. I thought my arms were going to be wrenched off, but I held on. The tall fellow with my suitcase leaned down, grabbed my shirt, and hoisted me to the top. "You've got to learn," he said with a grin, then stuck out a welcoming hand. "In the first place, you don't stand still when you're hopping a moving freight. You run alongside toward the engine. Get it?"

I was surprised to find that I was immediately accepted by everyone on top of this boxcar despite the Exeter and Williams stickers all over my suitcase. They all advised me to dump the suitcase and get a bindle—that is, wrap my belongings in a piece of canvas so they could be carried over my shoulder and I'd have two free hands.

At the next stop I decided to resume hitchhiking, and late in the afternoon was picked up by a young man from Kansas named Hulse. His goal was to homestead in Colorado. Until dark he talked of his dream of owning land of his own. By that time we were both hungry, and Hulse said he would get cold meat at a grocery store if I would get a loaf of bread. While I was paying for the bread I noticed Hulse slipping something into his pants pocket. It turned out to be a can of Ken-L Ration dog food, which Hulse insisted was edible if warmed up. He ate his portion with pleasure, but I could not finish my dog-food sandwich.

For the next week I stayed at Boulder with a couple of friends from Exeter, one of whom, the modest and quiet Dolph Coors, turned out to be the son of a beer baron. Then I continued my trek by thumb. It took only three hours to reach Cheyenne, but here I ran out of luck. No rides. As darkness approached I looked for a place to sleep. I ended up at the railroad station and settled down on a long bench, as if waiting for a train. I was soon told by an official that there wasn't another train going east until morning, and I could see that I was not welcome. In the nearby yards a freight was being made up. The scene was a nightmare: the smash of cars being hooked up; the brakemen with lights running on top of the boxcars; the swinging lanterns of crossing watchmen; the brilliant stabs of light when the firemen opened their firebox doors to feed the flames; the staccato whistles signaling messages; and the engineers leaning confidently out of their cabs as their engines backed and pulled with agility. A switch engine plunged toward me, bathing me in dazzling lights, and showered me with a slowly descending cloud of cinders as it passed. A brakeman leaped off into the darkness and pulled a switch.

"Where you going?" he asked in a friendly voice. "East or west?"

"West, sir."

"That man's going west in about fifteen minutes." He pointed at a line of cars. "Get up there a few hundred yards. Wait until you hear the highball. Keep outa sight or the yard bull might grab you."

"What's the highball?"

"Two sharp toots. That means the road hog's on and ready to go."

I was confused by the language but I cautiously moved into place. I heard two shrill toots and the engine lights slowly passed me. Boxcars, flatcars, tankcars rumbled past. I looked for an open boxcar. There weren't any, and I clumsily climbed into a gondola carrying gravel. This was traveling!

In the next two days I learned a number of hard lessons. For one thing, when going through the Rockies you should never sit in the rear of a gondola. When the train entered a tunnel, showers of hot cinders poured into the open car. And it was equally dangerous in a tankcar or a flatcar carrying machinery—which also provided no protection. The solution was to dig a hole in the gravel at the front of the gondola to protect your head.

When we finally reached Ogden, Utah, a dozen riders hopped off, half heading left and the others heading right. I learned that those going left were staying with the Union Pacific bound for Salt Lake City. The others were heading for the Western Pacific. I followed these and soon found myself in a "hobo jungle." I had seen movies about the fights bums had in these jungles and was surprised to find no conflicts. Everything was peaceful; I was accepted even though it was obvious that I was not one of them, and I was quickly warned that two yardbulls were keeping anybody from hopping a freight bound west.

The reason for this became apparent in the morning when two police officers arrived and arrested all of us for trespassing. A judge immediately sentenced us to three days in jail, and we were taken to the site of the Fourth of July Ogden Rodeo. Here we were put to work cleaning up the area and repairing broken seats. At dusk we were returned to jail and given a meager meal. In the movies prisoners were inevitably beaten, but not in Ogden. Our breakfast was a sticky sort of oatmeal, bread, and bitter coffee.

To me the highlight of our three-day sentence was meeting a tall, rangy youngster of eighteen who called himself the Pocatello Kid. He had been on the road for three years and knew all the angles. Learning I was in college, he asked me to correct his English so he could eventually get a good job. In payment he would teach me the lingo of the road: *yard bulls,* railroad detectives; *shacks,* cops, detectives; *town clown,* local cop; *stemming the drag,* panhandling on the main street; *deck,* roof of a boxcar; *Jesus stiff,* anyone eating at the Salvation Army (Sally's); *yard hog,* small engine shifting cars in the yards; *road hog,* large engine on full train; *doubleheader,* two road hogs used for heavy loads; *riding the blinds,* riding in a blocked doorway of the first car behind the coal car of a passenger train; *riding the rods,* an obsolete term meaning riding underneath a freight car; *crummy,* caboose; *conductor,* boss of freight (his office, the crummy); *hustle buggy,* police car; *on the fritz,* broke; *misery,* coffee. The most common term for those on the road was "bindle stiff," replacing the obsolete "hobo."

Pokey also sang road songs. His favorite, "Pie in the Sky," had a melodious final stanza:

> *You will eat, by-and-by,*
> *In that glorious land in the sky*
> *Work and pray, live on hay,*
> *You'll get pie in the sky when you die.*

When we were finally released, we discovered that the yard bulls for some reason were still preventing anyone from taking the Western Pacific, but Pokey insisted that he could get everyone aboard. Once the highball sounded and the freight started slowly, he said, he would hop aboard and run along the tops, leading the two bulls forward. Then the rest of us could safely climb aboard at the back. Pokey would leap off, followed by the bulls, and then hop back on again.

"But the train will be going too fast by then," I said.

"Let me worry about that."

It all worked exactly as planned. Pokey was on top of a boxcar thumbing his nose at the bulls, like Till Eulenspiegel. Then two farm boys carried my suitcase while I clumsily climbed up the ladder to the decks. I watched Pokey hop off, and although the train was going thirty miles an hour by then, he gracefully leaped at a ladder and hung on. Once on top, he stood up and again thumbed his nose.

By now it was warm, and I wondered how we could survive when we hit the desert without cover. All the boxcars were sealed and the rest were refrigerator cars (reefers). "They're not sealed," said Pokey.

"So what? Who wants to freeze?"

"Going east, these reefers carry fruit and are iced at both ends. But going west, they're empty—they're the bindle stiff's Pullman."

He opened the roof door at the end of one reefer and climbed inside. I followed and found myself in a compartment about three feet wide and big enough for two. It was bone-dry and comfortable. Pokey had pulled down the rod that secured the door and tied one end of a rope to the rod and the other end to the wire meshing inside. "That's to keep you and me from being cold meat. The train crew will see someone's inside and won't lock us in."

Pokey explained that when the train stopped at the next division point for examination of journal boxes and any repairs, we could find cardboard and heavy wrapping paper for bedding. While Pokey was doing this at the next stop, I scrounged the yards and found a gallon jug, which I filled with water.

The night was as pleasant as Pokey had promised. Outside, the desert air was cold, but we were snug—and I had never before known the pleasure of watching the moon and stars glide by through an open hatch.

During the day I would ride on top of the reefer drinking in the wonders of the desert until I began to sweat, and then would descend into my refuge. For hours Pokey described his adventures on the road and sang songs he had learned—like the saga of the immortal engineer Casey Jones. I particularly liked the final lines:

> *Casey Jones, he mounted to his cabin*
> *With his orders in his hand.*
> *Casey Jones, he mounted to his cabin*
> *And took his farewell trip into the promised land.*

Pokey gave me many tips on how to *batter the drag* (beg money on the main street) and use a *California blanket* (newspapers) on cold nights.

At last, late at night, we pulled into Reno, with its famous sign, THE BIGGEST LITTLE CITY IN THE WORLD, and soon we began our steep, winding descent into California—an eerie and thrilling ride in the moonlight. The next morning we reached Stockton, a maze of tracks, shifting trains, and parked empties.

Pokey led me to a small shack that looked as if it had been made by a blind carpenter. At one side was a scrawny tree loaded with empty tobacco bags and empty cigarette packages, at the foot of which was a large sign, "The Tobacco Tree."

Pokey explained that this tree represented the dreams of long-ago hoboes. A sign scrawled on the door of the shack read: "Thousand-Mile Beans. Ten Cents. Guaranteed."

"Guaranteed for what?"

"To last a bindle stiff for a thousand miles on the road."

I bought us two dimes' worth and eagerly gulped down a huge plate of the most delicious beans I had ever tasted.

"Whenever you're hungry," predicted Pokey, "you'll dream of these beans. The next best thing is the po' boy sandwich of New Orleans." He'd never been there, but everybody on the road talked about the po' boy, a huge sandwich, stuffed with meats, guaranteed to last a stiff two days.

Pokey was heading north to Portland and Seattle, so he brought me to a long one-story structure which had probably once housed machinery.

"You'll be safe in here," he assured me. "And it only costs two cents." Inside some fifty men, women, and children were huddled in corners or sitting at a long bar where cheap food, mostly day-old bread and butt ends of cold meat, was served.

I finally boarded my freight, and it was dark by the time I found Aunt Floss's new dwelling in Los Angeles. At first she was horrified to learn that I had been riding freights, but soon she was avidly pressing for details of my trip. She relished both my account of the dangers and my delight in the luxury of riding inside a refrigerator car, eating thousand-mile beans, and traveling with colorful and friendly people. She washed and pressed my filthy jeans and shirts, but when I slipped into the jeans I discovered she had ironed the legs so they were wide in front.

The days with Floss passed quickly. We would talk until late into the night about her bizarre life, which was as adventurous as my own. She had held a dozen odd jobs, from selling cosmetics door-to-door to taking care of crotchety old ladies. She had close friends in both high and low places and was welcome everywhere. She was enthusiastic about almost every crackpot fad that flourished in California—from plans to make the poor rich overnight to stories of religious miracles. Naturally she believed in flying anything fantastic and above all, she was confident that I would become a successful writer. I felt honored to be on her list of crackpots.

After two weeks I headed back east by freight, using the same route I had followed to go west. Because I had been warned that it was almost impossible to ride freights east of the Mississippi without getting picked up, I hitched to New York, again arriving at West 143rd Street in the midst of a fight between Virginia and my father. Things were reassuringly predictable at home.

My senior year, which began in the fall of 1935 with Jim Wood again my roommate, was primarily devoted to running the Garfield Club dining room and the bookstore, as well as writing three plays. The Yale Drama School informed me that I would be accepted if approved by the new head of play-writing, Walter Pritchard Eaton, who had succeeded the late George Pierce Baker. Eaton's weekend home was an hour's drive to the south, and a faculty wife offered to transport me for an interview.

The interview was brief. Eaton, former drama critic for the *New York Times,* had liked the play I had submitted, and I wondered why he couldn't simply have sent me a letter. My major problem was to make more money for tuition and expenses, most of which would come from ju-dicious purchases of textbooks from students at the end of the school year. The bookstore would buy books for one-third the original cost and sell them the next year for two-thirds. I had supervised the buying operation the previous spring, and 95 percent of the books bought had been used the following year. Those not chosen again for a particular course had to be "eaten." In my junior year I had persuaded a group of intellectual din-ers at the Garfield Club to find out what books would be used by their fa-vorite professors, who had refused to give out this information to any of the bookstores. Since I had such good relations with this group of intel-lectuals, I was sure I could get their help again, and it looked as though I could easily make enough for drama school.

Then came a blow. I was summoned to the office of President Dennett. Some of his staff had insisted that I be denied my full scholarship for senior year because I was making so much money. Dennett held a piece of paper. "I see you're headwaiter at the Garfield Club, work at the biology laboratory, and run the WCA Bookstore with your roommate. Is this true?"

"Yes, sir. I also run a typing agency." My case looked hopeless. Moreover, Dennett had publicly announced that he wanted more high school graduates at Williams and fewer from prep schools like Exeter and Andover.

"I see you went to Exeter," he remarked.

I exploded. "Yes! I lived at Abbott Hall in the cheapest room on the campus, was a waiter, worked in the chem lab, got a full scholarship, and graduated *cum laude.* I also worked in a factory so I could pay the first se-mester's expenses."

The president was not offended by my outburst. "What are your plans for the future, Mr. Toland?"

"I'm going to the Yale Drama School to be a playwright."

Dennett was amused. "Then you're going to need all the money you earn!" He crumpled the paper, threw it in a wastebasket, and held out his hand. "Good luck!"

Then I learned that the drama course would run for three years, and I realized I had to make even more money. One night I had an inspiration. I would invite one of my favorite movie stars, Binnie Barnes, to the spring houseparties. I wrote her that I was hoping to be a playwright and needed money to go to the Yale Drama School. I would sell tickets to the wealthy fraternity men for various houseparty occasions such as meals and dances. I guaranteed that she would have a wonderful time and I would personally oversee every event. The grand finale would be the big prom at a nearby dance hall, where a name band would play and a large gold wooden key would be presented to "Miss Houseparty." If she did not get it I promised to shoot myself.

For two months there was no answer. Then two weeks before the house-party a letter arrived from Hollywood. Binnie Barnes said she would be delighted to support such a good cause. But no sooner had I begun arranging dates than a telegram arrived: Binnie had just been offered a big part and had to leave immediately for location.

Undeterred, Jim and I attended the finale dance, where the four-foot, thirty-pound wooden key was displayed on the stage. Suddenly the lights went out, thanks to Jim. In the darkness I grabbed the key and darted out the side door unseen. I mailed the key to Binnie, who sent her heartfelt thanks.

This failure stimulated me to devise another scheme. I hitched to New York to see Mr. Barnes of Barnes & Noble. He was a Williams College alumnus. I told him of the numerous textbooks that would have to be "eaten" in a few weeks, and handed him a list. Almost all in top condition, I pointed out. How much would he offer? Mr. Barnes wrote down a figure. It was far more than I had imagined.

The students crowded into our WCA Bookstore to get rid of their books, and the four "compets" bought all those that had been approved by my spies. The rejects were dumped onto the other two stores in town. Within a week my compets and spies at the Garfield Club were buying back the rejected books from the other bookstores for almost nothing, and a large shipment was sent to Barnes & Noble.

Then I received astounding news from Vac. A wealthy friend had just endowed a two-year scholarship for graduate study in writing, and I had been selected as the first recipient.

My name was on the list of those selected for Phi Beta Kappa, but I declined the honor when I discovered I had to pay fifty dollars for a key and dues. Astronomy professor Willis Isbister Milham summoned me. He assumed that I, being an obvious radical, had refused for political reasons. Not at all, I explained. It was the fifty dollars. "We have a fund for young men in your situation," said the relieved professor.

I gave my Phi Beta Kappa key to my mother, who had come up for graduation day. Late that morning I got a phone call from Vac. His voice was choked. Because of some technicality, he said, the two-year scholarship I had been awarded could not be started until 1937, when I would not be eligible. I told him not to worry. I had plenty of money to see me through drama school. At the commencement ceremony in Chapin Hall I was awarded the Kaufmann Prize in English: the complete plays of two of my favorite playwrights, Aristophanes and Shaw.

As I was leaving the hall a stranger introduced himself. He was a representative of Esso. "Mr. Barnes told us about you," he said, and offered me a job that would send me immediately to the South Pacific. In a few years I would be a junior executive.

I thanked him. "It's a great honor, sir. But I'm going to the Yale Drama School and plan to be a playwright."

The Esso man shook his head.

"What a waste of talent!"

[Part Three]

A Fool There Was (1936–1942)

{8}

On the Road

I spent most of the summer of 1936 in New York City trying to peddle Singer sewing machines. On my first day I sold one and received as down payment an old Singer treadle which had a high resale value in countries without electricity. In only one day I had earned more than fifty dollars! But during the next two months, after trudging through scores of apartment houses in the Washington Heights area and using my most persuasive sales techniques, I made not another cent. I finally gave up and went to the Singer office on 145th Street and turned in my equipment.

I bought an old Chevrolet for thirty-five dollars and taught myself to drive. I piled my big typewriter and gear into it and set out for New Haven. The next morning I headed for the drama school, convinced that I was making the best move of my life. I was enrolled in the Class of 1939 and found there were eight others in my playwriting course. By the end of the first week I was troubled. The new director, Walter Pritchard Eaton, had been a top critic, but he was no George Pierce Baker. Baker had been inspirational, but Eaton could only point out flaws. Baker had encouraged originality and movement, while Eaton preached form. Moreover, there was only one gifted playwright in the class, a fellow named Larry Dugan, who had never been to college but had written several plays that had been produced in Philadelphia. The two of us paired off in Halsted Welles's directing class, where we were told to act the part of an expectant father in a hospital. Larry first directed me, and I was fairly credible as the father; I then directed Larry, who was more than credible—he was totally believable. Larry had a theatrical sixth sense.

I worked as a waiter in the freshman dining hall in return for free meals. It became quickly apparent that I was the only experienced waiter. The others, like me, were graduate students. I offered to take the farthest table, and within a week I had instructed the waiters working near me how to stack dishes and glasses so they could carry a tray with one hand. They caught on quickly, and the woman in charge was so impressed that she asked me if I would be her assistant. I accepted, and soon the dining room was well organized. With all running smoothly, I could spend much of my time at my desk working on my courses.

When I returned to Yale at the beginning of 1937 after the Christmas vacation, I wrote two more one-act comedies including one called *No, No, Nero!* and began the year's final project, a full-length play. All these plays were exercises in the craft of writing, and they only existed on paper. In early spring, however, one of my plays was finally produced. A girl from Texas in the playwriting class was so taken with *The Last Song of Solomon,* not realizing that it was a spoof, that she and her boyfriend, a director in the Class of '38, insisted on performing it over a New Haven radio station. They were entranced by my "wonderful" poetry and regarded me as excessively modest when I insisted that it all came from the Bible. I started listening to the program and soon began to pray that I was the only person tuned to that station, for it was a disaster. I did, however, learn something: that it would probably never be a good idea to cast an all-American Texas girl as a romantic Sheba.

I left New Haven early that June and vowed never to return until one of my plays had been tried out for Broadway at the local Shubert Theater. I would stay home and write. Looking back, I realize it was a good decision, since Eaton had nothing more to offer me. Even though I never did write a successful play, I later saw that my efforts to master the discipline of writing plays had been a necessary part of my development toward a successful career as an historian.

I now look back on the next year or so as a period of transition. I doggedly presevered in my attempts to learn playwriting on my own, but I also grew restless as I began to face the possibility of turning from drama to other forms of writing. I was now back on West 143rd Street. My father had moved downtown and was living with his girlfriend.

Following Dr. Johnson's advice ("Few things are impossible to diligence and skill"), I was soon at work on another play and seeing at least three Broadway shows every week at no cost. First I would pick up a free meal at Horn & Hardart's: cup, saucer, and hot water at the tea stand (my own tea bag) and a collection of rolls and bread left on abandoned tables. I would then wash up at my favorite hotel, the Astor. (There was no washroom attendant to tip.) By that time the first act had just ended at a theater, where I would walk in with the others, check around for an empty seat, and try to reconstruct the first act as the second proceeded.

I refused to have dinner at 572 Broome Street with my father and his mistress. The Pyroil job had petered out, and he was now working for a printing firm. Virginia spent much of her time with the couple, but I would see my father only on weekends when I would drive him out to Neshanic Station in New Jersey to visit the farm of distant relatives.

In the spring of 1938, Professor Licklider wrote me to get in touch with Mark Reed, one of his former students at Dartmouth, whose play *Yes, My Darling Daughter* had been a big hit on Broadway. I was invited to lunch in a small town near New York and found to my amazement that Mr. Reed was living in a boardinghouse. He reminded me of Jim in Marquand's *Wickford Point.* His car was just as ancient as mine but was treated by the restaurant's car attendant as if it were a new Rolls-Royce.

Reed spent lunch talking about his own difficult climb to the top. He'd had several plays produced on Broadway and one had sold to the movies, but at home he was still regarded as a failure. Refusing to borrow money from his father, he made a living laying linoleum in bathrooms. It was a perfect job, he explained, because he could think about his plays as he did this mechanical work. He found that he could not write in his boardinghouse, so in his free time he would drive to an abandoned spot in the country and write in his car.

Spurred by Reed's encouragement, I sent him two of my plays and went back to my writing. During the summer of 1938 I returned with my friend Bob Frank to New Hampshire, where we had done some hiking the previous year. Bob had received a master's degree in English at Yale, and in our spare time we had written several one-act plays. We stayed in the attic of Roxy Heath on Little Squam Lake and started a comedy based on my Binnie Barnes caper at Williams. We called it *Fraternity Row.* Bob, who had been in a fraternity at college, wrote the fraternity scenes and I wrote the rest.

Late that fall I took *Fraternity Row* to George Abbot, the master of comedy. After three months it was returned. No sale. Later Abbot came out with another big hit—*Best Foot Forward*—using my plot about a college student who invites a film star to a houseparty weekend. I was advised to sue, but I remembered the counsel of Porter Emerson Browne: "Suing is for lawyers, not writers. You'll waste time and energy that should go into your writing."

While I was still in New Hampshire that summer a letter from Mark Reed was forwarded to me: "You have the right attitude: just keep knocking shows off until increased experience and a happy combination of theater elements result in a hit. One encouraging factor: at no time in the past thirty years have there been so few good scripts." The producer of *Yes, My Darling Daughter* had just written him that out of two hundred plays read, there was not even one with a good idea. "Get a good dramatic idea, John, and you're set!"

Early in the fall my mother took a week's vacation from her job at Consolidated Edison, where she was doing her best to keep the lights burning for people who were slow in paying their bills. Already she was known all over the building as "Miss Bleeding Heart." I drove again to Little Squam Lake, where we were the only guests at Roxy's, and I spent the first evening rereading *The Vicar of Wakefield.* I was so engrossed by its possibilities that I decided to write a dramatization. Within several months I had finished *The Vicar* and acquired an agent from Curtis Brown, Edith Haggard, primarily notable for the novel cigarette holder attached to her middle finger.

I also sent a copy to Mark Reed, who was spending the winter in a trailer in Florida. "In letting me read the play," he replied, "I feel you want my honest reaction. The adaptation didn't strike me as worth spending so much time on—if you want a commercial success. Aren't you making a mistake in tackling the old costume subjects?

"Why not stick to 1938? Here is a world dizzying and palpitating with unmined drama and comedy. The stage needs your new-generation reaction to the people facing conditions of today. Why not dig your teeth into 'right now' and see what you can do—not necessarily brutal realism, and certainly not propaganda—but America of 1938 in character action!"

What Mark Reed wanted me to write about was constantly boiling inside of me: the tragedy of more than ten million Americans driven out of their farms and homes by the Depression and forced to live on the road. I had the perfect setting—Seattle's skid row. I'd call it *Pie in the Sky.*

Even though I had decided to take Mark's advice and write *Pie in the Sky,* I woke up one night with the idea for a comedy that seemed surefire. In the first act the central character, a descendant of a famous Revolutionary hero, likable but a bit weak, gets into trouble; suddenly (accompanied by Bach's "Come, Sweet Death") he is transported to Revolutionary days and finds himself inside the body of his famous ancestor in the American Revolution. In the next scene his ancestor is flung into the twentieth century and faces our hero's problems.

After reading the first two acts, Mark Reed telephoned to say, "I think you've got a hit." The next day he called again. "Sorry, John," he said. "The third act just doesn't work. And I don't know how you can fix it." I had never bristled at Mark's conclusions because I always realized he was right. I could then reread a play and see its flaws.

In early June 1939, I sewed yet another ten-dollar bill into my jeans, packed a bindle, said goodbye to my mother, who handed me another pack of stamped blank postcards addressed to her, and started hitchhiking.

I was worried about my father. The previous fall he had unexpectedly announced he was going back to La Crosse. I had noticed a loss of vitality, but he ridiculed my concern. I then offered to drive him all the way to Wisconsin, but he said he preferred the bus to my rattletrap Ford. Why was it, I wondered, as I had for my entire life, that he always brushed off any attempt I made to get closer to him? I recalled the time I had taken him to one of Philip Barry's plays and during the intermission he had ridiculed my enthusiasm for Barry's craftsmanship. What was wrong between us? I recognized that it was not all my father's fault, for I always reacted too sharply to his rebuffs and our quarrels always ended in a prolonged, cold truce.

Once I reached Chicago, I got a freight that would eventually get me to La Crosse, where my father was living at Putch's little house near the river. But somehow I couldn't make myself get off at La Crosse and face my father, so I headed out to Montana. As usual, I made friends with my fellow bindle stiffs; all of us knew that our welfare and safety were founded on cooperation and reasonably decent behavior.

At this time there must have been, according to estimates by historians, some seven or eight million people on the road in America, people of all ages and both sexes looking for a new start or just to survive. Apart from the hobo camps (and the jails!) and flophouses of various degrees of cleanliness and cost, there were always the missions, run mostly by Sally's (the Salvation Army).

I could see why the road kids hated the missions. The people who ran them seemed to bring out the worst in everyone. They weren't unfriendly, only detached. They treated us as if we were prisoners to be kept in order until we left town.

Along with some friends I made on the road, I took a southbound train, but at Klamath Falls I got off and headed back north toward Seattle. For the next ten days I wanted to soak in the sights and sounds. Every jungle along the way was different, but there was one constant: nowhere did I find (as in the movies) hostility. In skid rows, although there was a natural coolness between the home guards and the riders, they were all essentially victims of what they called the Big Trouble—the Depression.

From Seattle I moved on to Portland. The jungle near town was far different. It was a colorful group: old and young, men and women, boys and girls, and several complete families with crying babies. There were cowboys in broad-brimmed hats and wild-colored neckerchiefs, spurs, and boots. There were boys with guitars slung over their backs, and Chinese, Filipinos, and Hindus with heads swathed in cloth.

A boy of about twelve nudged me. "These old birds," he said softly, "they're always eating pie in the sky."

The next morning we all boarded a freight. After several miles it went into the hole (pulled off onto a siding) to allow a passenger train to pass through. Someone yelled, "Hey, look! There's a bakery truck on the highway! The guy is waving at us!"

A man in white was holding up two loaves of bread. "He's giving stuff away!" shouted a road kid, and streaked toward the truck. I followed, as did thirty other stiffs, including the dustbowl family. "Here, Shorty," called the truck driver, and threw me a loaf of bread.

The driver tossed out rolls, sweet buns, bread, and a few pies. "I made all my rounds. This's mostly day-old stuff. And hell, the boss'll never know."

A passenger train moaned in the distance. "We'd better get back, Pop," I warned the family. "Here comes what we're waiting for."

The passenger moaned again and then stuck its fantastic orange head around the bend. The stalled freight in the hole rattled as the streamliner hurtled past.

All the stiffs—the old and the young, the cowboys, the Hindus, the Filipinos, the girls and boys—were sitting on top of the freight as it slowly pulled away. The white-coated truck driver waved at us. A few of the stiffs waved back, but the others were too busy eating their miraculous breakfast.

I made my way west, enjoying the people and new adventures I encountered every hour, every day on the road—riding freights, staying in everything from flophouses to haystacks. One day on the road was equivalent to several months of "respectable" life. Every day was an entirely new act in an unfolding drama. This was life in the raw, and I loved it. I wanted to write about this life I had discovered. This could make a great novel, I thought. But the truth, I found, was more vivid than any fiction.

After briefly visiting my two aunts in Los Angeles I drifted around for a while, at one point hitching a ride with a young man in Nebraska who wanted to be a singer. He gave a demonstration at his home, and I was so impressed by his voice that I advised him to bum his way to La Crosse and get advice from my father.

I had carried along a copy of *Crime and Punishment,* and when I had finished reading it I decided to give it to my father. Perhaps I should have given a copy of *The Brothers Karamazov* instead! On the long trip east over the Big Goat line (the Great Northern) and the CB&Q, I often brooded on our strange relationship. During this summer I had come to realize that I still loved my father, but I wished we could talk as equals.

Mark Reed had confessed that he'd had a similar relationship with his father, a successful man who regarded writing plays as a blot on the family escutcheon. After he sold *Yes, My Darling Daughter* to the movies, he had taken the check for $100,000 (an extravagantly large amount in those days) and driven his rattletrap car to Elmsford, Massachusetts, to hand it to his father. "It was the greatest moment in my life," he told me.

But I had no big check to hand my father—only a battered copy of *Crime and Punishment*. When he came to the front door at Putch's, I was almost speechless. He looked at me eye to eye. He had shrunken to my size. But his voice was as vibrant and his spirit as cocky as ever. For once he listened to my recent adventures, and then he retreated to his room with Dostoevsky. He didn't come down to breakfast, and Putch's wife was worried. She came downstairs shaking her head. "He's reading that book as if it's glued to his fingers."

Late that afternoon my father emerged. "It's the goddamnedest thing I ever read," he told me, and I immediately thought we were finally on the same wavelength. "I never read such crap!" he added. He then began to analyze the central characters with brilliant exaggerations and to point out the faulty structure of scene after scene.

At first I was stunned, then it struck me as wonderful. My father might have shrunk, but he was still full of piss and vinegar. I burst out laughing and would have hugged him—except that I had never hugged him and didn't know how to.

My father was shocked by my laughter, but then grinned. "But I couldn't put it down," he admitted.

This produced another explosion from me, and I did something unbelievable—I punched him in the side. Neither of us said anything more, but we both knew we had suddenly—at least for the moment—wound up on equal ground. During the next week we were inseparable, arguing incessantly but with good humor.

I stayed in La Crosse an extra week and then set out for New Orleans. My father accompanied me to the freightyards. I learned from two road kids that a manifest was leaving in ten minutes, and I introduced my father. He shook hands and wished us all a safe trip. As the train slowly pulled away, the three of us atop a boxcar waved at him, and he casually but gallantly touched his hat. The gesture reminded me of Franklin D. Roosevelt.

———

The trip south was uneventful the first day, and then the two road kids went off toward their own destination. The next day a young black man joined me in a gondola. He told me a lot about New Orleans, what lines to avoid, and the wonders of the famous po' boy sandwich.

As we were nearing the next junction point, Jackson, Mississippi, a shack—a cop—suddenly leaped into the gondola. "Whites don't ride with niggers!" he yelled as he grabbed me and held me in a firm grip. The freight was pulling into the yards but still going at a good clip, and I was wondering what the shack was going to do when he unexpectedly shoved me off the train. I hit the cinders facedown and rolled down a steep embankment. I heard bells ringing in my head. My legs felt okay and so did my arms, and I was surprised to see that my bindle was gripped tightly in my right hand. But my head throbbed and blood was dripping from my nose.

"Okay, bo," said a voice. "C'mon along." It was a town clown—a local cop—who escorted me to the city jail. An officer took me to a bathroom and gently helped me clean off my face. "I think you busted it, sonny. You're just staying here the night. We need the streets cleaned."

There were two main cells containing about twenty men and boys. We were all given a good meal, and at dark we were led outside. Each of us was given a large pushbroom and assigned a section of the main road. We worked quietly all night under the supervision of good-natured cops who gave us frequent rests. A new moon cast a romantic light over the bizarre scene, and an indescribably sweet smell came from the roadside trees and bushes. All in all it was an enjoyable night, and we were treated to a genuine breakfast with real coffee, then transported back to the yards.

Soon most of us were heading for New Orleans. It was dark by the time we got to the outskirts of the city. The freight slowed down at the crossing of the Southern and the Louisville-and-Nashville railroads. I jumped off and started running forward. This time I didn't fall. My nose ached, but I felt excited about the prospect of seeing the wonders of New Orleans. To my right the Southern railroad yards were erupting with activity. A road kid named Mac and I followed the tracks as they curved to the left toward the L&N yards, and from a swampy field came the glow of a hundred lit-up cabins. The high-pitched voices of laughing women and the deep laughs of men mixed with sounds of music. "A Creole settlement," said Mac. In the opposite direction, from the brush and brambles of the city dump, came a long, almost hysterical woman's laugh. A dog howled and a guitar was softly strummed. "The jungle," said Mac.

As we approached I heard the half-drunken talk of men and the soft wail of a baby. We broke through the bushes and saw dozens of scattered lights.

The moon lit up scores of rickety shacks made of corrugated iron, packing boxes, and burlap. It was, I thought, a strange city of distorted ingenuity.

"This's the best damned jungle in the world," said Mac.

A dark-skinned woman reeled out of the first shack, an old dog at her heels. She glared at us with intense hostility. From inside the shack a man, cursing drunkenly, staggered to the doorway. He was white.

"What'n hell you looking at, boys?" drawled the woman.

We went deeper into the jungle. A black was sitting on the steps of the next shack, his harmonica wailing a song so blue it hung like a cloud. Nearby was a campfire, and I smelled stew bubbling in a big pot. Tending it was an old man huddling close to the pot and shielding it with his shoulder.

"How about a taste?" asked Mac.

"Damn road kids!" grumbled the old man. "Damn fresh road kids! Go get your own poke! I worked all day tooling bells"—ringing doorbells—"for this stew. Beat it!" Mac made a move toward the pot. "Hit the road, kid! Hit the road!"

We slept on cardboard in the jungle. It was warm and pleasant, and at first light we started hiking toward New Orleans. An hour or so later we were on Jackson Street. I scanned the area for cops and then started moving toward a man who was heading for a restaurant. Mac stopped me. "Never bum a rushing crowd," he said. "People in a hurry got no time for stemmers. And never hit a guy going into a restaurant. He's thinking of his stomach, not yours."

I had planned to stay in New Orleans for two or three days, but I'd already had enough of the city and headed alone for the yards, where I learned I was in luck: the Banana Express was making up for its run to Chicago. It was called the Mae West because it was the fastest freight in the world, consisting of about fifteen loaded reefers and making only stops for water at division points. Few stiffs ever rode her, because you had to stay perched on top of a reefer, and so I was the only one who boarded her as she slowly left the yards.

At last we sped into Illinois. I'd been told the Mae West would stop at Champaign, and I planned to hop off there and hitch to Danville for a decent bed and bath with the Ludwicks. I had long since passed beyond the fullest meaning of the word "filthy."

When the train slowed, I had trouble untying my bindle. My hands had lost their strength. I desperately yanked at the knots. The train started moving again, and I was about to abandon my precious bindle when it flopped loose. My legs were like rubber as I cautiously descended, and I tumbled when I hit the cinders. People looked at me as if I were one of Gorki's

"Creatures That Once Were Men," and before noon I was greeted at the door of 1603 North Logan Boulevard, Danville, by a startled grandmother. "John!" she exclaimed. "Is this *really* necessary!" I spent the next hour relating my recent experiences while my aunt and Dammy clucked around me like two hens. My sister, Virginia, there for the summer, was as keenly interested as George in all the gritty details of riding freights.

I stayed there for ten days. Although I had never before gotten along well with Dammy, this time I persuaded her to tell me a lot about my great-grandparents and the legendary Colonel Melvin Grigsby. Aunt Jeanette even gave me her precious signed copy of Grigsby's book, *The Smoked Yank,* which I still have.

Just before I left town, Virginia and I borrowed the Ludwicks' car and went to the Danville Country Club for a big dance. I met a very attractive redhead, Elaine, and by the end of the dance I had persuaded her to let us take her home. Her date agreed and sat up front with Virginia while Elaine and I sat in the back. Virginia predictably stopped at a lonesome place and took Elaine's date for a long walk while I told Elaine about my adventures on the road. She was enthralled, and I immediately fell hopelessly in love with her. As I was saying good night at her door, she suddenly vomited. Yet I still loved her. She agreed to drive me to the yards in Indianapolis the next morning, since I was determined to continue riding the freights on the east side of the Mississippi.

There were only three other stiffs on my freight, and they were suspicious and cool. The camaraderie of those west of the Mississippi had disappeared.

It was a dirty ride in a gondola carrying iron pipes, and I was filthy again by the time we reached Ohio late in the afternoon. As I was heading for a drink of water at the station, a middle-aged man asked if I would like a dinner and a place to flop. I accompanied him to his home half a mile away, learning en route that he had formerly been a lion tamer with Ringling Brothers. I wondered if this was a gag, since the man didn't look the part, but pictures in his home showed him using a chair to hold off a fierce lion.

The first thing I wanted was a shower, and I didn't think it odd that my host—his name was Eugene—stayed in the bathroom asking questions about the road. Nor did it seem odd when the lion tamer took off his shirt and showed me the ugly scars on his muscular chest and back.

After a good meal and a long talk, Eugene explained that his wife was out of town and they had only one bed. Would I mind sleeping with him? For fear of offending my host, I did not suggest that I'd just as soon flop on the floor. No sooner were we in bed than Eugene pointed out that he could make it better than any woman. Uh oh, a jocker! I didn't want to offend

Eugene, since he had been very kind, and he hadn't yet made a pass. Furthermore, if he got mean, he was more than a match for me. How to get out of this without hurting the man's feelings? I suddenly got an inspiration.

"Eugene," I said in tones of deep sincerity, "I'm awfully sorry, but I promised my mother I would never do that thing."

There was a pause, and I hoped I had sounded convincing.

Finally Eugene said quietly, "John, I understand," and turned over. I also turned over and we slept back-to-back until morning. Eugene made a big breakfast and insisted on giving me two meat sandwiches. On the way to the station I talked about my writing ambitions. At the yards I held out my hand to say goodbye, but Eugene insisted on staying until my freight pulled out. More than an hour later I said, "There goes the highball. So long, Eugene. I really enjoyed myself."

It was the slowest freight in America, and didn't pull into the Pittsburgh yards until dark. No sooner had I hopped off than a town cop collared me, and I was brought to a justice of the peace who read me some garbage about trespassing and endangering the lives of innocent people. After signing a paper I was transported to the Allegheny County Jail and was put in a cell with a huge man who was asleep on the only bed—a plank with one end resting on an open toilet and the other end on a chair. I curled up on the cement and slept until breakfast: an unspeakable blob masquerading as hot cereal, plus a hard roll and bitter coffee.

I had never been in such an enormous jail. There must have been three stories of cells. Across the way I could see prisoners living in luxury. They were all clean and had radios, books, curtains, and pictures in their cells. My roommate explained that these were criminals, and had been given first-class treatment. Our side held homeguards, drunks, exhibitionists, and bindle stiffs. A guard lined me up with other freight riders and homeguards and we were marched to a bus and driven for about an hour into the country.

We drove through a high wire gate to a big, sprawling brick building in the center of a huge tomato field. This was Blawnox Workhouse, my home for the next ten days. On the other side of the field some forbidding stone walls enclosed a huge stone fortress.

"The Big School," explained a road kid. "The state pen. That's where the big shots go. The Big House."

I knew I was entering a new world. First we all went through the ritual of surrendering razors and handkerchiefs. I protested when they wanted my soap, and the guard—after a quizzical look as if I were mad—let me keep it. Another guard with a moon face, looking like a grown-up baby, brought three others and me to the second floor of the barnlike building, where we went through a large dayroom containing a dozen scarred chairs, several tottering card tables, and a mountain of dog-eared magazines. Beyond, in an alcove, there were two double-deckers. "You-uns is lucky," said the guard in a twangy mountain voice. "This here is real private." He nudged me. "You-un take the top bunk nigh the window."

I had heard the clatter and clank of utensils and crockery on the main floor and knew the prisoners were eating. "When do we eat, mister?"

Moon-face was surprised. "Tomorrow morning. What the hell you-uns think?" He pointed to a towel on each bunk. "Them's you-un's. Take a shower every day if you-uns want," he noted proudly, then left without any further instructions.

I peered out of the wide, barred window. A tomato field stretched for a quarter of a mile, and just below was a baseball diamond with a wire backstop. In the fading light the massive gray fortress in the distance looked medieval.

Soon inmates sauntered up to the dayroom, griping and gossiping. Exhausted, I climbed up to my bunk and closed my eyes. The voices in the dayroom grew louder, turning my alcove into a madhouse. Someone shook my leg, and I opened my eyes. A man of about thirty, with a nose smashed to one side of his face like my father's and wearing a white jacket, was grinning at me. He held up a can. "This here is crum powder, Shorty. Better give your mattress a good spraying. God knows what the previous customer left behind. He was a filthy bastard. Bet your mattress is crawling with them li'l old sharks of the night!" He gave me another lopsided grin. "Bedbugs. You look clean. Good deal on the road." He lowered his voice. "Half these birds are old dingbats. They make a thing outa the workhouse. It's their country club. And their folks likes to have 'em here, too. You stick with the riders, kid. Need anything, just come to old Slim."

I thanked him for the crum juice, then squeezed the rubbery can, spraying powder over the straw mattress.

Slim pulled the mattress to the floor and cautiously sprayed the corners and cracks. "You gotta get way down in, Shorty. It's not only the bedbugs, it's the lice. Gimme a hand." We flung the bulky mattress onto the top bunk. "Now we do the same with your blanket." He pulled down the worn army blanket and repeated the process. "You got a pretty good place. Don't stink as much up there and you get a good view." He reached into the pocket of his white jacket. "You new guys got screwed outa supper. They always manage to bring you out so's you miss a meal. Saves the county money." He handed me a piece of white bread.

I thanked him, wondering if the guy was a jocker setting me up.

"Tomorrow you get assigned. They's three groups. The pickers, they pick the tomatoes; the sweepers, they clean up the joint; and the canners, they stew and can the tomatoes. I'm a canner. Everybody wants to be a canner. You get to wear a white jacket all the time." I asked about the baseball diamond outside. "Yeah, it's a big thing around here. We got a real league, like the major leagues. Each group has a team and we play just 'fore supper. That's why we eat late around here. The winner of the league gets to play the Blawnox Steelers. You know, outsiders. You'd think it was the World Series."

The din lessened as the men in the dayroom began drifting back to their bunks. Slim continued to give advice. "Riders has got to stick together. Most these birds are homeguards or stewpots or troublemakers. Only about a third of us is floaters. We follow the crops and keep on the move. Don't never trust one of them big homeguards. They're allus looking for a snag party, specially in the shower room." Prisoners were allowed to take showers until ten at night. "So wait until after nine when you'll be alone. If you get real dirty at a game go in with a partner and wash back-to-back close together. And remember, you *never* stoop to pick up a piece of soap—you squat! Them big jockers are rough on your asshole!"

Early the next morning I wrote my mother: "Fate reared its ugly head and I got arrested in Pittsburgh for riding a freight. I'm in for ten days." I'd be home August 21 or 22. "For Lord's sake don't worry about me for this is a mighty fine jail—and I can get rested up here as well as at home."

After breakfast Slim introduced me to Bill, the guard in charge of the canners. "Unnerstan' you-un went to college," said Bill with the same accent as the other guard. "I'm putting you in charge of a three-man team. Slim here will show you-un the ropes."

The process was simple. First the tomatoes were cleaned, with the rotten parts cut out, and put in a pot to be stewed. After stewing, the tomatoes were dumped into cans and sealed. Slim, as supervisor, went from team to team.

At eleven the canning operations stopped and the canners helped serve up the noonday meal. I felt at home as I ladled soup into outstretched bowls, careful to give everyone a full helping. At the end of the meal we canners cleared away two tables and set up our own lunch. It reminded me of the Garfield Club waiters at college.

"Pretty soft," gloated one man as he stuffed himself. Being a canner was something!

That afternoon the Canners were to play the Sweepers. There was a crisis: the Canners' manager had been released the previous morning and the season would end in eight days. The Canners and Pickers were tied in the playoff, and every game was important. Slim convinced Bill, the guard, that I should be the new manager. I'd been a big brain at college, said Slim. I was also to play. What position did I want? Second base, I said, aware that I would do the least damage there since I had a poor throwing arm and was slow.

That day's game with the Sweepers was a runaway 21–1; I fortunately had only two easy grounders to handle, and at bat I did manage to hit two foul balls. After a week it seemed as if I had been at Blawnox for a month. The games were the highlights of the day, and the Canners had beaten the Pickers once and lost once. By now it was obvious that I was a flop as a player, but my decisions as manager were good.

By the end of the first week the Canners and Pickers were still tied. I got a letter from my mother telling me not to worry—she had written the governor of Pennsylvania that her son was a Phi Beta Kappa and should be released. Over the years I had learned that my mother, in her own original way, often managed to influence people, and I prayed that no action would be taken until after the big final game.

The hours crept by slower than ever. The entire workhouse was excited about the game. Every man was betting whatever he might have on hand. The old-timers put their tobacco and pennies on the Canners, who always gave them extras at mealtime; but the newcomers put their treasures on the Pickers, who had won recently because of my failure to hit in a pinch. So far I had not gotten a single hit, although I had managed to wangle four walks. The two guards in charge of the teams had waged a huge twenty-dollar bet.

The afternoon of the final game arrived. When the workhouse bell clanged at four o'clock the place was in an uproar. The Pickers had come in from the field a half hour earlier. They hadn't picked a dozen bushels all day. The Canners who were on the team ran to the second floor and took off their white jackets, threw them on their cots, and joined the writhing mass blocking the wide staircase.

Those who weren't ballplayers were carrying folding chairs, since there was no grandstand, and the pushing, eager mob was excited in a good-natured way. Canners and Pickers razzed each other. The old Sweepers by that time had taken sides and rooted as vociferously for the Canners as alumni returning to the annual Yale-Harvard game.

By game time both sides of the diamond were lined with spectators. The two teams were evenly matched. The Pickers were mostly wild road kids who played baseball as though engaged in a gang fight. Every time they slid into a base they kicked their feet, and when they tagged out an opponent they did it sharply. The Canners, steadier and more competent, played carefully and calmly. No one was a star except the pitcher, a lanky twenty-year-old called Stretch who reminded me of the Pocatello Kid. He was a lefty with a good fastball and a variety of curves, but gave up quite a few walks.

The score was knotted at 4–4 in the top of the ninth inning. The first Picker hit a screaming drive that carried all the way to the wire fence near the railroad tracks. The ball was relayed in quickly, but the Picker made third. Stretch walked the next two batters, filling the bases. I walked over to Stretch, and we conferred for a long minute. Everyone imagined I was giving complicated instructions. Instead I merely told Stretch not to try so hard to strike out everyone. Stretch proceeded to fan the next three men.

In the bottom of the ninth, the first two Canners grounded out and I came to the plate. I had suggested that someone pinch-hit for me, but Stretch walked up and told me not to try and hit a homer. I swung wildly at the first two pitches and missed by a mile. The next ball came floating at me like a basketball. It had to be a roundhouse curve, and curves were my Waterloo. I shifted my feet and held up my bat. The ball was dumped down the first-base line. No one had expected a bunt with two strikes on me, and I managed to reach first base safely. The Canner rooters shouted as Stretch came to the plate, and I was still elated at finally getting a hit. Just then the afternoon freight tooted. The smoke of the engine climbed into the air in big puffballs, the Picker road kids instinctively turned to watch the oncoming freight, and I quietly walked to second base. Now a single would drive me in. On the first pitch Stretch hit a liner over first base and, slow as I was, I managed to score the winning run.

On my last day the Canners' reward came. Several trucks arrived with a crowd of players and fans from the Blawnox Steel Mill. I imagined they would be big, strapping monsters, but they were gaunt and worn. We won, 14–0. It was a letdown.

The next morning I was released on schedule, and I said farewell to my friends. Stretch was also released, and he suggested we ride the blinds to Pittsburgh. But I said we'd surely be picked up in Carnegie, and I took to the highway. I wanted no more jail adventures. The summer of 1939 had finally ended.

[9]

Going Left

On February 4, 1940, I received a telegram from La Crosse: my father had died. I had known this was coming, but it seemed impossible that the man who had been one of the heroes of my life was no longer with me.

Today, after more than half a century, those two weeks in the summer of 1939 with my father in La Crosse remain my most precious memory, and my deepest regret is that he did not live to share in whatever success I later enjoyed. When my books were finally published and I was awarded the Pulitzer Prize, he would have been proud of me. I can imagine no higher praise than his.

In May of 1940 I wrote long, introspective, and adolescently self-indulgent letters to my cousin Pat about my youthful ambitions and fantasies. I was sarcastically critical of current successful playwrights like Saroyan and Sherwood, and I was absolutely persuaded that my forthcoming brilliant career as a dramatist ("I've decided," I wrote, "to do to the American stage what Dostoevsky did for the Russian novel") would grow out of my experiences on the road—an aspect of American life that no writer had as yet properly presented.

Today I reread these letters with embarrassment and some amusement. How naive and pompous I was. I should have been past the age of arrogance and conceit but was hopelessly immature. Yet I also realize that without this adolescent self-glorification I would never have pushed on with my writing career. This youthful romanticism, in the long run, paid off, because it lay behind my perseverance. I had inherited a stubborn streak from both sides of my family, and I stubbornly clung to my vow to be a writer. That was good. But I also stubbornly clung to my conviction that I was going to be a playwright or novelist. At the same time I was also determined to be a factual, straightforward writer who didn't go in for stylistic improvisation and freewheeling imagination. I had complete confidence that I could be a "creative" writer, a playwright or novelist, despite my strong distaste for "subjective" writing in which the author's fancies or his private views were prominent. In an odd way, I now realize, I was self-centered and "selfless" at the same time. I was both right and wrong, and that, I am sure, is why it took me so long to finally become something I had never anticipated— an historian. In 1940 I was only at the beginning of my slow, gradual, groping, indefatigable journey of self-discovery.

Thanks to a fellow member of the Williams College Garfield Club, I got a big break.

He was so impressed by my play *The New Woman* that he convinced a friend of his, the actor Van Heflin, to read it. Heflin was in turn so impressed that he invited the two of us to attend a performance on Broadway of *The Philadelphia Story,* starring Katharine Hepburn.

For years she had been my ideal; when I was in New Haven at the drama school I often drove past her home. After the play, which I loved, the two of us went backstage to Heflin's small dressing room. While we were talking, Katharine Hepburn sailed out of her large dressing room like the Snow Queen. Ignoring my friend and me, she said she was ready for her coffee. Heflin said he'd be free soon.

In a few minutes she was back again, again ignoring my friend and me as if we were flies. Heflin made an attempt to introduce us, but in her "the calla lilies are in bloom" tone of voice, Miss Hepburn trod on his lines. He told me he would talk to Theresa Helburn of the Theatre Guild, and excused himself. I was stunned. My Dream Woman had evaporated. But my pal was chuckling as we made our way out the stage door. "What a great performance!" he exclaimed. "The Snow Queen! The Bitch!" He paraded out to the street, his scarf flying dramatically behind him as if he were the star of *The Philadelphia Story.*

For years I carried a grudge, but I relented after seeing *The African Queen.* Now I can watch her good movies with pleasure while consoling myself with how awful she had been in the play *The Lake.* One New York critic, Dorothy Parker, stated that Katharine Hepburn had "run the gamut of emotions from A to B." Another said she should have jumped into the lake. But she was always delightful with Cary Grant, and I (like God) forgave her her trespasses.

By the end of May of 1940 my high hopes for *The New Woman* had ended. I finally had a talk with Theresa Helburn, but the Theater Guild had a full schedule. I knew this was a kiss-off and decided it was time to get back on the road; by that time I had made enough to finance the venture by tutoring a wealthy kid so he could get into Exeter and by selling blood at a clinic every two weeks.

After driving to Illinois and spending a few weeks with the Ludwicks, I hit the road and the freights again, heading west on the Union Pacific with friends I made as I rode the rails. Once again I crossed the immensity and stern beauty of the desert. The heat by day was indescribable—and one's hope for relief in the cool of the night was often dashed when a freight would pass through an area of hot, dead air that persisted during the night. I made it to Reno, and the heat became less lethal as we climbed into the mountains, only to return with equal force when we descended and reached Stockton.

I led one road kid to the Tobacco Tree and its famous thousand-mile beans. For a place that catered to the less than affluent (and on a cash-only basis), it was surprisingly clean, pleasant, and colorful. They even gave you as much free ice water as you could drink on the spot. Yet it was in this unusually attractive spot that we first heard about the Stockton Killer's latest victim—his fifteenth.

I had heard of the Killer, but wondered if much of the talk wasn't exaggerated. He would apparently ambush the road kids and cut off their private parts. That night I ditched my companion and slept alone in a nearby field. The moon was so bright I could have read a newspaper. I recalled an article I had seen quoting a well-known psychiatrist who claimed that the Stockton Killer would kill and kill until caught. Each killing only whetted the maniac's appetite. The psychiatrist also warned that the Stockton Killer would be difficult to find, because he had no identifiable motive for his crimes. Ordinary police methods would continue to fail. Except during his rare moments of "ecstasy," it would be impossible to pick him from a crowd of ordinary men.

I couldn't sleep, and headed back to the yards so I could hop the next freight to the friendly Northwest. In the long wait I tried to convince myself that the killings had been more rumor than fact, and that little was actually known about the Killer. Perhaps there had only been two or three victims, but this thought did not relieve my fear, and I broke into a trot.

I spent the next two weeks touring my favorite area, then headed south to see Aunt Floss in Los Angeles, riding a train carrying two heavy loads of lumber and one boxcar bearing a scary warning: EXPLOSIVES—DANGER—DO NOT HUMP. About thirty lumberjacks shared a flatcar or the tops of boxcars, keeping to themselves. It was quite a thrill when we got a hotbox and the train started to catch fire. Fortunately the brakeman and the lumberjacks put out the fire quickly. Very quickly!

After too short a short visit with Aunt Floss, I left to follow the fruit harvest, taking part in a migration that Steinbeck later stunningly captured in *The Grapes of Wrath*. My first job was at a pleasant peach farm in the heart of a rich valley. I started working in the cutting sheds, where I would slice in two the firm, heavy peaches, then lay the halves in orderly rows on trays. I felt sorry for the women cutters, who coughed and sweated. The work was particularly difficult for the shorter ones, because the trays were stacked high above their heads and they had to stand on boxes. The morning started cheerfully, but by midafternoon everyone was in a bad humor. As hustler it was my duty to speed up the cutters, but I wasn't very good at this, because I didn't have the heart to put pressure on them. Their skins, covered with fuzz, itched and burned where they had scratched themselves with sticky fingers.

After work we all cleaned up at an irrigation ditch, had dinner with the farmer and his family under a large eucalyptus tree, and then wandered back to our beds in the hay. By the end of a week I felt I had learned enough about peaches, and I headed for Oregon. On the way I worked in a lettuce field. I had never before harvested lettuce, and at the end of my first ten-hour day my back ached from stooping over in the sweltering field. I had to drag two cases after me—one for the small heads and one for large. I would have collapsed if two Filipino boys hadn't shown me the proper technique. These boys—the others called them Goo-goos—won my admiration for their great strength, their skill, and their desire to be helpful.

A few days of lettuce-cutting was enough, and I flipped a freight for Klamath Falls and again visited the skid rows of Portland and Seattle. By early September, I decided to head back east. I picked the Northern Pacific, known as the Hungry Route because its division points provided little food at bakeries and meat markets, and stemming was fruitless. I had already mailed my change of clothes to the Ludwicks in Danville, but I still had ten dollars sewed in my jeans. In a dire necessity I would use it. But a con man soon relieved me of it and left me dead broke by boasting he could throw three sevens in a row with his dice. He did.

On the long trip east I managed to survive, along with two young road kids, on a few handouts. I decided to write a novel about these road kids and how they managed to endure the life on the road. I had ridden freights during three summers, but they had to stay on the road during the hard winter. How could they deal with such hardships?

I had seen so much injustice and hardship that I wanted the "people who lived in houses" to know what was going on in the most democratic nation in the world. My single driving force had previously been to be a writer—at all costs. But now I had a second drive—social reform. Once safely home,

I could think of little except the coming winter on the road for these young people. I spent several weeks brooding on the problem and writing down my thoughts. Here are a few samples, pompous but heartfelt:

"When Depression II comes," I pontificated, "you can pass these helpful hints along to your children. For governments, like people, seldom learn from experience and no doubt the next time two million or more kids wander over the face of our fertile land, once again welfare workers will spend their time filling out fat notebooks with spurious or unimportant information instead of just helping. Breadlines will again form to the right, although probably a pledge will have to be taken that neither you nor any of your relatives belong—or have ever belonged—to any subversive organization."

I felt bitter about the smug self-righteousness of those in power. When a left-wing girl in my playwriting class at Yale was kicked out because she handed out Red pamphlets at a New Haven strike, Larry Dugan and I had been the only ones in the class who were willing to sign a protest. I thought she wrote boring plays, but that was no crime; nor was being a member of the Communist Party.

Looking for literary material in my four summers on the road had been only a small, rather vague ingredient of my motive. I hadn't been researching subject matter for a future sociological thesis. I had hit the road because it was the last frontier open to someone with wanderlust and no money. But without realizing it I had become involved in a civil war that was given little publicity and would soon be forgotten. What particularly angered me was the treatment of the horde of boys and girls from twelve to nineteen years old, driven from their families by the Big Trouble, and I threw myself into my new project. I would write about how they had been reluctantly pushed out of their homes and forced to wander as penniless vagabonds over an indifferent and even hostile land baked by the sun, soused by the rain, and frozen by the winter winds. These children of the Depression roamed the Midwest and Far West on foot and on freights in search of food, clothing, and a future. They were hounded by their natural enemies: hunger, cold, railroad detectives, and the municipal police. Many were killed. Many more were maimed, losing arms, legs, and eyes in railroad accidents and fights. Many graduated into the ranks of the permanently dispossessed, the home-guards of countless skid rows. Others, well educated in the school of the road, rose to high positions in the petty criminal world.

But the amazing fact was that many more, through their own courage and character, the kindness of strangers, and pure luck, were managing to survive in body and mind. They were generally lively, bright, and volatile, and though they had their moments of hopelessness and bitterness, they faced life with a defiant, rough humor.

By late September 1940, I was ripe for Communism. The previous fall my mother had brought home from Consolidated Edison a Chinese, Yung Ying Hsu (pronounced Shu), who had come from China to work at the Institute of Pacific Relations. He was writing a history of two key Chinese provinces, and I had been fascinated by his stories of the Long March. Y.Y., as he liked to be called, had become friends with Edgar Snow, author of *Red Star over China,* and was a protégé of Chou En-lai. I had listened for hours to stories of the differences between Mao and Stalin. Y.Y. had taken me to meet Snow, who lived in the city, and I was awed by Snow's understanding of the Orient. I also accepted Y.Y.'s offer to let me work at the Chinatown paper, the *Red Star,* where my unpaid job was to turn the writers' prose into better English.

Early in October I joined the American Communist Party. It was the only party, I was assured, that was pro-labor and against the war in Europe, Jim Crow, and anti-Semitism. Another young man and I were given our cards at a brief ceremony in which both of us, in front of an American flag, were asked to pledge allegiance to the U.S.A.

On the subway back to 143rd Street I was still absorbed by what I had just done. It had, I reasoned, been inevitable. This would mean a great change in my life, but the step had to be taken. I would still write the novel, of course. Yet how could I write of the inequities of the road and stay out of the battlefield? The answer was that I had to do both simultaneously.

{10}

With Confused Confidence

At that moment my highest priority was peace, and I agreed to join the Washington Heights chapter of the American Peace Mobilization. On paper it was labeled "Progressive" but in truth it was run by the Communists. The leader, Manny Block, an energetic lawyer, put me in charge of staking out positions for the nightly street speech by planting a small podium and an American flag on a busy corner half an hour before the start of the meeting. The speaker was usually Manny, whose voice was loud, clear, and persuasive. But occasionally he insisted that I take over as a change of pace.

My first effort was pitiful. I had stage fright in front of thirty people, and I spoke either too fast or too slowly, too loud or too softly. But Manny was pleased. "At least you kept going," he said, having quickly learned something about me that I myself had not yet fully recognized: that one of my strongest traits was dogged perseverance.

My worst chore was trying to plow through Stalin's *Dialectical Materialism,* required reading for all new Party members. We also had to record our reactions, and I was called down to Fourteenth Street to explain why I had described the book as "impressive and inspiring but too complex, and most difficult to understand."

By that time my new mentors had also persuaded me to believe that capitalistic propaganda had portrayed Stalin falsely, and that he was not guilty of murdering his own associates—that, in fact, the Russian people loved him and called him Papa Joe. In my naiveté I was even convinced that the Stalin-Hitler nonaggression pact of August 23, 1939, was a blow to capitalism, and that Papa Joe would know how to handle the Germans.

My own writing suffered from my involvement with APM. I had laid aside the road-kid novel to write short stories and a play. "I'm afraid when I become famous, and it's only a question of time, naturally," I wrote with my usual bravado to my cousin Pat, "that my poor relatives will be torn between pride and horror at the things I'll say." I went on to tell her of stories I had written about bindle stiffs and road kids. I even called these stories "classic," although none of them had been published or was likely to be. I was sure as always that I was soon to become a public figure, although I said that the play on which I was then at work was "either a real masterpiece or a piece of cheese." I did not mention a word about joining the Communist Party and casting my first vote for president to Earl Browder. And I denied Putch's report to her that I was probably secretly married to a girl in Illinois. "But don't tell Putch," I wrote her. ". . . his little secrets may give him something to live for."

Ironically, a week or so later I did get a letter from Elaine, who had been writing me every week and had sent me a Christmas present—a ring. The letter announced that she had found someone else. I was crushed. But I finally recovered from my broken heart. I also attended rallies at Madison Square Garden and other large halls. As a friend and I were leaving one enthusiastic meeting, we saw John Garfield come out with two very attractive girls.

"Julie!" exclaimed my friend.

Garfield smiled and shook hands, and they chatted for a minute or two after Garfield had affably introduced us to the two girls.

"You called him Julie," I said later.

"We went to school together. His real name is Jules Garfinkle. Nice guy."

Many theatrical and movie personalities were supporting APM. They were called fellow travelers and helped our cause although they insisted they were not Communists. Some wealthy "travelers" in New York would even allow their mansions to be used for benefits.

In the spring of 1941 I volunteered to represent our chapter of APM in an antiwar protest in front of the White House. The reporters who met us at Union Station treated us with open scorn and arrogance. I was aroused, but Manny restrained me from retorting. There were about fifty men and a few women representing various chapters and unions. A Hollywood director was the leader of our group. To date he had not deigned to speak to anyone except two of his lieutenants, and now he was so distraught by the hostile reception accorded us by the press and the public that he was about to leave us to our fate when a dignified lady stepped out of the house next to Blair House, strode across Pennsylvania Avenue as if she owned it, and announced in a queenly manner that her home was at our disposal. As she recrossed the avenue she was followed by the twenty-five or so homeless, who found cots, beds, or mattresses neatly laid out on two floors. Our hostess apologized to us for not having prepared dinner, but promised us a good breakfast.

APM activities came to an abrupt halt on June 22, 1941, when word arrived that Hitler had invaded Russia. Manny Bloch phoned me and revealed that APM was now AAF, Americans Against Fascism. "The hell you say!" I retorted. "How can you call it an imperialistic war on Saturday and a democratic war on Sunday?"

Later we had a long talk, and as a result I agreed to sell the *Daily Worker* at the uptown IRT yards to subway employees leaving work late in the afternoon. No one ever bought a paper until one big guy stopped and grinned at me. "Ah, hell!" he said. "Let's buy one from the kid."

By the end of the week I was selling five or six copies a day, and I received a call of commendation from Manny. "They're impressed with you," he said. Most of the salesmen, he added, rarely sold any copies at all but secretly paid for them personally.

A week later I drove my mother to Roxy's in New Hampshire for a week's vacation, and when I returned I found a letter from my former teacher at Williams, Stanley Young, now an editor at Harcourt, Brace. I had sent him the rough draft of my sketches on bindle stiffs and two plays. Young liked both plays and suggested I send *The Banyan Tree,* the first play I had shown Mark Reed, to the legendary agent Audrey Wood, "one of the few agents in town," he wrote, "who is interested in young writers and knows what she is doing."

I was so encouraged that I sent all my road sketches to the *Atlantic Monthly* short story contest. All were politely returned in due course. One might say that I was "banned in Boston."

In the meantime I had finished another play, an American version of Dostoevsky's *The Idiot.* A Communist woman with influence in the Party liked everything but the ending. It should finish, she insisted, with the triumph of the people. Dialectical materialism demanded it. My refusal to change the ending brought a lecture on Party discipline. I tore up the play and returned to the task of making a novel out of my road sketches.

Everything changed on the afternoon of December 7, 1941, while I was listening to the Giants—Dodgers football game (yes, there *was* a Dodgers football team!). The broadcast was interrupted for an announcement that the Japanese had bombed American warships in some place called Pearl Harbor.

On the 10th of January, 1942, I finally heard from Audrey Wood, the agent Stanley Young had suggested for my two plays, *The Banyan Tree* and *Pie in the Sky.* "You seem to have a flair for character as well as knowledge of what is theatric," she wrote. "However, in my opinion, because of present-day conditions, I would be at a loss to know where to submit either play." I appreciated her encouraging words, but felt depressed. I was still only a "promising" writer.

A few days later I had my tonsils removed by the father-in-law of Bob

Frank, coauthor of *Fraternity Row*. The surgeon and I had become good friends, and he agreed to remove my tonsils for nothing at the Morrisania Hospital on Worth Street.

Once I was on the operating table, the doctor explained that he was going to place mirrors around my head so I could watch the entire process. "You can use this in a story sometime," he said. I wanted to close my eyes but decided that would be impolite. The doctor hooked a strand of wire around the diseased tonsils and then jerked with both hands. Nothing happened. "Toughest tonsils I ever saw!" he observed, and yanked again. Now what? I thought. The doctor set himself and gave a tremendous jerk. The tonsils yielded a bit. Another yank did the job. No longer would I have to pick pus out of those damned things! I thanked the doctor and spent two nights in the hospital, which charged me only six dollars for "general institutional care."

While waiting to be called up I thrashed around in a final desperate attempt to rework my road-kids material into a novel, asking my friends for advice and fretting over such problems as whether to use a first-person narrator, the kind of person to use as my central character, and the possibility of including a key strike in California as a major event.

During this time my sister came to dinner. In the past few years, Virginia had gone emotionally downhill, and quite rapidly. On several occasions I'd had to bail her out of dingy hotels where some man had left her after a bout with the bottle. Three men had figured prominently in her life. One of them was a handyman named Joe whose electricity had been turned off because he hadn't paid Consolidated Edison. My mother had solved the problem by putting him on a strict budget and persuading her boss to give him time to pay. Joe had repaid Mother by coming down from the Bronx each weekend to fix sundry things that had gone wrong with the little house on 143rd Street. He also promised to dry out Virginia and put her on a liquor budget. After several months he took her to Alcoholics Anonymous, where she was the pet of the chapter for about a month. Then I got a phone call requesting that she stay away from all future meetings. She was too "disruptive," said the caller, without telling me exactly what he meant.

The next man in her life was a middle-aged salesman whose droning stories put me to sleep. He was crazy about Virginia and finally persuaded her to marry him. But after two days Virginia was back—his endless stories were driving her mad. As always, it was my mother who solved the problem; she persuaded one of her clients, a struggling lawyer, to get the marriage annulled. Virginia's third man was even more elderly—an author named Roberts who had published several novels and had begun writing a biography of Raphael Semmes, the famed Confederate admiral. I tried to like him, but him pomposity was unbearable. Marriage was never mentioned, but Roberts took her to New Orleans for research.

By 1942 she and the author were back, living in Brooklyn. Although I had gotten along very well with her in the past, I now felt very strange when she came to dinner, for she had become a snob. We got into a violent argument about equality. She obviously thought of herself as superior to people of almost all other races and of every other class—which eliminated about 90 percent of the world. And so I said she was a Fascist because she believed in the master race and the master class of "superior" administrators. After the fight I felt disgusted with both her and myself. Even then I could realize how self-righteous I was. There was one definite improvement, however— she was not drinking so much. Evidently Roberts knew how to handle her.

On March 13, 1942, I received orders to report in a week to Dr. F. Smith at St. Luke's Hospital on Amsterdam Avenue for a final physical examination at 3:45 P.M. I passed, and on the day I enlisted the Senate voted to raise the GIs' pay to eighteen dollars a month. I was particularly pleased that my dog-tag number began with 1—which meant that I hadn't been drafted, but had volunteered. I soon found myself a member of the 491st Squadron in a bombardier school near Midland, Texas, facing a month of basic training, which meant marching, mopping, and movies on syphilis. I stood out in the drilling, for my name apparently fascinated the corporal in charge of drills, and "TO-LAND!" was heard all over the drilling field whenever anything went wrong. Of course, I looked on all my experiences as material for the Great Army Novel I would someday write.

In early June, basic training ended and my group was transferred to several different destinations. My best friend, Van Auker, and I were sent to the Waco Army Flying School. I made another friend, Mort Hunt, whose IQ was extraordinary. He loved music, and the two of us hitchhiked to the music building of Baylor University and persuaded the woman in charge to give us a key so we could spend evenings listening to classical music.

A few days later I was assigned to Public Relations as a reporter, and I devised a scheme not only to help a group of young actors in Waco but to get myself rides in the training planes that were designed for aerobatics: I promised one of the young instructors that I would write a story with photos about his activities for his local newspaper. He was delighted, and I not only got an hour of aerobatics but was introduced to a lieutenant in charge of supply. I offered to do a hometown story for him too if I could borrow equipment for a worthwhile local show about the army. I left with a truck-load of equipment.

When I heard that glider schools had upped the age limit and I was eligible, I immediately applied, took all the exams, passed, and awaited my assignment, although I did not tell my mother of my plans. But in early August the glider program was cut, and I had to continue my boring life in Public Relations, occasionally clipping a paragraph or running to the message center. One day a civilian plane landed, almost out of gas. I happened to be on the line and recognized the pilot—"Wrong Way" Corrigan, who had been refused permission to take off on a flight across the Atlantic, and then announced he was going west but headed across the Atlantic anyway. When reporters queried him in Europe he said, "I guess I came the wrong way."

While Corrigan was arguing for some fuel, I took the ground chief aside and told him this was a great opportunity for a story. He summoned a photographer. I interviewed Corrigan and then had a picture taken with Corrigan, the ground crew, and several mechanics. "Now let's get one for AP," I said, and asked Corrigan to sit like a cowboy on the tail of his ship— facing the tail. Unfortunately some officers thought this would make fun of the Army Air Forces and the picture was destroyed.

I was so disgusted that I formed a club to carry a message throughout the air force once we left Waco. I named it BIOYA, and members were pledged to write it on walls, hangars, and other buildings. It stood for "Blow It Out Your Ass."

I became so bored that I decided to enter office candidate school. Hunt and VanAuker agreed to do the same. Mort was accepted at the top-level air force school in Florida, which claimed such celebrities as Clark Gable. Van, an expert in armament, went to school in the East, and I was sent to a new school for men in all branches of the army located in Fargo, North Dakota.

Early in September 1942 I boarded a train for Fargo with several other Waco candidates. Three months later I emerged as a second lieutenant in the Army Air Forces.

I spent my ten-day leave in New York, and my mother insisted I go to Wanamaker's to have my picture taken in my uniform. As I look at this picture today I see an incredibly innocent young man completely unprepared for combat. Brimming with eagerness to at least be in a position to get into a battle zone, in December 1942 I boarded a train for my new station: Basic Training Center No. 6, AAF Technical Training Camp, St. Petersburg, Florida, where I could finally thaw out from the arctic winter in Fargo.

The war I was so eager to participate in would soon move past the point of no return for the Axis powers. Italy would soon no longer be a significant force. Japan first was crushed at Midway, then stopped at Guadaleanal. And Germany would begin to experience the terrifying retribution of the Red Army.

I did not know it then, but I would never experience combat personally, though over many years to come I would relive it through the eyes of those who did.

Part Four

At War with the Army (1943–1957)

{11}

At Ease

My war would be waged on the home front with Army brass who did not find most of my ideas about democracy and its values acceptable. I thought we were fighting for these values. I was on occasion, to be disillusioned.

A few days after my arrival in St. Petersburg, another second lieutenant and I were assigned to the 588th Technical School Squadron in Clearwater, where our mission was to train enlisted men for service as members of ground crews, chiefly by means of lectures and drilling. Since there was no officers' club or bachelor officers' quarters, my mate and I had to rent a small bungalow near the Clearwater Hotel, which housed some five hundred enlisted men. Captain Dix, the commander, put me in charge of insurance, VD, and special services. The last meant that I was to run sports and entertainment programs, which was the start of my show business career.

Captain Dix told me to put on a soldier show. I spent the next week in the hotel's enlisted recreation room rounding up a dozen entertainers and Ed Baxter, the piano player from a big-name band. We started writing songs with lyrics which I provided, and every night the crowd around the piano increased.

An older private, who never knew why he had been drafted, offered to direct the show. This was Private Frank R. Brown, the Hollywood Reporter. He and Sergeant Persuitte presented the idea of a public performance to Captain Dix, who wavered until Brown promised to give the show wide publicity. I spent the next week in the plush suite on the top floor of the hotel as night duty officer, writing the book of *At Ease*—a series of scenes depicting the adventures of Private George Brick in the 588th Squadron. There would be two girl walk-ons and one girl to play Private Brick's girlfriend, Lena.

I went to the Clearwater Amateur Theater and was told that the one girl in the group who could sing and dance was then working in the perfume department of the local Woolworth's. I went there and behind the counter

I found an attractive girl with red hair. Dorothy Peaslack, whose father was a retired army band leader, had been a professional roller skater, was an acrobat, and could play six musical instruments. She readily agreed to fill the role of Lena. When I saw her in action onstage I was captivated.

For the next three weeks, fifty-two men spent most of every day rehearsing, making scenery and props, and setting up the lighting. Dix came to several rehearsals, his face stern with misgivings. He was also apparently annoyed that I had fallen in love with Dorothy, and that she had reciprocated. She was the most talented woman I'd ever met.

Then I decided that the "Dream Sequence" at the end of the first act had to be drastically changed. I insisted that Lena, wearing long black stockings, come out on roller skates playing the "Bachanal" from *Samson and Delilah* on a clarinet. Then as Brick arises from his cot, eight GIs in beautiful ballet costumes dance around him to the "Bachanal" (played by pianist Baxter) as Lena skates off. Her role had even more elaborate variations as the scene built to a flamboyant finale.

At the first night's performance the Army Induction Center scene worked beautifully. Brown and Baxter had done a professional job with a group of talented young enthusiasts. The complicated Dream Sequence also came off without a flaw, and there was tremendous applause at the end of Act One. Yet despite this ovation I felt sure that this was the end of my career. I knew Dix would get back at me.

Brown had brilliantly staged the final number with the entire cast marching around carrying various national flags and singing "Fight On, United Nations!" I had persuaded the commander of a Soviet naval school in St. Petersburg to provide the Soviet flag. It was stirring, and the crowd of GIs and civilians cheered. Even so, I was prepared for the worst as the grim-faced Captain Dix approached me after the show. But before he could open his mouth, the commanding general of the area and his wife appeared backstage. "Lieutenant Toland," said the general sternly, "were you imitating me in the inspection scene?" (In the middle of the second act I played a white-gloved officer inspecting a barracks.)

"Yes, sir."

"Next time do it properly." He illustrated with a twist of his right wrist.

"We loved everything!" gushed his wife. "That girl was simply darling!"

"Your show is a good morale-builder, and I want every man in my command to see it," said the general, and turned to Captain Dix. "I want three more performances." He then turned back to me. "That was a good idea letting civilians in free." I said it was the idea of the director, Private Brown.

There was so much publicity about *At Ease* that the leader of the nearby

Coast Guard installation band urged us to give a performance for the Coast Guard. The show was an even greater success this time around.

But my relations with Captain Dix were only worsened by the success of *At Ease,* and he, after submitting a scathing efficiency report on me, insisted that I be shipped to St. Petersburg. This would mean, of course, that I would have difficulty seeing Dorothy.

I was assigned to the 603rd Training Group, billeted in the Vinoy Hotel at the edge of the city. My commander, Major W. F. Bull, was small, wiry, and energetic. He was noted for touring the area on his bicycle wearing a pith helmet and slapping a leg with his riding crop while whipping his scattered charges into order. "I've heard all about you," he told me, and brought out my 201 file—the personnel file maintained for each officer. Captain Dix had shown me no mercy. "I can see you're a can-do officer, and I'm giving you free rein. You'll be my supply officer, and I want you to see that when this command finishes its mission I'm not charged for missing blankets, sheets, and cots." I would also be special services officer, in charge of athletics and entertainment. Morale throughout BTC 6, he said, was poor because of the cold, wet weather, and he wanted me to put on shows not only for the 603rd Training Group but for the poor devils camping out in "Tent City." The men there had no barracks and lived in tents with inadequate sanitary facilities. I was to place a notice on the bulletin board asking for volunteers.

"How many?"

"As many as you need. Welcome aboard!"

The next morning I was flooded with applicants. Half of them were performers, including the best accordion player in San Francisco (who had played at a gay bar, but was not gay), an accomplished pianist, a juggler, a natural comic from Pittsburgh named Marty Alpern, and an athletic sergeant with a familiar face who turned out to be Bob Gregory, former light-heavyweight wrestling champion of the world and husband of the ranee (queen) of Sarawak, a British protectorate in northwest Borneo. Bob had left the Orient with his bride to open a successful restaurant in England and somehow had ended up in St. Petersburg. He offered to be stage manager.

Others volunteered to make scenery, work behind stage—anything to avoid the incessant drilling. I started organizing shows for the hotel while Gregory prepared for the Tent City performances.

I was in my element, but I missed seeing Dorothy. I volunteered to take night duty every two to three days. This consisted of being driven in a staff car throughout the entire area to check on bars, dance halls, and recreation centers. On the first night I instructed the driver to head for Clearwater, where we picked up Dorothy, who accompanied us on our rounds. Before the next trip I suggested that the driver pick up his girl too. There was never any trouble. If anyone approached the car, the girls would simply slip down out of sight.

Our next show was *Jeeps,* the story of the average American in the Army Air Forces. In the next four months I put on numerous successful shows, climaxing with a special soldier show in the huge outdoor theater in the middle of St. Petersburg. Other groups had been putting on performances there, but the major wanted the one from the 603rd to surpass them all. I suggested getting volunteers from the Soviet naval school for a joint U.S.–Soviet extravaganza. The idea appealed to him. I had attended two dances given by the Soviet officers, had learned how to say "I love you" in Russian, and was on good terms with the commandant. I suggested that the show start with a slam-bang GI number to be followed by Soviet dancers. Alternating U.S. and Russian performances would follow. Each act had to be rehearsed separately, and it was up to me to see that everything fit together at showtime. Every seat was taken, and although air force brass was not seated in a block, many stars and eagles were in evidence. The overture was music from *At Ease.* Then the first act—Marty Alpern. As he came shuffling onstage as Gwendolyn, there were shrieks from his old-lady club, and he immediately captivated the entire audience, including the Soviet officers sitting near the front. What followed was a wild dance by eight young Russians that brought cheers. Everything worked like a charm—even the mistakes. I knew from the beginning that no matter what went wrong the audience was with us.

In early June 1943, Major Bull told me that Basic Training Camp 6 would soon close down. An officer from Washington was then in town looking for a talented junior officer for an important Washington job in public relations, and the major urged me to get an interview. I was summarily turned down.

A few days later, something even more important than my brilliant military career (in show business!) took place. I married Dorothy in a church in St. Petersburg. The rain that had failed to fall on the U.S.–Soviet show poured down, but Bob Gregory saved the day by commandeering a staff car and driving us safely to the church. That night Gregory and Marty redecorated the recreation room at the officer's club and prepared a show for the reception. All the officers were invited, and most attended even though they knew a crowd of enlisted men would also be on hand. Later I drove Dorothy to a house I had rented on the Gulf of Mexico for my ten-day leave. The honeymoon was shared by my large staff, who made our house their headquarters and somehow, probably through Bob Gregory, got passes to visit us almost every day.

It was also time to get ready to leave St. Petersburg. Major Bull was relieved to find that he still had a full complement of sheets, towels, blankets, mattresses, and cots. He did not know that the wily Sergeant Marco had also stored away an additional supply for his private use. By chance the sergeant, two other enlisted men, and I were assigned to Keesler Field in Biloxi, Mississippi.

Now I would see the *real* South.

{12}

Riding the Air Force Roller Coaster

I found myself finally in show business in a big way, but hardly in the way I'd expected. I was also in the Deep South, an area I was encountering for the first time. Biloxi was a beautiful city, and Keesler Field was a big and impressive base. My three enlisted men from Florida received good assignments and reported that my share of the blankets was safely stored away. To my own surprise I was warmly welcomed on all sides and was put in charge of entertainment.

Apparently news of *At Ease* had preceded me, for the commandant, Colonel Robert E. M. Goolrick, gave me *carte blanche* to produce an extravaganza to celebrate the opening of a huge outdoor theater seating ten thousand. I would also have the services of the Keesler Field Concert Orchestra, along with a group of some sixty male and female singers from Biloxi.

I was appalled. All this big-time talent did not fit my concept of a true GI soldier show, but I knew I had to do it.

Most of my men were not enthusiastic about staging a show for an audience of ten thousand until the hillbilly band suggested they turn it into a rodeo. All of them could perform such stunts as riding two horses, Roman style. I began writing sketches and blackouts, as well as blocking out production numbers.

But the whole setup disturbed me. We plowed ahead, overcoming countless difficulties until rain turned the ground around the stage into a morass. On the day of the show I inwardly groaned as I watched the front rows of the benches fill with officers in white dress uniforms. Hillbillies on horses suddenly appeared in the rear, racing down both sides of the bench section. Great globs of mud splattered over those on the aisles. Then followed one hillbilly riding two horses. It was a bravura performance. He made a sharp turn in front of the benches, spraying fresh mud over the first two rows of white-clad officers. The next hour and a half was pure torture for me even though the individual acts were very good. The show as a whole was a fiasco.

I slept little, wondering what would happen now. In the morning I was informed that I was being shipped on temporary duty to Washington and Lee University in Lexington, Virginia, to attend officer courses at the Special Service School. I would be there for two weeks before returning to Keesler. I was as glad to get out of there as my superiors were to see me go.

My favorite class in Lexington was with Major Herzberg, who called on every man to return to his post determined to promote the message of democracy within the ranks. Herzberg, reputed to be the choice of Eleanor Roosevelt for the post, reiterated that all personnel in the army, regardless of race or color, should be treated equally.

On the way back to Keesler, I was inspired to insist on doing soldier shows his way—that is, if I was still head of the Recreation Department. I was greeted enthusiastically by my men, but my superior was cool.

The next day I observed a one-armed black captain lunching at a small stand open to all personnel. He was reading Dostoevsky. I introduced myself and asked why he wasn't eating at the officers' club. The captain, whose name was Clark, smiled. "Gentlemen's agreement, lieutenant."

Remembering the words of Major Herzberg, I said, "What would happen if I brought you to the officers' club for dinner?"

"All hell would break loose," observed Clark, and smiled. "It would be a sight to behold."

"Let's do it," I said.

Learning that I was married, Clark insisted that my wife agree. We drove in Clark's car to the large boardinghouse where Dorothy and I lived. It was off base but not far from the officers' club. Although Dorothy had been raised in the South, she made no objection and agreed to accompany us. On the trip to the officers' club, Clark revealed that he had lost his arm in the First World War and had been awarded the Distinguished Service Medal. He had then become a professor of English at a black university.

When the three of us entered the club I could feel the shock. As we sat down, a black waiter turned pale. Occupants of nearby tables were aghast, and the tension in the room was electric. Then came an announcement over the intercom for Lieutenant Toland to report to the front desk. The post executive officer, whom I will call Colonel Redd, was waiting for me. "Get that Nigra out of here, lieutenant!" he snarled, almost overcome with anger.

"We'll be happy to leave, colonel," I said in a somewhat shaky voice, "once we've finished our meal." I went back to the table and quietly explained what had happened.

The three of us hastily finished eating and started out of the room. Redd was still at the desk. "Toland!" he called. I approached. "If it's the last thing I ever do, I'll have you court-martialed. Report to Colonel Goolrick at nine o'clock!"

We drove around for more than an hour wondering what was going to happen, assuming that I was to report at 9:00 A.M. the next morning. But as we approached headquarters all lights were ablaze. Redd must have meant 9:00 P.M.! It was several minutes after nine as I darted into the building. "Hi, John!" said the duty officer, a friend from the North. "What's the big rush?" It would be the last time he would ever say a kind word to me.

I found Colonel Goolrick with knitted brows. He was not angry, only terribly disturbed. "Don't I treat my Negroes well?" he asked plaintively.

"Yes, sir."

"How could you have done this terrible thing in Mississippi? I deeply regret the consequences of your . . . rashness. The executive officer will give you your next assignment."

During the next two months, Dorothy and I underwent a variety of punishments. She was kept off the post and I was assigned to the toughest squadron. My task was to supervise the drill field, and the four Southern redneck sergeants made my life hell.

Next came a genuine crisis. I was charged with assaulting a GI at the enlisted men's service club. The previous Sunday, Dorothy and I had attended a record concert open to everyone on the base. The door had been closed, and when I pushed it open, it brushed against a staff sergeant. Although I apologized, the sergeant, half a foot taller, had rudely pushed me away.

At the hearing my testimony was not taken seriously. Then two Jewish psychiatrists appeared and stated that the door had barely touched the sergeant, who had returned my apology with a vigorous shove. The case was dropped.

A week later I was charged with stealing several books that had disappeared from the library. But the man in charge of the library, a talented poet and my good friend, Sergeant Weston McDaniel, reported that he had already found the supposedly stolen books, which had been misplaced in the shelves.

Then I was investigated by an intelligence officer who was concerned about several entries in my statements when I enlisted in New York, starting with my various arrests. He was so confused by my complicated explanations that he dismissed me. Thank God I hadn't revealed in New York that I was a member of the Communist Party and the American Peace Mobilization.

By that time I had sent a letter to Major Herzberg in Lexington, telling of the attempts to court-martial me. So far I'd escaped trial, but I feared that Colonel Redd would redouble his efforts.

On the bright side, the two psychiatrists and their wives had become fast friends, and my enlisted men, with very few exceptions, stuck by me. Knowing that our night life was dull, the hillbilly band suggested that Dorothy and I attend a play date they had at the warrant officers' club. We were driven in the battered hillbilly station wagon to a lonely structure in the middle of a bayou, where the moss-hung trees surrounding the house made it look like the scene of a murder mystery.

For an hour Dorothy and I joined in the dancing and games such as passing an orange under the chin to someone of the opposite sex. One very thin young woman took a fancy to me, and I ducked into the men's room to escape. Upon emerging, there she was, holding two wineglasses. "Have a drinky," she said, and as I took one glass her husband, at least six foot six but also skinny, approached, his face contorted.

"Aren't you the New York Jew who took the nigger into the officers' club?"

I had to strain my neck to look up at the tall man. "What's it to you?" I said.

"You bastard!" The warrant officer swung at my head, but I ducked slightly and his fist struck the wineglass I was holding. The broken glass smashed into his wife's face. Blood spattered. There were shouts of rage, and angry warrant officers converged on me. I knew I was in for a beating— perhaps worse. Then the lights blacked out. One of the hillbillies, accustomed to such crises, had doused them. Screams and shouts added to the confusion. I felt a hand on my right arm. "Come with me," said a calm hillbilly voice. "Someone's taking Dorothy out."

I was led in the dark through the shouting mass and safely deposited in the rear of the station wagon containing some of the band's musical gear. Dorothy was already there. For the next hour or so we waited until the dance was over, occasionally bumping into a drum or cymbal. The hillbillies advised me to go to the Red Cross and ask for an emergency leave before something else happened. I did, and was turned down; my case wasn't considered that serious.

The future looked bleak, but early in December 1943, Marco, my sergeant from St. Petersburg, who had access to headquarters, reported that a message had just arrived from Washington signed by Army Chief of Staff G. C. Marshall, ordering 2d Lt. John Toland, O184459AC, to report to the Special Service School in Lexington, Virginia. Major Herzberg must have worked the miracle.

(Later I would receive a letter from my one-armed friend Captain Clark, who had been promoted to major and was doing very well: "I'm enclosing something which you can show your children when they ask, 'What did you do in the war, Daddy?' " It was a 1944 Army Air Forces regulation stating that all officers, regardless of color, race, or creed, would henceforth be admitted to all officers' clubs, not only in the continental United States but overseas.)

We stayed only two days at the Special Service School before continuing to Washington, where I was almost immediately sent on a sixty-day assignment to help develop soldier shows in New England.

While I was visiting air bases as far north as Presque Isle, Maine, a young black officer invited Dorothy and me to attend a dinner and dance held by a black fighter squadron that was leaving for Europe. I danced with Colonel Chappie James's lady and he danced with Dorothy. He would become the first black four-star general.

On March 1, 1944, another order arrived ordering me to proceed "soonest" to the Special Services Division at 25 West Forty-third Street, New York, for approximately thirty days. The last two months had been like an endless roller coaster ride, and I didn't know what to expect in New York City. What most impressed me was the Special Services Division address—the same building as *The New Yorker.*

I was brought to the office of the executive officer, Colonel Warburg, who was scanning my 201 file. "I understand this is the worst 201 file in the air force," he said sternly. I didn't doubt it and expected a blast—until Warburg smiled. "But it looks good in New York City." I was temporarily assigned to the Entertainment Section, which was headed by Lieutenant Colonel Marvin Young, who had been, I later learned, a talent agent in Hollywood. Young was friendly and turned me over to his executive officer, Captain John Shubert.

I certainly knew who *he* was, and wondered what on earth I would be doing for the next thirty days. Shubert shuffled some papers and then said, "For the time being you'll be in charge of Domestic. Miss Voltz can explain." She was his secretary, a very competent-looking individual. She was in her late twenties and attractive, but reminded me of a top sergeant. In the next hour I discovered that she practically ran that office. She explained what "Domestic" meant—the USO Camp Shows units and celebrities in the continental United States: the Victory Circuit, composed of some dozen or so performers; the Blue Circuit, five performers; the Hospital Circuit, special performers; and Personal Appearances—which meant stars.

I was dazed by the constant activity in that large office. Colonel Young was protected by a private office, but Captain Shubert, who was also in charge of Professional Entertainment, was protected only by Miss Voltz. He always looked as if he wished he weren't there.

Within a week, Berenice Voltz and I understood each other. She had heard about me and thought the two of us could handle the office. "Look," she said, pointing to the officers from other sections who were crowding around Shubert's desk and asking for tickets to the Shubert shows. Berenice explained that he passed out several hundred free tickets to the Shubert theaters each week. "He can't say no."

It offended me that the bulk of the officers demanding tickets were field grade—majors and colonels—and were using their rank to put pressure on Shubert for free tickets. What a waste of a talented man's time! I wanted to do all I could to help him do what he could do better than anyone else.

My daily routine was fascinating. Every morning I would call my opposite number at USO Camp Shows, Papa Drescher, a longtime stage manager for the Shuberts. He would tell me if any stars were available for visits to the GIs. If so, I was to decide where the star should be sent and then make all travel and housing arrangements. At first I consulted Berenice, but she said I was better qualified, since I was the only one in the entire office who had "served in the field." Almost everyone else had been plucked out of civilian life, attended a brief officer training program, and then been sent to New York. Most of them didn't even know how to wear their insignia. But I had been in Texas and Mississippi and knew about the actual conditions at such places. I decided to send the stars to the dreariest, most forlorn places.

One day I requested a few minutes alone with Captain Shubert. "I've noticed that much of your time is taken up with passing out free tickets, sir. Why don't you let me take care of it?" Shubert seemed dubious. "I've also noticed that practically everyone who gets tickets is a field-grade officer." Shubert looked uncomfortable. "It wouldn't look good if this were generally known. I believe I can take care of this with no trouble. Miss Voltz agrees with me." The final remark turned the trick.

"Good idea, lieutenant," he said, and he reached into his drawer and pulled out a box of tickets.

Miss Voltz also had told me Shubert was deathly afraid of being shipped overseas. I headed to the office of the man in charge of shipping, an unpopular warrant officer. When we were alone, I held out four tickets. "How would you like to get four more *every* week?"

The warrant officer checked for listeners, then asked, "What do I have to do?"

"Keep Captain Shubert off the shipping list," I said softly.

The warrant officer grinned. "No sweat."

I knew I couldn't tell Shubert that he need no longer be afraid of being shipped out, but I did inform Berenice—who said nothing but gave me a conspiratorial wink and nod.

On May 6, Colonel Young informed me that I was now on permanent duty and shook my hand. "We're pleased with your work, lieutenant." By that time I had also convinced Papa Drescher at USO Camp Shows that the plan to send stars to the dreariest camps in the country was working—except with a few superstars who insisted on performing to huge audiences in or near large cities. But I did have some trouble with travel arrangements. Most of the stars wanted to travel by air, even for short distances, because it made them look important. But I already had many connections with bus and train agents and I could prove that air actually took longer because of weather conditions, schedules, and transportation to and from airports.

For a long time I wondered why Papa Drescher at USO Camp Shows always accepted my advice. The reason for this, I eventually discovered, was a chain—not a chain of command, but a chain of friendship. Working under me in the Entertainment Section was Sammy Weisbord, who had formerly been one of the best talent agents at the William Morris Agency. He had discovered, for example, Red Skelton and Betty Hutton. Like so many in show business, he had been sent to the officers' training program and, though very bright and able, had been turned down. I was sure this was because he was a Jew. He was now a sergeant doing clerical work—essentially no more than a typist. It was ridiculous. We became good friends, and at one point he praised my work to Abe Lastfogel, chief of the William Morris Agency and now head of USO Camp Shows, who regarded Sammy as a son. Abe in turn had congratulated Papa Drescher on his good relations with Lieutenant Toland, who was doing such a good job. This was why Drescher so readily accepted my advice.

Another new friend was Second Lieutenant Alex North, the composer. He and Sammy had introduced me to lox and bagels, and in turn I introduced them to the Yale Club, only a short walk away. The three of us would spend most of the long lunch period in the steam room of the Yale Club, discussing Colonel Young's madhouse.

During one of these steam-room sessions I asked Sammy if it was true that the novel *What Makes Sammy Run* was based on him.

"I've had to make some tough decisions," he replied. "Everyone is free to draw his own conclusions."

On July 4 there was a celebration in the office. Young was promoted to full colonel, Shubert to major, and Alex and I to first lieutenant. I'd never dreamed that I'd ever wear silver bars.

I also discovered that Alex North's brother was Joe North, editor of *The New Masses*. But Alex was not at all political. He had, however, studied in the Soviet Union with Prokofiev and had written music for his own first wife, a renowned dancer. Alex was a close friend of Charles Weidman, and he persuaded Weidman to give Dorothy private dancing lessons if she had talent. Weidman was impressed by her complete control of her body and taught her several modern routines, the best one to "I'm Only a Motherless Child."

The number of celebrities I had to manage gradually increased, and they occupied more and more of my time. The most memorable addition was Alan Ladd, who had been released from the air force because of ill health. When he offered to give us two weeks in between movies, Papa Drescher proposed a series of performances at camps and bases, but I insisted on sending Ladd and his wife to general hospitals, not as performers but to talk at length to each patient. Both Ladds enthusiastically approved, and every three or four months during the rest of the war they visited general hospitals. They were willing to travel by bus, train, or plane and wanted no publicity. The Ladds not only treated the men as friends but gave each one a gift. I never met them or talked to them on the phone, but I felt I knew them better than any of my other celebrities. And I was delighted to receive dozens of commendations from patients and hospital authorities.

Despite the ravages of war that we learned of in the newspapers, life in New York was pleasant. My mother was now operating a successful gift shop in Pennsylvania, and Winnie, our landlady, still charged those of us in the family who stayed on only thirty-five dollars a month at 618 West 143rd Street; Dorothy was now expecting a baby in July; and Sam Weisbord had volunteered as godfather. Every week he would come to dinner bearing diapers, or a crib, or a playpen, or sundry garments and shoes. By that time I had become close enough to Sammy that he told me about his youth. He had been so poor that when he finally got a good job with the William Morris Agency, he put a hundred-dollar bill in his pants pocket and kept it there—just in case he was broke. He drew out the bill and showed it to me.

Then on May 7, 1945, came news that Germany had surrendered, and Fifth Avenue was soon jammed with celebrators. Sammy, Alex, and I dashed to the street and were immediately hugged and kissed by girls as if we had been in overseas combat.

A month later I started typing my novel, it was about a young bindle stiff in the depression days on the road. I worked from early morning to late afternoon, and after two weeks it was two-thirds finished.

In July, I took Dorothy to a hospital in the Bronx and kept myself awake the whole night by writing a long section by hand. In the morning Diana (no middle initial) Toland was born. Dorothy was disturbed to learn that I had spent the night working on my book.

The first weeks at home were difficult, owing in part to the arrival of Dorothy's young niece. One evening while I was working in the living room I heard a thud followed by a baby's shriek. I rushed into the kitchen and found Diana on the floor howling in pain. Apparently the niece had left the baby on the ironing board, and she had rolled off. I wrapped her in a blanket and hurried up the hill to the avenue for a taxi. When no taxi appeared I rushed on foot all the way uptown to the Children's Hospital, where I had been getting special milk for Diana. She had a broken leg and was put in traction.

This experience did not leave me in a very agreeable mood, and during an argument in the kitchen a few days later I became so incensed that I smashed my right fist into the wall, making a hole in the plaster. When I arrived at the office the next morning with my right hand swollen, I explained that a filing cabinet had fallen on my hand, and I was taken to the Army hospital on Staten Island. With my little finger badly broken and the entire hand bruised, I was put in the officers' ward with about fifteen Americans and one captured Italian officer. A host of relatives visiting him every day and deluged him with good food, which he shared with the rest of us, and this former "enemy" became the best-liked man in the room. Unable to write with my right hand, I finished the last pages of the novel with my left hand.

The next great event came on August 14, V-J Day, celebrating victory over Japan, when everyone rushed once more to the streets. This time, though, there was little kissing of men in uniform; the celebration was more thoughtful, as if no one could really believe the long war was finally at an end.

Officers and enlisted men now spent a lot of time calculating how many discharge points they had accumulated for getting out of the army. Since none of us had served overseas, it would be a long wait. On October 8, however, came another mass promotion; I was a captain and Shubert became a lieutenant colonel.

For some time, Sammy Weisbord and I had mulled over possible special projects, and eventually Sammy came up with the brilliant idea of getting some leading cartoonists to portray the lives of men and women who had overcome physical disabilities. Small collections of these drawings could be passed out as an inspiration to every man in the general hospitals. I proposed to Colonel Young that Sammy be relieved of his clerical duties and assigned to me for special projects. The colonel approved, and within a month Sammy had a group of noted cartoonists working for nothing. The success of this project inspired Sammy to develop an even more original idea: to send out teams to the general hospitals for inducing men with the worst injuries to reenact their experiences in psychodramas. The first attempts were not too successful, but before long, hospital attendants joined in and reports were enthusiastic. Sammy also encouraged Peg-Leg Bates, the one-legged black dancer, to perform at hospitals, and his amazing pyrotechnics always brought down the house.

Before the end of 1945 Sammy had come up with another potential triumph: a plan to send one ring of the Barnum and Bailey Circus to France to entertain the troops. After a number of conferences with officials of the circus, Sammy worked out the logistics, and final acceptance was up to the man in charge, Mr. North. Sammy and I appeared at his office, with Sammy doing most of the talking and I vigorously nodding my assent. Mr. North, bursting with the patriotic fervor that Sammy inspired, gave his approval, and the offer was transmitted to Eisenhower's headquarters. The answer was, sorry, but the GIs were too busy being processed out of the service to watch a circus. They would appreciate, however, the arrival of several Fifth Avenue buses for touring Paris. This Sammy promptly arranged.

I didn't realize it at the time, but I had changed radically since taking over as Shubert's assistant. I had left behind me indecision and a feeling of being unfit. I had also left much of the gaucherie, shyness, and bewilderment of youth. I had stepped across a boundary into another land. I'd turned one of those corners which everyone rounds in life without being conscious there had been a turning. For the first time in my life everyone thought well of me, but I only thought, what a wonderful office this is! We all looked on one another with respect.

Sergeants Arnold Auerbach and Arnold Horwitt had just shown me their latest soldier show, *Call Me Mister,* with music by Sergeant Harold Rome, who now worked in our office. This one was so good that I did not pass it on to Colonel Shubert. I knew he would insist it be issued immediately as just another soldier show. I felt that the three creators deserved a chance to get back in show business. And this show, if a hit, could be a welcome symbol to all those about to reenter the life of a civilian.

Auerbach, Horwitt, and Rome asked me to join them in a visit to Major

Melvin Douglas at the Algonquin Hotel. He had just returned from the Far East, and we found him enthusiastic about producing the show on Broadway, but he feared that Shubert might block the venture. I assured Douglas that I could persuade Colonel Shubert to be reasonable. The skits secretly went into rehearsal while Rome was orchestrating the music. All went well until Shubert discovered what was going on. Rome had just been released from the army on points, but the two Arnolds still had some time to go. Shubert ordered them sent immediately to the Fourth Service Command, thus halting the show.

I told Shubert that all his life he would regret what he had done and said I was going to get the two men released from Fourth Service Command. Shubert said nothing. A few minutes later I was telephoning my friend Percy Johnson, Jr., still chief of Entertainment and Recreation, that he owed me many favors for all the celebrities and units I had sent to the Fourth Service Command. "How would you like to repay them all with one big favor?"

"What?"

"Arnold Auerbach and Arnold Horwitt will be checking into Atlanta in a few days." I then told him about *Call Me Mister.* "I'd like them back as civilians soonest."

"No problem," said Percy. "Consider it done."

By January 1946, the Special Services Division was only a shadow of itself. Everyone was making plans for the future. On the 23rd I was awarded the Army Commendation Ribbon for "outstanding service." I never wore the ribbon, considering it equivalent to the Good Conduct Ribbon given to almost every enlisted man who had not shot himself in the foot.

On February 15 I signed a three-year contract with the William Morris Agency and three days later received forty-five dollars for a radio script I had written for *Suspense.* Berenice had typed the final draft of my novel. I was eager to return to civilian life.

In late February I journeyed to Reception Station No. 2, Fort Dix, New Jersey, where I became a civilian, receiving a ruptured duck, that brass pin proving I had served in the war, as well as the "heartfelt thanks" of President Truman for my "fortitude, resourcefulness and calm judgment" in carrying out my task. "Fortitude" and "resourcefulness"—okay. But I had my doubts about the "calm judgment."

{13}

Return to Duty

From a feeling of assurance and success under military auspices I plunged into discouragement and failure as a civilian. I understood neither the new postwar world I was entering nor the nature of my own abilities. By the 4th of March of 1946, our money from eighty-four days of untaken terminal leave had been invested in a gift shop, and our second daughter, Marcia, was born in July of that year; but the gift shop lasted less than a year.

My career as a writer went nowhere. I first wrote a comic script for *Suspense.* It was rejected. Then came what I thought were genuine good tidings. Helen Strauss of William Morris called to tell me that two publishers had bid for my novel, *Blood's a Rover.* She recommended the one from Pascal Covici of Viking Press with an advance payment of five hundred dollars, because he was considered the best editor in the business, and I immediately phoned to make an appointment to talk to him. He was enthusiastic about my future. "Some of your work reminds me of Steinbeck and Faulkner," he said. And he should have known, since he was editor of them both. I glowed to be compared with the first; but because I knew very well that I had nothing in common with Faulkner, his remark made me uneasy. Even so, his enthusiasm was reassuring.

During the long luncheon he entertained me with anecdotes about the idiosyncrasies of both men. One loved the bottle and the other loved chorus girls. Then Covici announced that they were going to hold up my *Blood's a Rover,* which needed, he said, a complete rewrite. I was disappointed but tried not to show it, and I promised to get to work on a revision immediately. As we parted, Covici asked my age.

"Thirty-six in June."

Covici was stunned. "You look twenty-six." He was obviously disappointed.

"I'm a late starter, Mr. Covici. I didn't make love until I was twenty-five."

Covici laughed. "Shaw didn't start until he was older." He held out his hand. "And call me Pat."

I started home with mixed feelings, but I was determined to start revising. After all, to be compared with Steinbeck was really something! I sent my revision of *Blood's a Rover* to Helen Strauss, but Pat Covici still did not think it was ready for publication and suggested that I start a new novel. This was yet another blow, but I recalled an idea for a novel that I once considered after Dorothy had told me details of the life of a professional roller skater. I sent to Covici the outline of a story about a skater whose partner was extremely jealous. He liked it and urged me to start at once.

But the new novel did not go well; radio producers and people in Hollywood merely expressed "interest" in my work, and I gradually realized that I was obviously still playing the long-familiar role of the "promising," albeit unpublished, young writer, and I was discouraged.

Meanwhile my sister, Virginia, had returned to live with Mother, having been expelled from the navy. After leaving the novelist, Roberts, she had volunteered as a Wave and had done well for nine months until drink again took over. I was grateful to the navy for giving her a Very Honorable Discharge for "inaptitude" and declaring that she was "not physically qualified for reenlistment." I accepted the reality, with great sadness, that there was nothing I could do to could stop Virginia from destroying herself. She soon moved in with a second husband, Bob. He was a likable, sober man who had published a number of pulp stories and tried in vain to sell some of my rejected pieces. Bob was a good influence on Virginia, who claimed she was now on the wagon permanently.

In the fall of 1946, I finally wrote Tom Ireland, who was now back in Washington, and was elated to learn that there would be an opening for me at the new Special Services School for officers at Fort Monmouth, New Jersey. I would be in charge of soldier shows and would reenter the military, retaining in my rank as captain. The first class would not start until September 1947, but I was to report to Fort Monmouth in a month and prepare myself for a new career.

Dorothy was delighted. She was in good shape and could surely get a job dancing in a New York nightclub, and as I was packing my flight bag, she got word that she could dance in the chorus line at Leon and Eddie's. And some friends who had baby-sat Diana and had come to love Marcia were happy to take care of the two girls until we found a home near Fort Monmouth.

I hitchhiked to New York City in 1947 and took the train to New Jersey.

I was warmly greeted at the new school by Colonel Roger Goldsmith, the commandant, who explained that some thirty-five officers and fifteen civilians would attend the first class. They would be prepared to become recreational officers or work in Army Exchange as salesmen.

Once a week I journeyed to New York to watch Dorothy perform at Leon and Eddie's, and back at bachelor officers' quarters I started searching for a home nearby. In July I met an enterprising realtor, Joseph Carlone, who found a large mansard-roofed house at 201 Bergen Place in Red Bank where two of the downstairs rooms could be turned into a dance studio for Dorothy.

Dorothy left Leon and Eddie's with enough money to keep our chins above water, and by early October we had retrieved Diana and Marcia. Herb Trattner and one of his sergeants had turned our two downstairs rooms into a studio, and Dorothy had put an ad in the *Red Bank Register* announcing the opening of the Dorothy Toland Dance Studio.

Our efforts in the first class were fairly successful and I felt I could do better when the second class arrived in January 1948, and the routine resumed. I suggested to Colonel Goldsmith that this time I would like to take the entire recreational group to New York City to visit backstage at several theaters during the day and then attend a show at night. Who would pay for it? "I think I can persuade John Shubert to cooperate," I said. Goldsmith gave his permission, and the next day I walked into Shubert's office just off Shubert Alley. His secretary turned out to be a girl from the Special Services Division. She rushed into the inner office, and soon Johnny appeared. He took to the plan immediately, promising not only to escort the students to at least three theaters but to talk about the problems of show business. At night they would have orchestra seats for the best Shubert show.

The visit to New York was the high point of the second class. Shubert spent several hours lecturing and even let my pupils come backstage during a rehearsal. They were fascinated by the agile changing of sets, the military precision achieved in the semidarkness, and the lightning costume changes, some in small protected areas.

Afterward Shubert took me aside. "Thank you for getting Auerbach and Horwitt back to New York," he said.

"Thanks for letting me do it."

"What if I hadn't?"

"I was sure you would, colonel."

"When are you going to start calling me Johnny?"

"Right now, Johnny."

A decent guy, I thought. And the tragedy was that Auerbach, Horwitt, and Rome still hated his guts and would always hate his guts. I told all three that they should be grateful, since it was Shubert who had *allowed* me to call Percy Johnson in the Fourth Service Command and arrange for their return to New York.

By early 1948, Dorothy had about twenty pupils, and I took care of Diana and Marcia when I returned from work. I managed to keep them amused with a never-ending tale of Blacky the Cat, based on our own cat, who was fascinated by television.

The shows by now had become a major feature at Fort Monmouth. And Johnny Shubert continued to entrance the students with his backstage lectures.

But one morning the string of army theatrical successes came to an abrupt end when the new chief of recreation discovered that one of our staff, Sergeant George Chiasson, was a homosexual. George was indignantly summoned to the office of the lieutenant colonel, who, in the presence of several officers and men, loudly declared that Sergeant Chiasson was a disgrace to the army, and that he would be tried and kicked out of the service.

When I returned early that afternoon from arranging a special show at a local hospital, I was shocked. A sports sergeant told me that George had taken off for New York, and I knew he was going to the Astor Hotel, where he always took a room on the top floor. I telephoned the New York police and told them Sergeant Chiasson might be trying to commit suicide. I then stormed into the office of the recreation chief and announced that I would not serve one more minute with such a mean son of a bitch. I then stalked over to the administration building and told Goldsmith I was quitting the army. The colonel tried to calm me, but it was obvious that I could not be swayed. Then came the news that the police had grabbed George as he was going out the window. He was returned to Fort Monmouth and put in the stockade.

I urged Colonel Goldsmith to let George stay with us in Red Bank until he was expelled from the army. The colonel agreed, and after a few days George was back to his old self. He was subsequently dismissed without publicity and left for the South. (We would remain close friends until his death twenty-nine years later.) And I once more became a civilian. I would now become the manager of the Dorothy Toland Dance Studio, and the next five years would be the most frustrating period of my life.

{14}

Life Begins at Forty-two

During the next five years, from 1949 on, I taught dramatics, elocution, and baton-twirling at Dorothy's school, received rejection slips for one more novel and fourteen short stories, sold my first short story (at age forty-two), and finally stumbled into a career in writing for which I was suited but which had never entered my imagination.

During these years it also became clear that Dorothy and I were not meant for each other, even though I was grateful for her strong support—especially at crucial moments.

By the beginning of 1953, my pile of rejection slips made me realize that there was only one thing to do—write something that would sell. I enjoyed reading science fiction, but found most of it humorless and heavy-handed. Well, why not use the Thorne Smith tongue-in-cheek method? Ideas flourished, and by the end of the year I had written a science fiction novel for a contest, as well as fourteen short stories. All were rejected.

Undeterred, I kept plugging away, and finally I wrote a long story about a little man with an overbearing wife who tries to commit suicide by jumping from a boat into the Hudson River, and discovers he can walk on water. I sent it off in early 1954 to Ziff Davis's *Fantastic* and was stunned to receive from the editor, Howard Browne, the letter I had been dreaming about for almost thirty years: "We're buying your novelette, 'Water Cure,' and I'd like to tell you how much we enjoyed reading it here. . . . Stories with a light humorous touch and concerning ordinary people are always welcome with us. . . . Just remember to keep them light, fast-paced, and with plenty of dialogue."

Despite this sale, which brought $165, I felt discouraged. On June 29, 1954, I would be forty-two, and not one of my twenty-five plays had ever been produced nor one of my six novels published. I had been writing for twenty-nine years and the best I could do was sell a story to the pulps!

Learning that a well-known science fiction writer lived only half a mile away, I took him several stories. He told me I was writing for the wrong market and suggested I see a literary agent named Rogers Terrill who had just moved into a summer house on the shore.

"Is he your agent?" I asked.

"He would never take me. But I think he'll take someone who could write 'Water Cure.' "

I didn't realize it at the time, but this was the greatest crisis of my life. I felt so depressed I didn't even phone Mr. Terrill. What was the use? I had hit bottom not only with my work but in my personal life. Dorothy and I were driven by separate dreams; dancing and writing didn't mix. We were strangers. On the day after my birthday I told her I was going to drive up to New Hampshire in my mother's car for a few days.

It was dark when I pitched my pup tent near a small river in pouring rain. Half soaked, I was unable to sleep and threw up twice. But in the morning, with the sun shining, I felt strangely alive, almost as if reborn. I drove to a small hotel in Plymouth, New Hampshire, and spent the next week climbing mountains and thinking. Porter had told me I should write a million words as my apprenticeship. I had already done more than that, with puny results, but I knew he would tell me to write another million. Porter had once remarked that a writer had to be able to be a part of things, yet stand aloof outside them. It was like living a double life, he explained, and would be both a curse and a blessing.

On returning to Red Bank I found a letter from Rogers Terrill asking me to come to his summer home. My mother had taken it on herself to send him some of my stories. He was about my height but heavier. For years he had edited *Argosy,* a men's magazine, and had now become an agent. "If you had sent me 'Water Cure,' " he said, "I think I could have sold it to *The Saturday Evening Post.*" He urged me to come to his New York office.

By this time I was determined to start a new life. Taking a change of clothes, my typewriter, and fifty dollars, I set out for New York City. I found a room for eight dollars a week in a boardinghouse for Columbia University graduate students, and the next morning I was at Terrill's office. After he gave me an hour of valuable advice about writing short stories for the leading magazines, I returned to my room and began to think of the kind of plot Rogers had suggested. In two days I emerged with the idea of a tale about a young man working in a Madison Avenue advertising firm whose girl won't marry him because he spends his working day dreaming up lies to deceive the public. "You couldn't tell the truth for a single day!" she says. "If I can," he asks, "will you marry me?" And so for one whole day he tells the awful truth, and nothing but the truth.

It took another two days to write the story. I brought "Nothing but the Truth" to Rogers and a week later learned that it had been sold to *American Magazine* for $750. They loved it. It was a great day in my life. My worries were over! I could write two stories a week and make so much I could then go back to novels!

I was resolved to spend none of the $750, and kept living on the budget I had set up: meals $1.25 a day, entertainment twenty-five cents a day. I completed three stories in the next two weeks—all of them, I thought, at least as good as "Nothing but the Truth." But nothing sold. Rogers soothed my feelings by explaining that the bottom had abruptly dropped out of the fiction market and the major magazines were now featuring factual articles. I did sell four more science fiction stories to Howard Browne, but so many readers objected to my comic approach to science fiction that Howard was fired partly on my account. Years later, however, he would write me from Hollywood thanking me for getting him canned from the magazine. He went on to become a very successful screenwriter.

I was now getting one good meal a month at the apartment of Morton Hunt, my old air force buddy. Mort had become a very successful article writer and was appearing in the top magazines, including *The New Yorker*. He offered me a job helping him research one of his articles, and when this had been completed he suggested that I take over one of his assignments, a piece on "suppressed inventions" for *Cavalier*. Mort gave me a lesson in how to write articles: hook the reader in the first paragraph and nail him in the last paragraph, and keep everything in between both factual and interesting.

I returned to Red Bank confident that I could make a living by writing articles and never again have to teach baton-twirling. (I had known nothing about the arcane arts of twirling, but the army had showed me that you could teach anything if you taught yourself and kept one step ahead of your students.) I interviewed a number of people involved in suppressed inventions and came up with an article showing that the so-called inventions I had investigated were actually fakes. It made such a stir that I was offered a large sum by the National Association of Manufacturers for reprints of the article for national distribution. Although I had long detested this capitalistic organization, what I had written was the truth—and I could use the money.

I then found a larger and more comfortable apartment on West Seventy-first Street in New York. There I began producing articles on subjects ranging from epilepsy to the first flight over the Atlantic by two navy aviators, doing most of my research at the New York Public Library. Almost everything sold, and in March "Nothing but the Truth" (with a new title, "Cross

My Heart") appeared in *American Magazine,* followed unexpectedly by several reprint sales overseas. I also climbed up from men's to general magazines with the publication of "40,000 Fortune-Hunters" in *Coronet.* The editor, Gerald Frank, persuaded me to try again, and I succeeded with a lively story about a young man who had cornered the wheat market.

But soon I phoned Rog Terrill and said I was tired of writing articles, even though I had just sold another one (and it brought a bonus) to Gerald Frank about people who tattled on diamond smugglers. "I want to write a *book,*" I complained. "And I'm sick of getting everything from the public library."

A week later Rog called to say that he had a contract for me with Henry Holt to write a book on dirigibles, for which I would get an advance of two thousand dollars once a satisfactory outline was accepted. Within a week I had scoured the New York Public Library at Fifth Avenue and Forty-second Street and had written an outline that more than pleased Holt. Realizing that the outline was only window dressing, I telephoned the information officer at the U.S. Naval Air Station in Lakehurst, New Jersey. It turned out to be Lieutenant Bess Bryant, whom I had known when I was Shubert's assistant, and she told me to come to Lakehurst in a week for interviews that she would set up.

During all this my life was further complicated by a divorce. In the fourteen years of our marriage Dorothy and I had many good times, and I will never forget how stoutly she supported me in the dark days after I took the black captain into the Biloxi officers' club, and how she had approved my foolhardy battle with Colonel Shubert over *Call Me Mister.*

Dorothy was both one of the physically strongest and the most talented women I had ever met. She had many gifts, including unusual abilities as a dancer and a musician. Music was in her genes—her father had been a bandleader in the army, and she had learned to play six different instruments, including the violin, piano, and flute. She had a dancer's instinctive grace; her body was capable of amazing expressiveness—as John Donne said of one of his beloveds, "You might have said her body thought."

After the divorce, both daughters continued to live with their mother in Red Bank; my mother moved there as well and lived a block away from our house. I would see the girls on Sunday and take them to Broadway shows. And I also took them on trips to places I loved, like Squam Lake in New Hampshire. I have remained close to them to this day—and to my wonderful grandchildren.

But their mother and I had been simply incompatible. We continued to have a complicated but necessary relationship for the sake of our daughters—and perhaps because of what we had shared in the younger and less affluent years of our life together.

At about this time, late 1957, for three straight nights I had nightmares of the *Hindenburg* explosion, and to get these harrowing scenes out of my system I sat down and, in two days and far into the nights, wrote the first draft of a ten-thousand-word last chapter for my book.

The next five months were the busiest of my life. A new friend, Walter Henry Nelson, persuaded me to do an article on "Dad" Joiner, who had opened up the East Texas oil fields, and I was making many interview trips for this and other articles. Research for the dirigible book, which I called *Ships in the Sky,* was also going well. When I was told by enlisted men about the the great U.S. Navy dirigible *Los Angeles* suddenly breaking loose from her mooring in 1926 and actually standing on her nose for a few seconds before gracefully twisting around and slowly descending belly down, I found several enlisted men who had been inside the ship. At first they were reluctant to tell their stories, because the top brass wanted this incident buried. But I induced them to talk and soon guessed that someone must have taken a picture of the nose stand. During every subsequent interview I asked if my interviewee was the man who had taken the picture. The first half-dozen or so denied the charge. But the next one said, "How the devil did you find out?"

"I have my ways," I cryptically replied, and persuaded the man to let me use the picture he had taken, with the provision that I was never to tell the navy where I had obtained the photo. I vowed I would keep my word, and I meant it. At first Holt protested that it was too ridiculous a picture to put in the book, but for once I refused to budge. It had to go in.

Foreign sources also provided valuable material. With the help of European newsmen and foreign embassies I located airshipmen in Germany, Sweden, Norway, England, and Italy. In Rome I discovered General Umberto Nobile, who wrote me a lengthy account of his two controversial flights to the North Pole, including details of his epic thirty days on polar ice with the survivors of the *Italia,* an account that answered the charges by writers who had concocted lies about him because he was Italian and therefore was regarded as a Fascist even though he was nothing of the sort.

By the end of May, 1957 I had finished *Ships in the Sky,* which Mother had been typing chapter by chapter. Rog phoned to compliment me, and two weeks later he called again, this time in a voice so excited I could not at first understand what he was saying. "The *Post!*" he shouted. *"The Saturday*

Evening Post! Yes! They've bought the entire last chapter! They're going to feature it!"

When I heard the price, six thousand dollars, I tingled. In one day I had made more than I had earned in a year as a captain! But I regarded *Ships in the Sky* as only a passing phase in my career. I would keep writing factual books to make money, but I was sure I would eventually return to plays and novels. My book was featured on the cover of the December 8 *Saturday Evening Post:* LAST CRUISE OF AIRSHIP *HINDENBURG*. The editors had not deleted a single scene from the double-length article. At the end of the magazine, in the "Keeping Posted" section, there was a story telling how as a boy I had seen the *Shenandoah* fly past and later watched the *Hindenburg* swing serenely over New York City just a few hours before it had gone up in flames at Lakehurst. This is what had inspired me, it said, to write about the last hours of the *Hindenburg.*

Within a few days I was on my way to Washington to start interviewing for a book on the Depression. I had decided to make a feature of the Bonus Army March of the destitute World War I veterans. "To assist you," promised Major Victor Walker of the U.S. Army Magazine and Book Branch, "we have sent out requests to the agencies of record in order to locate material, and thereby the participants, in the Washington portion of the affair. By the time you arrive here, we should have at least a handful of officers involved located for you to interview."

At the Military History Office I received a warm welcome from the army writers. At the Pentagon, Walker had gathered together for me a War Department press release with an interview with Secretary of War Patrick J. Hurley and General Douglas MacArthur, news clips on the topic ranging from the time of the Bonus Act through the end of the tragic affair, and background material on the Bonus Act itself, as well as the official record in the National Archives.

After I had interviewed half a dozen participants, Major Walker abruptly suggested that I do a book on the Battle of the Bulge. People in the Pentagon, he said, had been impressed by the way I had portrayed naval enlisted personnel in *Ships in the Sky.* "We'd like you to do the same for the army," he said. He promised full support, and Dr. Hugh Cole, who had been working for several years on the official history of the Bulge, would let me use all his material.

I was then introduced to Brigadier General Ted Clifton, chief of the Information Office. He said my research would be facilitated in both the United States and Europe. I could travel on space-available flights and get inexpensive lodging and food at BOQs and officers' clubs. In Europe the commander of the Seventh Army, General Bruce Clarke, who had fought at St. Vith, would be eager to clear the way for me. I would also be able to interview Germans, from privates to the top generals. In this battle, Clifton explained, Americans were caught napping and were almost wiped out. Men ran in terror and commanders were confused. "All we want you to do is to tell the truth. Tell what happened. That's all." The army would check the facts if I wished. "But nothing—*nothing*—will be censored."

"I'll do it," I said.

(General Clifton later became the aide of President Kennedy. It was he who put a copy of my second war history, *But Not in Shame,* on Air Force One for Kennedy to read. The president sent me a letter of commendation.)

I didn't realize it at the time, but the intense interviews I conducted while preparing *Ships in the Sky* had introduced me to a new career. At last I was viewing life through the eyes of others with no thought of myself. Similarly, only now—near the end of my career—have I finally realized that the sheer variety of experience during my first forty years had taught me how to be a sympathetic listener as well as to distinguish truth-tellers from fakers, capacities which have been indispensable for my later work. I was eventually to be awarded, when I was fifty-nine, a Pulitzer Prize—not as a novelist or playwright, but as an historian, even though I had not taken a single course in history while in college. History—what I was to call "living history," based on hundreds of interviews with people who were present at crucial historical events—was to become the center of my life as a writer.

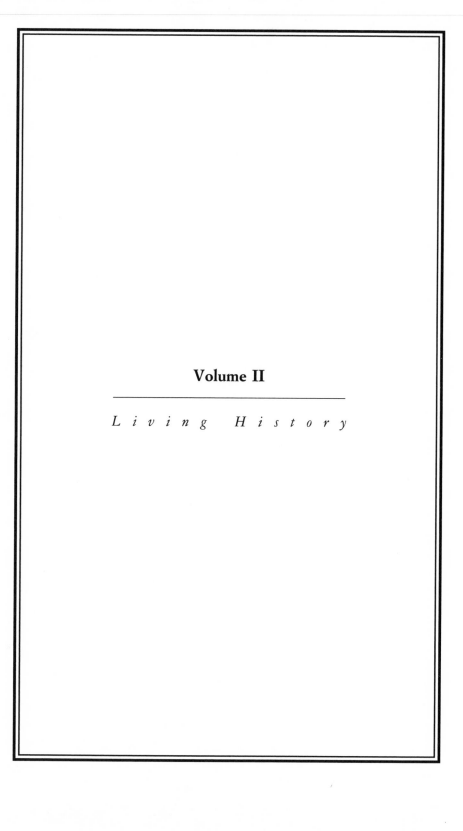

Volume II

Living History

[Part One]

New Ventures (1958–1965)

{1}

The Battle of the Bulge

In 1954, the year I sold my first story, my sister, Virginia, had appeared in Red Bank with her third husband, Jed, whom she had met in a gay bar. He too was an alcoholic, but they both—with the encouragement of my mother—had gone on the wagon, and I got Jed a job in a friend's gas station. They moved into a neat little house on the edge of town, and Jed worked so well for several years that he was given a Christmas bonus in 1958. But the celebration of this bonus plunged them once more into the depths of liquor. A month or so later they disappeared, and in early 1959 my mother learned that they were living in Greenwich Village. After several weeks she received a telephone message from the New York police that utterly crushed her: Virginia had been found dead from gas inhalation. Beside her was Jed, but he had been revived by the medics.

The Red Bank newspaper printed a brief item with no embellishments, but the next morning, reporters and photographers from nearby cities were at my mother's front door. I stepped out, closed the door, and refused their loud requests to interview her. Behind my back, one of the reporters opened the door and started to enter the house, followed by a photographer. Incensed, I seized the reporter's arm, caught him off balance, and flung him off the porch. Then a sympathetic and hulking neighbor arrived and persuaded the others to leave.

Late in the day another call came from New York. Where did Mrs. Toland want the body of her daughter sent? I knew the arrival of Virginia's body would destroy my mother, and told the authorities to bury the body in an unmarked grave. I was following Christian Science belief that there is no death so there is to be no acknowledgment of death through ceremony.

Then came Jed's trial for murder a few months later in 1959, which hit the front pages of the tabloids. Fortunately I was able to keep my mother ignorant of the circus going on in New York by intercepting all phone calls. A magazine wanted to do a story, but I refused to be interviewed. Jed's testimony, that it had been a joint suicide, was finally believed, and he was acquitted. But on the evening of his release, a friend informed me that Jed had leaped out of his third-floor window, and fatally impaled himself on an iron fence.

Those days remain embedded in my mind, and looking back, I believe I might have helped Virginia if I hadn't felt, wrongly, so ashamed of her. I knew her much better than my father and mother did. When I was eight I could see that she was faking injury in the Hillside tennis match while my parents were comforting her. As we grew up I saw her steal as if it were a game, and make up tall stories as a lark. I also saw how courageous she could be as my protector.

Perhaps Virginia's charm and talent worked against her, since they always enabled her to find some man who could come to her rescue. Perhaps success as a dancer came too quickly; perhaps it was show business that made the bottle a fatal attraction.

Whatever the causes, I now see I was no help. I should have loved her more and been less troubled by shame. The only one in the family who remained unswervingly loyal to Virginia and gave her unconditional love was our mother, who couldn't add or subtract and crucified the English language but never wavered in her belief that Virginia was God's perfect child.

Ships in the Sky was enthusiastically received in early February 1958. *Life* called me for permission to use the picture I'd unearthed of the *Los Angeles* standing on her nose. When I agreed, I was asked to write about 250 words of explanation in the next half hour because the magazine was going to press. I complied, and *Life* did what it had never done before: reproduced sideways the huge dirigible on two pages of "Speaking of Pictures," with the headline AN INCREDIBLE NOSESTAND. Half a dozen men's magazines also ran sections of the book, and I appeared on television and radio. The first few shows were exciting, but I soon found myself repeating the same things, and I was relieved to hear from the Pentagon that on March 5 I was to report to McGuire Air Force Base, New Jersey, and take off for Frankfurt, Germany, to start work on *Battle: The Story of the Bulge.* I could forget dirigibles and move on to warfare.

When I learned that I would have to get a passport on short notice, I hurried to Washington to expedite the process through a friend in the State Department. I filled out an application, admitting I'd once been a Communist. Because it was such a rush I gave the application to a friend in the State Department, who took one look at it and tore it up. "Take my word for it," he said, "you'll be turned down." He handed me another application, and I realized that if I had submitted my request through normal channels I would never have been able to get the army's complete cooperation, which I needed to write about the Battle of the Bulge—so this time I omitted "Member of the Communist Party, 1940–1945."

The plane left in midafternoon on March 5, 1958, and it was dark by mid-Atlantic. Others were sleeping, but I was too excited. I had hated the Nazis for years, and now I was going to interview them. How could I hide my repugnance? It was daylight as we flew over England, and soon we were over France and then landing in Germany.

I was picked up at the Frankfurt air base by a young U.S. second lieutenant and his driver. The trip through the city was shocking. Entire blocks still gave witness to the horrendous Allied bombings. Somehow this lessened my animus toward the survivors I saw plodding along in worn-out clothes. After a short stay in Heidelberg, I was driven to Seventh Army headquarters in Stuttgart.

General Clifton had not exaggerated the warm welcome I would receive. A captain, James Haslam, a decorated war veteran who had been assigned to look after me, quickly installed me at the BOQ while giving me a run-down on the preparations already made for interviews. Then he took me to his home for dinner. The next morning Haslam escorted me to the office of General Bruce Clarke, an imposing man who spent the next two hours telling me about his own experiences. At a crucial point in the Bulge campaign in late 1944, his Combat Command B had stalled General von Manteuffel's panzers at St. Vith, thereby giving the Americans a chance to build up defenses in the west.

I felt almost exhausted by the time I emerged from Clarke's barrage of detailed memories. But I was elated. Clifton was right. This man Haslam was going to give me full support—and knew what he was talking about. In the next two weeks I interviewed many GIs and officers who had fought in the Bulge, as well as a dozen important German officers. Then I was summoned to Clarke's office. "Now," he proclaimed, "you are ready to meet the man I held up in St. Vith with a single combat command, Baron Hasso von Manteuffel." He was now one of the leaders of the Deutsche Partei, serving as a representative in Bonn, the capital of West Germany. Clarke was soon on the phone telling the baron that an American author wished to interview him and suggesting that Manteuffel meet me next day at 1300 hours at the American embassy. He was sure General von Manteuffel would want to talk to Mr. Toland for at least three or four afternoons, and thanked him for his cooperation.

It was obvious that the baron had contributed little to this conversation, and I guessed I would be given a very frosty welcome by the descendant of a famous family of Prussian generals.

I took a train north and checked in at the embassy at noon. After lunch, at exactly 1300 hours, Baron von Manteuffel strode into the interview room. He was smaller than I but walked with the vigor and agility of an athlete. A former gentleman jockey and German pentathlon champion, he had commanded the Fifth Panzer Army. General Clarke had told me he was tough-minded, had formidable energy, and was one of the few who ever dared to disagree openly with Hitler.

He shook hands politely but with disdain, then sat down to arrange papers on the table as if he were planning a campaign and I were one of his junior officers. I disliked him on sight. Here was Prussian arrogance personified! It was obvious that he regarded the interpreter provided by the consulate as incompetent, and he corrected the man's introductory words in fairly good English.

"First," he began crisply in German, "I shall explain the plan of Operation Watch on the Rhine, which you people call the Battle of the Bulge." He spoke the second term as if it were vulgar. On December 16, 1944, he said, three great German armies were to break through the Ardennes front, the hilly terrain in Belgium and Luxembourg that reminded some Americans of the Berkshires and the Green Mountains. This had been the highway to German victory in 1870, 1914, and 1940. It was anticipated by the Germans that their forces would swiftly cross the Meuse River and reach Antwerp within a week. The western Allies, unable to recover from the initial surprise, would be smashed and sue for an immediate peace.

"The Sixth Panzer Army was to be led by General Sepp Dietrich, the Fifth Panzer Army by myself, and the Seventh Army, largely infantry, by General Ernst Brandenberger." Dietrich would be in charge of the northern flank and the main effort of Watch on the Rhine. He would have a preponderance of the best troops of the Waffen (Weapon) SS, scraped together to form an army as formidable as those which had won the great victories on the Russian front. He would also have a special unit: the brigade of SS Lieutenant Colonel Otto Skorzeny, famed for his daring rescue of Mussolini. His men would be dressed in American uniforms and drive American vehicles. These men of Operation Greif (Griffin), as Hitler named it, would seize bridges, spread rumors, give false orders, and generally breed confusion and panic.

On Dietrich's left, to the south, would be the Fifth Panzer Army under General Manteuffel. He would have two objectives. On his right he was to trap the U.S. 106th Division in the snowy mountain area called the Schnee

Eifel, just east of the boundary between Germany and Belgium, and then capture St. Vith, the most vital rail and road center east of Bastogne, the strategic city in the center of the Ardennes. The rest of his army, three panzer and two infantry divisions, would race south of the Schnee Eifel, through Luxembourg. Farther south, Brandenberger's Seventh Army, the lightest of the three, was to protect Manteuffel's left flank.

That was the plan, concluded Manteuffel. "Then the Führer told us that this battle was to decide whether we [Germany] should live or die. 'I want all my soldiers to fight hard and without pity. The battle must be fought with brutality and all resistance must be broken in a wave of terror. In this most serious hour of the Fatherland I expect every one of my soldiers to be courageous and again courageous. The enemy must be beaten—now or never! Thus lives our Germany!' "

I felt a chill. Then Manteuffel raised his voice. "That was the plan. Now I tell you what happened. Disaster! The man directing the main effort, Sepp Dietrich, an old crony of the Führer's, was only fit to command a company! He was courageous but stupid!"

On the first day, December 16, Dietrich was stopped cold at the Losheim Gap, the seven-mile corridor leading into Belgium through which invading Germans had already passed three times in the twentieth century. By dusk there was a great traffic jam extending back miles to the east. Behind the stalled panzers was Skorzeny's brigade dressed in U.S. uniforms, fully prepared to create confusion behind enemy lines. He sent seven jeeploads of his men to look for a hole in the line, but with each passing moment the chances for Operation Greif waned. A few hours later, after getting no encouraging reports from his advance troops, he knew the plan was hopeless and demanded that Dietrich allow his three battle groups to change into their own uniforms and join the battle. Dietrich glumly approved.

By the end of the afternoon that March in 1958 I felt exhausted, but the general was still fresh. "Tomorrow same time?" he asked in English. He bowed slightly and strode out without looking back or waiting for a response.

The next day Manteuffel was as distant and formal as ever. I dismissed the interpreter and tried to get more personal observations. The baron loosened up slightly and, in good English, told how Brigadier General Bruce Clarke, Combat Command B of the 7th Armored Division, had rushed to St. Vith and hastily set up a defense that held him off for almost a week.

I interrupted to ask for details on the many meetings he had with Hitler. But he cut me off abruptly. I persisted, realizing that I had one of the best sources on how the secret attack was planned and launched without anyone tipping off the Allies. My persistence finally caused Manteuffel to exclaim in obvious surprise, "You don't seem to have made up your mind about these events."

"Of course not." I told him I had read several U.S. reports about the battle but I had to know the German side. "I only want to know what happened and why it happened."

He looked at me closely as if seeing me for the first time. I felt I had at last reached him. "General Clarke told me you were the best tank commander in the Wehrmacht," I said.

He almost smiled. "General Clarke was tough and resourceful," he replied, and then, for the first time, he openly smiled. "He only had the equivalent of a regiment and was holding off several panzer divisions!"

From then on the coolness vanished. He began to speak more colloquially and less like a general to a second lieutenant.

On the next day he explained that SS Lieutenant Colonel Jochen Peiper, commander of the spearhead of the 1st SS Panzer Division, was the only one in Dietrich's vaunted army that managed to break through the Losheim Gap into Belgium. By midnight of December 17, Peiper was racing confidently toward the English Channel, only some twenty air miles from the border of Holland. But the rest of Dietrich's tanks were stalled far behind.

To the south, although Manteuffel's right flank was still held up at St. Vith, the rest of his army was advancing even faster than Peiper, and by midnight of the 18th some of his tanks had reached the outskirts of Bastogne. "By that time," said Manteuffel, "I realized it was all up to me."

To his north, Kampfgruppe Peiper would soon be at the end of its supplies. To the south, Brandenberger was useful only as defense against a possible attack from the south by Patton. Only Manteuffel's own panzers could cross the Meuse and reach Antwerp. But first he had to take St. Vith, now in his rear. On the 19th, Field Marshal Erhard Milch ordered Manteuffel to take this city within twenty-four hours. Dietrich was making complaints to Hitler. "He said even his 1st SS Panzer Division was being tied up because of the road jam.

"But," added Manteuffel, "Milch had as little respect for Dietrich as I did and told me he would set the Führer straight.

"By December 20," he continued, "the spearhead of my 2nd Panzer Division had driven a few miles north of Bastogne and was approaching the Ourthe River, which ran some five miles behind Bastogne." Here was the most important bridge in the Ardennes. Once it was crossed, only a few companies of U.S. engineers and antiaircraft troops would stand between the panzers and the Meuse River. And once across that barrier, the road would be clear to the English Channel. "On that 20th of December my tanks rolled across the bridge." His eyes were gleaming.

Then he slapped his right fist into his left hand. "But St. Vith in my rear was still holding out!" Although many U.S. troops had fled, others, in small groups, were also stubbornly holding out. And to the north, Kampfgruppe Peiper was fighting for its life with no chance at all of reaching Antwerp. A good portion of Manteuffel's own troops were still engaged in surrounding the U.S. units holding out in the area just behind St. Vith. "You Americans called it the Fortified Goose Egg." He shook his head. Never before had he seen such a confused battle. "That same day Clarke pulled his people back into this Egg. And I finally had St. Vith but no Clarke. And Hitler was still demanding that I take Bastogne. It was asinine!" He was no longer the calm tactician briefing a subordinate.

He was still angry at Hitler's failure to face facts. "On December 24, I phoned Jodl at the Führer's headquarters and told him that time was running short and the situation was virtually irretrievable unless a whole new battle plan could be concocted at once. . . . Jodl replied that the Führer would never give up the drive to Antwerp, and I told him there was still a chance for a great victory if they'd follow my plan. 'I'll wheel north,' I said, 'on this side of the Meuse. We'll trap all Allies east of the river.' But Jodl was shocked. I said to give me reserves and I'd take Bastogne, reach the Meuse, and swing north. Jodl reluctantly said he'd speak to the Führer. The next day, Christmas, Jodl told me the Führer hadn't yet made his decision. I said I needed immediate replacements but he said he could only give me one more armored division . . . which would mean nothing. Then Jodl said, 'And remember, Manteuffel, the Führer doesn't want you to move back one foot. Go forward! Not back!' And I banged down the receiver. That was the end of Watch on the Rhine."

I was more exhausted than he was. In four long afternoons I had lived through the German side of the battle. On that last day Manteuffel brought pictures he was going to use in the coming election campaign, showing him in uniform with his rows of ribbons. I smiled. "If you use this picture you're sure to lose. Those days are gone forever."

Manteuffel was amused. "Do you always say what you think?"

"Unfortunately, I usually do."

"Call me Hasso," he said, and held out his hand.

Later the baron wrote to say he had indeed been badly beaten in the election and he was quitting politics. I suggested he move from the north, get a place south of Munich, and enjoy life.

On the train back to Stuttgart my mind was churning after my four days with Manteuffel, who had epitomized the German version of the battle. Now I had to meld what he'd told me with the U.S. versions.

In the next eight months I would interview almost four hundred more survivors of the battle, including more than seventy-five civilians caught up in the fray. I would travel more than 100,000 miles in the United States, Great Britain, France, Spain, Belgium, Luxembourg, and Germany. I would gather material in a Senate hearing chamber of the U.S. Capitol, in the West German senate building in Bonn, in the gas chambers of Dachau, at West Point, at the Player's Club on New York City's Gramercy Park, in great castles and huts in the Ardennes, in the Pentagon, at Louisiana State and Norwich universities, in a slate mine in Belgium, in the baths of Spa, in the winding Siegfried Line, on the battlefields of Wiltz, St. Vith, Bastogne, Clervaux, and the Schnee Eifel. I would also study material in the U.S. National Archives, the libraries of the Army Historical Section at Fort McNair and the Air University at Maxwell Air Force Base, the Library of Congress, the Main Branch of the New York Public Library, the British Museum, the Historical Library of the British Army, the U.S. Army Infantry School Library at Fort Benning, Georgia, and, of course, the Red Bank, New Jersey, Public Library.

After digesting Manteuffel's story, I was ready to fill in not only with Allied military materials on high and low levels, but also with human-interest stories from all ranks. Because the wealth of materials was overwhelming, I began concentrating on the most important segments. First came in-depth research on the only successful German attack in the north—the breakthrough of Kampfgruppe Peiper, which left in its wake the infamous Malmédy Massacre. I was told what happened by a local man, Henri Joly. Moments after Peiper left Malmédy for his next objective, Joly had watched from the doorway of a café as about 125 American prisoners were herded into an open field. Hands still in the air, they chatted with an unconcern that baffled Joly. Then more vehicles, the main body of Kampfgruppe Peiper, began rolling out of the east and turning south at the café. "Later a supply half-track stopped. A German soldier in the rear stood up, aimed a pistol, and fired at the group of prisoners. One fell. Joly heard an American officer shout, "Stand fast!" The prisoners, suddenly terrified, huddled together.

Joly saw an armored car skid to a stop. Then came a second pistol shot followed by the dry hacking of a machine gun. The Americans moaned and screamed. Joly watched in horror as the Americans were brutally cut down. Several wounded men tried to crawl away. These and others, writhing in pain, were shot by pistol. In two minutes the 125 men were a tangled, blood-spattered mass of still bodies. Germans now began setting the café on fire, and Joly fled to his farm.

After my long interview with Joly I learned that in a nearby village the elderly host of the Hôtel du Moulin, Peter Rupp, had later saved a number of U.S. prisoners. I drove to the inn and found Rupp and his wife, Balbina, eager to talk. That afternoon and evening in their chalet behind the inn they told how they had previously smuggled out twenty-two Allied aviators during the German occupation.

Then they revealed what had happened soon after the Malmédy Massacre. The rear echelon of Colonel Peiper's *Kampfgruppe* set up a command post in their hotel. Rupp excitedly described how he had seen a German sergeant executing Americans behind the hotel. "Murderer! You killed eight of them! I saw you put the pistol in their mouths!" Balbina cut in to exclaim that the bully punched her husband in the jaw and knocked out two teeth. An officer then ordered everyone shot, including the Belgian swine. As Rupp and the others were being led off, a second SS officer said, "Leave them alone." He put a hand on Rupp's back. "You're right, *mein Herr.* It's a shame how some people treat prisoners." He ordered the sergeant to put the prisoners in a room. "And treat them as you'd want the Amis [Americans] to treat you." Still fearing that the fourteen prisoners might be killed, Rupp ordered hundreds of bottles of the finest cognac and champagne brought up from a secret wine cellar and liberally passed out drinks to the Germans. Rupp told me I could get more information on the event from an American captain named Green who lived in Ardmore, Pennsylvania.

I later interviewed one of the Americans who had been a prisoner at the Rupps' inn. He had been among those herded into the adjacent room and was sure he was going to be executed when the door opened and a big face looked down at him and said in English, "You are now my prisoners, gentlemen." It was SS Lieutenant Colonel Otto Skorzeny. After the cancelation of Operation Greif he had led his SS brigade into the wake of Peiper and was setting up his headquarters at the Rupps'. The American sergeant assured me that Skorzeny saved the lives of the remaining prisoners at the Rupps' and personally saw to it that they were given proper treatment. He gave me the name of another man who could vouch for the story, and then revealed that Skorzeny, a war criminal, could be found in Spain. Why hadn't he been discovered and sent back to Germany? I asked. Because the Spaniards regarded him as a great hero. I was determined to find Skorzeny, and the next day I was on a plane bound for Madrid. The sergeant had given me one tip—Skorzeny was involved in a business that dealt in scrap metal. I could speak some Spanish, and for half a day I visited a number of scrap-metal firms without success. But then I found an office with a sign on the door: "O. Skorzeny. Engineer." Eureka!

I entered to see a large man, well over six feet, with a prominent scar on his cheek. "My name is Toland and I'm writing a book on the Battle of the Bulge from both sides." The big man flung out his arms. "I've been waiting for you!" An hour later we were bound for Skorzeny's home. His wife was away, so the man who had been described as "the most dangerous Nazi" made dinner. We talked until well after midnight. Skorzeny told in detail of his exploits—snatching Mussolini from the Allies by landing a glider on top of an Italian mountain where Mussolini was being held captive by his own countrymen; kidnapping Admiral Miklós Horthy's son and seizing the Citadel, seat of the Hungarian government, when Horthy was planning to deal with the Russians. Skorzeny was most proud of the fact that both these deeds of daring had cost few lives. The kidnapping of young Horthy, for instance, had been inspired by Shaw's play *Caesar and Cleopatra,* in which young Cleopatra escaped capture by being wrapped in a carpet. He arrived at the Citadel with a carpet and then wrapped up young Horthy, took him to the airfield, and telephoned his father. "I am taking your son to the Führer," he said, "unless you denounce the Russians and let me take the Citadel." Horthy agreed, and Skorzeny's small force suddenly smashed into the Citadel, occupying it at the cost of only seven lives.

I spent two more days with Skorzeny, concentrating on the scenes with Hitler and the training for Operation Greif. After he told about the failure of the operation, he broke into laughter. Only *after* the war had he learned that the seven jeeploads of his American-dressed commandos had actually broken through and wreaked havoc. One of his teams was directing an American regiment down the wrong road and then changing signposts and tearing up telephone wires. Another team, which pretended to be terrified, induced an American column to turn around and retreat, while still another team was tearing up the main telephone cables connecting the headquarters of Generals Hodges and Bradley.

"And I thought everything had gone wrong!" he exclaimed. The worst damage, I told him, was done by one of his teams that was captured. When the four men revealed to an intelligence officer why they were in U.S. uniforms, a warning was broadcast that thousands of Germans in American uniforms were operating behind the lines. Hitler's plan of spreading chaos and terror was working.

I also revealed that on the third day of the battle there was terror in Paris, and an excited security colonel had insisted that Eisenhower wear a bullet-proof cap. The colonel had positive knowledge that Otto Skorzeny, Hitler's favorite commando, had sent teams of American-dressed commandos to assassinate Ike. Five German parachutes had been sighted in Eparnay! SHEAF headquarters was surrounded with barbed wire! Tanks stood at the gates! Skorzeny already knew that throughout the area U.S. trucks and jeeps had been stopped, and the men had to prove they were Americans by answering questions about baseball and movie stars; but he had not known about the panicked reports that parachutes had been spotted in a half-dozen places and that the emergence of Skorzeny's men at the Café de la Paix was expected momentarily. One report from the Paris police, I said, indicated that Skorzeny and his men had been sighted floating down in their parachutes dressed as nuns and priests. Skorzeny roared. The picture of himself as a nun particularly delighted him. I also revealed that as General Bruce Clarke was jeeping to his headquarters in St. Vith, he was stopped by an MP who asked what league the Chicago White Sox were in. His answer, "The National League," put him under arrest for half a day. This also appealed to Skorzeny's sense of humor.

I learned more about Manteuffel's drive to the banks of the Meuse by conducting several hundred interviews with Americans who had stopped him and then launched the counterattack that wiped out the fearsome Bulge in a few weeks. I talked to many generals, including Bradley, Ridgway, Collins, and Hodges. To get the story of Bastogne, which had fatally delayed Manteuffel's drive, I listened to General Maxwell Taylor talk regretfully of the fate that had taken him to Washington during the battle, and then to General McAuliffe, who had replaced him and uttered the immortal reply "Nuts!" to the Germans' demand for surrender.

In the Pentagon I met Creighton Abrams, Patton's tank commander who had broken into Bastogne from the south to relieve this bastion. He was celebrating his first day as a general and talked freely, as he smoked several huge cigars, about the goof-ups that had preceded his success. I mentioned that I had talked to a 101st Airborne sergeant who described Abrams entering the Bastogne perimeter, erect in the turret of his tank with a big cigar in his mouth that "stuck out aggressively like another gun." The new general burst out laughing.

I spent several weeks interviewing officers and privates all over the United States. Among them was Matthew Ridgway, commander of the XVIII Airborne Corps. He had a reputation as being a top—if not the top—commander in the army. I entered his office at the Mellon Institute with some trepidation, but in five minutes the general was kneeling on the floor with me, examining a large map of the Bulge. He talked frankly of everything that went right and of everything that went wrong; and when I brought up the stories I had heard of his swift dismissal of high-ranking officers during the Bulge, he said, "I'd have ousted my own grandmother if she couldn't deliver." If an officer made a mistake it could mean the lives of many men. "And so I had to sack some of my own friends."

I was soon ready to write, and I first made a detailed chronological outline of the material I had collected. Using this, I began to arrange everything into a sequence of dramatic chapters (with few flashbacks), trying to tell it as if I had been there. After so many interviews with men and women in Germany I felt able, at last, to empathize with their personal feelings during a battle, just as I could with Americans and British.

On Christmas day of 1958 I turned on the classical station WQXR for the music that would insulate me from the rest of the world and started to type in the basement of my mother's house in Red Bank:

BATTLE, The Story of the Bulge
Chapter 1 THE GHOST FRONT
15 December 1944
The night of December 15, 1944, was cold and
quiet along the Ardennes Front . . .

By the end of the day I'd written some ten pages. The story seemed to flow by itself. I left the basement and drove out to a hilly country section of New Jersey that reminded me of the hills in the Ardennes. The next day I did another ten pages. Again I drove out to the hills, which were now lightly covered with snow, like the hills of the Schnee Eifel. It was an omen.

I finished the book in July 1959 and once more took the girls and my mother to the Little Holland Cabins on Little Squam Lake. During the day I took the girls boating or hiking. At night I revised the book. On my return I brought the manuscript to Rog Terrill, who was enthusiastic. My editor for *Ships in the Sky,* Gerry Simons, was no longer with Holt, and the new editor returned the manuscript with a short note stating that it was a very poor job. Rog suggested that they hire Gerry Simons to work on the revision. But after more than a month, I told Rog it wasn't working. I still liked the first draft and was convinced that the Holt editor was wrong. I insisted on paying Holt back the $2,500 advance and trying another publisher.

About this time I was invited by a war correspondent to attend a session at the Overseas Press Club, where I was introduced to a number of correspondents who had covered the Bulge. A small, attractive young woman approached me, smiling. "You're John Toland," she said and introduced herself: Jean Ennis, head of publicity for Random House. "I loved *Ships in the Sky,*" she said, and invited me to the Algonquin Hotel for a late dinner that Random House was giving for James Michener. I accepted, since this hotel was then the mecca for literary people. Jean introduced me to Michener, and I sat next to his wife. She was the first Japanese I'd ever met and was both friendly and charming. After I had thanked Jean, she smiled. "Someday I'm going to get you for Random House."

For some strange reason it never occurred to me until I was writing the above that Jean was probably the one who was responsible for the next upward step in my career. For not long after our meeting, Robert Loomis of Random House called Rog and said he had been impressed by *Ships in the Sky* and wondered if my new book was available. On October 15 I signed a contract with Random, receiving an advance for *Battle: The Story of the Bulge* that was much larger than the one from Holt. For the next three months I spent much of each day with Loomis, an excellent editor. Now all I had to do was get pictures and draw rough maps.

Bob Loomis then suggested that I try a book on the first six months of the war in the Pacific. I liked the idea. I had never been west of Los Angeles and longed to see the Orient. A contract was signed in March 1959 and the book was given the temporary title of *Island of Resistance.*

I set off to Washington and asked the Book and Magazine branches of the air force and navy for lists of officers who had served in the Pacific. By this time the Pentagon knew me well enough for the Defense Department's Office of News Services to make arrangements for me to be flown around the country at no cost to me before I set out for the Pacific.

On June 1, I began interviewing at Maxwell Air Force Base, Alabama, and three days later was at Elgin, where I took one afternoon off to fly in a jet for the first time. It was like riding in a glider at tremendous speed. The pilot asked if I'd like to try it out, and I found there was no need to keep pressure to the right. "No torque," explained the pilot. "No prop." I was given a paper with the honorary title "Jet Jockey."

During the next three months I conducted interviews in southern and western states, encountering in Fort Sam Houston, Texas, a host of men who had served in the Pacific, and in Carlsbad, New Mexico, a dozen men whose antiaircraft unit had been based at Clark Field in the Philippines.

By now advance copies of *Battle* were available. On the back cover was a photograph of me and General Manteuffel. Also coming out was an article in *Coronet,* "The Bottles of the Bulge," on the heroic rescue of American prisoners by the Rupps. The first and most important review from the Sunday

New York Times was mixed. "The book contains as much conversation as a historical novel," complained the reviewer, but added, "The brunt was taken by men in small units fighting greatly. Their story is told better than it has ever been told before." *The New Yorker* went further in its distrust of "Mr. Toland's cheery national self-congratulations." That review pained me, since this was my favorite magazine. But Bill Mauldin, the idol of combat GIs, wrote in the *St. Louis Dispatch:* "Far more fascinating than any war novel. The pace is rapid, crackling, like battle itself. . . . it contains the best description of the American combat soldier I have ever read."

Despite all this and other praise, it was obvious that my work was controversial and was particularly irksome to many academicians and intellectuals. Even so, or perhaps because of this, the book was sold in England, France, Italy, Germany, Israel, and Japan. Enthusiastic letters came from veterans of the Bulge from both sides. And the Pentagon was delighted. The American Legion did vigorously object to the scene describing the murder of German prisoners in retaliation for the Malmédy Massacre, but when the army revealed it had checked the facts and found I was telling the truth, the Legion sent me a letter of apology.

Thanks to Jean Ennis of Random House, I was mentioned in the gossip columns and introduced to some of the leading critics, including John Barkham, who would become my good friend. Jean also sent me out on a strenuous publicity tour, arranged book-and-author luncheons, and put me on the best TV and radio shows.

Before long I was exhausted by touring, and I yearned to get on with the war in the Pacific. At last, in early December, the long-awaited word arrived that I would be picked up at Floyd Bennett Field on Long Island and taken to California, where I would board a plane for Hawaii. Soon I would be bound for the other side of the world and new adventures. I was already forty-seven, and still far from maturity, but felt I was beginning a new life. The coming months in Asia were destined to take me much farther, personally, professionally, and geographically, than I dreamed. Without being fully aware of it, I was deeply engaged in what was to become the most important work of my career.

[2]

My Bridge to the Orient

As I left the coast of California, I somehow perceived that I was starting a new life with daunting obstacles and new challenges. Halfway to Hawaii I was asked to visit the pilot. "Understand you're doing something about Pearl Harbor," he said, and revealed that a good friend of his had been in one of the twelve Flying Fortresses that were arriving just as the first bombs fell.

When I first saw Oahu I tried to picture the twelve bombers scurrying for safety. I stayed a week at the officers' club near Pearl Harbor and interviewed some twenty men who had seen the attack, but my most important interview was with General Emmett "Rosie" O'Donnell, commander in chief of the Pacific Air Force. He had been a bomber pilot in the Philippines at Clark Field, which was taken by surprise. Not a single pursuit plane was flying cover over the parked Flying Fortresses, even though the commander of the Far East Air Force had reported the bombing of Pearl Harbor to MacArthur more than seven hours earlier.

O'Donnell was still incensed. Then he closed the door. "I'm now going to tell you something that you can't print until the death of one of the most important officers in our army, George C. Marshall." I promised. "Because of Marshall, almost every one of my pilot friends was killed in the first few days of the war." He revealed that late in 1940, months before Pearl Harbor, Claire Chennault, who had been privately fighting for the Chinese and getting handsomely paid for each Japanese plane he shot down, reported that he had solved the problem of how to defeat the Japanese Zero fighter, which was far more maneuverable than any American plane. Because it had little protective armor, it was much lighter and could easily outclimb the heavily armored American fighter planes. The U.S. pilots should therefore be instructed never to climb but to dive, since their weight enabled them to dive faster than the Japanese. From his notes he outlined to Marshall and the Army Air Corps officers how they could attack from above, preferably two on one; if they used their present tactics they would be wiped out.

When Chennault left, according to O'Donnell, Marshall tossed his conclusions in a wastebasket. "And that," concluded O'Donnell, "was why I lost so many good friends."

The next stop on my long trip to the Orient was Wake Island. The pilot assured me that I would have at least four hours to explore the island while a minor repair was being made. I borrowed a truck and a map. The visible top of an inactive volcano was a V-shaped atoll. Each arm was about five miles long. Narrow channels cut off the tips, forming three islands whose total area was only two and a half square miles, about the size of New York City's Central Park. Wake was the main island.

I had seen many battlefields, but this scene of an early victory by the Japanese was one of the most evocative. Ruined gun emplacements, foxholes, and shell cases were still strewn over the coral island. Walking along the deserted beach during the fading light, I could picture the Japanese destroyers stealthily heading for the shore while the surf boomed.

After a two-day stop in Guam I landed at Clark Field, about fifty air miles northwest of Manila. I spent a week following, by air, the first Japanese attacks on the Philippines, and several times I induced one pilot to imagine he was a Japanese attacking the airfield. On the last simulated attack we landed so heavily that a tire burst and our plane was wrenched off the strip with one wing barely missing the ground.

During another flight I was taken over nearby Mount Arayat, which stuck up like a huge traffic marker. This lonely 3,867-foot peak stood in the middle of miles of plains, its cone dented—according to native lore—where Noah's ark landed. The pilot pointed to a nearby dirt road. "That's where Colin Kelly crashed," he said.

I was astounded. Kelly had been awarded a medal, so I had heard, for diving his plane into the smokestack of the battleship *Haruna*. When I mentioned this the pilot said, "Then how come I know a man who was on the plane?" I checked the records and learned that Kelly had located a Japanese ship near the north end of Luzon and dropped a bomb into its smokestack. Everyone aboard the B-17 was sure the ship was sunk, and they headed for home. En route they were attacked by a Zero pilot, Sabura Sakai, and Kelly's radio operator had his head shot off. Then the left wing gas tanks broke into flames, another shot severed the bomber's elevator cables, and the plane plunged into a steep dive.

Kelly ordered the men to bail out, staying at the controls while his men jumped. The plane burst into flames and crashed on a dirt road. Men of the 26th Cavalry found Kelly's body near the wreckage, his chute unopened. He had sacrificed his life so his men could live. The survivors reported that Kelly's bombs had opened the seams of a battleship and forced it to be beached. This was reported by MacArthur, and Kelly became the first great hero of World War II. He was posthumously awarded the DSC, which he deserved. But as General O'Donnell had told me, the fanfare of publicity was bad for the morale of other American air units whose pilots had also performed heroically over the Philippines that same day but were never honored by a single line of public acclaim.

When I awoke on the morning of December 25, 1959, at the spartan BOQ at Clark Field, I could faintly smell tropical flowers and feel a pleasant warm breeze. It took me some time to realize it was Christmas Day. I'd spent most of my life in New York City and New England, far from frangipani, poinsettia, water buffaloes, and ninety-degree Decembers. After trying unsuccessfully to telephone my two daughters in Red Bank, I decided to combat nostalgia by working. I persuaded Dr. W.T.T. "Chips" Ward, the able historian of the 406th Fighter Wing, to wangle transportation for a trip to see his friend Tony Aquino, who had been a third lieutenant in the Philippine army. I also wanted to ask Tony about his father, the late Benigno Aquino, member of President Quezon's cabinet at the outbreak of war and later a leading member of the quisling Filipino government set up by the Japanese.

The following morning, Tony unexpectedly appeared at the BOQ and invited me to spend the next few days at his family residence. Here I met Tony's younger half brother, Benigno Jr., not yet thirty and already governor of Pampagna Province. Unlike the happy-go-lucky Tony, he was serious and devoted to serving the people. His wife was an attractive, pleasant hostess and housewife who one day would be president of the Philippines. I listened to Tony's fascinating story at his private lake in the shadow of Mount Arayat. He'd gone off to war in his brand-new car, fought as a third lieutenant in the first battles on Luzon, and joined the retreating U.S.–Filipino troops into the Bataan peninsula. When the defenses crumbled, he was a prisoner on the Death March. As he was about to be loaded on a train to prison camp he was met by his father, a so-called quisling. But when a Japanese officer said he could go home, Tony refused. "I told Papa I couldn't leave my men but he could help me by giving all of the prisoners food and medicine." When his father told him he and other Filipino officials in the new Japanese regime were working with General Homma for early release of all Filipinos from prison camp, "I told him, 'Hurry, Papa, we are dying like flies!'"

On January 3, 1960, I started my research on the momentous battle of the Bataan peninsula. In Balanga I met the constabulary commander of Iloilo,

Lieutenant Colonel Wilfredo Encarnacion, who suggested I lodge in the abandoned chicken coop behind his home. It contained a cot protected by mosquito netting, and I could have breakfast and dinner in his house. I accepted, and would never forget the next eleven days.

With the help of Encarnacion I traveled the entire length of the U.S.–Filipino defense positions in the middle of the peninsula, the Abucay Line, by truck and foot. A long winding trench, reminiscent of World War I, was still there. Several farmers had built their shacks, made from nipa palms, directly over the trenches. Protecting the middle of this line was Mount Natib, scarred by innumerable ravines and covered with huge trees and dense jungle growth. It had not been defended, since it was assumed that no military force could possibly come over that matted mass of precipitous crags, ravines, and cliffs. That was why Lieutenant General Akira Nara ordered one of his regiments to climb over the mountain, circle behind the American positions, and join another of his regiments coming down the eastern coastal highway. Nara's "impossible" plan worked, and the American and Philippine troops were forced to retreat. It was the turning point of the Battle of Bataan. I told Encarnacion I must climb up Mount Natib. He reluctantly agreed, but insisted I take along half a dozen of his men armed with rifles and submachine guns. After four hours my hands were bloody from grasping prickly bamboo shoots to pull myself up steep inclines, and I was not too disappointed when the leader of the constabulary abruptly called a halt.

Six months after leaving Bataan I learned from Colonel Encarnacion why I had needed such a large armed guard. I learned that Mount Natib was the hiding place of diehard Huks, Communist outlaws. My expedition up Mount Natib had been stopped halfway because a scout had spotted several Huks waiting to ambush us.

A few days later I did climb to the top of Mount Samat, near the end of the peninsula, where the last catastrophic battles were fought. I was also paddled up the west coast in an outrigger canoe to the scene of the crucial Battles of the Points, inaccessible by road. Then I drove down the eastern coastal road with Colonel Encarnacion to the southern end of Bataan to see the remnants of the two U.S. hospitals. As we neared Cabcaben, people began shouting "Nihon! Nihon!" and pointing at me.

"What's the matter?"

Encarnacion was amused. Vice President Nixon reportedly had arrived in Manila the previous day. "They think you're Nixon. Stand up and wave." I did, wondering what my mother, an avid Nixon-hater, would think.

The last two days on the peninsula were spent in walking over much of the fifty-five-mile route of the Death March during the hottest hours of the day. Along the way I stopped for water and found some people who had risked their lives to give water to the prisoners. Others told of seeing Japanese shoot men who dropped from exhaustion; still others told of Japanese acts of kindness.

When I returned to Clark Field I learned from a friend at headquarters that some of the air force officials were unhappy with my behavior on Bataan. I had been seen washing myself early in the morning at a town pump with half a dozen local bathers. At another town I had caused a stir by playing chess with a thirteen-year-old boy on the main street. The boy had beaten me and people were shouting that Carlos had outwitted the American champion.

When I requested transportation to Manila, I was turned down, so I took a bus, sharing the packed vehicle with men, women carrying babies, children, six chickens, and two goats—all munching on tidbits. Once in Manila I would attempt to get help from the embassy. But my reception there was also cool, and when I asked to stay overnight in one of the little cabins on the grounds, as I had done previously, I was told there were no vacancies.

I had already been helped by three unorthodox officers in Manila: Colonels Gaffney, Bohannan, and Lonsdale, the original "Ugly American." I can't remember which one suggested that I ask President Garcia for help during a break in a meeting he was holding with top Filipino military officers. The next morning I waited for several hours outside the hall until my helpful colonel brought me inside and explained to the president that John Toland, an American historian, had come to get the Filipino story of the war. Garcia instructed all four chiefs to assist me. Major Ramos, a West Pointer, would help arrange matters.

On January 19 I boarded a worn-out former U.S. bomber with Lieutenant Aurelio Repato, the air force historian, who would be my guide in a tour of the southern islands. The plane had a number of bullet holes, which made an eerie noise, a concern to no one but me. I was introduced to a senator who had been in the underground, and I interviewed him until we started to land in Mindanao, the southernmost island. As we were coming in, a horde of wild dogs rushed onto the field. No one seemed disturbed, and my seat mate explained that this, like the bullet holes, was a common phenomenon.

As Bataan was about to fall in March 1942, MacArthur had finally consented to leave Corregidor with his family. After a dangerous trip by torpedo boat to Mindanao, the MacArthurs were taken inland to the airfield near the Del Monte pineapple ranch. We visited the dock near the Del Monte pineapple factory where Lieutenant John Bulkeley's torpedo boat had landed with the MacArthurs.

Our next stop was the island of Cebu. Soon after we landed, Repato was informed that Sergio Osmeña, who had succeeded Manuel Quezon as president, would like to see Mr. Toland the next morning. It took almost an hour to drive to the president's beautiful home in the hills. He was a small man, and looked wan. He dismissed everyone and then told me that he was nearing the end of his life and it was time the world knew the hidden truth about the so-called collaborators. Just before President Quezon left for America in 1942 he had summoned Osmeña, Laurel, and Aquino and ordered the latter two to stay in Manila and deal with the Japanese. "He told us someone had to protect the people from the Japanese. You must tell the world that Laurel and Aquino were heroes, not traitors as everyone still believes. Both agreed to pretend they were quislings and never to reveal the truth. We all kept silent—until now." He held out a feeble hand. "I want you to tell the truth." When he learned that a group of reporters had arrived during our meeting, he made me promise to say nothing until my book was published. I was deeply moved.

Outside, the reporters converged on me. I tried to break through them. One shouted, "What do you think of the American representatives who just arrived in Manila and are so critical of everything?"

"They might have waited a day or two," I thoughtlessly replied, unaware that I had just tipped over an applecart.

Repato and I returned to Manila and took a boat to Corregidor, where we wandered all over the still-destroyed island. The next day we returned in a helicopter to investigate the famous tunnel where MacArthur and his men had taken refuge when the island was attacked. We were warned not to go in very far because of the snakes, but Repato got flashlights and we went until we were blocked by wreckage. Even though the battle was history, the atmosphere inside was still deathly eerie. I tried to imagine what it must have felt like to hear the muffled roars of battle outside and never know just when the Japanese would finally break in.

The following two days were spent in interviews. I had learned of the daring exploits of Jim Cushing, a miner who had become one of the leading underground leaders. Several Americans had warned me that he was a drunken bum who detested talking to reporters and could be very abusive, although Filipinos regarded him as a great hero and had given him a home. He was presently in an American hospital recovering from his latest binge. The warnings I had received only induced me to visit him. A nurse said he was at the end of the ward. There on a bed was perched a dark-skinned man who reminded me of an ill-tempered pixie.

"Colonel Cushing?" I said.

"Cushing is a disgusting drunk and a liar. I advise you to stay away from him."

I extended a carton of American cigarettes. "I understand this is Cushing's brand. Guess I'll have to give them to my driver."

Cushing grinned and grabbed the carton. During the next two hours he told me in detail about his experiences during the war. He was half Irish, half Mexican, an ex-boxer and, in his own words, "a damned hard-drinking, devilish individualist." Before the war he and his brother had been mining engineers. After the surrender by General Wainwright he had been persuaded by his Filipino wife to sit out the war in the mountains, but was eventually induced to unify the quarreling groups of guerrillas on Cebu. He was given the rank of major by MacArthur, and he accomplished near miracles through his daring and originality. His most noteworthy achievement came in March 1944 when he learned that a high-ranking Japanese naval officer and nine men had been captured by some of his men after a plane crash near Cebu city. Cushing immediately radioed MacArthur in Australia that there was also a briefcase of important documents, some of which looked like a cipher system. The admiral, Shigeru Fukudome, had to be carried in a litter to Cushing's mountain hideaway. In his briefcase was the battle plan for Operation Z, Japan's last hope for the Decisive Battle wherein all issues would be settled at one stroke.

The Japanese commander in Cebu city sent word to Cushing that the prisoners must be released at once or he would burn down villages and execute civilians. Cushing retreated further into the mountains with Fukudome and received another order from MacArthur: ENEMY PRISONERS MUST BE HELD AT ALL COSTS.

This was impossible, since Cushing had only twenty-five men and Japanese troops were closing in. He sent the precious documents to the island of Negros with two runners but informed MacArthur he would be forced to release the admiral in order to avoid continued reprisals. The enraged MacArthur relieved Cushing of his command and reduced him to the grade of private. But Fukudome's briefcase found its way to MacArthur via submarine, and its contents were among the most significant enemy documents seized during the war.

Although Jim Cushing was in disgrace and was subjected to worse punishment when MacArthur returned to the Philippines, he carried on brilliantly as a private. Owing largely to the efforts of General Courtney Whitney, head of the Allied Intelligence Bureau and onetime severe critic of Cushing, Jim was reinstated, and after the war he was awarded a substantial cash bonus for his significant contributions to victory. It should have

been enough to last Jim for life in the islands, but he spent it all in a few
months on a series of celebrations that ranged across the Pacific to California.
When Jim told me of these parties he beamed, then said he was being kept
alive by the Filipinos "and a few quirky Americans."

A couple of days later I persuaded the king of the Negritos, a tribe which
wore almost no clothing, to tell me of his battles against the Japanese. The
Negritos had been brought by the American military to Clark Field to stop
the thievery of everything from refrigerators to the nuts and bolts that held
up a communications tower—a theft that had caused its collapse. The king,
now fully dressed, first took me to his church, a place of worship for a small
Christian sect, and then brought out his bow and arrows to demonstrate how
he had killed more than a hundred Japanese from ambush. He was more
than a foot shorter than I and thin as a rail, but he had tremendous strength.
He gave me two arrows as a souvenir, noting that the tips had once been
poisoned but had probably lost most of their potency. They are among the
momentos that still decorate my studio.

His brother-in-law then offered to take me on a trip by mule through the
rugged Zambales Mountains northwest of Clark Field, where many American and Filipino guerrillas had established their wartime hideaway. The price
was five dollars and a year's subscription to *Life*. By the time we returned
from the ten-hour trip I could hardly walk—to the great amusement of the
Negritos. Even so, I was made an honorary member of the tribe—but I
would not have to dress like them.

I now had everything I needed, and on January 31 I finally returned to
my room at Clark and packed my flight bag. I walked to headquarters to
say goodbye and was taken aback to find the usual coolness replaced by icy
coldness. One secretary whispered that I was in big trouble: the commanding
general was going to have me shipped back to the United States. She showed
me a copy of the Communist newspaper with the headline AUTHOR FLAILS
AMERICAN REPRESENTATIVES. It was a belated report of what I had told
reporters after leaving President Osmeña.

"I only said they might have waited a day or so before sounding off," I
weakly explained.

A stony-faced colonel strode toward me from the general's office. I knew
I was cooked. Just then there was a hubbub outside and several officers, led
by a four-star general, burst into the room. "How are they treating you,
John?" boomed Rosie O'Donnell.

"Fine, general!"

"We're taking some R and R in Hong Kong. Want to come along?"

"You bet! I'll be back in a few minutes with my bag."

On the plane I told Rosie about the incident at President Osmeña's. He laughed. "Take a tip from me. Always say, 'No comment.' "

I was so elated upon landing at the Kowloon airport that I lost sight of my flight bag for a few minutes. It was snatched, and I lost not only all my clothes but my two notebooks on the Tony Aquino story. Fortunately I was carrying the other notebooks.

In the morning I got fitted for two suits, a pair of shoes, an overcoat, and a trench coat. Joe Lowe, the tailor, also agreed to guide me. We interviewed an English doctor who had helped hold off the Japanese, and then inspected the redoubts on the island and interviewed half a dozen survivors of the Battle of Hong Kong.

Although Hong Kong had soon come under siege, in 1941, they told me, life in the city had been going on normally, with shops open, buses running on schedule, and nightclubs filled to capacity. But on December 14 of that year the vaunted defense line on the mainland—its name was Gin-Drinkers' Line—collapsed, and four days later Japanese big guns began a heavy bombardment of the island. The end was imminent.

On February 4, 1960, a feature article in the local paper told about my search for material, and this brought a strange note at the front desk: "It would be to your advantage to call me at my room. Irving Hoffman." I had no idea who this was, but I was so intrigued that I telephoned Hoffman and was invited to his room.

In the middle was a huge empty box labeled "Marx Toys." "My filing cabinet," said Irving. It was already littered with hundreds of papers and letters. Irving explained that he was in town preparing publicity material for a movie, *The World of Suzie Wong.* He offered to buy all of my meals and taxis if I paid the tips. Chinese currency baffled him. During the next five days I spent half my time with Irving, who allowed himself to be taken all over the New Territories in search of war survivors; he then showed me a Hong Kong I never knew existed. We took pictures of the locations used in the movie and met those who knew the real-life Suzie.

By this time Irving's constant costume was a flowing black kimono. An illustrated story in *Time* described his antics in Hong Kong. Not mentioned was the day we brought the toys from the huge Marx box up three flights of stairs to a party for the children of the local prostitutes. It was a warm scene that I would never forget.

By the ninth day I had filled three notebooks, acquired new clothes and flight bag, and formed many friendships—one with an English journalist shunned by most of his countrymen because he had married a Chinese. He gave me a list of people who could help me at my next stop, Taiwan. One, "Newsreel" Wong, the famous photographer, would show me the ropes.

The next day Wong took charge. He told how he had taken the classic picture of the Chinese baby crying during a bombing. He knew it was a great shot, but his film had run out and he thought he'd missed it, since he'd sent the undeveloped film to New York. Then he gaped when he saw the cover of *Time.* Newsreel knew everyone and was trusted by everyone.

Newsreel arranged an interview with the minister of war, General Chen Chang, who had been head of the Nationalist army under Chiang Kai-shek. He seemed nervous in the presence of my two official escorts. After an hour of conversation, he asked if I would like to use his bathroom. Once we were in the bedroom he handed me a heavy document. It was his autobiography, he said softly, and would never be printed in Taiwan. I hid it under my jacket.

On February 12, 1960, I took off for Japan in a MATS (Military Air Transport Service) plane, arriving at Tachikawa Air Base at about 4:00 A.M. In the moonlight, the flak towers, which had appeared so ominous in Germany and Austria, reminded me of pagodas in the mist. We left in a staff car for Tokyo, and the next two hours shattered my concepts of Japan, a land I had come to detest even though I'd never known a Japanese. In New York I'd already met many Chinese and liked them, and a Korean couple had been close friends. Now I could see that the Japanese, too, were just people. Even so, the stories I'd heard in the Philippines about the Death March still rankled. And I still could not forget the sneak attack on Pearl Harbor.

Now I was passing villages where women in kimonos clopped around in *geta* (wooden clogs) and children were crossing the street carrying little flags. This was not the Japan I'd read about. By the time I reached my hotel I had begun to feel as if I'd been deliberately deceived. I'd had a similar experience in Germany.

The next morning a navy captain, Susumu Nishiura, chief of the War History Office of the Defense Agency, appeared at the Sanno Hotel, which was run by the U.S. military. He had brought two officers to be interviewed. I was taken aback by their willingness to reveal everything they knew. I had arrived expecting roadblocks to the truth, and they were spilling out details just as General von Manteuffel had done.

I was in heaven. The enlisted men running the information office at the hotel—Chief Master Sergeant Tom Rhone, Master Gunnery Sergeant Alan Sydow, and Master Sergeant Art Hicks—arranged for transportation of the interviewees and kept coffee and refreshments coming. I did not realize it, but I'd come at a most propitious moment: the Japanese were now ready and eager to tell their side of the war. The word spread that I had promised to return what I wrote to those I interviewed so that any mistakes could be corrected. In four days I had learned more about the Japanese military than I had learned from extensive reading in histories. One officer confided to me that he was telling me these things because I wasn't an enemy now running his country but an observer without prejudice—and that was why he had given me details he had never revealed to other Westerners. He added that it was a relief to unburden himself.

A junior officer, Lieutenant Haruka Iki, after a half hour of hesitation, told how his torpedo helped sink the great British ship the *Repulse.* Upon return he and the other pilots who had sunk at the same time the *Prince of Wales* were tossed in the air by their joyous ground crews. Iki's own exaltation, he told me, was short-lived. The following day he flew over the graves of the sunken ships and dropped bouquets of flowers. "I didn't want to launch my torpedo," Iki confessed in a choked voice. "It was such a beautiful ship, such a beautiful ship!"

On February 20, 1960, a Navy helicopter took me to Nagoya, where I interviewed Ensign Kazuo Sakamaki, commander of one of the midget submarines that attempted to break into Pearl Harbor. Sakamaki, the only survivor, was sent to a POW camp in Tennessee, and during his captivity he came to admire and respect Americans. "This realization," he said, "came like a hammer blow against the heart of my whole past." The entire history and culture of Japan, out of which he had been born, had abruptly collapsed. "It was the rebirth of reason." Now he was a Christian and a successful businessman. "I told myself in Tennessee that we had fought and lost. We could not blame others. We could not complain. It was all our fault. It was we who were weak, inadequate, and ignorant. We must rebuild our country with our own hands in silence. That is the only way we can pay our debts."

Upon returning to Tokyo I was greeted by Captain Nishiura and his close friend Colonel Takushiro Hattori, who had been operations officer for imperial general headquarters and was eager to tell everything. He was as explosive and unrestrained as Nishiura was cool and self-possessed. The most difficult thing was to copy down Hattori's explosive words, many of which were in Japanese. Nishiura, in good English, calmly filled in the blanks. By noon I was exhausted. "I've just begun," exclaimed Hattori, and Nishiura suggested we conduct the second interview in Hattori's office.

The excitement of the day had just started. In the afternoon my regular interpreter at the Sanno, Toki Koizumi, the grandson of Lafcadio Hearn, introduced me to General Akira Nara, commander of the troops which had broken through the Abucay Line on Bataan. Now I could find out how Nara's men had managed to climb over Mount Natib—something I myself had failed to do.

The interview went smoothly until I asked how Colonel Takechi had been able to cross the rugged mountain with his equipment and guns. Suddenly something seemed to have gone wrong between interpreter and interviewee. Ordinarily mild, Koizumi was expostulating vehemently.

"What's wrong, Koizumi?" I asked.

"He's telling things that no proper Japanese officer should tell!"

General Nara took a book from his briefcase. It was *Battle: The Story of the Bulge.* He pointed to a page at the back of the book marked "About the Author." "You Williams," he said. "Me Amherst. Lost English. Must tell secret of Bataan." he rattled off something to Koizumi, who said, "He says he was a classmate of President Coolidge's son at Amherst College. But he should *not* tell you the things about Bataan."

I looked at the general and pointed to myself. "Another interpreter. In one or two days." I indicated with my fingers.

Nara smiled and nodded. "Good interpreter?" he said.

I nodded. Once the general had left, I tried to calm down Koizumi, whom I was about to replace. I dismissed him with thanks.

That night I had a date at the Foreign Correspondents' Club on Shinbun Alley to have dinner with Igor Oganesoff, of the *Wall Street Journal,* whom I had met in Taipei. Igor had revealed he was married to a Japanese, and this intrigued me. At the table were several other correspondents, including Dan Kurzmann, former head in Tokyo of *McGraw-Hill World News.*

While I was complaining about the problem with my interpreter, I noticed a petite girl heading toward our table. She carried herself regally, floating like a princess. I had never seen such beauty. I fell in love with her the moment I saw her. Very few women I've ever seen had the gracefulness of her walk and gestures. The sound of her voice, its softness and clarity, enchanted my ears just as the exquisite beauty of her face captured my heart. Igor explained that this was Toshiko Matsumura, correspondent for *McGraw-Hill World News,* and she had come to the table to give Kurzmann some information for the book he was now writing. She politely asked what I was doing in Japan. I said I was writing a book about the war. "I've come to listen to the Japanese."

"In that case you're about the only American to do so. The others"—she looked around the table—"usually ask five pejorative questions." I must have been looking at her open-mouthed. "Could I help you in any way?" she asked.

I explained about General Nara and she agreed to be my interpreter after her own workday. I was advised by an air force major not to use a girl interpreter because the Japanese looked down on women. But I set up the appointment. From the first moment it was obvious that General Nara was delighted with Toshiko. During the hours that followed, Toshiko and I were spellbound by his story. He told how he had been ordered to launch an attack on the Abucay Line even though his men were exhausted from chasing the Americans into Bataan. After reconnoitering, he decided to keep one regiment in reserve and sent the 141st Infantry Regiment of Colonel Imai straight down the coastal highway. He then ordered his old and trusted friend Colonel Susumu Takechi to head inland with the 9th Infantry to the west, toward the slopes of Mount Natib, and to circle behind the American positions, finally joining Imai at the highway.

After an hour-long Japanese barrage, Imai started down the highway while Takechi struck off into the wild jungle. Suddenly, to Nara's dismay, American artillery rounds fell on the highway in front of Imai. Nara had not realized that General Homma's intelligence officers had mistakenly placed the American defenders too far north and that his men wouldn't reach the Abucay Line for another three miles. Imai was therefore forced to shunt his regiment into the fields to the west in order to escape the heavy American artillery.

Nara's dismay was confounded by the strange disappearance of Takechi's regiment into the heavy jungle of Mount Natib, but to save his friend's reputation Nara did not report this to Homma or record it in his war diary.

While Imai was fighting for his life, Takechi was lost. He had failed to go directly over the top. Instead, after six days he emerged from the jungled slopes on the east side of the mountain and began attacking the Americans who were trying to wipe out Imai coming up the east coast. Takechi soon found, however, that he was also attacking friends, and he rushed back to General Nara's field headquarters to make a personal report. Tattered and exhausted, he explained how he had become lost in the mountainous jungles.

"I'm putting you in reserve," said Nara, who realized that Takechi's men needed rest after their ordeal.

"*Hai*"—yes—said Takechi. He saluted. But instead of heading back to a rest area, as ordered, he was determined to take his men directly over Mount Natib this time or die trying, for he mistakenly thought—Nara explained to us—that Nara had ordered him into reserve as punishment for getting lost. There was no word from Takechi for five days, and once more Nara kept this information from Homma. Two days later there was still no word from Takechi, and Nara deduced that his friend must be trying to go over the top of Mount Natib and ordered bundles of food dropped at various points. None reached Takechi, who had finally succeeded in crossing the "impassable" mountain and continued to the Abo Abo River. Once there, he cut sharply to the east and headed for the coastal highway. The Americans and Filipinos hastily withdrew all forces to the south. When Takechi finally reported to Nara, he revealed that his men had not eaten for a week. Nara handed over his personal supply of bread and cigarettes, then watched his haggard officer being interviewed by a newspaperman who would report that, in a brilliant maneuver, Takechi's men had marched over rugged Mount Natib, completely surprising the Americans and causing a breakthrough of the Abucay Line. Realizing it would ruin Takechi's career if it was known he had disobeyed orders, Nara kept quiet. But now Takechi was dead, and Nara wanted his family to know what a hero he was.

By the end of the interview I felt as exhausted as Colonel Takechi must have after his breakthrough, but I knew I had the secret of the most crucial battle on Bataan. This was one of the most productive interviews of my career, thanks to Toshiko, who was still chatting with Nara. The general suggested we have another meeting so he could clear up details and answer questions.

During the next week I spent the days at the Sanno or with Hattori at his steaming office. During the evenings Toshiko and I interviewed important men, including Count Ian Muto; General Minoru Genda, head of the Self-Defense Force, who had led the attack on Pearl harbor as a navy commander; and Mrs. Homma, widow of the commander of the Philippine invasion force.

During this eventful week I also learned much about Toshiko and her family. Her father worked for Nippon Steel and as a young man had been secretary to Count Koyabama, head of a Japanese-English organization, since he was fluent in English. His own father, a samurai, had taught the tea ceremony. Her mother's father had been headman in a village, and her mother had been one of the early Japanese *moga* (modern) girls. Both parents had become Baptists, and Toshiko had graduated from Keisen, the well-known girls' school run by Miss Kawai, who had graduated from Bryn Mawr College. December 8, Japan's Pearl Harbor Day, had been Toshiko's twelfth birthday; when she learned of the war and heard the martial music while on her way to school, she did not feel that Japan had a chance of winning. A family friend, Felix Rothschild, had been sending them *Life* magazine, and thumbing through its ads for all sorts of vehicles and equipment, as well as pictorial stories of America's industrial power, had convinced her how impossible it would be for a tiny, just industrializing nation like Japan to challenge such a giant.

After the horrifying firebombing of Tokyo and later attacks, the family left for the inland, where, the day before the surrender, Toshiko's sister was almost cut down by a diving American navy pilot looking for a target of opportunity. During the occupation Toshiko had worked for the American army and was then chosen as a Garioa Scholar (a program that was the direct progenitor of the Fulbright scholarships) and sent to the United States for a year's study. On her return, after several jobs she became a correspondent for McGraw-Hill and was its expert on coal and steel. Her main job was interpreting for her present boss, Sol Sanders.

I also told her about myself and what I hoped to achieve with my writing. Matter-of-factly I revealed how my first marriage had come to an end because Dorothy and I were poorly matched. At present I was paying for support of the two children, and I planned to send them both to preparatory school and college when more money came in. I was equally candid about my finances. I had little in the bank, but prospects were good for a condensation of the Pacific book in *Look.* I added that I was also supporting my mother and helping two aunts. My chief need was to get enough money for research.

For more than a week we had been eating dinner together, and I had even forced myself to try sushi—which I detested. We saw several shows, and during our many taxi trips I kissed her despite the disapproval of the kamikaze drivers who whirled us around Tokyo.

Early one evening in March on our way back to Toshiko's tiny house I kissed her and then said, "Will you marry me?" She hesitated five or six seconds before saying, "Yes."

Our engagement caused a stir in several circles. Her parents were appalled, and several of my friends warned me that I was making a terrible mistake. Dr. Kazutaka Watanabe in the Office of Information Service assumed that I'd found some girl in a nightclub, and lectured me severely. The wife of the chief counsel at the U.S. embassy begged me to reconsider; she said, "At least have Madame Kurusu meet her." She was the American widow of the Japanese diplomat who, with Admiral Nomura, had delivered the final note to Cordell Hull on the Day of the Pearl Harbor attack.

After we enjoyed a pleasant dinner with Mrs. Kurusu at the Sanno, she reported that Toshiko was most suitable. Dr. Watanabe also heartily approved upon learning, to his amazement, that Toshiko was the daughter of his own best man.

When I learned that I needed the original document of my divorce proceedings, I telephoned my lawyer, Mort Abrams. He in turn called my mother, who responded with dead silence for some time. She had disapproved of Dorothy and would undoubtedly disapprove of Toshiko, but not because she was Asian, since my mother was not at all racist. She would have disapproved of anybody—even Mary Baker Eddy. I also guessed that it would take some time for my daughters, Marcia and Diana, to accept a new mother. I myself never had any second thoughts, for I was confident that Toshiko shared my dedication to work. And she was not daunted when I told her of the rigorous trips I had to take to gather material. And most important, she shared my need to dig out the truth regardless of nationality.

Toshiko's parents were also in shock, but not because I was an American. Both had many American friends, but they feared Toshiko might never return to Japan. Besides, I was much older and a mere writer, one of the lowliest forms of life in Japan. Appointments to meet me fell through several times, and finally Toshiko's younger sister, Eiko, married to a psychiatrist, was deputized to meet Mr. Toland. Both Eiko and her husband found me presentable, and at last the meeting with the parents was definitely set up. I was surprised to be greeted in Oxford English by her father. He was very formal and began asking the questions a father should ask.

"Why were you divorced?"

"My wife and I had different lives. She was a dancer and I was a writer."

"Can you afford to keep my daughter?"

"Yes, sir!" I said positively. "Things always pop up."

Mr. Matsumura fumbled around until interrupted by his wife, Orie, who sat next to him, reminding me of a plump goddess. She knew little English, and said slowly, "You—will—make—Toshiko—happy."

I beamed, and thought of kissing her but decided it was not yet the thing to do. Apparently Mr. Matsumura was also relieved, and when I presented him with a box of golf balls that I'd bought at the post exchange, he also beamed. Toshiko had told me her father was an ardent golfer and a charter member of the first golf club in Japan. "Ah," he said, holding up one ball, "the big American ball!"

The date for the wedding was indefinite, since the divorce papers had not yet arrived, but tentative arrangements were made for a church wedding on March 12, 1960, and on March 10 I finally received the divorce papers, along with a note that my mother had come to Mort expressing fear that I would now take away her house. Mort had replied that she didn't even know her own son. I moved to the Grand Hotel, and the next day Toshiko and I were married at the U.S. embassy, thanks to Sol Sanders. Champagne was served and we then drove the short distance to Toshiko's ward office for a civil ceremony, at which we were married at a cost of approximately ten cents.

We were married a third time at the Baptist church, and that afternoon a reception was held at a large union hall. Most of the guests were Japanese, but I was allowed to invite about a dozen of my American friends, including correspondents. Toshiko and I sat at the head table flanked by two go-betweens, a Japanese couple, while the guests sat at other tables eating and drinking. The formal ceremony began with the go-betweens giving long descriptions of Toshiko's life. Then they called upon the guests to add their comments. A teacher told what a perfect student Toshiko had been in grammar school. Then those from Keisen commented on the admirable things she had done in that school, and other friends offered illustrations of how she helped them with no thought of herself.

The male go-between then asked friends of Mr. Toland to make comments.

One correspondent rose and told a funny story of how I had wangled the truth from a reluctant American staff officer. The Americans laughed, but the Japanese were taken aback. Another American offered a second comic tale about me, and this time even the Japanese laughed. Then a Japanese girlfriend told of Toshiko's antics when she and her schoolmates spent the last year of the war ironing uniforms for the emperor. This brought another story of how she had slid down the clothing chute to the first floor to see how it felt, and had bumped into her teacher. The time passed quickly, and after the reception Toshiko and I moved to the Nikko Hotel, which was less formal and boasted a Japanese chanteuse.

Our honeymoon ended on March 15, and I set out for Tachikawa for the flight home. Toshiko insisted on staying in Japan until she could find a proper replacement for her job. Once aboard the MATS plane I began to go over the thirty-one days I had spent in Japan. I had with me a number of full notebooks, photographs, and maps. I'd managed to interview some of the most important survivors of the war, and I had found to my wonder that I believed what they said. I had arrived at Tachikawa hating Japanese and wondering how I could dig the truth out of them, and I had discovered that it was even easier than it had been in Germany. I was finding far more rapport with the Japanese than I had with the Germans. The Japanese seemed impelled to tell what they believed was the truth, with little thought of the consequences.

I felt as if I had literally come to a new world. Things happened to me haphazardly, almost as though by chance. Chance had brought me to the Foreign Correspondents' Club to complain about my interpreter. Was it also chance that had brought Toshiko to my table that night? Whatever it was, I knew that I now had a bridge not only to the East but to a level of personal understanding that I had never had previously.

{3}

Try, Try, Try Again

During the two months in the spring of 1960 before Toshiko would be able to join me, I conducted several extremely helpful interviews that would give great color and vitality to my book. While on the West Coast I managed to locate "Jitter Bill" Bradford, a pilot who had been operating an air taxi service known as the Bamboo Fleet between Bataan, Corregidor, and Del Monte in worn-out military and private planes. He had flown Colonel Arthur Fischer out of Corregidor in the desperate attempt to bring cinchona seed, from which quinine was produced, so that quinine could be available for our troops in the Pacific. A month later he had daringly snatched Colonel Carlos Romulo out of Ilo Ilo the morning the Japanese landed on the island of Panay.

By that time, 1942, Corregidor was under heavy attack, and Bill was asked to ferry badly needed medicine there. But he was down to one plane, an ancient Bellanca. The chances of arriving were exactly zero—and he knew it. Even so, he took the job. Somehow he managed to lumber over enemy territory at eighty miles an hour and softly touch down on the Corregidor airstrip. He met Wainwright in Malinta Tunnel and was told that morale was fairly high even though few of the thirteen thousand on the island had hopes of being saved. The men's favorite song, he reported with a wry grin, was "I'm Waiting for Ships That Never Come In."

One of the most moving stories came from Corporal Irving Strobing, the army radio operator in Malinta Tunnel. Concussion from the almost continuous Japanese shelling had knocked out most of his lines, and he was keying directly to the transmitters near the west mouth of the tunnel. He was still maintaining contact with station WTJ in Honolulu when on May 6, 1942, Wainwright nearby was composing his last message to President Roosevelt:

WITH BROKEN HEART AND HEAD BOWED IN SADNESS BUT NOT
IN SHAME I REPORT TO YOUR EXCELLENCY THAT TODAY I MUST

ARRANGE TERMS FOR THE SURRENDER OF THE FORTIFIED ISLANDS
OF MANILA BAY. . . .

When word came that General Wainwright and half a dozen officers were riding in a car up to the top of Denver Hill and about to surrender, Strobing tapped out his final message:

MY NAME IS IRVING STROBING. GET THIS TO MY MOTHER, MRS. MINNIE STROBING, 605 BARBEY STREET, BROOKLYN, NEW YORK. . . . MY LOVE TO PA, JOE, SUE, MAC, CARRY, JOYCE AND PAUL. ALSO TO ALL FAMILY AND FRIENDS. GOD BLESS 'EM ALL. HOPE THEY WILL BE THERE WHEN I COME HOME. TELL JOE WHEREVER HE IS TO GIVE 'EM HELL FOR US. GOD BLESS YOU. . . .

I also interviewed Carl Mydans of *Life,* who at one point had heard that the Japanese had landed at Lingayen Gulf the previous night and the bay was filled with floating bodies and the beaches strewn with Japanese dead. Learning at headquarters that the wild battle was still raging, Carl drove quickly to the scene, but found no bodies on the beaches and no signs of battle. Except for a few Filipino soldiers resting beside their weapons, the great expanse of sand was empty.

A smiling American major explained. At midnight several dark shapes had been seen approaching the mouth of the Agno River. (I later learned these were two small Japanese motorboats on reconnaissance.) Artillery fire opened up, and a moment later Lingayen Gulf was ablaze as every gun in the area, from 155mm guns to pistols, opened fire.

By the time Mydans returned to Manila, the other reporters were wiring their papers and magazines stories about the great victory. He buttonholed Major LeGrande Diller, MacArthur's press chief. "Pic," he protested, "I've just been to Lingayen and there's no battle there."

Diller pointed to the communiqué he had just read aloud to the press. "It says so here."

Carl gave me a picture he had taken of the peaceful beach at Lingayen Bay. "Use it with my blessings."

In mid-May 1960, Toshiko flew to New York with her clothes, a glass case containing a huge doll wearing a kimono, a record player, and a tape recorder the size of a portable typewriter. One of her first requests was to see *My Fair Lady* on Broadway. It was as wonderful as she had imagined. The hotel was another story: the cockroaches were not only plentiful but impudent. We spent as little time as possible in the cockroach arena, preferring the main branch of the New York Public Library, checking facts.

After a short visit to Red Bank, where my mother, frostily polite, staged a small party in honor of Toshiko and offered to teach her how to use a knife and fork, we eagerly left for three weeks of fact-checking and more interviews in Washington, and at the end of June we left for New Hampshire with my mother and the two girls. This time I had rented, for July and August, a house several hundred yards from Big Squam Lake. There was a small one-story cottage behind the house where Toshiko and I slept—and I began writing the book.

The swimming was perfect, and Toshiko learned to water-ski almost immediately, even though I was just teaching her to swim. The lake and its pleasures were constant, but the relationship between cottage and house grew more and more strained, and meals were often marred by squabbles. Despite this friction, I wrote rapidly, and by the beginning of August I had finished the first three hundred pages. As usual I followed my detailed chronological outline and put everything I knew on paper without any thought of correction or deletion. That would come in the second draft.

Toshiko liked what I had written and tried to get me to rest, realizing that I was already exhausted. One afternoon my mother asked to read what I had finished, and the next morning she solemnly appeared at our cottage and invited me to come into the house, where there was a fire burning. There she announced that what she had read was not up to my standard. It just didn't work.

When I returned to the cottage, sweating from the fire, I told Toshiko that the Squam Lake situation was impossible. Although we were supposed to stay until the end of August, I suggested we leave and find an apartment in New York. I knew what I had written was good.

On West Seventy-ninth Street we found a pleasant apartment featuring a large living room with beautiful mahogany floors. I knew I could write there in peace, even though the bedroom was so small there was only about a yard between the bed and the pathway to a tiny kitchen. But it was all ours. Toshiko had never learned to cook, so I had to serve up my favorite dish—tuna fish. I ate primarily so I could work, but after a week of this Toshiko sought recipes from Japanese friends and, while I worked, was on the phone tirelessly discussing the day's menu. By the end of the second week her meals far surpassed mine.

Before long I had finished the first draft and Toshiko had retyped a clean copy. Bob Loomis liked it and the editing began. We worked well together and finished the final draft early in 1961. A copy was sent to *Look,* and just as our money was running low, we received word from Rog Terrill that three parts would appear in that magazine. This meant even greater research funds for the next book.

I had recently talked with one of the men at the Pentagon who had launched me on the road to military history. He noted that although some of the more intellectual magazines criticized my books, the military liked them because they were down-to-earth. Could I describe my technique?

A phrase occurred to me. "I guess you could call it living history." I was only doing what Porter Emerson Browne had told me to do: I gazed down on my characters and let them do what they had to do, say what they had to say. The only difference was that my characters were real people, not products of my imagination. I was only an observer watching both sides and taking no sides. "It's really very easy. I only have to record." Actually, it was much more complicated. I had to keep sorting and arranging my materials, deciding what to leave in and what to omit. I was also trying to separate fact from fiction and to distinguish between what actually happened and what a narrator—or a governmental report or pronouncement—said happened. What I did my best to avoid was inserting personal judgments or interpretations—that is, either moral evaluations or attempts to get at any sort of "meaning" beyond or behind the events themselves. I had also learned a valuable lesson: never write "half-truths," which are, of course, half-lies.

On September 12, 1961, the first installment of *But Not in Shame* appeared in *Look*—advertised as a condensation of an important new book. Two weeks later, Jean Ennis, head of Random House publicity, phoned to report that there was an enthusiastic prepublication review in *The Kirkus Reviews.* Jean also reported that Walter Winchell, the then influential and famous columnist, had just praised the book at length. "His amount of research," wrote Winchell, "was enormous. . . . You'd think Mr. Toland would wind up hating the Japanese but he didn't. . . . he dedicates the book to his interpreter— a lovely girl named Toshiko Matsumura. . . . And not only did he dedicate it to her—he married her."

The book was published on that Friday, and the *New York Times Book Review* gave it a rave review on the front page. S.L.A. Marshall in the *New York Herald Tribune* stated that Toland was "a nonpareil" at emphasizing the human elements of war.

After all the work that had gone into these books, I reveled in these words of praise—which meant that I was no longer a "promising" writer. For the first time I really felt Porter Emerson Browne and Mark Reed would be proud of me. I never felt this initial thrill again, even when I won the Pulitzer Prize. This was something that could only happen once. At last I had made it!

Despite the pleasure of these accolades, however, I felt this was just the beginning, and I still believed that when I had saved enough money I could return to my chosen medium—plays and novels.

As I paused to look back over the long, hard road which had brought me to this success, I wondered what had kept me going after so many rejections and so many mistakes. When I told my father I was spending the summer riding freight trains, he had called me the "biggest damned fool in the Toland family." He later told me I was stupid to keep on writing plays and novels that nobody wanted. And why did I waste time picketing the White House and selling the *Daily Worker?* I had not flared up when he made such remarks because I was confident there was no substance in what he was saying—he was only worried about my future. Now he was dead and could not enjoy my day of success. I had persisted in my dogged way. Had it been my Irish blood that kept me rising from the floor, or sheer Scottish stubbornness? Perhaps both.

By the end of 1961 I was itching to start work on our next book—about the thirteen months during the 1930s when John Dillinger and his cronies terrorized the Middle West.

{4}

The Dillinger Days

Once I had finished the first draft of *But Not in Shame,* Toshiko and I had immediately begun work on the next project. Bob Loomis of Random House had suggested, in 1960, that I do a book on John Dillinger, and the idea was appealing. Until very recently, impressions of the violent criminals of the Depression years in America's heartland were formed largely from movies like *Bonnie and Clyde,* a colorful but largely inaccurate portrait of people who were far less handsome and a great deal more wicked than the glamorous movie stars who impersonated them. During my first year as a bindle stiff and hitchhiker on the road I had actually been picked up in the Midwest by police who thought I might *be* Dillinger. I told Loomis I'd like to do the thirteen months during the thirties when Dillinger and his contemporaries such as Ma Barker and her boys, Bonnie Parker, Pretty Boy Floyd, and Machine Gun Kelly terrorized America. Bennett Cerf, the cofounder of Random House, also liked the idea, and a contract was signed.

I wrote J. Edgar Hoover asking for help in interviewing FBI agents, but received only a reply from a subordinate stating that the FBI could not allow its agents to be interviewed or their names used, since it could endanger their lives and might hinder their operations. Undaunted, on my own I located a former agent living in Connecticut who had been connected with the Dillinger case but had since quit the agency. This man was willing to tell why he had left but would not let his name be used—although he did give me the name and address of a colleague in California who had also left the agency.

In March 1961 we packed clothes, notebooks, the tape recorder, and other supplies into an old Ford and set off for Chicago. For the first two weeks we spent almost every day collecting information about Dillinger's Chicago exploits. A prime source was Sergeant Frank Reynolds of the Dillinger Detail, which had been formed to track down Dillinger at any cost. A husky Irishman with cold blue eyes, he told Toshiko and me about killing twelve dangerous criminals in face-to-face duels. He pulled his gun from a drawer; it had twelve notches on the handle. "I'm eager for the thirteenth," he said.

He gave us a detailed story of the time he personally raided Dillinger's hideout and killed three men. For hours they were identified in the morgue as Dillinger, John Hamilton, and Harry Pierpont. Naturally, they turned out to be three other men. But Dillinger was only half a block away at the time.

We also traced down the manager of the Biograph Theater, where Dillinger was ambushed and killed in July 1934 as he emerged with his girlfriend and the "lady in red" who had betrayed him to FBI agents. The manager, whose name was Charles Shapiro, told us how he first got suspicious when Melvin Purvis, the head of the team of FBI agents assigned to track down Dillinger, bought a ticket and began poking around the foyer. Then the theater's engineer, who was checking the cooling system in the alley, noticed a man standing on the catwalk (a G-man) and a car in the alley containing four men (also G-men). The engineer was so scared that the manager locked him in the boiler room and told him he'd take care of things. Then the cashier reported seeing about ten suspicious men outside the theater. The manager called the Sheffield Avenue police station, and a few minutes later two plainclothesmen arrived. (There had been two holdups at the theater in the past year, and the manager had personally captured one of the bandits.) While the plainclothesmen were frisking the boyfriend of the lady in red, who should start walking out of the theater but Dillinger himself, along with two women! Afterward, Purvis came into Shapiro's office to make a call to Hoover, and Shapiro got on the phone to blast Hoover for not telling him what was going on. Shapiro had always refused to talk to any reporters or writers or radio and TV people. I think he talked to us because we came out to the suburbs by bus to see him.

Toshiko and I also visited the Cook County Morgue and talked our way into a personal tour. The supervisor insisted on showing us how Dillinger was processed. Corpses were arriving every few minutes. The sight of the bodies and the pungent smell of the morgue almost made me vomit. I turned white. We also found a doctor who had posed as the coroner for the news media when Dillinger's body was brought in so he could be photographed with the body and serve as the source of the story for the *Tribune*. To this day most people still think he was the coroner.

Our next task was to explore Dillinger's sensational escape from the Crown Point, Indiana, jail, supposedly with a wooden gun. Robert Estill, the Indiana prosecuting attorney, gave us the real story. Dillinger had been captured in Tucson, Arizona, and upon his arrival at the Chicago Municipal Airport, armed police from two states were waiting—including the eighty-five men of Chicago's Dillinger Detail.

Dillinger was taken to the sheriff's office at Crown Point, which was jammed with reporters—all shouting to get the bank robber's attention. Treated like a celebrity, Dillinger acted like one. His manner, recalled Estill, was good-natured but a bit condescending, as if he were superior to everyone in the room. Then a newsreel cameraman began to take movies. Estill said he was on Dillinger's left (he was, in fact, on the right) looking, he admitted, exhausted and a bit sheepish. On Estill's other side was the attractive Lake County sheriff, Lillian Holley. A freelance reporter called out to Estill, "Bob, put your arms around him." Estill told us that he didn't hear this but Dillinger did, and while the prosecuting attorney was saying something to Mrs. Holley, Dillinger impudently rested his right elbow on Estill's shoulder as if they were buddies. Estill admitted he had then put his left arm behind the gangster's back. Photographers and newsreel men took pictures of Dillinger grinning sardonically at Sheriff Holley and then at the man who had vowed to send him to the electric chair. He somewhat resembled a rising movie star, Humphrey Bogart, and when I saw a later snapshot of him deftly taking a puff on a cigarette, I recalled that Bogart had done it the same way in *The Petrified Forest*.

That tableau would rock Indiana politics, cost one man his chance to be governor, and kill another's hopes for the presidency. J. Edgar Hoover said that no picture ever made him more angry. Attorney General Homer Cummings called Estill's conduct disgraceful, and the *New York Times* described the episode as "a modern version of the Prodigal Son."

Estill informed us that he had managed to ignore the growing criticism so he could concentrate on his case against Dillinger. He was aware that Dillinger had already made one escape in Lima, Ohio, but he knew that Lake County's three-story brick jail was "safe." Dillinger was securely locked up in a new "escape-proof" section of the jail, and between him and freedom were a half-dozen barred doors and some fifty guards. Mrs. Holley had also buttressed the defenses with armed members of the local Farmers' Protective Association and a National Guard squad, and at night floodlights illuminated the area around the big building.

But Dillinger did escape. He had fourteen dollars and a gun, which had been smuggled in to him by his lawyer; he had no other help from the outside but really made his escape on his own. The story that he had only a wooden gun was, insisted Estill, just a myth.

We next visited the Indiana Reformatory in Pendleton, where Dillinger, then twenty years old, had been incarcerated for hitting a grocer with a bolt wrapped in a handkerchief and stealing the day's receipts. He was tried without a lawyer. Foolishly believing the prosecutor's assurance that he would receive a light sentence, he pleaded guilty and was sentenced to Pendleton for ten to twenty years. And so he was sent to live within the same walls as the two "big-time" criminals he most admired—Pierpont and Homer Van Meter. It was his admission into the College of Crime.

Our next penal visit, to the Indiana State Prison in Michigan City, brought us detailed accounts of all the escapades inside, letters received, letters sent, visitors, etc. I got permission to go back in and speak to an old man named Baldy Peyton, who was serving life for murder. His real name was Raymond Moseley, #10823, but he asked me to use an alias. He'd been in jail forty years, not counting a few months of freedom when he walked out the front gate, claiming he was going to fix the eaves on the warden's house. Baldy was a well-read, educated man, very bitter. He wouldn't give me the time of day at first, but he finally opened up. The old man said he knew the entire inside Dillinger story but wouldn't talk while he was inside. He was afraid that he'd be killed and also that it might affect a parole he was working on.

Moseley told us he had known Dillinger only while he was in Michigan City, but during that brief time they had become close friends. He knew that Pierpont and Van Meter had taught the tricks of the trade to Dillinger, who had agreed to help them escape once he had been released on parole. He would then join their gang. All this, Moseley pointed out, had given Dillinger a goal and a sense of responsibility. He had written home that he was staying out of trouble and was maturing. And in a sense, commented Moseley, he *had* matured. For the first time in his life he "belonged." Dillinger did, in fact, help the Pierpont gang to escape and in turn was captured; then they, in turn, helped him to escape.

Just before we left Michigan City the warden let us copy the official report of the escape, and Moseley gave us a chapter about the escape from the book he was writing, *In for Life.* During the next few days we made a number of miscellaneous visits: to the Biograph Theater neighborhood, where we saw the barber who shaved Dillinger two days before the killing, the Greek confectioner who served Dillinger a strawberry sundae that same day, and the man who sold Dillinger the silk shirt he wore when he met his death; to the office of Dr. Eye, where Dillinger was almost trapped; to the room in the Irving Hotel where Dr. Joe Moran performed facial operations on fugitive criminals; and to the house in Bensonville where Edward George Bremer, the beer magnate, was held during his kidnapping by Dillinger.

During the next two weeks we raced around in nearby Illinois and Wisconsin; most of our excursions were pleasant and successful, but occasionally we had a frustrating day. One of these was a Monday when we drove to Barrington, Illinois, where Baby Face Nelson killed two G-men and was mortally wounded. We chased six or seven cold leads—people not at home, wouldn't talk, or knew nothing. Finally in midafternoon we luckily found a man who had witnessed the whole thing.

After a brief stop in La Crosse we went to Iowa, where we unearthed more Dillinger stories. Probably the best of all came from a former bank telephone switchboard operator who, during the robbery, kept sending out calls until they shot at her; she then ran to the back window of the bank and shouted to a well-dressed man in the alley: "For goodness sake, get help! The bank is being robbed!" The man looked up and said, "Lady, you're telling *me?*" It was Baby Face Nelson.

Dillinger's getaway car, we learned, had sped away at ten miles an hour. It was a Buick, and it held about twenty people: seven robbers and the rest hostages (Dillinger jammed them inside and on the running boards). The cops were following at a respectful distance, also at ten miles an hour. At one point the Dillinger car stopped to let an old lady cross the street; it stopped again when an elderly woman on the running board noticed where they were and hysterically shouted, "Let me out! This is where I live!"; once again when Baby Face Nelson fired at the police and strewed roofing tacks on the highway (I managed to get three of them); and once more when another woman said she was getting sick and the robbers let her out because they didn't want their car messed up.

In Sioux Falls, South Dakota, we got the story of the bank robbery there in which Baby Face Nelson first appeared with the gang. On March 6, 1934, Dillinger, by that time the entire nation's Public Enemy Number One, had arrived in Sioux Falls in a new green Packard and parked in front of the imposing Security National Bank and Trust Company. A pretty stenographer jokingly remarked to a clerk, "There's a bunch of holdup men." But the clerk was suspicious and put his finger on the burglar alarm in readiness. The gang walked casually into the bank. Suddenly Baby Face shouted in his shrill voice, "This is a holdup! Lay down on the floor!" The alarm went off and Dillinger escorted the head teller back to the vaults. But the teller pretended to have trouble with the five-way combination of the money vault. Van Meter jammed a machine gun in his side. "Open it up, you son of a bitch, or I'll cut you in two!"

Then began a lethal comedy of errors. The desk sergeant at the police station got a telephone call about some trouble at the bank, but the caller forgot to mention that the alarm was ringing, and the sergeant figured some customer was making a fuss. He sent one patrolman to quell the disturbance. On entering the bank he was immediately disarmed and ordered to lie on the floor. The alarm was still ringing, and a fascinated crowd of about a thousand pressed around the bank, filling the streets.

Three of the bank employees described for us the chaos inside the bank. Baby Face was hopping around the lobby like an enraged bantam rooster, shouting that he would kill the man who had hit the alarm. The teller was trying to tell Dillinger he was innocent and was sharply told, "Forget it— just get the money!" Baby Face looked out a side window and saw a man in a khaki uniform getting out of a car. It was an off-duty policeman who was hitching up his belt. Baby Face, thinking he was reaching for his gun, hurdled over a waist-high railing, jumped up on a desk, and began firing through the plate-glass window.

Out front, one of the gang had captured two carloads of police and lined them up without firing a shot. By that time the robbers inside had gathered together almost fifty thousand dollars and were rounding up five women to use as hostages. One of them told us how they were ordered to surround the gangsters, thus serving as human shields. As the group neared the front door, Nelson, who had wanted to enter with guns blazing, unnecessarily shot the glass out of the front door. Outside he took over and ordered the five girls to stand on the running boards. One said she couldn't hold on, and Dillinger let her step off. A teller, Leo Olson, told us that he took her place. A rifle shot made a hole in the car's radiator. After a block the motor sputtered and stopped. The five hostages jumped off the running boards, but a shot in the air brought them back.

The Packard was restarted and off it went, followed by Sheriff Melvin Sells and three men. The teller on the running board thought a getaway car would career at top speed, but they were going less than twenty-five miles an hour. The driver even slowed cautiously when passing a milk wagon drawn by horses. The teller called out that the four girls on the running boards were freezing, and Dillinger said, "Well, come in the car." The shivering girls crammed themselves into the backseat, sitting on the laps of three robbers.

"What about me?" asked Olson, who was soaked with perspiration despite the cold.

Dillinger replied, "You're through!" and Olson was sure he'd be shot. But Dillinger merely told him to hop off.

A few miles later the car stalled for good. A farmer in a Dodge was waved down, and while the five girls waited fearfully on the road, gasoline cans were shifted from the Packard to the Dodge. Just then Sheriff Sells and his men approached, having been delayed by punctures from the roofing tacks tossed on the road by Baby Face Nelson. Sells explained to us that they were afraid to fire because of the girls, and watched as the gang scrambled into the Dodge and roared away.

After a brief vacation in St. Paul, Toshiko and I headed for northern Wisconsin—our goal Little Bohemia, the lodge where the FBI had trapped the remnants of the Dillinger gang. The owner of the lodge, Emil Wanatka, and his son both told all they knew. The son had liked Dillinger but detested Baby Face Nelson, who, while playing catch with him, would viciously burn in the ball. We then went back to the Indiana State Prison, where Toshiko was allowed to accompany me for another long session with Raymond Moseley.

In nearby Indianapolis our greatest discovery was Mary Kinder, a member of the Dillinger gang who knew far more about him than any other living person. During the first interview it was obvious that she was essential to the book, and for the first time I offered money for full disclosure. She agreed, for five hundred dollars. Realizing she was an alcoholic, I insisted that two full days of interviews take place in our motel so I could keep her sober. She took an adjoining room, and by the end of the first day Toshiko had several tapes. After dinner I doled out drinks, and the next morning Mary continued. A rounded view of Dillinger emerged, as well as a detailed picture of life as a gangster. When she met Dillinger, Mary had been twenty-two—slender, red-haired, and an inch under five feet. One of thirteen children, she had helped support the others after her father's death. Her ties with the Indiana State Prison were diverse. Within its walls she had, in addition to two brothers, the man she loved—Pierpont.

She had arranged to help with the mass breakout from Michigan City, provided her brother, Earl, was added to the list of escapees. Dillinger assigned her the job of finding a safe apartment in Indianapolis for the escapees. She was also to buy six suits in six different stores. She drove one of the two cars for the bank robbery in St. Mary's to get money to break Dillinger out of prison in Lima, Ohio. She recalled that as one of the gang was entering the bank that afternoon a radio was broadcasting the opening game of the World Series between the Washington Senators and the New York Giants.

She grinned as she revealed they hadn't known the bank was legally closed by the Treasury Department during the Bank Holiday and was just making change for local merchants. But by luck a fairly large sum of money had just arrived from the mint for use when the bank reopened. They got eleven thousand dollars—more than double the amount they expected. But the money was too new to spend. Mary delighted in telling how she baked the bills in an oven, sprinkled them with water, and then rebaked them. But they still looked new, and she had to repeat the process until, after several days, the bills looked worn enough to pass. "Oh," she said wistfully, "them was the good old days!"

After the gang was arrested in Tucson, bail for Mary was set at five thousand dollars, but the gallant Pierpont spoke up: "I don't care what you do to me, but that little woman had nothing to do with it." "He sure was a gentleman!" she soulfully noted.

When she was being interviewed at the courthouse, Mary regretfully said, according to the news story, "I presume no one understands us, but I love Harry Pierpont. . . . I realize that after we arrive in Indiana we may never meet again, for the law intends, if possible, to 'burn' him on a murder charge. That's why I want to marry him, and when the vows are taken by us we will be united forever—in spirit at least. If the worst comes, I shall love him more even in death than life."

Asked what she thought of Baby Face Nelson, she said he had been a lousy touring companion. But she liked Dillinger, who trusted her. After the Sioux Falls job he had sent her an envelope containing two thousand dollars, a good part of his cash share in that robbery. She wanted the money to help Pierpont, who was being tried in Lima. But that case was lost, she said with a sigh, and she knew her lover would be executed in the electric chair.

The next time she saw Dillinger he had just had his face changed. "You look like you got the mumps or something, Johnnie," she said. He laughed; but when Mary remarked that it was obvious Pierpont was going to be executed, he became serious. "Mary, of all the gang you're the only one that's lucky." Then, she recalled, he grinned crookedly. "My time's coming, but I don't know when it'll be."

By the end of our travels I knew we had enough material for our book. If the FBI would let us see its records, fine. But if it would not cooperate, we had plenty. The interviews with FBI men had all resulted from my own contacts. And I realized that the material they had given me in Washington was primarily the standard stuff passed out to every hick newspaper. They had given me not one line of "inside" information. But no matter—I felt that I knew a lot more about Dillinger than they did.

Eventually J. Edgar Hoover's office did make available the names and addresses of a number of agents who had participated not only in the Dillinger chase but in the kidnapping capers. I was impressed that Hoover wanted the truth to come out no matter how embarrassing for the FBI or himself. We interviewed two agents who were at the Biograph Theater and three who were at Little Bohemia, and we acquired additional rich material for the Ma Barker, Machine Gun Kelly, and Pretty Boy Floyd stories. At last I had what I needed to make the bank robberies and the final end of Dillinger come alive.

{5}

The Last 100 Days

By April 1962 I had sent off the final draft of *The Dillinger Days* and was already planning a new book—about the resistance in Europe before and during World War II. I went to Washington to spread the word of my intentions and ask for leads. When I returned to Red Bank I received a phone call from Cornelius Ryan, whom I had interviewed for *Battle*.

To my surprise, Connie pleaded with me to drop my project because he was almost finished with a book on the same subject based primarily on the papers of William Donovan, head of OSS. I agreed, and the next day I thought up my most ambitious undertaking to date—the last three months of World War II. The narrative would start in early February 1945, with the fateful Yalta Conference. Russian troops were only fifty miles from Berlin and powerful American and British forces were about to smash across the Rhine, yet Hitler delivered a fighting message to his generals: "We must not give up at five minutes before midnight!" I could picture one dramatic scene after another: the horrendous bombing of Dresden; the daring crossing at the Remagen Bridge; the death of a million German civilians in the east trying to escape the vengeful Red Army; Himmler's secret plans to save the remaining Jews and thereby save his own skin; Eisenhower's controversial decision not to take Berlin; the heroic defense of Prague by an army of Russian prisoners; and Hitler's final days in the Berlin bunker.

I immediately wrote Manteuffel and Skorzeny and got instant replies; Manteuffel would introduce me to Wehrmacht survivors and Skorzeny to the SS. Skorzeny also promised to bring Hitler's greatest hero, the pilot Hans-Ulrich Rudel, from South America to Madrid. I phoned Robert Meskill, the assistant managing director of *Look,* and gave him a brief outline. He told me to come to his office, and in a three-hour session with Bob and Mike Land, his assistant, I gave them an enthusiastic word picture featuring Skorzeny and Manteuffel, a proposal that a more cautious managing director would probably have turned down. Bob, who reminded me of a priest, turned to Mike, who nodded. "Sounds good," said Bob, and told me he'd take the idea to his chief.

"Half the things I now think are great," I warned him, "will probably not pan out, but I'm going to spend a year in Europe and will find even better material."

By that time Toshiko and I were so exhausted that we decided to spend a few months in Japan. After all, I had promised her parents I'd bring her back in a few years. Late in June we arrived in Tokyo, and after two weeks with her family we started on a tour, stopping over in Japanese hotels. Toshiko feared that I would be bothered by sleeping on the floor, but I had slept in boxcars and on cement floors, and I loved everything—including the bathing and the nightly massages. Upon returning to Tokyo, I received a call from Rog Terrill, my agent, inviting me to appear on a special TV show on Pearl Harbor, together with Drew Middleton, the military expert of the *New York Times,* and Joseph Heller, author of a satirical novel on the military, *Catch-22.* In a way, I think we disappointed our TV host because we liked each other and made no scathing rebuttals.

Leaving Toshiko in Japan to spend a few weeks with her family, I was greeted on arrival by good news: *Look* was going to run three installments of *The Last 100 Days* and I would be getting about five dollars a word. Now we'd have enough to do research all over Europe for a year. And as I was preparing to leave Red Bank I received more good news: I got word well ahead of time that *The Dillinger Days* was scheduled to be reviewed on the front page of the *New York Times Book Review,* and on page two would be a feature story about our research. I was interviewed, and I promised to lend the *Times* writer my tapes on Mary Kinder, the key member of the Dillinger gang we had met in Indiana.

Through the housing department at the Pentagon I rented a large apartment in one of the three buildings within easy walking distance of the Pentagon. I spent most of my time combing the Pentagon files as well as those at the National Archives and the Record Service in Alexandria. Allen Dulles gave me material on Operation Sunrise, the secret surrender of SS troops in Italy by General Karl Wolff. I could get all the details, he said, in Germany from his assistant, Gero von Gaevernitz, who had stage-managed the entire operation and might possibly arrange an interview with General Wolff, now in prison. By this time Toshiko had returned from Japan, and she took over the job of copying the material I had borrowed.

I left her alone for two days while I flew to Columbus, Ohio, to interview General William Hoge, who had taken the Remagen bridge, and by the end of three hours knew I would feature his story in the book. When General

Hoge learned that his men had reached the bridge, he ordered them to cross over and prevent it from being blown up. A few minutes later he received a message from III Corps, canceling his mission to cross the bridge.

"I was watching from the hill. I scanned the bridge. Before me lay one of the great opportunities of the war, and now I couldn't take it—if I followed orders. The infantry assault hadn't yet started across. I knew it was not too late to stop the entire operation, and I hesitated for a few seconds. It was a hard but clear choice for a soldier. If I succeeded, I'd be a hero; if I failed, I could very well lose my command and ruin my military career." He paused and was thoughtful, then said, "I was going to take the damned bridge. To hell with the consequences!"

The Hammelburg Disaster

As I was getting ready to leave, he stopped me. "You've come a long way, John," he said. He was very serious. "It's time I told the truth about Patton and Hammelburg." I was sure this concerned the suspicions that Patton had known that his son-in-law, Johnny Waters, was in a prison camp at Hammelburg and had organized a daring attack to free the prisoners. It had ended in disaster, with Patton persistently asserting he was unaware that Waters was in the camp.

"He knew," said Hoge. After taking the Remagen bridge, Hoge had been promoted and made commander of the 4th Armored Division. "I was given a strange mission. General Patton wanted a special expedition sent about sixty miles behind enemy lines to free nine hundred American prisoners in a POW camp at Hammelburg. I thought this was curious but said nothing. A few hours later, Patton himself telephoned me, and I noticed his voice was pitched even higher than usual. 'This is going to make MacArthur's raid on Cabanatuan [a prison camp in the Philippines recently liberated by MacArthur] look like peanuts!' I didn't say anything but complained to the corps commander, General Manton Eddy, that I didn't like the idea. Why take such a great risk at this late stage in the war? There were many POW camps, and what was so important about Hammelburg?

"I knew my feelings were shared by others and assumed the matter was dropped—until one of Patton's aides, Major Alexander Stiller, arrived and told me he was supposed to go along on the expedition." Stiller was a close friend of Patton's, having served on his staff in World War I. "The next morning Patton telephoned me with orders to carry out the plan. I said I couldn't spare even a single man or tank." Hoge shook his head. "It's hard to believe, but Patton didn't lose his temper. He began *wheedling* me, promising to replace every man and every vehicle I lost. I was embarrassed by the almost pleading tone in his voice, and I turned to look at Stiller, who was listening on another phone. I was baffled. Then Stiller said in a low voice, 'The Old Man is absolutely determined. Johnny Waters is one of the prisoners.' "

Hoge said he reluctantly sent a brigadier general to Lieutenant Colonel Creighton Abrams (who would later become army chief of staff), whose Combat Command B had just seized a bridge not too far from Hammelburg. It was up to him to send a special task force to Hammelburg. "Abrams immediately phoned me and said it would take his entire combat command to get through. And I had to tell him the corps commander, a three-star general in command of three divisions, refused to divert an entire combat team for such a mission. Disappointed as Abrams was by this order from the top, he complied. It was now his tough task to turn over the mission to Captain Abraham Baum of the Bronx and 307 men."

I knew I would have to get further confirmation of what could be a major story, and one day when we were in Frankfurt am Main a contingent of officers approached us as we were walking down a corridor of the huge headquarters building. In the center was Abrams. He greeted us warmly; and when I told him Bill Hoge had spilled the beans on Hammelburg, he swore.

"You others go on," he said and escorted Toshiko and me into the nearest office. He shooed out the occupants and for the next hour or so told us his story. His Combat Command B had just seized a bridge across the Main. He was ordered by Brigadier General W. L. Roberts, the assistant commander of his division, to send a special task force to Hammelburg. "I phoned Bill Hoge and told him that a reinforced company alone would be wiped out. If it had to be done, the entire combat command should go. But Hoge told me General Manton Eddy, the XII Corps commander, had already refused to divert a combat command for such a mission. And so I had to turn over the job to Captain Abe Baum, intelligence officer of the 10th Armored Infantry Battalion."

Abraham Baum, formerly a pattern cutter in a blouse factory, was six feet two, rangy, and extremely aggressive. His crewcut hair, mustache, and grin, explained Abrams, added to his cocksure appearance. "He was still yawning when I told him to take a task force behind enemy lines and bring back nine hundred American prisoners. I gave no reason and he didn't need one. He just turned to his battalion commander and jokingly said, 'This is no way to get rid of me. I'll be back.' I told him to pick his men and get going."

Later, in New York, I interviewed Abe Baum in his own factory in the garment district. He still looked just as Abrams had described him, and I got the extraordinary story of how Task Force Baum—307 men, all battle-tested and full of fight—plunged more than sixty miles through enemy lines with ten Shermans and six light tanks, three 105mm assault guns, twenty-seven half-tracks for hauling back the prisoners, and seven jeeps. It would have made a scenario for a hair-raising movie, and Baum gave me all the details of how they broke through villages and towns.

Later I interviewed several of his men. They told me that when one young officer saw that some of those killed were girls in uniform, he vomited. As they rolled into Gemunden, Sergeant Donald Yoerk was amazed to see German soldiers walking nonchalantly in the streets carrying briefcases. All the previous towns had been waiting for the Americans, but this town was completely unaware that an enemy task force was on the loose.

Sergeant Yoerk, in one of the last tanks, then saw a train coming out of the marshaling yards and heading in his direction. From the next tank Frank Malinski hit the engine with his first shot and then began blasting the cars. Suddenly an ammunition car blew up. Farther ahead the light tanks had already set fire to several barges on the river and ripped apart a combination passenger-freight train. The Shermans moved up and knocked out a dozen more trains, tying up the entire network of yards. By chance a German division was just detraining and was thrown into confusion by the small task force. At this point Baum and Lieutenant William Nutto were wounded by a panzerfaust explosion. Feeling pain in his right hand and knee, Baum yelled, "Let's get the hell out of here!" He pulled back the column.

The main road to Hammelburg was now cut off, and Baum quickly detoured north along the west bank of the Sinn River. Then they were lucky. A German paratrooper who was home on sick leave and tired of the war told Baum where they could cross the river eight miles down the road. A mile later the Volkswagen of a German general blundered into the column. "Get the son of a bitch into a half-track and let's get going," yelled Baum.

Finally, at 2:30 P.M., the town of Hammelburg came into view. As the column started up a steep hill to the prison camp, a German tank stuck its nose around the corner ahead, then another tank, and another. The fight for Oflag XIIIB was on. The object of this mission, Lieutenant Colonel John Waters, Patton's son-in-law, was watching the action from the POW headquarters building. He could see several American tanks roll across the field, firing into the Serbian barracks. The German camp commander, Major General Günther von Goeckel, told Waters that he was now an American prisoner and the war was over. He then asked if any American would volunteer to go out and stop the firing. "Okay, I'll go out," said Waters and went forward with a German interpreter and two U.S. volunteers, one carrying an American flag and the other a white sheet on a pole.

By now Baum had lost five half-tracks and three jeeps, but his six Shermans had knocked out three German tanks and three or four ammunition trucks. Smoke was billowing as the Waters party headed toward Task Force Baum. Just ahead a soldier in camouflage uniform ran toward them. Waters, not knowing whether he was German or American, called out, *"Amerikanisch!"*

The soldier was German and fired his rifle. Waters felt as if he had been hit with a baseball bat. He was then put in a blanket and carried back to camp.

The exhausted Task Force Baum started back with as many prisoners as they could carry, and by 2:00 A.M. they were in grave trouble. Baum now had only a hundred men who could fight, and he himself was wounded. He had six light and three medium tanks, three assault guns, and twenty-two half-tracks. They were also almost surrounded, and soon were being annihilated by an enemy they could not see. Baum yelled out to break up in groups of four and escape. He started off with one of the American prisoners they had rescued as well as Major Stiller, Patton's friend, who had proved to be a silent but efficient fighter. They were soon tracked down by dogs, and Baum was wounded for the third time. He had just enough time to throw away his dog tags lest the Germans find out he was Jewish. It was the end of Task Force Baum.

Task Force Baum appeared to have been a complete failure, but the gallant force had left such a path of destruction in its wake that the German Seventh Army headquarters had been deeply confused; it diverted the equivalent of several divisions to guard strategic crossroads and bridges while another large force was scouting the hills with dogs trying to round up about a hundred liberated Americans and Russians. Later I talked with General Waters, who had been severely wounded. "So Dad knew," he finally said sadly. I nodded. He didn't hold it against me that I was going to publish this story. It was a fact. Neither did the Patton family, who understood, and would become our good friends.

At about this time while we were in Washington I had learned that hopes of *The Dillinger Days* becoming a best-seller were dim owing to a New York City newspaper strike. There would be no chance now for my page-one review in the *Times Book Review.*

The newspaper strike of 1962–1963 delayed the publication of *The Dil-*

linger Days. Furthermore, the *Times* writer had lost my Mary Kinder tapes. But in mid-January two installments of *The Dillinger Days* did come out in *Look* and we were at long last solvent. The book was finally published in February 1963, but there were still no reviews in New York. Although I did eventually appear again on the *Today* show to plug *Dillinger,* and it did win the Mark Twain Award for the best book on an American, the book would obviously never get on the best-seller list.

Then we received tragic news: Rogers Terrill, my agent, had died. It seemed so sudden, even though we had long been concerned about his emphysema. He had done much for my career. His wife told us that his good friend Paul Reynolds had taken over his clients. I agreed to this, since Mr. Reynolds was one of the top agents in New York.

[6]

The Search Begins

In mid-April 1963 we boarded a plane for Frankfurt am Main. It was To-shiko's first trip to Europe. At Frankfurt we picked up the red Volvo we had ordered, then stopped over in Heidelberg for several days so I could show her my favorite German city. From there we proceeded to Stuttgart, where we checked in with Seventh Army before heading for our headquarters, Munich.

In the next eight months we would visit sixteen countries in Europe including five behind the Iron Curtain, interviewing more than four hundred people on both sides, some of them five and six times. They ranged from privates to generals and from German civilians who had fled the vengeful Red Army to a former prime minister of England. I would go to a prison in Munich to see SS General Karl Wolff, the central figure in Operation Sunrise, and to Count Folke Bernadotte's ancestral home near Stockholm to get details of his secret negotiations with Himmler to end the war. We would travel on both sides of the Oder River to inspect the battlefields near Frank-furt an der Oder; to the site of the Shell House in Copenhagen; to the Citadel in Budapest; to the Warsaw Ghetto; to Dachau, Buchenwald, Auschwitz, and Sachsenhausen; and to the home of Admiral Karl Dönitz near Hamburg. In the bar of the Hotel Sacher we would listen to Major Carl Szokoll's story of the Vienna Uprising; in the dining room of the House of Lords we would talk with Clement Attlee; and in the Madrid airport we would hear the incredible tale of Hitler's favorite fighter, Hans-Ulrich Rudel, with Hitler's other favorite, Otto Skorzeny, as interpreter.

Peacemaking Efforts by Himmler and Ribbentrop

One of our most complicated stories involved the attempts of high-ranking Nazis to secretly negotiate a peace settlement in the last chaotic months before the end of the war. In two long interviews in Munich with Dr. Peter

Kleist, a Ribbentrop assistant, we learned that both his chief and Himmler had been desperately trying to accomplish the same thing independently. Ribbentrop and Himmler had been rivals for years, each striving to outdo the other in the Führer's eyes.

The peacemaking effort had been started by one of Himmler's closest associates, Karl Wolff, the SS chief in Italy. He was encouraging his chief to come out in the open with Hitler, but the terrified Himmler would not listen. Wolff, a big, energetic, and rather simpleminded man who ardently believed in National Socialism, decided to approach the Führer personally and, on reporting to Hitler's office on February 6, found him with Ribbentrop. "My Führer," he said, "it is obvious from evidence I have gathered from my own particular field that there are natural differences among the unnatural allies." During an interview in his prison cell Wolff told me that he was referring to Roosevelt, Churchill, and Stalin. "But please do not feel offended if I say that I don't believe this alliance will split up of itself without our active intervention."

Hitler had cocked his head and kept snapping his fingers until finally he smiled and dismissed Ribbentrop and Wolff. These two began talking excitedly about the Führer's apparently receptive attitude toward the daring suggestion. He had not said a word, but he had not said no. The two then separated, Ribbentrop to explore possibilities for peace in Sweden and Wolff in Italy.

Wolff was convinced that the only valid procedure was to arrange an orderly surrender of German forces so that the allies could take over northern Italy before the left-wing partisans seized control. One of his trusted subordinates proposed that they contact Allen Dulles, who had opened an office in Berne as Donovan's OSS representative. This was the birth of Operation Sunrise in Italy.

But Wolff's forthright plunge into this scheme frightened Himmler, who didn't want to know any of the details. Instead he concentrated on setting up negotiations with the Allies which would save Jewish prisoners in the concentration camps. These efforts were not motivated by humanitarian feelings but were a form of blackmail, since it seemed obvious that one and a half million lives could be used ruthlessly as a strong bargaining factor in a negotiated peace.

Ribbentrop's approach to a negotiated peace also followed this path, and on his behalf Dr. Kleist started negotiations with the World Jewish Congress for the release of Jewish prisoners. "I first spoke to Count Folke Bernadotte, the vice president of the Swedish Red Cross. I then took up this touchy subject with Himmler's assistant, SS General Ernst Kaltenbrunner," Kleist recalled. Although Kaltenbrunner listened in stony silence, a few days later he sent for Kleist, pumped his hand, and told him that Himmler was "definitely willing to take up this Swedish possibility." To Kleist's amazement he than revealed that there were not *one* and a half, but *two* and a half million Jews in their hands. "In my excitement," said Kleist, "I also reported this information to Count Bernadotte."

This resulted in the count's first meeting with Himmler in Berlin on February 18, 1945. Kleist told us what little he knew about Himmler's meeting the next day with Bernadotte and the subsequent crucial meetings between Himmler and Bernadotte. Kleist urged us to go to Sweden and get the details of these meetings from Bernadotte's widow and his assistants. Consequently we started north in our Volvo, planning to spend several days in Holland before heading for Denmark and Sweden.

When we came to the German border on our way to Nijmegen, Holland, we had what we had to admit was a typical experience with a certain type of German. While waiting in line for customs, Toshiko left about ten yards of space between us and the car ahead. Instantly there was a terrific roar as two German cars darted from nowhere and squeezed in ahead of us. We had tried to be objective during recent weeks, but it was obvious that a large number of Germans acted as if they still owned the world. They merely tolerated foreigners, even when traveling in foreign countries.

In Holland we learned they were much hated and feared, for many were now buying up real estate in the best parts of that country. Amsterdam was delightful, its people a refreshing change after Germany—cheerful, humorous, and unobtrusively helpful.

Our next stop was Denmark, where we received excellent cooperation from the press division of the Foreign Office. One of the most vivid and horrifying wartime events, we discovered, had been the Allied pinpoint bombing in Copenhagen of Gestapo headquarters, located in the Shell House, for the purpose of burning incriminating evidence that the Nazis could use against Sweden, as well as other records. One British plane fell near a large convent school, and the following planes, believing this was the target, dropped their bombs on it, killing eighty-eight children.

The deputy chief of the Foreign Ministry, head of the Danish Information Section who had been the wartime leader of the illegal press, informed us that the Germans were hated as much now as ever. They crowded the beaches, which were state property, and built great sand barricades with flags on top warning others to keep off. We took a picture of a group of these *Festungen,* several of them actually featuring a cardboard sign, OCCUPIED.

I decided to fly to Stockholm alone to interview Countess Bernadotte. She had been widowed when, after surviving all the dangers of World War II, her husband was assassinated in Jerusalem when the Stern gang blew up the King David Hotel in 1948. She turned out to be an American and looked like a combination of Amelia Earhart and Katharine Hepburn. Her maiden name was Manville; her father was an asbestos and roofing magnate. She spoke freely about everything she knew concerning the Himmler-Bernadotte meetings.

My most important interviews were with Bernadotte's assistant, who had been present during the count's meetings with Himmler in March 1945. On the phone he told me he could only talk off the record, but upon learning I'd written *Battle,* he immediately thawed out and said that I could use whatever I wanted.

The count had firmly told Himmler that what had aroused great indignation even in neutral Sweden was the German seizure of hostages and the murder of innocent people. He also asked permission for the Swedish Red Cross to work in the concentration camps, and Himmler could see no reason this could not be arranged. After fencing on minor matters, Bernadotte politely questioned the Nazi treatment of Jews. "Won't you admit there are decent people among the Jews, just as there are among all races? I have Jewish friends."

"You're right, but you in Sweden have no Jewish problem and therefore can't understand the German point of view," Himmler replied.

Bernadotte then proceeded to Ribbentrop's office. The foreign minister was more than eager to help the count, but Ribbentrop's overbearing good humor only rankled Bernadotte, who finally politely excused himself. He could barely stand to be in the same room with this former liquor salesman.

Bernadotte's next meeting with Himmler, also in Berlin, came on March 31, 1945, when it seemed apparent that the Russians would soon charge across the Oder and head for Berlin. Even Bormann, Hitler's closest associate, was writing his wife that desperation hung over the city like a cloud. Yet Himmler still maintained that the military situation was not hopeless. The count thereafter restricted the conversation to his own mission, asking only that all Danes and Norwegians be transferred at once to Sweden. Himmler said he couldn't do this and changed the subject. The count still had not given up hope of turning Himmler around. He would try harder at the next and final meeting on April 23, a week before Hitler shot himself.

The description of this occasion by the count's assistant sounded like a movie directed by someone with a macabre sense of humor. The scene: the Swedish consulate in Lübeck, a German port on the Baltic north of Hamburg. The time: just before midnight. Himmler and Schellenburg entered the darkened house and were met by Bernadotte, who led them into a small room lit only by two flickering candles. In the ghostly atmosphere Himmler's face looked even more furtive and indecisive than usual. The Reichsführer said that if the German people were crushed, then Hitler would be remembered as a hero and martyr. Above all, Himmler was fixated on saving millions of Germans from a Russian occupation. Bernadotte agreed to take the capitulation message and Himmler's conditions to his government. "What will you do," he asked, "if your offer is turned down?"

"In that event I shall take over command on the eastern front and be killed in battle." All watched as Himmler strode purposefully into the dark and mounted his car as if it were a noble steed. He stepped on the gas and it lunged out of control through a hedge into a barbed-wire fence. It took all the Swedes and all the Germans to shove the car clear. As it lurched off in comical jerks, Bernadotte remarked, "There's something symbolic about all this!" And that was the end of the attempts by Ribbentrop and Himmler to negotiate peace through the Swedes.

Operation Sunrise

We soon discovered that while Himmler was futilely negotiating with Bernadotte in the north, his obstreperous SS commander in Italy, Karl Wolff, was successfully dickering in the south with Gero von Gaevernitz, the representative of Dulles. Toshiko and I had first learned about Operation Sunrise from Allen Dulles, who had given us Gaevernitz's address in a beautiful town south of Munich. He was as handsome and urbane as Dulles had described him and still had a dash of mystery about him. He claimed to have no ties with the CIA, the offspring of the OSS, but neither Toshiko nor I believed him. His father had been a noted university professor and political liberal, but Gero had come to America in 1924 to enter the international banking business and become an American citizen. In 1942 he was made Dulles's assistant in Berne, and a month after Yalta, in the spring of 1945, he secretly met with SS General Karl Wolff in Switzerland and listened to his offer to surrender all SS troops in Italy. When Wolff promised he would make no other Allied deals, both Dulles and Gaevernitz believed him. "We informed General Donovan in Washington of the deal," explained Gaevernitz, "and were instructed to continue negotiations under the code name Operation Sunrise. . . . On March 19, Wolff secretly crossed into Switzerland and came to my house in Ancona near Locarno. Here he met with Mr. Dulles and two generals from the staff of Field Marshal Harold Alexander, commander of all Allied forces in Italy. I served as the interpreter. Wolff was very worried. Kesselring had just been replaced by Vietinghof, and this threatened the whole operation. Had Hitler learned about the negotiations? Wolff feared he might be arrested on his return to Italy, but he promised to carry out the surrender if possible. I led him onto the terrace and asked how many political prisoners were in Italian concentration camps. Several thousand at least, he thought, adding, 'There are orders to kill them.' I asked if he would obey those orders. He said no, and I asked him to give his word of honor. He grabbed my hand and said, 'Yes, you can rely on me.' And I believed him."

Gaevernitz told us that this was just the beginning, and the rest of the story would require several more interviews. But first we should try to see General Wolff in his Munich prison. I was able to see him for thirty minutes. The head of the prison greeted me frostily and insisted on being present during the interview. By the end of the half hour, however, he had become so fascinated by Wolff's story that he let me continue for almost two hours. He even agreed to let me return the following day for another long interview. Wolff was to go on trial the following day, and the head of the prison suggested I return in several months, which I did.

At the trial Wolff was given a harsh sentence, but he was not bitter. Ironically, it was his effort on behalf of Sunrise that helped bring him to trial for atrocities. Field Marshall Alexander and Allen Dulles both felt that if he had been tried at Nuremberg, due consideration would have been given to what he had accomplished in Italy. But since there was also comparatively little evidence against Wolff at that time, he was not tried by the Allies.

At Wolff's trial, Gaevernitz testified for the defense, trying for two hours to impress upon the court what Wolff had done, and he later wrote that the entire atmosphere of the trial was unfavorable to Wolff, commenting, "This phenomenon may be explained by the fact that Wolff is the only one of the high Nazi hierarchy still alive."

During our three interviews Wolff never showed any bitterness—he appeared grateful that people like Gaevernitz, Dulles, and Alexander had trusted him.

Gero Gaevernitz had also given us the address of Major Max Waibel, an intelligence officer in the Swiss army. On his own initiative he had played a leading role in operation Sunrise. At the time he was a forty-four-year-old career officer who had studied at two universities and earned a doctorate in political science. At his home in Switzerland he told us that he knew his career would have been ruined if he had been caught in the conspiracy, but if he succeeded many thousands of lives would be saved. It was worth the risk.

It was Waibel who had invited Gaevernitz to dinner in 1945 and revealed that he had a well-connected friend (General Wolff) who wanted to discuss a matter of mutual interest with them. Once Wolff learned that Dulles was involved, he abandoned his efforts to negotiate through the Pope or the English.

On March 8, the day the bridge at Remagen was seized, one of Waibel's men brought General Wolff and several companions to Zürich, where they were ensconced in a private room at a hospital. That night Waibel took Dulles and Gaevernitz to the hospital. They all then moved, under cover of darkness, to an old-fashioned building near the lake where Dulles maintained an apartment for secret meetings. Wolff agreed that the war was irretrievably lost for Germany, and he'd made up his mind that peace must be bought—even at the price of personal humiliation. Was it clear that only an unconditional surrender could be considered? "Yes," said Wolff.

It was obvious to Dulles that Wolff, though an ardent National Socialist, was not a creature of either Hitler or Himmler. He therefore agreed to deal with Wolff—provided Wolff make no other Allied contacts. Wolff agreed, and also promised to protect the lives of prisoners and prevent the destruction of factories, power stations, and art treasures. Gaevernitz then had the German party escorted back to the border. Wolff told me that during this crucial period he had received a message from Kaltenbrunner instructing him to report at once to Innsbruck, a town just on the other side of the Austrian-Italian border. Wolff felt sure that Himmler's men had somehow learned about the negotiations with Dulles and that a trip to Innsbruck would end in jail or death. He therefore decided to ignore the instructions.

Then Himmler personally summoned him to Berlin, where he accused Wolff of treason; Kaltenbrunner's spies in Switzerland had indeed found out all about the negotiations with Dulles. Himmler also accused his erstwhile friend of stupidity; if Hitler found out he would kill them all.

"He was a coward!" Wolff stated flatly. Then Wolff suggested something that turned the Reichsführer pale: "We should both go to the Führer and tell him everything." For a moment Himmler couldn't speak, and finally said, "It's impossible for you to deal with Dulles." He flatly forbade Wolff to return to Switzerland. But Wolff assured me he was now so disgusted with Himmler that he disobeyed and continued the negotiations. When Himmler learned that Wolff was still negotiating, he again ordered him to Berlin "posthaste." Wolff first agreed, then wrote Himmler he could not come. The next day, April 14, Himmler phoned twice, again ordering Wolff to Berlin. He ignored both messages and then asked for advice from Dulles, who told Toshiko and me that he had warned Wolff not to go to Berlin but to flee to Switzerland with his family. Nevertheless, Wolff finally decided he had to go to Berlin and face both Hitler and Himmler.

On the evening of April 16 he flew to an airport sixteen miles south of the capital and the next morning drove to a nearby sanatorium and had lunch with Himmler. "I convinced him," he told me with a grim grin, "that I'd only done what Hitler wanted me to do." At that moment Kaltenbrunner burst in and said he'd just received a message from an agent who reported that Wolff and the Vatican were carrying on secret negotiations, and the final signing of a cease-fire on the entire Italian front could be expected in a few days. "I swore to the Reichsführer that I had never personally negotiated with the Pope, since I'd only done so through a delegate. I was so sincere that Himmler believed me, but Kaltenbrunner didn't, and all three of us had a mouth fight that lasted an hour. I finally insisted we all go to Berlin and see the Führer." Himmler refused to go, but Kaltenbrunner, still boiling, accompanied Wolff.

They encountered Hitler in the corridor of the bunker. He was not angry, only surprised to see Wolff. "Good!" he said in a normal tone. "Please wait until the briefing is over." A few hours later, Wolff was summoned into the conference room. "Kaltenbrunner and Himmler have told me of your negotiations in Switzerland with Mr. Dulles," the Führer said coolly. He stepped up close to Wolff. "What made you disregard my authority so flagrantly?"

Wolff reminded him of their meeting with Ribbentrop on February 6: "You heard me suggest," he said, "that if we could not be sure that these secret and special weapons would be ready in time, we should enter into negotiations with the Allies." Wolff explained that he didn't once break eye contact with Hitler. "I felt that if I did, I'd lose my life." He continued to address Hitler in a calm and frank tone. "Now I'm happy to report to you, my Führer, that I have succeeded in opening doors, through Mr. Dulles, to the president, Prime Minister Churchill, and Field Marshal Alexander. I request instructions for the future."

Wolff's bold manner seemed to stun Hitler. He stared at the general for a moment, then said, "Good. I accept your presentation. You're fantastically lucky. If you had failed, I would have had to drop you exactly as I dropped Hess."

"And that was the last I ever saw of my Führer," said Wolff. He had returned to Italy, and two days later Truman and Churchill ordered all future contact with General Wolff cut off in order to avoid friction with Stalin. The Combined Chiefs of Staff ordered the OSS to immediately "regard the whole matter as now closed." The excuse was that complications had "arisen with the Russians over this matter."

Unaware that he had been abandoned, General Wolff on April 23 secretly crossed the border to Switzerland with two trusted officers to arrange the surrender terms. They were met by Waibel, but the major did not reveal that the Allies had broken off all negotiations until they reached his home in Lucerne. The three Germans were furious. So was Waibel, but he tried to calm them down. He telephoned Dulles, who agreed to send a cable to Field Marshal Alexander in Naples, who would request the Combined Chiefs of Staff to let Dulles resume contact with Wolff.

The problem, Waibel told me at his home in Switzerland as if he were reliving the incident, was horrendous. How could he keep Wolff in his home until the matter was worked out? Wolff was already insisting that he could not stay away from his headquarters much longer. He had also just received a telegram from Himmler which had been phoned to him at Waibel's home. He was to hold the Italian front and undertake "no negotiations of any kind." Wolff was furious.

"I already knew," explained Waibel, "that the situation in Rome was also critical, with Mussolini threatening to negotiate a surrender himself by broadcasting to the world his denunciation of the Germans." That night ten cars loaded with Il Duce's entourage, including Marshal Rodolfo Graziani and the German escort, headed north to Lake Como. In one car was Clara Petacci, Mussolini's mistress, who had just written a friend, "I am following my destiny. I don't know what will become of me, but I cannot question my fate."

When no word had been received from Dulles by midnight, Wolff returned to Italy. By coincidence he was so exhausted that he decided to spend the night at SS border headquarters on the west shore of Lake Como. As he was preparing for bed, Marshal Graziani unexpectedly appeared. He had left Il Duce's party at Como, not five miles down the lake, and was seeking the protection of the SS. Once again I was hearing a story that sounded like a Hollywood thriller. Wolff persuaded the marshal to surrender all his troops in the best interests of Italy, and reluctantly Graziani wrote out a document granting Wolff the authority to surrender the entire Italian army.

"Later that morning," Waibel continued, "I received a report that 'a big fish' would soon be caught at Lake Como. I made a few discreet inquiries, and this verified my suspicion that the 'big fish' was Wolff. I arranged to meet an agent that evening at the Chiasso railroad station and we would try to find some way to save Wolff. I then phoned Gaevernitz and told him if we didn't act promptly Wolff would be killed and the show would be over."

Gero had already told us that he had then urged Dulles to help, but he had definite orders to make no further contacts. He then asked if he could get the help of an OSS agent, Donald James Jones, posing as the American vice-consul in Lugano. When Dulles said his hands were tied, Gaevernitz decided to act on his own and told his chief, "I'm going on a little trip and will return in two or three days." Dulles didn't ask where his aide was bound for, nor did he want to know. He merely said a casual goodbye, but Gero was sure there was a twinkle in his eye.

Gero located Waibel, and that evening they got off the train at Chiasso, a Swiss town on the Italian border not far from Como. To their surprise they were met by Jones, the OSS agent Gero had requested. "I've been waiting for you," said Jones. "I understand you want to liberate Wolff." Waibel pretended the matter had nothing to do with the Dulles office and said there was considerable Swiss interest in saving Wolff. Jones agreed, and also agreed to make a bold dash through the partisan lines, where he was well known.

Waibel and Gero now took a chance and phoned the hotel on Lake Como where Wolff was staying. Incredibly the line was open, and Wolff was told that two cars would soon attempt to break through and rescue him. At 10:00 P.M., Jones's raiding party drove out of Chiasso. Gaevernitz and Waibel waited in a small restaurant for two hours and then walked up to the border. At 2:00 A.M., two cars approached and stopped. It was Jones's party. A bulky man emerged from one of the cars and headed directly for Gaevernitz. It was Wolff. "I'll never forget what you have done for me," he said. He wrote a letter to the SS commander in Milan ordering him to stop fighting the partisans. He then handed over the document signed by Marshal Graziani and promised to use his influence to prevent destruction of property and to protect the lives of political prisoners.

"What would you have done," asked Gaevernitz, "if Himmler suddenly said, 'I'm taking over command and I arrest you'?"

"I would, of a course, turn around and arrest Himmler!"

Wolff headed for his new headquarters in northern Italy, and the exhausted Waibel and Gaevernitz returned to Switzerland. Gero drove to his home to get some sleep but was almost immediately wakened by a phone call from Dulles. A wire had just come from Washington permitting him to resume negotiations with Wolff! Now remained the risky business of carrying out the mass surrender. Dulles instructed Gaevernitz to take two of Wolff's emissaries by car and plane to Alexander's headquarters near Naples. One of the emissaries insisted that a message be sent to General Heinrich von Vietinghof, the army commander of all German forces in Italy, outlining the terms, but the other emissary was persuaded to sign the surrender document. Churchill wired Stalin: "We must rejoice together at the great surrender." But there was trouble ahead. Although Gaevernitz had managed to bring the two Germans back into Switzerland, he could not get them across the border to Austria, because the highest Swiss governing body had ordered all borders closed.

Then Dulles stepped in, abandoning protocol that morning to visit a Swiss official who happened to be shaving at that early hour. He authorized the passage. Wolff suddenly encountered further opposition, this time from fellow officers; but Hitler's death released all officers from their personal oaths of loyalty to their Führer, and eventually they allowed him to go through with the surrender.

Mussolini's Final Hours

After our interviews with Major Waibel in Switzerland in 1963, Toshiko and I headed for Italy, not only to explore the area where Wolff had met with the OSS but to get details on the last days of Mussolini in the Lake Como area. We spent the night in a small hotel and the next morning started over the Simplon Pass. We encountered dense fog, and in places we could see only a yard. But as soon as we started down the other side the weather cleared and was brilliantly bright. We passed beautiful Lake Maggiore and then entered Milan—which was soon my candidate for the worst city in the world for a stranger in a car. Our hotel was even worse than the traffic, and we were forced to eat a ghastly meal that night before returning to a losing battle with a squadron of well-armed mosquitoes.

The next day we had a long interview with Count Pier Luigi Bellini delle Stelle, head of the Italian partisan group which had captured Mussolini and Clara Petacci in a town on Lake Como. At the time I interviewed him, he was in public relations, and he was writing a book on the episode so everything was fresh in his mind.

Late that afternoon, six miles from the city of Como, along the winding road that skirted the west side of the lake, we found a hotel in a village a mile up a steep hill. It was perfect—inexpensive, comfortable, small, friendly, and with a sensational view of the lake from our window. I slept little that night as I went over Count Bellini's story in my head. He and his second-in-command, young Urbano Lazzaro, were not Party members and, in fact, strongly opposed Communism. Their main objective as partisans was to fight the Germans and Fascists and help bring back peace to Italy. At dawn on April 27, Mussolini had learned that most of his Black Shirts had surrendered to the partisans in Como. He left his hotel with Clara Petacci, his mistress, and several of his entourage to join a German convoy of twenty-eight trucks heading north up the lakeside road. By now Count Bellini had set up a roadblock at Dongo, and that afternoon young Lazzaro recognized Mussolini and arrested him before the angry crowd could kill him. (Four local partisans had recently been murdered by the Fascists.) It was several hours, the count had told us, before he realized the heavy responsibility Mussolini's capture entailed. Another German column might try to free Il Duce, or the townspeople might murder him.

Clara, who was kept in another hiding place, begged Bellini to turn Mussolini over to the Allies. "But I refused and said I'd do everything I could to see that he *didn't* fall into their hands. Il Duce's future only concerned Italians." She then spoke emotionally and at length about her love for Benito. The count admitted to us that he was deeply moved and assured her he had no intention of shooting Mussolini. He finally decided to hide them in a place near Como so they could be together.

Bellini then described the location of the house, which was not far from our own hotel on the lakeside. We took along an interpreter and soon found the three-story white building. The woman of the house, Lisa di Maria, agreed to talk. She was bright and attractive in a worn way. She told how Bellini and his men had begged her husband to shelter a wounded man. Her husband, Giacomo, had agreed. Lisa then brewed a pot of ersatz coffee. The man refused but the woman eagerly drank hers. When the man finally removed the bandages over his face she whispered to Giacomo, "It looks like Mussolini, but it's impossible. What would the Duce be doing in the home of farmers?" They finally concluded that he was a German prisoner.

She showed them to a bedroom, and she noted how he tried the bed with his hand like any tourist and said, "It's nice. Thank you." Then the pretty woman asked if she could have a second pillow. Her husband was used to sleeping with two, but she didn't use any. "And when I walked downstairs," Lisa told us, "I thought, 'What nice people they are!' "

Count Bellini had told us that on April 28 another group of partisans arrived in Dongo and surrounded the town hall. They had learned of the capture and had been ordered to shoot the pair. "I was staggered when I was told by Colonel Valerio of the National Committee of Liberation that they had been sentenced to be shot. I said it was unthinkable to shoot a woman who was only his mistress. But I was forced to take the prisoners to the town hall." At four that afternoon, Mussolini and Clara were brought to the little town square. Colonel Valerio suddenly cried out that he had been ordered to render justice to the Italian people.

Il Duce stood still, but Clara threw her arms around him and shouted, "*No!* He mustn't die!" Valerio told her to move away or she'd be shot. Sweat was running down her face as she stepped to her lover's right. Valerio aimed a machine pistol at Mussolini, but nothing happened. He grabbed his regular pistol, but this too jammed, and he called for another gun. From ten feet he then fired a burst of five shots. Mussolini crumpled to his knees, then pitched forward as Valerio swung the gun on Clara.

Bellini was furious, but the shooting had not ended. Clara's brother was found. He broke free and with a shout leaped into the lake and frantically began swimming for his life. But a volley of bullets smashed into him and he sank. It was a truly ghastly sight, said Bellini. Guns were fired in the air in a wild display of hatred. "When the shooting finally died down," recalled Bellini, "Valerio asked me to fish Petacci's body out of the lake. I told him to get someone else."

Early the next morning the bodies of Mussolini and Clara were carted to a half-built gas station in Milan. Mussolini, mouth open, was strung up by his feet on an overhanging girder. Clara was hung by her feet next to him, her skirt falling over her head. A woman climbed on a box and tucked the skirt between Clara's roped legs. One witness recalled that her face looked strangely at peace but Mussolini's battered, swollen face was cruelly distorted.

Toshiko and I drove up the lake to Dongo, where Mussolini and the Petaccis were executed. It was a beautiful spot resembling an operatic backdrop with a small public square right on the banks of the lake and a mountain rising behind like a weird cyclorama.

As twilight fell on the placid countryside my mind was full of images of what Mussolini must have seen in this area as he headed to his doom. The natural beauty around me seemed to be overshadowed by the memories of destruction and suffering that this one foolish man had brought to a land that already had experienced the heavy tread of too many armies in its crowded past.

7

Behind the Iron Curtain

Sometimes the writing of history requires a certain amount of real risk and adventure. In order to get stories that no one had gotten previously, Toshiko and I decided to go behind the Iron Curtain, even into East Germany, which U.S. citizens were prohibited—on their passports—from entering. By the end of May 1963 we felt ready to begin our trip. First we drove to Berchtesgaden, Hitler's famous mountain retreat on the Obersalzberg. The town itself, although a bit touristy, retained its medieval flavor, and every spot on the main street offered a spectacular view of the surrounding mountains. We stayed at a place called Evergreen Lodge, located on the mountain road leading to Hitler's Eagle's Nest—the steepest climb for a car I have ever seen. We had a lavish suite with a second-floor living room, a long-enclosed porch, a huge bedroom, and an oversized bathroom. I remarked to Toshiko that this place must have belonged to some bigwig Nazi, and we later learned it had been Albert Speer's summer home. I imagine he designed it.

Göring

By chance I found Göring's butler, Robert Kropp, and persuaded him in my broken German to give us an interview. He had been with Göring daily from 1933 until the Reichsmarschall was arrested in 1945 by the SS. Then we found Göring's chief housekeeper, who had also served him at Karin-hall—his country house, an enormous mansion that had ostensibly been built as a hunting lodge and was named after his dead first wife—and got confirmation of what we had learned about the Reichsmarschall's last days in Berchtesgaden, his arrest by the SS, and his home life. Kropp had told us about his great extravagance in clothing, particularly in dressing gowns. He amassed them as some people collect stamps. They were voluminous affairs, made after his own design, of velvet or brocade in blue, green, purple; one was covered with Egyptian hieroglyphics. For each coat there were matching leather boots in the same design and color, and around the middle he wore a belt and an old Germanic knife.

Kropp insisted that Göring was a good family man who played for hours with his nephews, particularly with an intricate electric train system at Karinhall. Both Kropp and the housekeeper were still indignant over the lurid stories that had been circulated about their master's putting on makeup and wearing fantastic costumes at wild bacchanalian parties. The housekeeper agreed that Göring was still regarded in Berchtesgaden as a jovial, friendly man, whereas everyone wholeheartedly detested his enemy Bormann.

Kropp concluded with a vivid description of the Görings' last day at Karinhall. They left with fourteen carloads of clothing and plundered art treasures. Göring gave orders to blow up the house so that the Russians couldn't enjoy his remaining treasures—including the huge room filled with miniature tracks and trains.

Vienna

We moved next to Salzburg, which despite its associations with Mozart and its baroque architecture we found dusty and depressing, and then on to Vienna, which we eventually came to love despite our initial disappointment with the filthy brown "Beautiful Blue" Danube. We were bent on getting a full account of the Vienna Uprising of resistance forces in the spring of 1945. It proved to be a great story, although it was still so potentially explosive a subject that each person had his own private version (usually determined by his politics) of what happened.

Most Viennese knew little about Major Carl Szokoll, who led the anti-Nazi resistance but was regarded by most Austrians as a traitor. We finally located him, and he agreed to meet us at the Sacher Hotel, across the street from our favorite pastry shop. It was a fitting place for our interview, and I kept hearing in my head the song from *The Third Man,* the Carol Reed film set in Vienna during the Allied occupation and featuring Orson Welles in one of his most memorable roles. Szokoll, who had gone into the film business after the war and produced a number of films, including *The Last Ten Days* and *The Last Bridge,* was a small, slight man. It was like interviewing a highly nervous bird who might fly off at any moment. He too had never before been persuaded to tell his personal story. It took enormous courage for him to go on the record, because what he had to tell us would enrage many of his fellow countrymen.

In our few spare moments we attended a Beethoven concert at the height of the Vienna Festival and spent an evening at a wine garden in Grinzing, where Beethoven wrote most of his symphonies. After midnight Toshiko did an improvised dance on top of the mountain in the shadows of an ancient monastery, and I hoped at least a few monks were watching. Toshiko also noted how different Vienna was from Munich; the people, although hard-working, did not forget to have fun. Austrians, she noted, obviously knew how to enjoy themselves no matter who was in power. So we enjoyed ourselves like Viennese but worked as hard as Americans; looking back, I can see how much pressure was on us to get essential stories from reluctant people. Telling the truth usually hurts—and we saw a great deal of the torment people experienced when they relived the war years. But few retracted their words when they saw their interviews in full.

On Sunday we started eastward toward Budapest, pausing to eat lunch in a small, baroque town on the border where we visited the birthplace of Haydn, and then went across the border into Hungary.

Hungary

Crossing the border into the mysterious East was a disorienting experience. I felt a chill entering a Communist country, but we had no trouble and soon found ourselves alone on the road to Budapest. We received a weird greeting in every village; children rushed to the road and waved frantically whenever they saw us coming. A few probably wanted money, but most seemed to be just waving in a woebegone, desperate way. We took turns driving, and once when we stopped the car to change places, three kids suddenly descended on us and wanted to see the inside of the car and stare at us. They were particularly fascinated with Toshiko.

The villages were dusty and quite poor, without a single automobile in sight, only bicycles, motorcycles, and horses and carts. Although two children angrily threw cherries at us (probably because we offered them neither money nor a ride), all the others were almost wildly friendly when they spotted the foreign license plate and the strange-looking car. (We had not seen another Volvo for two weeks.) It was a whole new look at the "other" Europe. To our surprise we liked it—and they liked us, particularly Toshiko.

Coming into a larger town, we finally saw a few automobiles. Then it grew dark and we ran into quite heavy traffic. Oncoming cars blinked their parking lights at us because we had turned on our headlights. We persisted, since we couldn't see well enough without additional light, but it was frightening to go through darkened villages. We noted crowds coming from at least one church in every town, and along the way we saw four or five roadside shrines, all of them run-down. Budapest itself, in semi-blackout, was the most frightening because we didn't know where we were supposed to go. But finally, after much tacking about, we found our hotel.

It turned out to be surprisingly comfortable, and the next day we were greeted warmly. Paul Nyiri, head of the Institute for Cultural Relations, took an instant liking to us, and when I learned he was Hungary's leading baritone we soon became friends. (For the next fifteen years he would send us recordings of his recitals in Hungary, Moscow, and Germany.) He was very gallant to Toshiko and told her he would do anything she wanted— but she must promise not to take pictures of the Soviet soldiers who cluttered up the scenic spots.

For the most part our interviews were not productive, but almost every time we entered a restaurant the little orchestra would play *Madame Butterfly,* and the people in offices and on the streets were always extremely friendly. Those who could speak English had one message for the West: "Peace." They considered us to be the nation that was threatening the world; and if only we wanted peace, all would be well. Toshiko innocently took many pictures of Soviet soldiers. One morning we discovered that the rear compartment of the Volvo had been forcibly opened. Nothing had been stolen, but our films had all been exposed.

The people in Hungary were well dressed, and they looked happy and healthy; there was no doubt that the average man was better off than in the Horthy days, and there was evidence of an attempt to provide more individual freedom. We were allowed to drive where we wanted and to talk with anyone we pleased.

Yugoslavia

Yugoslavia, however, was like a different universe. The customs officials were informal, cursory. It was almost like visiting Canada. The children no longer crowded around us; we were not a curiosity. The trip to Belgrade was dusty and dull. There was no evidence of intramural conflict or even ethnic discontent. Just dullness. There were more modern buildings and wider streets than in Hungary, and the people were neither curious nor friendly. They were more like those in the crowds in New York City—brisk and impersonal. Although the big red star appeared over many buildings, as in Hungary, the prevailing attitude was quite different. The people were pro-British, pro-American, and pro-Italian, but violently anti-Bulgarian and anti-Chinese. Many still hated the Hungarians for the excesses committed in World War II, and they openly criticized the USSR. Those I talked with feared the Soviets more than the United States as a threat to peace.

Look had requested I interview Tito, but the press chief of the Foreign Office told me that Tito had rejected my proposal. Bob Sherrod had recently interviewed him for *The Saturday Evening Post,* and Tito didn't want to see another American writer for a year. But I did meet the head of the Serbian government and finally the Serbs' leading new political novelist, who had fought the Chetniks (the enemies of Tito, led by Colonel Draja Mikhailovich) for four years and had just completed a thousand-page documentary novel on the subject. He supplied us with pictures of Mikhailovich and German commanders negotiating as early as 1941. The evidence against Mikhailovich was overwhelming, and I no longer had any doubts. Later, in London, I talked with Brigadier Fitzroy Maclean, who had been dispatched by Churchill to Yugoslavia to find out if Mikhailovich was really working with the Germans. MacLean discovered that he was, and at Tehran Churchill persuaded Roosevelt and Stalin to throw major support behind Tito.

On the Sunday before we left Yugoslavia we took a trip into the interior. On the way back we were waved down in a village where there had just been a car accident, and the headman of the village, a very efficient young man, asked if we would transport one of the victims, accompanied by his wife, to a Belgrade hospital. It was a blistering hot day, close to a hundred degrees, and because the victim—a barefooted farmer—couldn't stand any breeze, we had to keep all the windows closed. When we finally reached the city, nobody could direct us to the right hospital, and the farmer's wife knew nothing about Belgrade. For an hour and a quarter we went from one hospital to another. The fourth hospital turned out to be the right one, but we were told it was full. At this point I lost my temper and threatened to go directly to Tito. I finally had to give the farmer's wife some money and leave them both at hospital number four so we could move on to our hotel.

We found it packed with celebrities honoring the president of Liberia. Because the dining hall was jammed, we were sent to a nearby restaurant, where we tried to look out the window and were politely but firmly pushed away. Toshiko, however, got a peek at the African dignitary, William Tubman, and his wife. Outside our hotel thousands were lined along the street. When Tito eventually arrived there was clapping, but there were no cheers. The response might be characterized as extremely reserved.

A Visa Problem

Planning to stay in Budapest for two days before crossing into Czechoslovakia and starting for Poland, we finally headed for the Hungarian border. We passed through the Yugoslav gate with no difficulty, but the Hungarian border officials told us our visas were no good. This was a disaster. If we couldn't get into Hungary we'd have to find some roundabout route to Czechoslovakia and Poland. The only solution was somehow to talk our way back into Hungary.

I insisted on making a call to Budapest, even though the officials kept asserting—in a combination of Hungarian, German, and gestures—that there was only a restricted military phone line to the capital. I acted dumb and persisted in my efforts to call our former opera-singer friend Paul Nyiri. The officials finally gave up and put us through to him. Our friend, who had a magnificent and confident manner, said to wait an hour and all would be well, then hung up. But I was not hopeful, because it was almost noon and usually nothing can be done in Europe between noon and 2:30 P.M. In the meantime I had plotted a new route to Vienna of about a thousand miles—with hopes that we could persuade the Czech embassy in Vienna to change our point of entry from Austria.

But Paul soon called back to say that our passage to Budapest was all arranged and asked to speak to the head official. I saw this man shake his head in disbelief and say in German, *"Voice visa!* No such thing!" But he shrugged his shoulders and motioned us through the gate. Paradoxically, in a democracy this probably could not have been arranged in so short a time.

In Hungary, Paul greeted us with delight and said we were all going to the opera that evening. With us was Joseph Nemes, a well-known artist whom we were to interview in the morning. To my astonishment Paul loudly exclaimed as the curtain rose, "Ah, the Iron Curtain!" Nemes laughed with delight. "Yes, the Iron Curtain!"

Czechoslovakia

It was midafternoon by the time Paul bade us goodbye at the Czech border. He couldn't get us any Czech money but assured us that American traveler's checks would be cashed. Our plan was to travel until dark, find a hotel, then continue to the Polish border.

Lines of cherry trees were our first sight of Czechoslovakia. I couldn't resist, and gorged myself with the best red cherries I'd tasted since my youth in Oregon. Toshiko kept calling me to come back to the car, and I reluctantly did. People seemed aloof when we passed, and several kids threw rocks at us. It was seven-thirty in the evening when we came to the town of Nitra, a manufacturing center, very dusty and hot. The first hotel we went to was full, or so we were told. No one seemed interested in helping us find a place; we were coolly advised to keep driving. Nor would anyone change money.

We tried another hotel but were cavalierly waved away. I guessed that the proprietors were afraid of getting into trouble by giving a room to foreigners who had a car bearing German license plates.

By that time it was pitch dark and there was nothing to do but head for the next town. There were no other cars on the road, and we felt as though we had been abandoned on some distant planet. Both of us were uneasy until we saw a light in the distance that spelled out EDEN. A few minutes later we came to the Eden Hotel, where, to our relief, we were greeted with enthusiasm and shown a room containing about eight beds. We had our choice. The proprietor then led us downstairs to the dining room, where some fifty young people were celebrating something. Although they couldn't understand us and we could not understand them, we were soon enjoying the celebration and trying to sing their songs. Toshiko delighted everyone, and we had a rollicking good time.

In the morning we explained that we had no Czech money, but when I showed the proprietor a traveler's check he indicated that he could get someone in town who "handled" such negotiations. In a few minutes the negotiator arrived—a twelve-year-old boy with the look of a streetwise New Yorker. He professionally eyed the check, made some rapid mental calculations, and then handed me cash. This was my first clue that the flame of capitalism still burned in socialist Czechoslovakia.

Poland

It was a long, tedious trip to the border of Poland, and once again it was like entering an entirely different world. The people were friendly and cooperative, and we had no trouble getting money and information. We stopped at a small town, found a hotel on a side street, and were given a room containing four beds. Someone rushed us around the corner so we could get into a restaurant before it closed at 10:00 P.M. Nobody could speak English or French, and the waitress had to bring in samples of food from the kitchen in order to find out what we wanted. But everyone in the little restaurant was eager to help, and before long we were drinking their vodka.

First we went to Auschwitz, which, seen from a distance, reminded me of a small, tidy Midwestern college campus. It seemed so peaceful. Then this illusion was quickly dispelled; we inspected the buildings and found frightful heaps of false teeth, trinkets, shoes, clothing—the remnants of many thousands of brutally murdered Jews. After that sight the peaceful facade was nauseating. I came away feeling compelled to tell the full, horrific story for the sake of those who had died there and in the other camps.

Helen "Collie" Snow, the author's mother, before her marriage to Ralph Toland in 1909. She threw over Billy Pattee, whose father owned five banks in Iowa, for the good-looking Ralph Toland.

Toland's father, Ralph, looking debonair in 1909, just prior to marrying Helen Snow. A self-educated man who possessed both charm and an Irish temper, Ralph Toland also had a wonderful baritone voice.

John Toland, aged three in 1915. Toland's mischievous grin in this photo shows his troublemaking side.

Lell "Belle" Chandler Snow, Toland's maternal grandmother, known as "Dammy" to Toland. When Willard Snow was wooing Lell, he became so distracted that he stepped in a bear trap, and later nearly suffocated when he fell into a pile of sawdust.

Toland's maternal grandfather, Willard Snow, whom Toland called "Dadda." The son of a wealthy logger, Snow disliked earning a living by destroying trees, quit his father's timber business, and became an insurance investigator.

A family portrait (Helen; Virginia, age six; John, age four) taken in 1916, the year before the Tolands moved from La Crosse, Wisconsin, to Watertown, South Dakota. Soon thereafter, Ralph Toland took John to the barber, where John, to his great joy, was sheared of the Little Lord Fauntleroy look.

John Toland, playing "war" in
La Crosse, 1918. Toland was a patriotic six-year-old, and had his mother
make him both an army and a navy
uniform to wear as he imagined
killing "Kaiser Bill."

Virginia Toland, age eight in
La Crosse, 1918. Although she is
holding a doll, Virginia was, Toland
remembers, a tough and independent
girl—the kind who beat up bullies
who tormented her younger brother.

1918, La Crosse, "Dadda" Snow, Virginia, Helen, and Toland in his "navy" uniform. Soon after this, the Tolands moved to a farm near Norwalk, Connecticut,
where Toland found himself the only boy in an exclusive girls school!

Hewitt "Putch" Toland, Toland's favorite uncle. His nickname originated when as a child he mispronounced "pretty boy," his mother's term of endearment for him, as "putchy boy."

The Tolands (Helen, Ralph, Virginia, and John) in 1932 on Fire Island during the bittersweet summer when John dated a girl named Exotic and dreamed of getting back to playwriting at Williams.

John Toland, about 1935, around the time when he hopped a freight train and rode the rails with the hobos and bindle stiffs.

Lieutenant John Toland and Dorothy Peaslack on their wedding day in June 1943, in St. Petersburg, Florida. Toland was assigned to Keesler Field in Biloxi, Mississippi, shortly after the wedding.

Virginia, in the mid 1950s,
several years before her tragic death
in early 1959.

Dorothy with daughters Diana and Marcia, in the early 1950s. At this point,
Toland was the manager of Dorothy's dance studio, having resigned from the
army in 1948 over the ugly dismissal of a fellow staffer.

Toland and Toshiko Matsumura on their wedding day, March 11, 1960. They met while Toland was doing research in Japan for *But Not in Shame: The Six Months After Pearl Harbor*. Toland had just fired his interpreter when he met Toshiko, then a correspondent for *McGraw-Hill World News*. She became Toland's interpreter, fellow researcher, and the love of his life almost instantly.

The Tolands' daughter, Tamiko, around 1973 with her grandparents, the Matsumuras, who were visiting her in Danbury, Connecticut. When Toland first met Mr. Matsumura to ask for Toshiko's hand in marriage, he had the foresight to present his future father-in-law with a box of American golf balls, a move that greatly pleased Mr. Matsumura, a charter member of the first golf club in Japan.

Marcia and Diana with her daughter Gabi around the late 1970s. Toland now has three grandchildren: Gabi and Eric, Diana's children; and Heidi, Marcia's daughter.

Toland and Toshiko with their daughter, Tamiko, at Cornell University in 1988.

Still shaken by walking over an area where so much tragedy had unfolded, we headed for Warsaw. We were warmly greeted by a press official and given tickets to eat at various restaurants, including Warsaw's pride, the new Chinese emporium. We went there first, expecting a treat. There was no menu and everyone was served the same thing—an indescribable mess that no Chinese would have tolerated. Yet all those around us were stowing away this slop as if it were the finest Peking cuisine.

When I asked to interview Jewish survivors I was told they wouldn't talk to me, a non-Jew and a foreigner who they would feel could not begin to understand the unspeakable horrors they had endured. But somehow word of our arrival reached the Jewish community, and we were engulfed with survivors who showed us the numbers tattooed on their arms and recounted the horrors of their wartime experience.

Since we had no appointments for the weekend, we headed north through East Prussia toward Danzig. I'd read reports of the two greatest marine disasters in history and wanted to see where they both had started. Once we reached the Baltic seaport I could visualize the huge crowds attempting to get onto the 25,000-ton *Wilhelm Gustloff* in a desperate attempt to escape the onrushing Red Army. There had been at least eight thousand civilians and fifteen hundred young submarine trainees aboard. Everyone was supposed to have a ticket and evacuation papers, but hundreds had smuggled themselves onto the ship.

The Baltic was almost a dead calm, and we drove north along the coast so I could follow in my mind the escaping *Wilhelm Gustloff.* By luck the wind heightened and the sea became choppy, but not as rough as it had been in 1944. I looked far off. Some twenty-five miles to the north the sea had become rough and there had been a great explosion. A Nazi torpedo had sent this ship full of Germans to the bottom. Only a few survived, and they had left their memories on paper, so I could attempt to recreate the scene. Later another passenger ship, the *Goya,* left the Bay of Danzig with some seven thousand civilians, and it too was hit by a German torpedo. As one of the 170 survivors reported, the big vessel "all at once seemed to snap in two."

The next morning we headed south through East Prussia. It was June 29, 1963, and we celebrated my fifty-first birthday in the only restaurant to be found in a town called Graudens. The place was so crowded that we joined a dozen Poles at a large table. I sat next to a young shipbuilder who discovered it was my birthday, and for the next two hours everyone had a boisterous, merry time even though we shared few words in common. (Toshiko corresponded with the shipbuilder's wife for many years afterward.)

In Warsaw we found that the great majority of Poles were friendly, but the waiters and other hotel employees in that city were a strange, harried, rude lot. Eating places were hard to find, and we had to battle to obtain a simple meal. After leaving Warsaw we took a short drive to see the birthplace of Chopin, a spacious home by Polish standards. The curator noticed Toshiko eyeing the replica of Chopin's hand on top of the piano. It was about the size of her own, and the curator asked her to play something. It was good for the piano, he said, to be used occasionally. She had to be persuaded, but I will never forget the look of pleasure on the curator's face when she complied.

That night we stayed in the city of Poznan, where food was available without pressure and the people were more friendly. It was also the first city in that region we had seen that was lit up at night. On our way toward Stettin, we picked up a young hitchhiker, who reminded me of the Czech boy who had cashed our traveler's check. Despite protests from Toshiko, I took out one of our checks and asked how much he'd give for it. His rate was three times that given at hotels. It was a deal. This episode gave us a glimpse of what was going on in Poland's postwar economy.

The following morning we headed up along the border of East Germany, where the aftermath of the destruction was still evident and appalling. One former city, Kustrin, was still a wasteland; another city had been built nearby. Along the Polish side of the Oder River we were almost alone and had to drive carefully because we would often come upon people sunbathing on the pavement. The entire area felt eerie—as though it had been utterly abandoned.

The areas we had covered in the last two days bore silent witness to the horrendous battles that had raged during Russia's drive on Berlin. Block after block of cities like Wroclaw (Breslau) were empty and overgrown with weeds. Some towns on old maps no longer existed and large sections of the countryside were desolate. In the East Department of the Bundesarchiv in Koblenz we had read about the fate of millions of German civilians caught up in this turmoil. We had been shown the files of 55,000 refugees. A typical file ran 225 single-spaced typewritten pages, including photostats of all sorts of documents and pictures. Here it was that I found the stories of those few who had survived the two greatest sea disasters in history.

We gradually came to realize that our book should start not with Yalta but with the desperate westward flight of not only the civilians but all prisoners of war, to avoid seizure by the Russians. I had already interviewed several American POWs about their bitter westward trudge in a snowstorm a few days before the Yalta Conference. The motive for the fury of the Red Army, I quickly understood, was a thirst for vengeance for over four years of systematic and unrelenting Nazi brutality; the Nazis had regarded the Russians as subhuman vermin to be wiped out as quickly and efficiently as possible.

General Guderian's Quarrel with Hitler

We had already interviewed two key witnesses to the battles fought in the wake of this mammoth exodus, which became known as Floodtide East. One was Baron Bernd Freytag von Loringhoven, who told of the tempestuous Führer conference on February 9, 1945. He had been aide to General Heinz Guderian, the army chief of staff and commander at the eastern front, who openly opposed the Führer on that occasion. (The baron was now commanding a base in the new German army.)

Prior to this conference the young aide had watched his chief studying the situation reports, Guderian's face eloquently expressing his utter frustration. Defense was not Guderian's forte, nor was command on this high level. He was basically a leader of troops, a straightforward, hot-blooded soldier who led from the front and fought with such ability and gusto that his men—from staff officers to privates—followed him with unshakable devotion. Earlier in the war he had been one of the few who openly disagreed with Hitler. Despite Guderian's promotion, Freytag von Loringhoven realized that the rupture between general and Führer had been only superficially patched up, and with each conference it threatened to erupt again.

As he and Guderian drove to Berlin for the February 9 conference, the general fretted and said something had to be done. Two German armies in the north were cut off, and there was nothing to stop Marshal G.K. Zhukov's drive on Berlin but Army Group Vistula, which was now commanded by a total amateur, Himmler. It was little more than a paper force. Despite this direct threat to Berlin, Hitler had ordered the opening of a big offensive in Hungary against the Red Army. This was ridiculous, Guderian told his aide, who feared for his chief's life.

No sooner had the conference started than Guderian abruptly asked Hitler to postpone the Hungarian drive and, instead, launch a major counterattack against Zhukov's Berlin-bound spearhead. Simultaneous attacks against both flanks of this spearhead could cut it in two.

Hitler listened until Guderian revealed that this also meant pulling out divisions from the Balkans, Italy, and Norway and the Kurland Army Group, which had been cut off and stranded in Latvia. Then he curtly refused Guderian's request. But, to Freytag von Loringhoven's despair, his chief stubbornly continued his argument. "I can see no other way left to us for accumulating reserves," he contended, "and without reserves we can't hope to defend Berlin. I assure you I'm acting solely in Germany's interests."

Hitler struggled up from his chair, his left side trembling. "How dare you speak to me like that? Don't you know that *I'm* fighting for Germany? My whole life has been one long struggle for Germany!"

Göring took Guderian by the arm and led him into the next room, where the two drank coffee, Guderian struggling to control his temper. But once he returned to the conference he doggedly insisted on pulling out the Kurland Army Group. It would be simple to evacuate it by sea.

Hitler again struggled to his feet and shuffled up to Guderian. Face to face, the two glared at each other. The Führer shook his fist, but the general refused to budge. Finally one of Guderian's staff officers grabbed the tail of his jacket and yanked him back.

Then, to everyone's surprise, Hitler got control of himself and quietly agreed to let Guderian launch his counterattack. But it wouldn't be possible to withdraw the troops from Latvia. Freytag watched his chief start to object, then, to his aide's immense relief, he reluctantly agreed that it would be better to have a small attack than none at all. At least it would open a path to East Prussia.

A few days later, Freytag told us, came an even more violent argument. This one was also witnessed by General Walther Wenck, Guderian's youthful chief of staff. Wenck later told us that he feared his chief, Guderian, had gone too far when Hitler painfully hoisted himself from his chair and, in response to Guderian's statement (with Himmler present) that Himmler was unfit to command troops, angrily exclaimed, "The Reichsführer is man enough to lead the attack."

Hitler turned his back on Guderian, who still faced him fearlessly. "For two hours the argument went on," Wenck related, "and each time Hitler shouted 'How dare you!' Guderian repeated his demand that I be made Himmler's assistant. Finally Hitler sighed and said, 'Well, Himmler, Wenck is going to Army Group Vistula to take over as chief of staff.' Then the Führer looked at me and told me to start the attack on February 15. He then sat down heavily and smiled winningly at Guderian. 'Herr Generaloberst,' he said, 'today the Army General Staff won a battle.' "

After the battle on the Oder had raged for three days, Wenck was ordered late at night to return to Berlin and brief Hitler on the progress. In his race to get back to Berlin, Wenck's car smashed into the abutment of a bridge, and Wenck, badly injured, was out of action.

With Wenck gone, Himmler floundered; he didn't even protest when Hitler urged him to build up a front by any means whatsoever—even by mustering women: "Here behind the Rhine nobody can go over to the enemy. That's the beauty of it. From here they can only take off to the rear." Freytag sighed with relief when his outspoken boss somehow managed to keep his mouth shut. But as Guderian predicted, in less than three weeks Zhukov had three bridgeheads across the Oder River and was only fifty miles from Berlin. Since Wenck's auto accident, Guderian had not received a single report from Himmler, the man still responsible for holding back Zhukov. On March 22 the frustrated Guderian drove to Army Group Vistula headquarters. At the entrance he met Wenck's replacement, who begged, "Can't you rid us of our commander?"

Himmler gave Guderian his support and that evening suggested to Hitler that the "overworked" Reichsführer be replaced. Young Freytag was surprised when Hitler calmly asked who should take over Army Group Vistula. Guderian suggested General Gotthard Heinrici, commander of the First Panzer Army.

Heinrici, whom we interviewed in Stuttgart half a dozen times, was selected. The next day when Guderian met Hitler and Himmler walking in the Chancellery garden, he asked if he could speak to Himmler in private. Hitler good-naturedly walked off. "The war can no longer be won," said Guderian without preamble. "The only problem now is finding the quickest way to put an end to the senseless slaughter and bombing. Except for Ribbentrop, you are the only man with contacts in neutral countries. You must go with me to Hitler and urge him to arrange an armistice."

Himmler did not reveal that both he and Ribbentrop had already been negotiating with Count Bernadotte. He seemed tongue-tied and then said, "My dear general, it's too early for that."

At that evening's conference, Hitler asked Guderian to remain. "I understand that your heart trouble has taken a turn for the worse. You must immediately take four weeks' sick leave."

The battle between the two men, explained Freytag, came to a climax on the morning of March 28. "Today I will tell all," Guderian told Freytag as they descended into Hitler's bunker. At the noon conference, General Theodor Busse tried to explain why his three counterattacks on Kustrin, a city on the Oder only a fifty-two-mile drive from Berlin, had failed. Hitler broke in angrily, "I am the commander. Responsibility for orders lies with *me!*"

"Permit me to interrupt you," cut in Guderian. "Yesterday I explained to you in detail that Busse was not to blame for the failure of the Kustrin attack." His voice rose and his manner became violent. "Ninth Army used the ammunition that had been allotted to it. The troops did their duty— the unusually high casualty figures prove that! I therefore ask you not to make any accusation against General Busse!"

Stung by this attack, Hitler struggled to his feet, but Guderian held his ground. He boldly brought up the subject he and the Führer had fought about for weeks. "Is the Führer going to evacuate the Kurland army in Latvia?" He made it more a challenge than a question.

"Never!" shouted Hitler, waving his right arm. His face was deathly white, while Guderian's was red. He advanced threateningly toward Hitler. One general held Guderian back, while another tried to escort Hitler to his chair.

"I was afraid Guderian was going to be arrested," Freytag continued, "So I ran into the anteroom and phoned Guderian's chief of staff, General Krebs. I told Krebs to hold the wire, then rushed back to tell Guderian there was an urgent call from General Krebs." For the next twenty minutes Krebs talked to Guderian, and Guderian had control of himself when he returned to the conference room. Hitler had also regained his poise, but his face was pinched. He quietly said, "I must ask all of you gentlemen to leave the room with the exception of the Feldmarschall and the Generaloberst."

Later Guderian told Freytag that when he and Keitel were alone with the Führer, Hitler said, "General Guderian, the state of your health requires that you immediately take a six weeks' sick leave." Guderian extended his arm in a stiff salute and said, "I shall go."

Now it was time to get the Russians point of view, something little written about by historians in the West. Thus we planned to exploit a Soviet offer made to me in Washington to allow me access to people who could tell me the Russian side of the story. But when Toshiko and I went to the Russian embassy in Budapest, as instructed, to pick up our visas for the trip to the Soviet Union, we had been greeted coldly and told abruptly, and without explanation, that we were not welcome in their country. I later discovered this action was retribution following an American author's recent visit to Moscow. Apparently on his return he had revealed something to the Western press that angered the Soviets. To my surprise I also learned that the author had dropped his plans to write a book on the resistance forces in Europe and was now doing one on the Battle of Berlin.

Berlin and East Germany

Since we could not get into Russia, we headed for Berlin. We were instructed not to leave the highway that led directly to the capital. If any car turned off or stopped, the East German police would arrive in minutes. We were held up for about two hours, but it was owing to inefficiency, not intent. We had already learned that in Communist countries inefficiency was the key word. All you can do is relax and let things work out.

West Berlin was like an oven, well over a hundred degrees. But we had comfortable quarters provided by Berlin Command, and the major in charge proved to be very able. We visited the newly erected Berlin Wall, about which we had heard many dramatic stories. But everything was quiet, with soldiers of both sides about twenty yards apart just staring at each other. We also crossed through Checkpoint Charlie and toured East Berlin, which was less reconstructed than West Berlin. We were not allowed to go down into Hitler's bunker, but in the rubble above, in the ruined gardens of the Chancellery, one could easily imagine the turmoil and desperation of Hitler's final hours.

The AP bureau chief in West Berlin, who had written a story about our research, had been born in the beautiful and very old city of Dresden. I learned this when he mentioned that his home city was slowly rebuilding after almost total obliteration. I guessed that he had somehow crossed over from East Germany well before the Wall went up. I asked him to tell me how to set up an illegal tour of East Germany. Americans were allowed to spend only the day in East Berlin and had to return before midnight. Moreover, our passports were marked "Entry Forbidden into East Germany."

On our second trip through Checkpoint Charlie I brought a letter from the AP man to a woman government official, urging her to set up a tour throughout East Germany for an American historian who wanted to tell both sides of the war. She nodded and, in broken English, told us to return in two days. We were warned, however, to tell no one in West Berlin about our plans or there could be international difficulties.

Two days later we set off with some trepidation, crossed into East Berlin, and reported to our contact. She wrote out an address. It was the East German Informations und Organisation Büro. We found a small place attended by one young man, Edgar Oster. He locked up his little office, pulled out his notebook, and joined us as guide. He already had a schedule. First we would head northeast for the Sachsenhausen concentration camp. By the time we arrived there we realized that although Edgar was a sincere Communist he was intent on showing us everything we wanted despite protests from Soviet guards. At Sachsenhausen as well as Buchenwald, "everything" was a catalog of fragments of lives—the unspeakable remnants of human beings who had been literally pulverized by the greatest murder apparatus ever conceived through the triumph of evil. Eyeglasses, clothes, extracted gold teeth, even children's toys, all in orderly piles. Perhaps the orderliness was the most inhuman aspect of it all.

Our next goal was Neubrandenburg, site of the large POW camp Stalag IIA, where Father Francis Sampson an Army chaplain with the rank of captain, who had been captured during the Battle of the Bulge, had been imprisoned. It was off on a small road heavily posted with signs forbidding any foreign military missions from entering. Edgar told us to go right in, and we entered the middle of what was now an East German army camp.

As we were returning to the Volvo, a VOPO (national police) car came toward us. I didn't know what to expect, since Toshiko was holding her camera. But when Edgar explained our mission the officer shook hands with us, and we weren't even questioned about the camera.

After visiting Frankfurt we spent two days in Dresden. We interviewed many survivors of the bombings and were amazed at their determination to rebuild everything as it had once been. Upon reaching Weimar, one of the most beautiful and historic cities in all of Germany, we visited the homes of Goethe, Schiller, and Liszt before driving up a nearby mountain to another concentration camp, Buchenwald. It was unfortunate that it looked so unremarkable and ordinary from the outside; upon entering, its horrors were soon apparent. It was sickening to think that this now tranquil and abandoned place had been used for such an unspeakable purpose.

We drove down the mountain to Eisenach, a city close to the border of West Germany, and discussed with the guards how best to make our return entry. They informed us that once we passed their gate there would be a no-man's-land of a mile or so, and then we would come to the West German guards. They would surely be astounded to see a red Volvo with West German visitor plates coming from East Germany with a driver who could be American or Swedish and an Asian passenger. At that point we should slowly but surely drive past the guards while smiling and waving, and the guards would do nothing, because the West Germans were intensely bureaucratic. We bade farewell to Edgar, who urged us to have a mug of good cold beer in north Germany for him, and then safely breezed by the West German guards, who, as predicted, only gaped at us.

Late in the afternoon we arrived at Gero von Gaevernitz's country place near the Swiss border. He was astonished and asked where we had been for the past ten days. A report had come from West Berlin that we had left one morning and just disappeared. We'd been dinner guests of General James Polk, commandant of West Berlin, and when he'd asked where we were going in the morning, I had blithely answered, "Researching as usual."

"We've been in East Germany," I told Gero.

He scolded us. Didn't we know that it was forbidden for U.S. citizens to go into East Germany? Yes, we did know. He fumed and then, noticing Toshiko's ever-present camera, asked, "Did Madame Toshiko take her usual number of pictures?"

I said of course, and told how our helpful East German guide had often got the attention of Soviet guards while Toshiko was snapping bridges, buildings, and even areas marked with the skull-and-crossbones warning. I had often chided Gero about still being connected with the OSS—now CIA—and I knew I was correct when he said all would be forgiven if we brought all our film to an unmarked office door in a prominent Munich building the next morning. I had always felt that the word "urbane" had been invented for Gero—and he had never been more urbane.

"CIA headquarters?" I asked and didn't expect an answer.

We did as promised. The official thanked us profusely for the film and promised to send us eight-by-ten prints in a few weeks. On this calm and reassuring note our illegal adventure into mysterious East Germany ended happily, and we went on to ever-placid Switzerland.

8

The Last Days of the Nazis

The Berlin Defenses Collapse

After completing our research in Switzerland, we recrossed the Alps in the summer of 1963 and headed for Stuttgart, where we had been interviewing General Gotthard Heinrici, the man who succeeded Himmler on March 20, 1945, as commander of Army Group Vistula. A dozen Wehrmacht generals had told us that he was the key witness for the final days of the Battle of Berlin, and Manteuffel had assured me that he was painstakingly meticulous and could be relied upon. At our first meeting, Heinrici had sniffed me like a suspicious dog for half an hour and showed me a pile of manuscripts, including a 250-page account he had written about the Battle of Berlin.

I told him that if I received exclusive information I would pay something, but a large price was out of the question. He quickly replied that he didn't want much, only what I thought it was worth. The upshot was that we were to have our interviews and at the end I was to put a price on their value. Altogether we had six long interviews, punctuated by horrible "snacks" prepared by his wife, who constantly insisted that we eat her dried-out crusts of bread, scraps of meat, and assorted goodies.

In our last two interviews he completed his account of his involvement in the Russians' final assault on Berlin. From captured Red Army soldiers he had learned that it would begin on April 12. It did, and he put into effect the strategy he had borrowed from the French: he ordered the Ninth Army, commanded by Theodor Busse, to pull back—except for a skeleton force—under cover of darkness to the ridge behind the Oder.

A far more important interview was a night appointment, arranged by Peiper, with Erich Kempka, Hitler's private chauffeur. The evening started like a Hitchcock movie. Kempka had someone call to say he would send a guide to lead us to his home. The guide turned out to be a nervous character who drove like a madman through the fog. Somehow we managed to follow his twisting trail into Ludwigsburg. There our guide raced up a street that was torn up, and in his frantic turning around he first almost ran down an American couple and then nearly rammed us. We finally got parked and were led on foot across a series of ripped-up roads and into a house.

Kempka himself was very pleasant and soon began spilling all. It seems unbelievable, but I had shaved just before dinner, yet when we finally tottered out into the fog, I needed another shave. It was the longest interview of my career—eight hours.

On the trip back to Stuttgart I kept mulling over Kempka's chilling descriptions of the last days in Hitler's bunker in April 1945. As if he were seeing it all again, Kempka described how Hitler's personal servant, Heinz Linge, and Dr. Stumpfegger carried out Hitler's body in a dark brown army blanket. "The Führer's face was half covered, his left arm hung down. Bormann followed, carrying Eva. The sight of her in Bormann's arms was horrifying. I knew she hated him and I called to Günsche, 'I'll carry Eva.' I took her away from Bormann, whom I also hated, and noticed the left side of her body was moist. Blood, I thought, but I later learned from Günsche that it was water from a vase spilled when the Führer, after shooting himself, pitched forward and sent it flying. She had taken a poison pill."

Kempka gave us invaluable details of his years with Hitler and lent us a number of pictures he had taken of the Führer that had never been published. He also put us in touch with Günsche, who knew all the details of the deaths of Hitler and Eva Braun.

After Otto Günsche had changed the date of our appointment twice, we finally set out for his home, some twenty kilometers from Köln on a deserted road. It was boarded up and there was no sign of Herr Günsche. I persuaded a neighbor to phone him at his office. He in turn required some persuasion before the neighbor was permitted to lead us in his car to Günsche's place of business, a factory. He was much younger than I expected; he looked about thirty-five, although he was fifty. He was six feet three inches and big as a house, though not fat. He was the director of a large pharmaceutical firm and had a sharp mind. At first he was cagey, and we sparred for over an hour through the terrible interpreter he had supplied. Finally he decided to help me, with two provisos: I was not to use his name in the book and I could not identify him as a source. I agreed.

He stated that what had been written about the last hours of Hitler had come primarily from secondhand sources and was completely wrong, and that he was the only living source of the most important events of the bunker. By the end of the interview I knew I finally had the real story, and Günsche was convinced that I would write the truth. He agreed to check all the material about the bunker that I used. He also said he would send me a copy of the secret three-hundred-page report he had made to the German government when he returned from Russia. But he was starting a new life, had an excellent position, and didn't want any publicity at all. Months later, after reading my version of the last days in Hitler's bunker, he *did* give me permission to use his name but requested that I not state in the notes that I had interviewed him. I complied.

Admiral Karl Dönitz

Some historians have pictured Karl Dönitz as merely an ordinary naval commander with few qualities as a national leader—just another Nazi with high rank. Shirer, for example, has described him at Nuremberg as looking "like a shoe clerk."

But Admiral Nimitz, who knew Dönitz, had insisted I see him in person and judge for myself, claiming that he was a man of superior talents and no Nazi. We learned that his wife had just died, and I wondered whether our talk should be postponed. I had also been warned that he would rarely see anyone, and then was terse and uncommunicative. But for some reason, probably because of Toshiko's presence, he seemed eager to talk. To my surprise, I found that he had a good sense of humor. He was also energetic and positive, and his story clarified the complicated set of surrender negotiations he carried out with the Allies after Hitler's death. He showed me a copy of his own farewell address to the officers' corps, written after the surrender: "Comrades, we have been set back for a thousand years in our history. Land that was German for a thousand years has now fallen into Russian hands. Therefore the political line we must follow is very plain. It is clear that we have to go along with the Western powers and work with them in the occupied territories in the west, for it is only through working with them that we can have hopes of later retrieving our lands from the Russians. . . . The personal fate of each of us is uncertain. That, however, is unimportant. What is important is that we maintain at the highest level the comradeship amongst us that was created through the bombing attacks on our country. Only through this unity will it be possible for us to master the coming difficult times, and only in this manner can we be sure that the German people will not die."

He stared at me somberly. "I thought of my two sons who had died for the Führer. Like so many other Germans, I was just beginning to see the perils of the *Führerprinzip*"—the principle of dictatorship. "Perhaps human nature could not use the power of dictatorship without succumbing to the temptations of its abuse of power." He then said he read through the speech to his officers he had just finished. He could not send it to them. "I slowly folded it and locked it in my desk drawer."

I knew this would make the perfect ending for *The Last 100 Days*.

Bullock and Bohlen

We soon pushed on to London, in November 1963, where we relaxed with plays and movies and Toshiko convinced me to buy some new clothes. We also continued our interviewing with both military officers and others, including the Oxford historian Alan Bullock. I had admired his book on Hitler for its factual accuracy. Many years later I reviewed his dual biography of Stalin and Hitler. It was both creative and daring, and I gave it the very good review it deserved.

I had scheduled a meeting with Chip Bohlen, our ambassador in Paris, who had served in Moscow and was involved in the Yalta talks. When our meeting was suddenly postponed for twenty-four hours, Toshiko and I went to see a play. During the intermission I noticed some people observing me with genuine concern—as if I had just lost a member of my family. I wondered what was wrong. Later, as we were leaving the theater, I learned that President Kennedy had been shot. Others in the crowd also looked at me with feeling, since I was obviously an American, and their sympathy did help sustain me after the terrible shock.

The next day I flew to Paris for the interview with Bohlen. The embassy guards were somber, and I was escorted upstairs to the ambassador's office. He was pale and shaken. I apologized for intruding at such a dreadful time, but he seemed to welcome this opportunity to talk about the past. I had been cautioned that he was chary about revealing more about the Yalta talks than the bare essentials, but within a few minutes he was pouring out intimate portraits of the Big Three so fast that I had trouble scribbling down his words. I had hoped for one hour, but I was there for more than two, and he bade me a friendly farewell. Some five years later when we were returning from a year's research in the Orient, I again interviewed Bohlen. He was politely cool and I was whisked out of his office with an almost blank notebook after half an hour. I then realized that if he had not been so stunned by the death of Kennedy I probably would have been given only a routine story about Yalta.

Hitler's Favorite Pilot

While in London we heard from Otto Skorzeny, who had booked reservations for us in Madrid. His most exciting news was that Colonel Hans-Ulrich

Rudel, Hitler's favorite soldier and leader of a group of Stuka dive-bombers, had promised to stop off at Madrid on the way from South America in order to see me on December 1 at Skorzeny's home. After almost 2,500 combat missions in six years, he was legendary. He had sunk a Soviet battleship and destroyed some five hundred tanks. But he had not answered my letters, and I wondered if he would keep his word.

Soon after our arrival, Skorzeny informed me that Rudel would not stop in Madrid for his promised interview. I replied that Hitler's favorite fighter was afraid to see me, whereupon Skorzeny promptly picked up a phone, and a few minutes later he announced that Rudel would meet us at the Madrid airport in two days. We would have two or three hours, with Skorzeny himself as interpreter.

At the airport on the appointed day, I still had doubts. Then I saw a man of average height bounding up the steep slope toward us as if he were in the Olympics. Skorzeny stood up and called out, "Hans!"

Could this be the Rudel who had lost a leg in the last crash? It seemed impossible, but it *was* Rudel, the most vital man I had ever seen. He didn't talk; he spouted words in a high-pitched voice. He had wavy, light brown hair, light olive-green eyes, and strong, chiseled features. He greeted Toshiko gallantly and then shook my hand. I could hear my bones crunching. I knew I had a perfect specimen of a loyal follower of Hitler. I had read enough to know that while he had believed in Hitler without any reservation, he was openly critical of the many mistakes made by both party members and military leaders.

He spoke some English, and Otto Skorzeny acted as interpreter when he got stuck. In any case, I knew I had again struck gold. When I told him I wanted his memories of the last one hundred days, he insisted on starting with his meeting with the Führer during the Battle of the Bulge. "Hitler wanted to give me another decoration, then told me I'd done enough flying."

Rudel continued to fly despite Hitler's orders. In a single day he destroyed eleven tanks. While the Yalta Conference was nearing its climax, Rudel was still flying. By that time he had been shot down a dozen times and his left leg was encased in plaster of Paris as a result of machine-gun wounds.

As the interview went on, Skorzeny had become as excited as Rudel in telling the story. They were oblivious to the presence of Toshiko and me. We had both learned, when such an unexpected flood of human memory rushed forth, to evaporate from the scene and not interrupt by asking questions.

Rudel then told the full story of the crash that ended his flying days. While still in a cast, Rudel took off on February 9, 1945, to attack Russian tanks. This time antiaircraft tore up his plane, set it on fire, and got his *right* leg. Still, half unconscious from pain, he attempted a crash landing that would save the life of his rear gunner and, possibly, himself. He grinned at Skorzeny and said, "I'd forgotten my left leg was already in a plaster cast. The plane was burning as I gently brought up its nose to make a pancake landing. I felt a jarring crash, a lurch, a screeching skid. I passed out, but came to almost immediately because of pain and then passed out again. When I next came to, I was on an operating table. I asked the surgeon, "Is it gone?" and he nodded. You can guess what I felt, Otto. No more skiing, diving, pole vaulting. Then I thought, 'What the hell! So many comrades wounded worse. What's the loss of a leg for the Fatherland?' "

We were all exhausted from his long, harrowing story. Rudel recovered first. "Göring's personal physician came a few days later and told me that when Göring had told the Führer about the crash, he was greatly relieved that I had escaped so lightly. He said, 'Of course, if the chick wants to be wiser than the hen . . . ' He was the hen," explained Rudel with a grin, "and I was the chick. Mother knows best."

Both he and Skorzeny laughed. Then Skorzeny told us how he had visited Rudel in a Berlin hospital, expecting to see him depressed. "Instead, he was laughing and hopping around on one leg, saying he had to fly again."

Rudel turned somber as he described the last day of the war. "I assembled my men and thanked them for their gallantry and loyalty, and shook hands with everyone. Six other pilots and I flew in three Junker 87s and four Focke-Wulf 190s toward the American lines. I hoped to get medical attention for my leg. When I saw American soldiers parading on the Kitzingen airfield in Bavaria, I led my group on a low sweep over the runway before we landed. After giving us a bit of a hard time, the Amis let us wash, and while we were eating, the interpreter told me that the U.S. commandant wondered if we would like to have a friendly talk with him and his officers. And we did have a good talk." When Douglas Bader, the renowned British pilot who had lost two legs, heard about Rudel, he sent him a mechanical leg.

Publication and Critical Reception

After our return to Washington for a few weeks of further research, we moved in 1964 to South Kent, Connecticut, where we had rented a small cottage out in the country. The work went well, and I sent off the first section to Bob Loomis at Random House. He telephoned to say he was coming up to talk things over, and from his voice I knew he was unhappy. As I listened to the criticism, I thought of the letter I had written Bob stating that I would need his guiding hand to keep me steady and I wanted to write this book under his whip. Our subsequent conversation showed clearly that Bob wanted me to make certain changes I didn't agree with, but with the help of my agent, Paul Reynolds, we worked it all out.

By late September we had moved to a rented house several miles out of Sharon, Connecticut. I finished the final draft in November, and by April 1965 I was doing the final revisions. The book had already been sold to several foreign countries, and *Look* would start serialization in the May 4 issue.

The Last 100 Days was again selected as an "A" book by the Book-of-the-Month Club; as usual, my book was not taken as a selection—but the Literary Guild picked it up, and Bennett Cerf was delighted by the three spreads in *Look* as well as the substantial paperback sale. By that time my mind was on our next book. I already had a title for it: *The Rising Sun.*

I had not been entirely pleased with my picture of Japan in *But Not in Shame,* and this time I wanted to spend five years, if necessary, finding out what really happened during the war in the East. *Look* agreed to do another three-part serialization at the same price; this, together with the sales from *The Last 100 Days,* would provide plenty to keep us going for the next five years.

But the first major review, by Robert Kirsch, was devastating. LAST 100 DAYS FLAWS [sic] AS HISTORY was the headline. I was stunned, for I knew that Kirsch was an excellent reviewer. Then other reviews from all over the country began pouring in. A few agreed with Kirsch, but the vast majority, including the Sunday *New York Times,* praised the book, and within a week it was on the best-seller lists and I was on many TV and radio shows. Kirsch's review is the only one I kept in my files—perhaps because I knew he was a good critic and he could have been partially right. As usual, though, I was eager to get on with the next book, and early in 1966 Toshiko and I took off for Tokyo.

We had become a beautifully matched research team. Toshiko had an uncanny ability to detect fabrications and evasions. I could persuade interviewees to confide, and do so in great detail. But in Japan I not only would have Toshiko's insights into her native culture but would also find out that getting the truth depended on penetrating the mystery that surrounded the emperor and his court and the nature of his relationships with the military and diplomatic players. Most of them had not opened up to any historians, even Japanese researchers. I was determined to break through this barrier of reserve.

[Part Two]

The Rising Sun (1 9 6 6 – 1 9 7 0)

{9}

Abandon Self

Getting to Work

By the time Toshiko and I arrived in Tokyo in February 1966, we were both exhausted, not only by jet lag but also from the strain of getting *The Last 100 Days* published. Fortunately Toshiko soon found a perfect headquarters: the penthouse apartment of the Co-op Olympia, located in Shibuya near the Olympic Stadium. It was only a block from the entrance to the Meiji Shrine, an ideal place for a daily walk. And within one block was a bookstore full of worn books in English, as well as two excellent restaurants. For lunch we could also get delicious takeout meals from the Olympia's Chinese restaurant.

My father-in-law, Tokiji Matsumura, who had spent the war years in China running a mill for Nippon Steel, had already drawn up a long list of people we should see, especially those remote, key players of the highest rank whom he knew personally. Soon we were interviewing six days a week. During the following year we accomplished far more than we had in our travels in Europe while doing research for *The Last 100 Days.*

We spent most of our time in the Tokyo area, but we uncovered much vital information throughout the four main islands of Japan as well as a number of small ones in the Sea of Japan. I also made solo visits to Okinawa, Iwo Jima, Taiwan, Guam, and Tarawa, and went twice to the Philippines. On my second trip I accompanied a group of Japanese survivors of the battles in Leyte in which 90 percent of the Japanese soldiers had been killed. I joined these veterans, together with a dozen mothers and fathers of the dead, to visit the scenes of havoc and witnessed the ceremonies in which they bid farewell to loved ones.

In our first visit to the American embassy in Tokyo we were greeted enthusiastically by Ambassador Edwin O. Reischauer and his first consul, John Emmerson. During the next year they would set up many interviews with key survivors, arrange two trips to Okinawa, and assist us in our effort to establish friendly relations between Washington and Beijing. Equally supportive were members of the Foreign Press Club, including Robert Trumbull *(New York Times),* John Rich (NBC), and Lewis Bush (NHK), as well as representatives of the three principal Japanese newspapers. The Japan Self-Defense Force War History Office and the Historical Research Institute opened their files; and my father-in-law, together with his group of Meiji men, translated for us all sorts of books and documents, including the thousand-page "Notes" of Field Marshal General Sugiyama, chief of the Army General Staff.

Our main source, the Japanese people, came from all walks of life—from fifty survivors of Hiroshima and Nagasaki to Marquis Kido, the emperor's chief adviser, who had unjustly been sentenced to life imprisonment despite his efforts to prevent the war and then bring peace. We listened to harrowing tales of those who survived the firebombing of Tokyo and those who commanded the Japanese army and navy. Gone was the reluctance, apparent only a few years earlier, to discuss certain sensitive subjects, and all were patient with my repetitious questions nailing down details. Admiral Ryunosuke Kusaka, the *de facto* commander at Pearl Harbor and Midway, and General Kenryo Sato, perhaps Tojo's most trusted confidant, spoke openly in six all-day sessions; they were convinced that Westerners, after their postwar experiences in Asia, would now more readily understand the Japanese ruthlessness in Manchuria and China. Those Japanese who fought the war—from privates to generals—were now more willing to talk of their mistakes and speak of the unspeakable: cowardice, murder, cannibalism, surrender, and desertion.

A Buddhist priest sent me a talisman that hangs on my study wall to this day: Sogen, the head priest in Kamakura, showed me by example how to overcome the vast problems I faced in this undertaking. He gave me an ideogram that he made with brush and ink. Translated, it said: "Abandon self." I looked at it and reflected on its wisdom every morning before starting to write.

A Rebellion That Failed

Before conducting our hundreds of interviews dealing with episodes occurring at different times before and during the war, I had decided to start our narrative with a crucial incident which took place early in 1936: the attempt by idealistic young officers, opposed to expansion in China, to take over Tokyo. The failure of their revolt, which is known as the 2/26 Incident, would eventually lead to war with the United States.

In blunt terms, it was a coup d'état. On February 26, 1936, the officers went forth bent on killing prominent members of the government and the imperial household who, they felt, were responsible for an indefensible and imperialistic assault on China. Their ambition—overreaching ambition is perhaps an accurate term—is stunning in retrospect. Six groups of officers headed for their assigned objectives as a thick and highly unusual fall of snow shrouded Tokyo in white silence. One group intended to seize the war minister's official residence and then force high-ranking officers to support them; another would seize police headquarters; and four other groups would assassinate the prime minister, the finance minister, the lord keeper of the privy seal (the emperor's chief adviser), and the grand chamberlain.

The coup was an inevitable and bloody failure. One of the supreme ironies of this attempt to alter the fatal direction of Japan's foreign policy was the fate of the grand chamberlain, Admiral Kantaro Suzuki, who was awakened to find himself surrounded by rebels. He told them to go ahead and shoot. Three shots rang out; one bullet missed, one hit him in the crotch, and the third went through his heart. By nothing less than a miracle, Suzuki survived, and he would play a key role as prime minister in Japan's final days as an empire.

The rebels in the 2/26 Incident had failed, and their opponents' program of expansion grew in popularity and eventually led to the Japanese invasion of China. On the battlefield the Japanese won easily, and by 1939 they had taken Hankow and Canton. But the cost of victory was to prove enormous. Japan lost thousands of men and millions of yen while incurring the wrath of the Western world, especially the Americans.

Stumbling Toward War

I realized that in order to understand the origins of the Japanese-American conflict, we had to somehow uncover the Japanese side of the subsequent bitter U.S.–Japan relationship, and we soon had a lead: Tomohiko Ushiba, private secretary to the prime minister, Prince Fumimaro Konoye. Ushiba told us that almost everything about Konoye seemed contradictory. He felt ill at ease with Americans yet sent his eldest son to the Lawrenceville School and Princeton University. His marriage was a genuine love match (rather than an arranged one), but he also treated his mistress, a geisha, with great affection and respect. At the same time he upset family tradition by abolishing the system of having rooms in the main house for second, third, and fourth "wives," and he discontinued the family diary. "How could I possibly write the truth if it were unfavorable to me?" he told Ushiba. The product of an elegant society, Konoye had one foot in the past and one in the future.

Ushiba said that Konoye was looking desperately for a negotiated peace, preferably with England, but he faced a threat to stability in Japan if he acted without a consensus behind him. The idealistic young officers had acted without authority in the 1936 uprising, thereby breaking a major Japanese taboo against *gekokujo,* literally "inferiors overthrowing their superiors." I asked Ushiba why a liberal like Konoye had allowed the army to gain ascendancy. "A Churchill or a Kennedy might have succeeded in controlling the army," replied Ushiba, "but given the Japanese constitutional system by which the supreme command was independent of the prime minister, it is doubtful if even Churchill could have succeeded."

Ushiba had been present at the critical meeting on September 6, 1941, when the emperor was presented with the request of the army and navy to wage war against the United States, Great Britain, and the Netherlands. He told us how shocked the military men had been when the emperor responded to their recommendations not by the dutiful assent of a constitutional monarch but by extracting a piece of paper from his pocket and reading from it. It was a poem written by his grandfather, Emperor Meiji—and it was a poem about the desirability of peace. This led to frantic efforts by Konoye to work out something by way of a compromise with U.S. Ambassador Joseph Clark Grew. (Toshiko and I would later meet with Grew at his home in Connecticut. He was then quite elderly but possessed of a remarkable memory which added color and detail to those desperate days and hours. Grew told us how he tried to convince Secretary of State Hull and President Roosevelt that Konoye was not only willing but able to deliver a peaceful *modus vivendi* if only he could personally meet with Roosevelt. The meeting was never held and Konoye was relieved as prime minister.)

The next scene in the tragic drama, said Ushiba, would be created by the permanent confidential adviser to the emperor on all affairs, the lord keeper of the privy seal, the Marquis Koichi Kido. I was dismayed to hear this, since Kido had refused to see me when I was doing research for *But Not in Shame,* nor had he replied to any of my letters, and his testimony would obviously be crucial for this book.

While I was moaning about all this to my father-in-law, he said, "That will be no problem. We play at the same golf course." He then made several phone calls and reported that the marquis would see us at his summer home in Oiso.

Kido was smaller than I, rigid and proud. Although Toshiko was there to interpret, he spoke English. The first interview was stiff, and I could not get him to give me the personal observations I wanted. But he did read excerpts from his famous diary, which had been used at length in the Tokyo Trials, and showed us how the U.S. translations had been grossly incorrect. In the middle of the next day's interview, however, the marquis abruptly stopped, looked at me, and said something like "You only want to know what happened." At that moment he reminded me of General von Manteuffel, and from then on he relaxed and talked freely, giving me all the details.

Kido told us he had felt that the best choice to replace Konoye was General Hideki Tojo, the war minister, nicknamed "the Razor." He knew Tojo could control the army and would follow the emperor's desire to reconsider the September 6 decision to wage war.

On October 17, 1941, the *jushin*—the seven former premiers—met in the palace to help select a prime minister. Kido attended as lord privy seal and managed, after two hours of argument, to persuade the others to pick Tojo, who would also retain his position as war minister.

Tojo's wife had told us that when Tojo got word that he was to report at once to the palace, he was expecting to be reprimanded by the emperor, and was confounded when his majesty ordered him to form a cabinet. Tojo requested time to consider and went into the waiting room, where he was soon joined by Admiral Oikawa, head of the navy, who had just been instructed by the emperor to work in "closer cooperation" with the army. Then Kido entered. "I assume the emperor has just talked to you about army-navy cooperation," he said, and explicitly stated what his majesty could only imply. "With regard to the decision on our *kokutai* [national essence], it is the emperor's wish that you make an exhaustive study of domestic and foreign conditions—without regard to the September 6 imperial conference. I convey this to you as an order of the emperor."

This was unprecedented in Japanese history. No emperor had ever before rescinded a decision of the imperial conference. Tojo was ordered to "go back to blank paper"—that is, to start negotiating peace with a clean slate.

Tojo's wife had also told us that her husband had gone to the Yasukuni Shrine, where the souls of Japan's war dead were enshrined. He bowed his head in prayer, realizing that he faced a completely new life. From now on he would think as a civilian, not as a soldier. He must form a cabinet representing all segments of Japanese life—a national, not a military cabinet. He vowed to live by a new motto: "To Let the Emperor Be the Mirror of My Judgment."

To the Western world he still would remain the chief Japanese villain of the war, even though he kept his pledge. He insisted, to the dismay of his fellow military leaders, on carrying out the emperor's order to go back to blank paper by sending a proposal to Washington. Although Secretary of State Cordell Hull turned it down, President Roosevelt, a practitioner of *Realpolitik,* responded with a *modus vivendi.* He wrote it in pencil and sent it off to Hull: the United States would resume economic relations with Japan, in return for which the Japanese would not dispatch additional forces to any other countries and would refrain from joining with Germany and Italy, under the terms of the tripartite pact (i.e., the Axis), even if the United States went to war in Europe.

But Roosevelt's 1941 *modus vivendi* was never sent to Japan—the British and the Chinese were not agreeable to the proposal—so Tojo never had the opportunity to use this compromise to carry out the emperor's wishes and thus avoid war, at least in the near term. Additional Japanese deployments resulted in a stern demand from FDR to withdraw Japanese forces from China and Indochina and to support the Chiang Kai-shek regime.

Thus plans for war were set in motion. The war that need not have been fought would soon change world history.

Operation Z—Pearl Harbor

In *But Not in Shame* I had written about Operation Z, the attack on Pearl Harbor. But I knew I had to dig far deeper to find those who knew all the details. The most important interviews were with Admiral Ryunosuke Kusaka, an acquaintance of my father-in-law. He had been put in charge of the operation and later was made chief of staff of Admiral Chuichi Nagumo, commander of the fleet that would carry out Operation Z. Kusaka would be the *de facto* commander, because Admiral Nagumo dealt only with final decisions, leaving all tactical matters to his chief to staff. It took five long interviews to cover all of Kusaka's activities throughout the war, and he told us many things he had never before revealed.

It was Kusaka who had ordered the Z flag raised above the flagship *Akagi* to set off the attack on Pearl Harbor. This was an exact copy of the flag Admiral Heihachiro Togo had used in the Battle of Tsushima when the Russian fleet was destroyed, but in the intervening years it had become an ordinary tactical signal. "I was sure that every man in the Striking Force would realize its symbolic significance." But several staff officers, including Commander Minoru Genda, the aviation staff officer, protested that when the men saw the flag go up it would cause confusion. "I reluctantly revoked the command," he revealed to us. At the time of our interview he was a general in charge of the Japanese Self-Defense Force. Genda added that he'd ordered raised another flag that had vaguely resembled Togo's signal. When the sailors on the nearby *Kaga* had seen the Z flag, they had excitedly hoisted their own. It was going to be another Tsushima! Then, inexplicably, *Akagi*'s flag fluttered down, and with it some of their enthusiasm.

The attack had to be coordinated by a single flight officer, and Commander Mitsuo Fuchida of *Akagi* had been selected to give this signal. Upon returning an hour after takeoff, he reported to Nagumo and Kusaka that at least two battleships had been sunk and four seriously damaged. He urged the admirals to launch another attack at once, this time concentrating on the oil tanks.

Kusaka told us he had seriously considered Fuchida's suggestion but believed a commander should not be obsessed by such temptations. "And so I advised General Nagumo to retire as planned," he said. Opinion on the bridge was divided, but as usual Nagumo relied on his chief of staff. "We will withdraw," Nagumo said, and the second attack, which probably would have wiped out all the fuel tanks and raised havoc with the submarines, was not made. Kusaka denied the stories that Fuchida and Genda had repeatedly pleaded with Nagumo to return. "They merely suggested a second attack and never expressed a forceful opinion after Nagumo had said, 'We will withdraw.' "

The Battle of Midway

Kusaka also described the June 1942 Battle of Midway, which turned the tide against Japan. Fuchida, who had led the attack on Pearl Harbor, was in sick bay, stricken by appendicitis, and his good friend Minoru Genda was scheduled to replace him. But he too was in sick bay with a bad cold. He managed to shuffle up to the bridge, apologizing to Captain Nomura for being late. At 4:30 A.M., June 4, Kusaka gave word to commence launching for an attack on the island of Midway.

As historians now know, this was the battle that sealed the fate of Japan in the Pacific war. The American fleet was closer than the Japanese thought; the first American torpedo attacks were brushed off, and the Japanese counterattack was insufficient—and it resulted in their carriers being caught at the most vulnerable moment of refueling and rearming aircraft. These irreplaceable ships—four carriers—and their equally irreplaceable air crews were lost. In one of the greatest sea-air battles of all time, America had gained control of the Pacific.

A Tactical Victory

Kusaka was again serving as Nagumo's chief of staff in the battle for Guadalcanal four months later. For weeks, Yamamoto had pressed Nagumo, without making it a direct order, to take his carriers south and engage the American carriers. This would be one of the central battles centering on Guadalcanal, the Battle of Santa Cruz. "But I persuaded him each time that it would be too risky and would end in another Midway." Few Westerners, even those in the military, understand the crucial role of a chief of staff. The commander, as in Nagumo's case, is a remote and godlike figure who plans the grand strategy and turns over its execution to his chief of staff. This is a reflection of the entire Japanese way of life and ancient tradition.

Late in the afternoon of October 25, 1942, Yamamoto decided to force Nagumo into action and sent him a message, insulting in tone, "urging" him to attack "with vigor." Nagumo summoned Kusaka to his battle room under the bridge. "I could see that my chief was upset. He said he couldn't ignore Yamamoto's latest message and wanted my support. I replied that it was his battle. 'If you really want to head south, I'll go along with the verdict.' But I reminded him that we hadn't even located the enemy fleet and we, in turn, would undoubtedly be discovered by B-17s operating nearby. 'But now that your mind is made up,' I added, 'I want you to know that we shall not be destroyed without first destroying the enemy.' "

Kusaka ordered the Carrier Striking Force—three flattops, a heavy cruiser, and eight destroyers—and the Vanguard Group of two battleships, four cruisers, and seven destroyers to turn south toward the enemy at twenty knots.

Again, as in Midway, the opposing forces were closer than they knew. The battle was, like Midway, fought by aircraft launched from opposing carriers and supporting warships that mostly were too far apart to make visual contact. Kusaka vividly recounted how he kept asking himself, "*Was* this another Midway?" He told us how he felt after he ordered a second attacking wave of Japanese torpedo- and dive-bombers: "On that day I was so conscious of the mistakes of Midway that I kept shouting impatiently from the bridge for the pilots to move faster." He ranged around the bridge until the last of the torpedo- and dive-bombers and fighters of the second wave were airborne. "From my window I shouted orders to hose down the deck and prepare for enemy attack. Not a single fighter was left to protect the carriers, but I was so caught up in the battle that I didn't care and muttered to myself, 'Bring spears, enemy! Anything!' "

Again the Japanese overestimated American losses—they counted four American carriers and three battleships sunk when in fact the United States had lost only one carrier, *Hornet,* and gained valuable time in this delaying action that was a momentary tactical victory for Japan. It would merely postpone the ultimate day of reckoning.

Green Hell—Guadalcanal

The Americans did not regard this Japanese naval victory as significant, since they still held Henderson Field on Guadalcanal, and even Yamamoto privately concluded that it would be next to impossible to retake the island from the U.S. Marines. Moreover, the Japanese bitterly holding on to half of the island were almost out of ammunition and food.

Toshiko and I had been fortunate enough to persuade Gen (pronounced with hard G) Nishino, the correspondent for *Mainichi,* to reveal his personal experiences during the savage battle waged on Guadalcanal that began in August 1942 and soon was known as Green Hell. Then thirty-seven, he was a slight man, about five feet tall and seemingly frail. But he was a born leader who had already survived arduous months in China reporting that war; his greatest concern there, he said, was not for his life but for the $25,000 worth of yen he was carrying for expenses. Soon after his arrival on Guadalcanal, General Kawaguchi had told him that the American marines were well dug in and had almost endless supplies. "Imperial headquarters," the general said contemptuously, "belittles the enemy on Guadalcanal and declares that once we land safely, the marines will surrender." Then he abruptly stopped as if alarmed by his own words. "It's not a problem for us to discuss here."

As Nishino feared, the next two attacks on Henderson Field failed, with heavy losses.

A captain named Kokusho ordered a charge. What came next was terrifying to watch. "The men were caught in a crossfire," recalled Nishino, "but Kokusho managed to reach one of the guns, followed by a handful of his own troops and a group of artillerymen armed with bamboo spears." Kokusho was hit in the face. His uniform was covered with blood. He cried out, "Banzai!" and headed for the next gun position. Staggered by a bullet, he leaped onto a gun platform. As he raised his sword in triumph, a grenade exploded in his face. From the ground he mumbled *"Totsugeki! Totsugeki!"*— "charge!"—and then died, sword still grasped tightly.

Dawn revealed a slaughterhouse. Six hundred Japanese and forty marines lay dead, and the marines would nickname the place Bloody Ridge. Despite the heavy losses, continued Nishino, General Kawaguchi was resolved to make a suicidal effort in a second attack. At dusk he led his men toward Henderson Field.

Nishino found it hard to keep his eyes open in the blinding sun. "My eyes burned and everything looked milky." What had been a jungle was now a barren wasteland. A few tree trunks reminded him of Grecian columns. "Then I saw Yoshino, my liaison man, stagger to his feet, and I shouted in a croaking voice to hit the dirt. He dropped beside me as a mortar round exploded yards away. I covered my eyes and ears. I shivered from malaria chills."

He felt his body slowly rise in the air and fall—again and again—as in a slow-motion movie. Overcome by an irresistible drowsiness, he let his head come to rest on the leaves. "My body seemed to be sinking into something unknown, and I wondered if I was going to sleep or was dying. Faces came to my mind: first my city editor, Honda; then my wife, looking very sad. Then followed a procession of friends and, strangely, Verlaine and François Villon." He heard distant thunder like a crash of a tidal wave, and his body was again slowly lifted from the ground. "I felt my breast pocket; a sea-shell rosary was still there, and the amulet Honda had given me for luck at the time when he told me not to get killed. I could see a little better." Less than half a mile a way was the end of a runway. "We had almost made it to the airfield. As if in a dream, I started to creep back."

He joined survivors from other battalions in the brutal trip to the coast. He came upon hundreds of wounded, still alive but unable to move. Men were traveling in groups of fifteen or twenty, each group at its own pace. There was no order. "By the sixth day the noncoms had to lash the younger soldiers with switches to keep them moving. I could hardly put one foot in front of the other. Then just before noon I emerged from the dark jungle into a palm grove. Ahead was an endless expanse of green sea!" They had come out at Point Cruz, seven miles from the airfield.

By luck, Nishino was evacuated to Rabaul. When he checked in at Seventeenth Army headquarters he tried to tell the truth about Guadalcanal to an army officer. "I began to feel dizzy and put my hands on the adjutant's desk to steady myself."

"Why are you so pale?" barked the adjutant.

"I've been in the jungle. There's no sunlight there."

"You just lack *seishin*"—guts, courage.

"My *seishin* saved me from the hell of Gadarukanaru. If you go there you'll see." Noshino turned to leave.

"Eat tomatoes! That'll do you good!" The adjutant's taunt then turned into a threat. "Just remember, we'll never let you return to Japan. It would be like sending a spy back home."

The end on Guadalcanal would not come until early February 1943. Thanks to courageous naval men, more than 13,000 emaciated soldiers were safely evacuated. But 25,000 others were left dead or dying. Although the imperial navy had fought well, it lost as many warships as it managed to sink, and the vessels it lost were irreplaceable.

General Kawaguchi was taken to a Manila hospital, where he slowly recovered from malaria and malnutrition. One of his visitors was Nishino, who had managed to get safely out of Rabaul. The two grasped hands and stared at each other. The general confided to the correspondent that on his arrival at Rabaul he had been treated as an incompetent coward. His career was over.

"I know how you feel better than anyone else does," said Nishino. "But the day is bound to come when the truth about Guadalcanal will be known and people will realize you were right."

"We lost the battle and Japan lost the war." Tears spilled on the general's pillow.

Nishino gripped his feeble hand and told him he must think of himself and get well. "I gave him a box of sushi. To be polite, the general took a mouthful; but then a smile came on his face and he exclaimed, *'Umai!'*"— delicious!

Earlier this year I got a phone call from one of Gen's daughters. Their mother had died and Nishino, now in his nineties, wanted to see me before he died. We three spent four fruitful days in Danbury recalling the past.

{10}

The Last Battles

Saipan

To get material on the crucial battle on Saipan, I set out alone for the most strategically located island in the Marianas. At Guam I discovered there were only occasional flights to Saipan, but luckily one was about to take off. I was the only passenger, and the pilot cheerily asked me to sit next to him—and then handed me a map. This was his first flight to Saipan. After buzzing a small island, he headed for another, and this time he set down. It wasn't Saipan, but half an hour later we were at our destination. In the principal city, Garapan, I rented one of the four Japanese cars that serviced the island and drove up the west coast to the only hotel. (I understand that today hotels litter the little island to handle the heavy Japanese tourist traffic.)

Of the many survivors of Saipan we had interviewed in Japan, the most important was Shizuku Miura. A young volunteer nurse, a tomboy with a round merry face, she had stared in terror out the window of the first-aid station when the first shells from American battleships exploded on June 14, 1944. "Then I thought calmly that I had lived for eighteen years and my time to die had come," she told me. She staggered outside and was knocked to the ground by the next exploding shell. Garapan was aflame with a heat so intense she could hardly breathe. "I made my way through the rubbled streets littered with bodies, and climbed up to a cave overlooking the city." She hid there all night with other civilians.

In the morning a soldier peered into the cave and told her the Americans were landing just below Garapan and the Japanese tank corps was moving out to stop them. She hurried out. Her brother was inside one of those tanks. The soldier warned her to get back in the cave, but she pushed forward to get a better look. "I saw enemy tanks at the pier, firing at our tanks. Americans were wading across the lagoon, holding their guns high, and were soon scrambling up the piers. Their faces seemed to be blackened." Then the enemy tanks were suddenly silent. "I realized that my brother and the other tankers must have been killed." She looked across the water at the nearby island of Tinian, where she had last seen her family. Had that island been invaded? "I and my elder sister, who had evacuated Garapan a week earlier, must be the only ones in our family alive. I couldn't go back to the cave, and that's when I decided to volunteer as a nurse at the main field hospital on the east side of the island."

Her memories of the days that followed were harrowing—it was painful merely to listen to them. At first she was overwhelmed by the terrible wounds she was seeing as she helped treat a seemingly endless line of Japanese soldiers. "If you're afraid of a wound," the doctor told her sternly, "and feel so much pity that you can't hurt a patient, you're useless." She gritted her teeth and within an hour she was helping a surgeon sever a young soldier's foot. When they were finished, the surgeon put in a few stitches, bandaged the stump, and injected the patient. "Then I heard the young soldier whisper, 'Thank you very much.' "

The next morning Shizuku could see that the hospital area was surrounded by rocky little peaks. It looked like a stadium, with no protection from air raids. She walked down the lane of wounded soldiers lying on the ground, doling out water.

"I bent over a man wearing only a loincloth, a Japanese army lieutenant. He kept his face hidden with his hands. His left eye was black, as big as a Ping-Pong ball. It was covered with squirming maggots." His other eye had been gouged out by the worms. "My hands trembled. 'Let me treat you, soldier,' I said, and he let me pick out the maggots one by one with pincers." She told him her brother was a tank man and had died in Garapan fighting the enemy. " 'That's why I can't see a soldier without thinking of him as my brother.' And when I told him that's why I had become a nurse, tears flowed out of his terrible left eye and he said, 'Thank you.' " The next day she found him a uniform. When she changed his eye bandage she discovered that the dressing had done no good. The gauze itself was alive with maggots. "But I assured him he wouldn't die; I would surely cure him. And reinforcements were coming. Then I told him stories about my four sisters. I was the only tomboy and mother kept telling me, 'Shizuko, behave like a woman!' "

She lost count of the days. On one of her daily visits to the lieutenant with maggots, a comrade berated her. "Why didn't you see him last night? Poor Lieutenant Shinoda called you all through the night and died just an hour ago." She crouched beside his body. There wasn't a maggot on his face. He looked pale and beautiful.

On June 30, 1944, the Americans finally broke through the main Japanese line, and an order came to evacuate the field hospital to a village on the west coast near Tanapag.

"When I told the chief surgeon I was going to stay and kill myself with my patients, he ordered me to leave. All the soldiers crowded around me to say goodbye. Those who couldn't walk crawled nearer. Every man tried to tell me something about his family. I promised over and over to tell what had happened if I ever got back to Japan. Then a young officer, his uniform dyed with blood, painfully asked if I knew the song of Kudanzaka. I did, and began to sing the song of the mother who had walked miles to say farewell to her dead son in Kudanzaka."

> *I was a black hen who gave birth to a hawk.*
> *And such good fortune is more than I deserve.*
> *I wanted to show you your Order of the Golden Kite,*
> *And have come to see you, my son, in Kudanzaka.*

When she stopped, there was silence, except for stifled sobs.

As she reached the end of the field, Shizuko heard a voice cry out, "Goodbye, Mother!" Then there was a sharp blast—a grenade.

"I crouched on the ground and flinched as grenade after grenade exploded in rapid succession."

The trek to the new hospital took several days, and by July 6 it was obvious that the end had come. Shizuko had crouched in her foxhole throughout the night. Then in the early daylight she saw movement on the heights above. Darkened faces peered through the undergrowth. They were black GIs, the first blacks she had ever seen. The surgeon ordered her to wave a white handkerchief and surrender, but she believed the Americans would rape her. The group of men charged forward, lobbing grenades. The surgeon shot himself in the throat, and the lieutenant slashed his neck three times. Warm blood flowed over her legs. She picked up a grenade. She tried to cry "Mother," but nothing came out. She pulled the safety pin, rapped the grenade against a rock to activate it, and threw herself on top of it.

"Then I heard voices I couldn't understand and discovered I was in a house. A young American officer told me in Japanese that I was wounded and shouldn't move. I couldn't believe that Japanese words were coming out of an enemy. Why hadn't I died?"

"All died but you," said the young officer, who was an interpreter. He was referring to the soldiers she had been with. Then he said, "We believe in humanity, even in war," and assured her that many Japanese civilians had been saved, but she didn't believe him. Everyone knew that the American devils tore Japanese prisoners apart with tanks. She blurted out that she was afraid of all Americans, particularly those who were black.

But he laughed and said, "It was the black troops who saved you."

———

Almost 22,000 Japanese civilians—two out of every three—perished needlessly at Saipan. And almost the entire garrison—at least 30,000—died. I drove or walked over the battlefields and followed the retreat from the field hospital to Garapan. Americans killed, wounded, or missing in action numbered 14,111—more than double the losses at Guadalcanal. But we had seized the main bastion protecting Japan's homeland, and the enemy's carrier-based striking power had been crippled. Even more important, the lowlands of Saipan offered us the first site from which massive B-29 bombing raids could be launched at the heart of the Japanese Empire, Tokyo. In addition, the nearby island of Tinian was already being leveled and would be used for launching the planes carrying our atom bombs.

Tojo Resigns

It also meant the end of the Tojo government. On my return to Tokyo, Toshiko and I interviewed Mrs. Tojo in their modest one-story home, testimony to the falsity of rumors that he had made a fortune.

Mrs. Tojo told us that she herself had been nicknamed "To Bi-rei," a play on the Japanese version of Madame Chiang Kai-shek's name, "So Bi-rei." After the disaster at Saipan, she told us, she had been inundated by anonymous phone calls asking if her husband had committed suicide yet.

On the morning of July 18, 1944, Tojo had told his cabinet in a weary voice that he had decided to resign because of the loss of Saipan, and he then asked for and got the written resignations of all the rest. He delivered the documents to Kido, who asked whom he would like to succeed him. "I won't say whom *I* want," he replied with sarcasm. "I imagine the *jushin* have already decided who it will be."

"The resignation," Mrs. Tojo told us, "brought me a sense of relief. Now at last the daily chance of assassination was over."

Breakneck Ridge—Leyte

One of the most compelling stories about Japan's last days in the Philippines came from a man who would become a close friend, Corporal Kiyoshi Kamiko. I left Toshiko behind sometimes when I went to see him; his English was good enough to paint an unforgettable self-portrait. He would become one of the main characters in my book.

The Battle of Leyte, spelled the virtual end of Japanese resistance in the Philippines. On October 20, 1944, MacArthur landed a large force and

100,000 tons of cargo on Leyte at a minimal cost—the loss of forty-nine GIs. The next day, four divisions pressed forward against little resistance.

In an attempt to isolate MacArthur, a large Japanese force set out to devastate shipping in Leyte Gulf, but four carriers, three battleships, six heavy cruisers, three light cruisers, and ten destroyers were sunk by the U.S. Navy. Never again would Japan's navy play more than a minor role in defense of the homeland.

General Sosaku Suzuki, in charge of the defense of the central islands, received misleading reports that a number of U.S. carriers had been sunk; he therefore sent the 1st Division, eleven thousand men, by transport to Leyte. Corporal Kamiko, a squad leader, provided me with a vivid report of what followed. Kamiko had been a primary-school teacher before being conscripted just after Pearl Harbor. Determined and idealistic, he had enjoyed the period of training in Manchuria, accepting most of the brutalities inflicted on noncoms as necessary conditioning. Like the other men of the Gem Division, he was eager to prove himself in battle and do his duty for Japan and the emperor. Long past midnight, after a long march across Leyte on Highway 20, he found himself on the highest point of the road. The jagged ridge to the north was covered with shoulder-high cogon grass. It was a natural fortress. A number of spurs branched off it toward the sea on the other side. In between the steep rises were dense woods. Here the march ended.

The sky lightened with dramatic suddenness. With the sun came intolerable heat, and the air was acrid with powder smoke. He figured the battlefield must be near, but the ridge above them was silent. A rifle cracked. Then it was quiet again and Kamiko heard the chirping of birds. The former schoolteacher's heart beat faster. His chest felt constricted. He turned to his companions, their eyes glittering—for three years they had been preparing to fight and they were as eager as he was. Then a whispered order came up to leave the road and climb the ridge.

On the other side, GIs were also nearing the top of the ridge. Kamiko pushed through and began the ascent. Behind, someone shouted, "Squad Leader Kamiko! Wrong direction!" It was the platoon sergeant. A grenade exploded and the sergeant stumbled, clutching his thigh.

"I was showered with debris," recalled Kamiko. "I heard a soldier grunt and say he was hit. Blinded, I tripped over him. I forced myself to be calm and gradually recovered my vision." It was exactly ten o'clock on November 5 in the nineteenth year of Showa (i.e., the nineteenth year of the reign of Emperor Hirohito.) "It might be my last moment as a human being. I fired blindly, round after round, and then stopped to reload and peeked above the brush." At that moment came a thundering shock, a blinding flash, and darkness. "Earth and sand showered down on me, but I was not hurt. The mortar barrage abruptly ceased. I held up my helmet on a bayonet, and a hail of bullets battered the helmet like a wind bell. I crouched down again, but the firing from the top of the hill had stopped. I wondered why the GIs, after pinning us down, had fallen back. I told my men to eat while they had the chance. We had hardtack but no water. At dusk I gathered my remaining five men and told them they alone held the hill. I ordered them to collect ammunition, arms, and supplies from dead comrades."

By midnight they were prepared for the attack that was certain to come at dawn, but their thirst had become unbearable. "I remembered seeing a coconut tree near the crest. I removed all clothing except my loincloth, tied a washcloth around my head, and stealthily crawled up the hill. In the moonlight I found a coconut tree and started shinnying up it." He managed to get eleven coconuts, and his men "chopped off the tops and distributed the milk. It reminded me of a soft drink."

Kamiko roused his five-man squad before dawn and was as ready as he could be when a withering attack was launched by American troops supported by heavy machine guns, which were in turn hit by a large Japanese artillery piece. Somehow the scattered Japanese remnants held the line and were finally joined by the main force of his company.

Casualties on the American side were horrific, particularly among the men manning the heavy machine gun positions, and the remaining troops had rapidly withdrawn down their side of the ridge. A single platoon, with the help of a dozen artillery shells, had blunted a determined enemy attack and given the strung-out regiment time to reach the front and make the ridge— soon to be nicknamed Breakneck Ridge by the Americans—into a fortress. "I remembered how the samurai of the civil war era took the head of an enemy, and I reached for an American officer's helmet. The liner was wet with blood, and I hesitated. Was it proper for a modern man to take booty? But I still had helmet in hand when I reported to my company commander."

That night Kamiko was appointed platoon leader. He couldn't sleep; the unattended corpses lying out in front nauseated him. From the darkness he heard someone say, "Why do American soldiers die on their backs?" Another voice answered, "The Japanese are well-mannered—even after they've died they hide their private parts." Both laughed.

In the morning the Americans resumed their assault on Breakneck Ridge. "We held again, but only twenty-five in our company were now alive." The survivors were sent back in relays down to a stream on the other side of Highway 2. "We washed our faces in the cool water, filled canteens, and ate hardtack. I thought: 'This is the pleasure of nothingness.' "

The next morning typhoon winds and rain swept the ridge. Palms bent like bows; some snapped, others were uprooted. The cogon grass lashed like a turbulent sea. Even so, the Americans rushed over the top of the ridge, to the accompaniment of booming artillery. But once again the Japanese resisted, first withdrawing down their side of the ridge and then firing at the Americans who swarmed over the top.

Once all the Americans had disappeared, the Japanese clambered up the muddy slope to reoccupy their positions along the crest. Then the deadly struggle resumed, and a friendly unit on Kamiko's right was pushed back. Even so, by morning most of Breakneck Ridge was still in Japanese hands. The rain increased, and American shells plowed into the crest line for the next two days. "It reminded me of the earthquake of 1923, which I'd never been able to forget."

Then the senior Japanese officer present issued an order that astounded Kamiko—*tenshin,* literally "turn around and advance," which was a euphemism for "retreat." But somehow the Japanese forces ignored the order and stunned the superior American force by a direct and sudden attack. As the Americans fell back, Kamiko found himself thinking: We could win, with one machine gun! "But the absurdity of the idea jerked me back to reality. I was leading my men to a meaningless death."

"Follow me!" Kamiko yelled, and dodged back down the hill toward Highway 2 with his men. "I jumped into the ditch by the road, then looked back. Helmeted enemy heads were poking up all along the crest. I began to lead the remaining eleven men in the ditch down the highway toward Ormoc, but the shame of retreat still gnawed at my conscience. I had even abandoned the body of my own commander. I had valued my own life above honor." He was tormented by every step to the rear. "Then, for some reason, I started to feel defiant. Why die needlessly? It wouldn't help the nation. I began to feel almost light at heart. No one was hurt, and we broke into a run. A few hundred yards down the road we came to a culvert. A stream was running underneath. It was all fate, I reminded myself. The only thing was to do one's best and not worry about the future. We were still alive."

Two weeks later, Kamiko's regiment was reduced to less than four hundred men and the Battle of Breakneck Ridge was over. On November 25 the remnants of Gem Division were ordered to regroup down the highway. Organized resistance on Leyte was at the point of collapse, and on December 15, MacArthur announced that the Leyte campaign was over except for mopping up. On Christmas night, Kamiko and four companions came to a beach. They could hear GIs playing Christmas carols on the hills above. In the dark they found a *banca,* an outrigger canoe, and made a sail for it out of a tent.

There was a heated argument about whether they were doing the honorable thing in escaping from the island. One man, who was wounded, shot himself because he did not wish to burden his comrades—and other men were tempted to commit suicide. But in the end their instincts for self-preservation won out.

The *banca* sailed out of the inlet in the moonlight. Abruptly the moonlight was cut off and rain slapped their faces. Dark clouds gathered ominously. "Let's go back," one man cried out.

"We're at sea, Nakamura, and determined to die," I said. "So keep going."

The frail outrigger tossed erratically as they frantically bailed with their canteens. Just before dawn the rain stopped and they found themselves surrounded by small, bare-rock islets. To the south emerged the vague outline of a large island. It had to be Cebu, their first goal. "And I began to sing my favorite song, one I had taught my pupils:

> *"From a far-off island whose name I don't know*
> *A coconut comes floating.*
> *How many months have you been tossing in the waves*
> *Far from the shores of your native land?*
> *I think about tides far away*
> *And wonder when I will return to my native land."*

I accompanied Kamiko, a dozen other survivors, and a number of relatives of those who had died to Leyte. We first called on the governor in the capital. As I was passing a crowd of belligerent Filipinos, one stepped forward and yanked my arm. "Since when have you become a Jap, Toland?" he said. I had interviewed him years ago, and I told him that I was just looking for the facts.

After our meeting with the governor we piled into a large bus and set off for the battlefields, accompanied by a dozen cases of orange drink. By the time we got to Breakneck Ridge the orange drink was very warm, but the Japanese gulped it down as if it were nectar. One gulp was enough for me.

The ridge was just as Kamiko and four other men had described it. Some of the foxholes on the slope were still there after twenty-two years, and the view of Carigara Bay was still breathtaking. Even more memorable was the ceremony held for the survivors. Some of the men talked to their dead comrades about their families, and one mother scolded her son for taking so many chances. Among us was a student priest who assured the dead that their souls were now at Yasukuni Shrine with those of other heroes. I stood apart with a group of Filipinos who had come to jeer and were soon in tears. At the end they helped us enjoy more of the warm orange drink, which even I had come to savor in the 120-degree temperature.

Our next visit was down the highway to what had become known as Death Valley. Kamiko pointed out where he had seen thousands of swollen bodies scattered all over the road and in both ditches. "At first glance," he explained, "the bodies looked as if they had been attacked by snakes—the dead snakes were tubes from gas masks. The place stank of death." Here, with deadly accuracy, American artillery had caught Japanese troops moving up to the front.

During another brief ceremony, a wife told her husband that the children were now grown up and he was a three-time grandfather. One boy looked just like him. All this was being translated to me, and as she said this the Filipino next to me burst into tears. I had trouble holding back my own tears; but I felt that, as a foreigner, I had no right to mourn with them. Once we were back on the bus the last of the precious orange drink was passed around and the men began singing a song that made some of the women blush. It was remarkable that these people could unburden themselves while talking to their dead sons and comrades, yet they brought no sense of gloom to the bus.

Kamiko pointed out all the places he had described previously, and often would recall things he had neglected to tell me. In the villages where we slept, the Japanese were soon treated as friends, and the Filipino mothers who had known some of the Japanese now had daughters of marriageable age. Kamiko, in particular, was a target, for it was known that when he left Leyte he had taken a vow never to get married. It would be a betrayal of those friends he had left behind. He was also good-looking and educated. But a few comrades and I helped him to keep his vow.

Within a week our bus had become known throughout Leyte, and wherever we went we were now greeted warmly. But in one city, which had been a Filipino guerrilla center during the war, I expected our reception to be cool. While gathering material for *But Not in Shame,* I had interviewed a number of the guerrillas, and I knew how they hated the Japanese, but to my surprise they now asked if I could persuade the Japanese to put on a show the next day. I agreed, with one proviso: that it be a joint Japanese-Filipino show.

The next morning I rounded up Filipino talent and arranged for half a dozen acts. Then I assembled the Japanese, who were delighted to make it a joint performance. The open-air school auditorium was packed that night, and the first act—a rousing song by the Japanese soldiers—brought an explosion of applause. This was followed by an equally rousing song from my guerrilla friends. For the next hour and a half the show rollicked on, with more songs, dances, and comic bits. Instead of finishing with a number combining both groups, the show ended with a Japanese mother under a single spotlight singing the song of the mother who had walked miles to say farewell to her dead son in Kudansaka:

"I was a black hen who gave birth to a hawk. . . ."

There was absolute quiet when she finished, and then an emotional display by the audience such as I had never before witnessed. It seemed to encompass the tragedies of both Filipinos and Japanese. One stout woman had finally united them a thousand miles from home.

A Tokyo newspaper had assigned me the job of covering this expedition, and I had already sent it some material. My last story was supposed to be on the yearly ceremony honoring MacArthur's landing on Leyte. This year, for the first time, the Japanese ambassador was invited to appear. I was asked to speak briefly. Everything went smoothly, with no anti-Japanese demonstration, owing—I am sure—to the impression made by our busload. But I had to add a postscript to my news story. That night the Japanese set up a shrine in one room of our hotel. On this shrine were placed hundreds of items our group had picked up at various battle sites in memory of those who had died. Dozens of candles were lit, and then we all went to our own rooms, leaving that room guarded by several men.

I was in the next room with Kamiko. It was so hot that by midnight I had already taken two cold baths. I was still awake an hour later when I heard a loud commotion in the next room. We rushed in and found that all the candles had been blown out. Yet there hadn't been a breath of wind. I sent the story, and when we finally arrived in Tokyo the question lingered: What had caused all the candles to be blown out so mysteriously? All of us who had gone to Leyte knew that the men on guard had not tried to play a trick. That was unthinkable after all we had gone through together. It was generally felt that this phenomenon had been a message to us. When asked my opinion about this, I tried in vain to think of something appropriate about the supernatural—preferably from Shakespeare. I don't recall exactly what I said, but my own life had been so full of incredible coincidences that I was inclined to agree.

Perhaps the message was revealed when, not long afterward, Kamiko wrote us that he was finally getting married. He no longer felt bound by his vow to his dead comrades. We would remain friends, and he became a leading character in my first published novel.

Iwo Jima

The next major battle had taken place on a small island. As our plane approached Iwo Jima, it looked like no more than a dot, and I marveled that it could have played such an important role in our victory. I was welcomed by the small U.S. staff from our air force and Coast Guard. They not only lent me a jeep to scour the island but escorted me down several deep caves where the Japanese had hidden during and after the bitter battle. We went down with a flashlight, the last man holding on to a very long rope so that we could find our way out of the many underground side trails.

From the sea, Iwo Jima ("Sulfur Island") resembled a half-submerged whale, but from the air it looked like a fat pork chop, its most distinct feature being Mount Suribachi ("Cone-Shaped Bowl"), the extinct volcano at the narrow southern end. Only 556 feet high, it seemed more imposing when seen from the sea, jutting straight up from the water. Several times I made the short but stiff climb to the marker on top where our flag had been planted.

The island was nearly five miles long and two and a half miles wide—a third the area of Manhattan. Though its volcano was inactive, the entire island seemed to be alive with jets of steam and boiling sulfur pits. The combination of coastal cliffs and rugged Suribachi gave the appearance of another Rock of Gibraltar, but after wandering around for two days I had the queasy feeling that the island might disappear at any moment into the ocean. I was warned about one dirt road leading to Suribachi. At one point it was a foot or so under water. If the water got much deeper it could mean that part of the island was disintegrating.

The fat northern part of the triangular island was a plateau some 350 feet high, with inaccessible rocky shores, but at the narrow end toward Suribachi there were wide stretches of beach suitable for amphibious landings. I already knew that the beach on the east side was the one selected for the marines to assault. I found it difficult to plow through what looked like black sand but was actually volcanic ash and cinders from nearby Suribachi, so light and powdery that I sank to my calves. I imagined that a big marine with a heavy pack would sink to at least his knees. I borrowed a pack and went out in the water to my waist. Wading back, holding a rifle, was exhausting. On the beach there was still evidence of the battle, and I brought back empty shells, several rifle clips, and a jar of volcanic ash.

I had already interviewed several Japanese who had defended the island, and I wandered from one end to the other marveling at the terrain. While the sterile soil provided little natural cover for the windswept beaches and plateau, the small hills and valleys surrounding the tableland were dense with jungle growth.

Iwo was one of a chain of islands hanging like a loose necklace from the entrance to Tokyo Bay to within three hundred miles of the Marianas. The last three islands were volcanic, with Iwo in the center. Of the entire chain, Iwo alone was suitable for airfields. We needed it desperately as a base for fighter planes escorting the big bombers to Japan, as well as a haven for bombers limping home.

Navy Lieutenant Toshihiko Ohno told us that he and his men had been driven from place to place by the advancing Americans. Ohno had commanded an antiaircraft battery of fifty-four men, but after two weeks only five were left. In some ways Ohno, who was six feet tall and slender, looked more like a young American officer fresh from OCS than a typical Japanese. A recent college graduate, sensitive and gentle, he seemed unsuited for commanding men, but under fire he had matured. After several weeks of retreat, he and his men were hiding in a pillbox about eleven feet square. The entrance was closed and they had crawled in through the gun port. They were sprawled on the concrete floor, sleeping off a feast; that night they had found two cases of hardtack and candy, three large bags of sugar, and a half-gallon can half full of water.

"I was awakened by a noise and through the porthole saw a marine helmet. As I drew my pistol, the helmet disappeared. Then there was a hissing noise and a grenade bounced off the floor. Someone leaped in front of me and tossed a blanket over the grenade just before it detonated. Fortunately it exploded upward and no one was hurt. I was dazed and didn't at first realize a bundle of dynamite sticks had just been shoved into the porthole. I leaped back, hugged the wall, and shouted a warning. Everyone stuck thumbs in ears, middle fingers on noses, and last two fingers over mouths." He said, *"Tenno Heika banzai!"* ("Long live the Emperor!") to himself and visualized his wife and mother. The pillbox seemed to rise three feet in the air. It was as if his body were being pressed together by some unearthly force. He heard himself cry out, "Ahhh!" The pillbox swirled with smoke. "I asked if everyone was all right. All but one enlisted man named Kitagata replied." Through a hole where the ventilator had blown out, a shaft of light illuminated Kitagata. His head was bleeding and sand peppered his face. He moaned. A shadow interposed in the foggy shaft of light; a marine was peering down. "I clamped a hand over Kitagata's mouth. The shadow withdrew and I heard someone outside shouting, 'Let's go!' We were safe for the moment."

Ohno told us they had hidden in a cave until the battle was over in mid-March. Then he sneaked out front and found the Americans building airstrips. "I still wanted to be a trader or a diplomat and decided to escape even though everyone said it was impossible." He fabricated a compass by magnetizing a needle with the magnet in a telephone receiver, and with four others collected enough material for a raft. They hoped they could sail north at six knots and in twelve hours catch the wind which swept past Japan. But the bulky craft was smashed by a towering breaker, and all hope of escape was gone.

A few days later, two of his men left one evening for food and ammunition but never returned. He was alone with Kitagata. For endless hours they endured a solitary confinement in their cave. They were so close to Seabee work parties that they could hear jazz music piped over a loudspeaker, and once it seemed that they would surely be discovered by Americans gossiping overhead when Kitagata farted.

On May 27, Japan's Navy Day, they prayed that there would be a major Japanese counterattack from the sea. When nothing happened they decided to leave their cave with three grenades apiece and a determination to make their own deaths as costly as possible. They intercepted two wandering GIs who fled before Ohno could activate the first grenade—the two "GIs" were his own men who had left for food and never returned. Discouraged, Ohno and Kitagata returned to their cave and slept. "Suddenly I was alerted by a hissing. Grenade! I grabbed a blanket and was only half covered before it exploded. My clothes were smoldering. A phosphorus grenade had showered me with burning red specks." He brushed at them frantically. When bits stuck under his fingernails, in agony he dug his inflamed fingers into the ground. A package of dynamite tumbled through the cave entrance, and there was a thumping concussion that flattened them against the ground. Through the dust and smoke they saw that the cave entrance had been blasted open. Then everything was dark. They had been sealed in by a bulldozer. At dusk they crept out through another exit, armed with six grenades. A complex of tents had magically mushroomed nearby; Kitagata thought grenades were not sufficient for a proper assault, but a search for land mines proved futile. Now Kitagata refused to attack altogether, but Ohno remained resolved to end it all that night. "You need only one grenade to kill yourself," he said.

Cowering in the predawn fog, Ohno smeared himself with stolen toothpaste and Lux soap so he would smell like an American. As he hung a necklace of three grenades around his neck, he said, "We'll meet at Yasukuni Shrine." He then began crawling toward the barbed-wire fence enclosing the tents.

"I was confident I could deceive the enemy with my Yankee odor, and made for the largest tent. I peered inside. It was a mess hall." He then crept to the next tent and cautiously rolled up a canvas side. A man was lying on a cot. "I struck the grenade with a stone and waited for the hiss. But apparently the fuse had deteriorated. I tried a second. This one hissed briefly but fizzled out. I tied the two duds to a third grenade and tried to activate it. Nothing happened. I looked around for weapons but couldn't even find a trenching tool. What kind of soldiers were these?"

He slipped into another tent. No guns. Someone approached, whistling a tune. "I ducked behind the empty cot." A heavyset man went directly to Ohno's cot and started making it. "I was sure I'd been discovered and sprang to my feet." The big American leaped out of the tent with a scream. Then two men in cots leaped at Ohno and clung to him until the big American returned with half a dozen armed men. "I just waited to be shot and asked the big American in my stumbling English for his name. The big man mumbled, 'Bill,' and the others burst into laughter."

One of them said, "Please," and casually motioned Ohno to follow. "For some reason, I felt as if I had found new friends. I turned to Bill and said, 'How is Gary Cooper?'"

Ohno was a prisoner for almost a year and a half. On the day he returned home, his father had just received ashes marked with his son's name. "A remarkable day," remarked the father as they bowed. "Suddenly I have two sons."

Navy Lieutenant Satoru Omagari had been hiding in a cave not far away. In the final battle he had volunteered to make himself a human bomb and throw himself under the treads of an enemy tank, and for two days he had tried in vain to do this. Now he thrust a pistol into his mouth and pulled the trigger. There was an empty click. He had long since given his troops permission to surrender, but few had done so. It would have meant eternal disgrace to a man's family. Driven from hiding place to hiding place by the Americans, Omagari decided to return to the navy aviation cave, whose occupants guarded its entrances against Japanese as well as Americans, for their squadron leader, a lieutenant, and his staff refused to share with anyone the spacious cave and its plentiful supply of food and water. But tonight Omagari and his men surprised the guards and broke in. There were at least 150 sailors in the rambling cave, and few of them had seen daylight in the past two months. The heat had grown so intense that they had ripped off their clothes and reverted to nakedness.

Several days later the Americans finally discovered the cave. Grenades and smoke bombs drove the occupants into its deepest recesses. Then an American warned over a loudspeaker that the cave would be flooded the next day. When there was no answer, seawater was pumped in, and only Omagari and those who had retreated to the highest level survived. A yellowish beam suddenly probed their smoke-filled cavern. "I fumbled for a light machine gun," Omagari told us, "then I saw it was one of my petty officers with a flashlight." Two more Japanese, also in U.S. fatigues, came forward; they had cigarettes and said there were many Japanese prisoners, including a major. They had been treated well by the Americans. Then they left to allow their countrymen to arrive at their own decision.

"If you want to live," Omagari said, brandishing the machine gun, "surrender." All left the cave except Omagari and an old friend, Ensign Kakuta, who was severely wounded. "I asked him what we should do and suggested we die together. But Kakuta said he didn't want to die. Neither did I, but I couldn't turn myself over to the enemy naked. I found a bolt of cotton loincloth and crept out of the cave, pistol and bolt of loincloth in hand." Half a dozen Americans, grinning broadly, came toward him. One stretched out a hand. "Wait!" said Omagari in Japanese. "I am an officer and must be clothed before I greet you." He modestly turned his back, ripped off six feet of material, and adroitly fashioned himself a loincloth. Then he too extended a hand.

Omagari remained composed until he had showered; then he broke down. "It was the first time I had ever wept." He was put under restraint. "I bit my tongue to choke on my own blood, but each attempt became feebler. It was weeks before I finally accepted the degradation of surrender."

He was among the prisoners of war that John Rich of NBC, himself a U.S. Marine interpreter during the war, brought to us. All had been despised by their fellow countrymen for surrendering and still could not go home. One told a harrowing story. He and two comrades had found a hideaway far underground. When two other Japanese tried to join them, they were shot, because air and water were scarce. After telling me this, the man who killed them asked me not to use the story. I agreed. The next day he said I could use the story but not his name. The following day he called to say, "Use my name."

Hundreds of other stragglers on Iwo could not bring themselves to surrender, nor could they bring themselves to commit suicide. They continued to hide beneath the crust of the little island, like dead souls on a distant planet. Among them were Ohno's two men. Six years later they were the last of the Iwo Jima garrison to surrender. They had held out until 1951. Ohno told me about how one of them, named Yamakage, returned years later to Iwo with an American journalist. They had come to find the diary Yamakage insisted he had kept for five years. They methodically searched Yamakage's last cave but found nothing. When the journalist expressed doubt that there ever was a diary, Yamakage searched all night in vain to find it. In the morning he and the journalist drove to the summit of Mount Surabachi to take pictures. At the crest, Yamakage started trotting with eyes on the ground. He paused, turned, and slowly walked back. Then he again loped toward the edge of the cliff overlooking the sea. Picking up speed, he threw his arms in the air, shouted something, and leaped. The journalist ran to the edge of the cliff. A hundred and twenty yards below, the body of Yamakage lay on a ledge.

Tokyo Bombed

Now I began to learn about what it was like to be a civilian on the home islands. One witness would pass me on to another, forging a chain of human links that bound this complex book together.

By the beginning of March 1945, Japan was being ravaged by bombings, but General Curtis LeMay realized that their primary purpose—to obliterate all production facilities—had not been achieved. He therefore hit upon a radical scheme: his planes would go in low at night, stripped of most armament to increase the payload, and scatter incendiary bombs into tinderbox targets over a wide area. On March 9, 333 bombers from Saipan and Tinian headed for Tokyo. A blazing X was etched by Pathfinders in downtown Tokyo. Then more Pathfinders dropped their napalm on the X, followed by the main force, three wings in orderly but random formation, dropping their loads. Whipped by a stiffening wind, the fires spread rapidly as succeeding bombers fanned out toward the residential area (where Toshiko and her family lived) to unload their sticks of napalm. The result was an unbelievable hellfire.

"The red glow that spread over the southeastern horizon quickly bulged up and filled the entire sky," Sumie Mishima told us, "so that even where we were, on the opposite edge of the city, an eerie pink light settled on the earth and clearly lit up the deep-lined faces of the awestruck people. The burning seemed to go on all night."

The Sekimura family lived less than two miles from the center of the fiery X. They bundled up their four children in quilted, hooded fire capes and joined a stream of people heading for one of the branches of the Sumida River. Walking through crisply falling debris that was beginning to come down like black snow reminded Mrs. Sekimura of the great fires after the earthquake of 1923, when she was twelve. The sight of the bombs bursting overhead like bunches of bananas entranced rather than terrified her.

It had taken Mrs. Sekimura a long time to even start telling us her story, and I was convinced that it was a lost cause. But Toshiko's patience and understanding finally relaxed her, and she spilled out her story like a dam bursting. She was in tears, but she later thanked us for finally helping her to let loose all that had been tormenting her through the years.

She told how they had pushed their way across the bridge to escape the roaring blaze that was pursuing them like a wild animal. A strong wind, sucked into the flames, swept a stinging storm of pebbles into their faces. They turned, backs to the gale, and slowly plodded away from the conflagration, fascinated by the sight of oil drums rocketing through the roof of a cable factory near the river and exploding into balls of fire a hundred feet in the air.

Mrs. Sekimura, baby on her back, later returned over the bridge to try to recover the belongings she had buried in the ground. The bridge was clogged with the bodies of those who had been trapped. The river itself, almost evaporated, was choked with swollen corpses and household possessions. "The places I had known most of my life were all gone. All I could recognize was the cable factory, twisted and deformed like melted candy. Bodies were all over, some naked and black." A few were oddly upright, crouched as if trying to run; some were clasping hands in prayer; others were seated as if in contemplation. One man's head had shrunk to the size of a grapefruit. The dead, covered with straw, were piled high in schoolyards. The stink of death permeated the air.

"I finally found the ashes of our house, but the ground was still too hot to dig. I looked around carefully, since it was impossible to buy even a piece of paper or a pair of chopsticks." The loss of all one's possessions meant a retreat to an animal level of existence. "All I could save was a *kama* for cooking rice. I picked it up with a stick so it wouldn't scorch my hands." Curiously, the sight of so much death, she said, left her untouched. "I walked mechanically by the corpses of neighbors, unable to shed a tear. There were the mother and daughter who lived across the street, completely black except for white rings around their eyes. And they had always been so neat!" Dazed, she passed the hospital and its emergency pool of water, now filled with layer upon layer of sprawling bodies. A man stopped her and remarked that he had been in that human heap. "Everyone else is dead," he said in a toneless voice. "Miraculously, I didn't even get hurt."

Sixteen square miles of Tokyo had been burned to the ground, and city officials estimated that there were 130,000 dead. I wished all those in the free world who had rejoiced at this great victory, like myself, could have heard Mrs. Sekimura's story, listened to her sobs, and seen the pain engraved on her face.

The next night, 313 bombers dumped napalm on Nagoya. This was followed by incendiary raids on Osaka and Kobe. In one week, forty-five square miles of crucial industrial centers had been incinerated. But more than Japanese military power had been destroyed. A multitude of defenseless civilians had already been killed—and this was just the beginning.

Okinawa

Still the Japanese fought on. One bastion remained, the island of Okinawa. The crossroads of the Orient, lying almost equidistant from Japan, China, and Formosa, it had been influenced by all three as well as by the islands of the South Pacific. It was an integral part of Japan and was represented in the Diet as one of Japan's forty-seven prefectures. The Okinawans, despite their mixed heritage, regarded themselves as Japanese and were as loyal to the emperor as any Tokyo resident.

To protect this key island, the super-battleship *Yamato* and nine other ships of the Ninth Fleet left the Inland Sea and soon launched a mass air raid on U.S. ships clustered off Okinawa. Three hundred and forty-one bombers dropped their explosives while 355 kamikaze plummeted down on the Americans, wiping out three destroyers and two ammunition ships. Nine other mass air raids followed, with damage to the Americans but at the cost of destruction of the great *Yamato* and her companion ships. It was the end of the Japanese navy—and the beginning of the end of Okinawa.

Toshiko and I were first sent to Okinawa in mid-1966 by the State Department so that I could lecture to the universities on history. With the help of officials, particularly Dr. Samuel Mukaida of the Public Affairs Department, we located a number of people who had lived through the bitter battle that ensued on Okinawa. For an entire day a helicopter toured us all over the island at low level, and we even visited Ie Shima, the small island just off the southern coast where Ernie Pyle had been killed. The monument read: "On this spot President Truman expressed the thoughts of those who fought and those who wrote about fighting when he said that Ernie Pyle 'became the spokesman of the ordinary American in arms doing so many extraordinary things.' "

After landing on Okinawa with few losses, the U.S. Army headed south, encountering little difficulty until approaching the main Japanese defenses, a rugged little escarpment that stuck up like a segment of the Great Wall of China. This was Maeda Ridge, with its forbidding sheer cliffs that made it a fortress in fact as well as in appearance. After two costly attacks, a third was mounted on the morning of April 27. Infantry, tanks, and flamethrowers assaulted the remaining Japanese positions, and before dusk the U.S. forces held the entire eastern segment of the escarpment.

General Mitsuru Ushijima, commander of Japanese forces, ordered a regiment to clear the ridge, and the center position was given to a battalion commanded by one of the youngest captains in the Japanese army, Tsuneo Shimura. "Most of my six hundred enlisted men," he told us, "had never before been in battle. One of these men, nineteen-year-old Shuzen Hokama, was still attending normal school, but like so many patriotic Okinawans had volunteered for front-line duty."

The story Shimura told us was one that staggered the imagination. More than one hundred of his men were killed in the first few moments of daylight when American tanks opened fire on them at point-blank range. Shimura and seven others found shelter in a tomb; other surviving Japanese soldiers took refuge in makeshift air raid shelters and in spaces behind rocks. Next morning the remnants of Japanese forces, armed only with rifles, grenades, and bayonets, counterattacked. "I didn't know then," Shimura recalled, "but the American units had taken a bad beating and some platoons were down to half a dozen men."

Despite losses at the Maeda Ridge, the American forces on the island had increased to 170,000 men, and they had endless quantities of ammunition and food. To those just arriving it seemed to turn the war into an adventure. Then on May 3, kamikaze planes struck at U.S. shipping, sinking the destroyer *Little* and LSM-195 and damaging four other ships. At the same time, Japanese artillery began to pound the U.S. front-line positions. Then came an infantry attack by two thousand men. The Japanese thought they were winning, since their accurate artillery fire had immobilized all the U.S. medium tanks, and a six-hundred-man battalion commanded by Captain Koichi Ito pierced the American lines in the predawn gloom. But only his unit had achieved a breakthrough. He was ordered to stay in place, but it was already obvious to General Cho, Ushijima's chief of staff, that the counterattack had failed. He knew defeat was certain.

The American assaults continued, and Ito had fewer than a quarter of the six hundred men he had started with. "While I was preparing myself for death, a message wrapped around a rock landed in my foxhole." It was from his radioman: an order had just been received to fall back. "I took leave of the wounded and distributed hand grenades among them." At midnight the battered battalion moved south in the darkness. It was a mile through enemy territory when the order was finally given to withdraw. Only Ito and a dozen others got back safely.

By that time young Captain Shimura too had fewer than a quarter left from his six-hundred-man battalion, and most of them were wounded. But he refused to surrender. "Regiment insisted I withdraw, but I wanted to die where most of my battalion had been killed." He told his men of the order to withdraw but stated that he was going to remain as a guerrilla. "Those who wish to stay with me can do so. We'll stick it out here on this ridge until we die." Some of the men went underground with Shimura and the rest withdrew, leaving Maeda Ridge to the Americans.

Many other Japanese shared Shimura's spirit. During these last days, kamikaze pilots were still diving into the American ships protecting Okinawa. Ensign Yasunori Aoki, born in Tokyo twenty-two years earlier, believed in the kamikaze slogan "One plane, one warship." He went to bed on May 26 knowing that the next day he would head for Okinawa and it would be his last day on earth. He awakened, composed, just before dawn. "I'm all right!" he thought. He felt extraordinarily refreshed and keen. He had already put aside fingernail clippings and a lock of his hair for his family. Now he wrote postcards to each of his parents, his four younger sisters, and his younger brother. "Our divine country will not be destroyed," he told them, and then prayed that Japan would survive total defeat.

Aoki was an aircraft commander. He had been given a slow, bulky two-seat trainer with a seventeen-year-old pilot. They took off in a flight with fourteen other aircraft in the afternoon and hours later were still droning on at a thousand feet for what was supposed to be a coordinated attack at midnight. Aoki ordered his pilot to attack at eleven-thirty and watched in the moonlight as antiaircraft fire began groping its way toward the plane. Spying a U.S. destroyer that seemed oblivious to their presence, the two men aimed their bomb-laden plane toward it. The ship fired not a single shot at them but did manage to evade the kamikaze attack, and the plane hit the water, remaining intact because the armed bombs had not detonated.

Both men were picked up by another destroyer. Feeling disgraced, they planned to commit suicide. On deck they refused cigarettes and bread. "We were transferred to a larger ship, and I showed Yokoyama how to commit suicide by biting the tongue and choking on the blood." With tongue extended, Aoki punched his chin again and again. For all the pain, there was little blood. Then he tried to strangle himself with a thick strand of twisted rope. A guard rushed in as he was blacking out. "I concluded that it was my fate to live and become a model prisoner." When he returned to Japan in late 1946 he was greeted by his uncle, a lieutenant general, with joy and understanding, and for the first time Aoki was glad to be alive. "I've had two lives," he told us. "Now every moment is precious."

On Okinawa the fighting had degenerated into a cruel hunt as the Americans went after the Japanese, entombed in large caves, with satchel charges and flamethrowers. General Ushijama's last words to his troops were "to fight to the last and die for the eternal cause of loyalty to the emperor." They were not to die in a useless suicide charge, but to filter through enemy lines in civilian clothes and join the small group of guerrillas in the north of the island. He himself sent a farewell message to imperial headquarters, got a final haircut, and then kneeled beside his chief of staff, Cho, and committed *seppuku*—ritual disembowelment.

Thousands of civilians, as well as soldiers, were still in caves. Shigeru Kinjo, then thirteen years old, told us how he was huddled with his family in a small cave packed with soldiers. Someone outside activated a grenade against a rock and threw it in the midst of the family. "I thought the world had exploded. I heard my mother say something, then her death rattle. Someone said, 'I'm not dead,' and then, pleadingly, 'Explode another!' "

Late that night, a few miles away in thorny brush near the shoreline, thirteen Okinawan student nurses, led by Seizen Nakasone, a music instructor at the normal school, were preparing for suicide. While his charges sat in a circle singing "Sayonara," a haunting song which he had composed, Nakasone went off by himself to sort out his thoughts. "How futile to die with nobody knowing anything about it!" The dew on the trees shone in the moonlight, beautiful and mysterious.

"At dawn," he told us, "I noticed Americans in green fatigues stealthily approaching. These were the Anglo-Saxon devils, but for some reason I no longer feared them, and I thought, 'Why should the girls and I kill ourselves?' I crept back to the huddling student nurses. One of them asked if it was all right to die now. She had a grenade and wanted to use it. I asked her to wait, hoping to stall them until the Americans arrived. One by one the girls left the circle—all except the resolute girl with the grenade. I stepped close to her and suddenly wrenched it from her hand, whereupon she raced to the beach and flung herself into the water."

Soldiers dragged her out, bleeding from coral cuts and still struggling. "Imagining I was the only Okinawan man who had surrendered, I was overcome with shame. But at least I had saved my students."

By July 2, the Okinawan campaign was officially declared ended. In three months, the Americans had lost 12,520 GIs, marines, and sailors. It was our greatest toll in the Pacific. The Japanese had lost 110,000 troops. In addition, the number of civilian casualties was horrendous. Caught between two armies, 75,000 defenseless men, women, and children had died. And their sacrifice was in vain, for Japan had lost the last major battle she could fight outside the homeland.

Toshiko and I became even closer to one another as we relived the story of her country's modern history. It is a tragic story, replete with the Greek fatal flaw of hubris and the stoic survival of those who paid the price for it. Through the pain of ordinary Japanese, civilians and soldiers alike, I came to an understanding of and feeling for the interwoven, inescapable bonds of a society that could, in the emperor's words, "endure the unendurable."

{11}

The Road to Peace

Circumventing the Militarists

While researching *The Rising Sun* in 1966, Toshiko and I faced our greatest challenge when we attempted to tell the story of the fantastic, intricate path to peace. Fortunately, she had persuaded those at the core of truth to reveal exactly what happened. Although Marquis Koichi Kido, the privy seal (Emperor Hirohito's chief adviser), was found guilty of war crimes, from early in 1941 he had worked with the emperor for peace. Prince Fumimaro Konoye, demeaned by some historians, had also been working for peace. After the fall of Saipan on July 9, 1944, he tried to enlist Kido in this cause, but the privy seal, though sympathetic, privately thought it would be precipitate at that time to use his influence on the emperor.

But the fall of Leyte in February 1945 and Iwo Jima in March so roused the concern of his majesty over the future of his nation that he had summoned Kido and suggested that he might find it necessary to consult the *jushin,* the former prime ministers, about the deteriorating war situation. Only once before, on the eve of war itself, had the emperor convened the *jushin* to discuss any subject except the selection of a new premier.

I was very grateful to Marquis Kido, because through him I finally got at the truth. Once he accepted me I knew I would be able to talk to the other leaders who had remained silent since 1945 and would get the story as it was seen by those on the inside.

"I had the *jushin* brought to the emperor's office one at a time," Kido told us. If they had appeared as a group, the military would have become suspicious. "This arrangement would also make it easier for each man to speak freely." Except for Konoye's, however, the advice of the elderly members of the *jushin* was vague and poorly thought through. Konoye's appraisal was a closely reasoned statement of the political and military abyss into which Japan would fall unless peace was concluded shortly. Konoye's position, explained Kido, was inescapable: peace could be negotiated only if the hard-core militarists were circumvented.

In April 1945, just before the last naval sortie of the Imperial Fleet in a futile attempt to stop the enemy landing on Okinawa, Prime Minister Kuniaki Koiso, who had replaced Tojo, was forced to resign. At the *jushin* meeting to select a new premier, Kido put forward the name of Kantaro Suzuki, who in the 2/26 Incident back in 1936 had miraculously survived three deadly wounds. He was a devout Taoist and free of ambition. "I knew this man would help us make peace."

Through the efforts of Kido and the emperor, the possibility of peace had at last been brought into the open, and Suzuki, the new prime minister, realized that his appointment was an unspoken directive from his majesty to end the conflict as soon as possible. In early May 1945, when the Japanese forces on Okinawa were fighting desperately to hold Maeda Ridge, a peace effort was under way in Switzerland, involving Allen Dulles. He suggested that the Japanese send a fully authorized representative to Switzerland. America would guarantee safe air transportation. This promising offer was transmitted directly to Navy Minister Mitsumasa Yonai. He took the proposal to the Foreign Minister Shigenori Togo, who asked Yonai to explore the proposal more thoroughly.

While Japan was searching hesitatantly for peace, her cities were being reduced to ashes. On May 12, four days after the surrender of Germany, Admiral Yonai made a suggestion at a meeting of the "Big Six," the Supreme Council for the Conduct of the War (comprising the premier, Foreign Minister Togo, and the four military chiefs), that could have caused his dismissal. He proposed that they ask Russia to mediate a settlement of the war. The forbidden subject of peace was again out in the open. The Soviet ambassador was sounded out, and he appeared willing, but the following morning, June 6, at another Big Six meeting, Togo was handed a document composed by the Supreme Command demanding an official reaffirmation of the policy of carrying the war to its ultimate conclusion. Although Togo argued heatedly, the resolution to fight to the end was passed. And two days later an imperial conference was convened to present the resolution to the emperor for his approval.

Unprepared, the emperor sat silent on his dais with a grave look on his face. He said nothing. "As he emerged from the meeting," Kido revealed, "I was puzzled by the concern on his face and asked why. 'They have made their decision,' replied his majesty, and showed me a copy of the new policy. I was stunned and knew I could no longer depend on the aging prime minister, even with the support of Togo, to take the initiative for peace. As confidential adviser to the throne, I was required by tradition to remain above politics. In the past I had managed to circumvent this restriction indirectly, but now I somehow knew I had to take positive action."

All that afternoon and into the night, Kido searched for a solution. "Finally I realized there was one source no one could oppose—the throne. I decided to confront his majesty with candor. I felt that in this crisis such an unprecedented approach was necessary in order to persuade him to end the war by personal intervention. At last I could go to sleep."

Early the next afternoon he presented a document to the emperor entitled "Tentative Plan to Cope with the Situation." The emperor studied it and appeared to be greatly satisfied by what he read. Kido asked permission to discuss the proposal with Prime Minister Suzuki and other leaders. "I would need the support of key men in the cabinet before the emperor could be openly involved. His majesty said, 'Do it at once.' " When the military still dragged their feet, the emperor on June 22, at the instigation of the privy seal, abruptly summoned the Big Six. He defined the unique informality of the occasion by speaking first. "This is not an imperial command," he said, "but merely a discussion. At the last meeting of the Supreme Council it was decided to adopt a new policy and prepare the homeland for defense. But now I have deemed it necessary to consider a move toward peace, an unprecedented one, and I ask you to take steps at once to realize my wish."

The emperor made it clear that he did not want undue caution to cost Japan an opportunity for this "move toward peace." But in the following week a great deal of time was consumed by Japan's initiative to get the Soviet Union to broker some sort of cessation of hostilities on terms Japan could accept. The emperor called Prince Konoye in, at Kido's suggestion, for an unprecedented private meeting between the two men. An obviously distraught Hirohito wanted Konoye to go as an envoy to Moscow. The prince quickly assented.

I could now understand just how these final days played out only because I had the trust of the key participants. Very little of this was documented— only the memories of elderly men could supply me with the priceless details.

In Moscow, Ambassador Naotake Sato was advised by cable of the prince's imminent arrival: "His majesty is extremely anxious to terminate the war as soon as possible. Should, however, the United States and Great Britain insist on unconditional surrender, Japan would be forced to fight to the bitter end."

Sato told us that when he got this message he knew the Russians well enough to doubt that anything good would come of this maneuver, and he cabled a reply to Togo with the caustic observation that if Konoye was merely coming to enunciate "previous abstractions, lacking in concreteness," he had better stay at home. "We have no alternative but to accept unconditional surrender or something close to it."

Hiroshima

One of my most difficult tasks was to do the research behind the story of the two A-bomb attacks, a story that began in July 1995 in Potsdam, where Truman had just received good news from Alamagordo, New Mexico: the uranium gun-type atomic bomb that would be dropped on Japan had just been successfully exploded. In his meeting that afternoon with Stalin, the president made no mention of the bomb, but Stalin had a secret to confide that was already known to Truman because we had broken the Japanese diplomatic code. Stalin showed him the emperor's confidential message requesting that Prince Konoye be received as an emissary of peace. Stalin wondered if he shouldn't ignore it, since the USSR was planning eventually to declare war on Japan. Truman told him to do what he thought best.

By late July the atomic bomb was on Tinian Island and the orders for its use drawn up. Now all that remained was to dispatch the Potsdam Declaration to Japan—the final warning which threatened "utter devastation of the Japanese homeland" unless Japan unconditionally surrendered. It also limited Japanese sovereignty to the four main islands but did promise that the Japanese would not be "enslaved as a race or destroyed as a nation" and would be allowed "to maintain such industries as will sustain her economy."

Japanese monitors picked up the broadcast of the proclamation on the morning of July 27, Tokyo time, and Prime Minister Suzuki decided to read a statement that in effect minimized the significance of the Allied terms without rejecting them outright. He told reporters the government didn't consider it of great importance. "We must *mokusatsu* it," he said. This word literally meant "kill with silence," but Suzuki's son told us that his father had intended it to mean the English phrase "No comment," for which there is no Japanese equivalent. Americans, however, understandably applied the dictionary meanings: "ignore" and "treat with contempt." And on July 30 the *New York Times* headline read: JAPAN OFFICIALLY TURNS DOWN ALLIED SURRENDER ULTIMATUM.

And so at exactly 2:45 A.M. on August 6, 1945, the *Enola Gay*, carrying the atom bomb, took off from Tinian for Hiroshima. Toshiko and I interviewed twenty-five survivors. It took many hours of our time just to track them down and many more to elicit full accounts. On the first day I found it difficult to remain composed while listening to people whose faces still bore witness to the horrors they had undergone. When we found that the first four would have lunch with us and then continue the interviewing throughout the afternoon, I couldn't imagine being able to eat a bite. But by lunchtime I was no longer repelled by their physical deformities and saw them only as people who had endured hell and emerged without any discernible rage and resentment against Americans. I saw their stoicism and spirit. They had not lost their humanity; in fact, they seemed to have gained something by their experiences.

Yasuko Nukushina told how she had been trapped in the ruins of the family sake store. Her first thought was of her four-year-old daughter, Ikuko, who she thought was playing outside somewhere. Unaccountably, she heard Ikuko's voice beside her: "I'm afraid, Mama!" She told the child they were buried and would die there. Her own words made her claw desperately at the wreckage. She was a slight woman, four feet six inches tall, but in her frenzy she broke into the yard. All around was devastation. Somehow she felt responsible—"her" bomb had also destroyed the neighborhood. People drifted by, expressionless and silent, like sleepwalkers, in tattered, smoldering clothing. It was a parade of wraiths, an evocation of a Buddhist hell. She watched, mesmerized, until someone touched her. Grasping Ikuko's hand, she joined the procession. In her confusion she had the illusion that vast numbers of planes were roaring over the city, dropping bomb after bomb with no letup.

Dr. Fumio Shigeto, head of internal medicine at the Red Cross hospital, told us that he never reached his office that morning. On the way to work, he was waiting for a trolley at the end of a long line which bent around the corner of the Hiroshima railway station. The flash seemed to make a group of girls, just ahead of him, almost invisible. "An incendiary bomb, I thought. As I dropped to the sidewalk, covering my eyes and ears, a heavy slate slammed into my back and whirls of smoke blotted out the sun. In the darkness I groped blindly to reach the shelter before the next wave of attackers came in." Fearing poison gas, he covered his mouth with a handkerchief.

A breeze from the east gradually cleared the area as though it were dawn, revealing an incredible scene: the buildings in front of the station were collapsed; half-naked and smoldering bodies covered the ground. "Of the people at the trolley stop, I alone, the last one in line, was unhurt, protected by the corner of the station building. I started for the hospital but was stopped by an impenetrable wall of advancing flames. I turned and ran for the open space—toward an army drill ground behind the station." He saw scores of survivors milling around, crying hysterically; and to ease the pain of their burns, they extended their arms, from which dangled long curls of skin.

"A nurse approached me." She figured Shigeto must be a doctor, since he carried a black bag and had a trim little mustache. "She begged me to help another doctor and his wife lying on the ground, and I thought, 'What if this mob discovers I'm a physician?' I couldn't treat them all. The injured doctor, who was bleeding profusely, told me to please treat his wife first. I gave the woman a camphor shot for shock, followed by another injection to stop the bleeding. I rearranged the bandages the nurse had applied and then turned to the other wounded." He treated them until he ran out of morphine and supplies. "There was nothing more I could do. I fled toward the hills."

Story after story followed during the next week of interviews, and my chief problem was to pick out the most typical and dramatic. I had already been told by Marquis Kido that he had immediately informed the emperor that Hiroshima had been laid waste by some secret weapon. "Under these circumstances," said his majesty, "we must bow to the inevitable." This tragedy must not be repeated, he declared, and was unable to hide his anguish. Yet both agreed that the psychological moment had not yet come for the emperor to take personal action.

On August 7, the day after the bombing of Hiroshima, Professor Shogo Nagaoka, formerly a geologist at the university, was trying to get through the rubble to the campus. Exhausted, he could barely fathom the endless devastation, and at the Gokoku Shrine he slumped at the foot of the huge stone lantern that illuminated the shrine. He felt a stinging sensation. He sprang to his feet. Then he noticed a strange silhouette on the structure. The awful revelation came to him—he was in the presence of radiation from an atomic bomb! Japan must surrender at once or be wiped out. (He later became the first curator of the Peace Memorial in Hiroshima and assured us that at least 200,000 human beings had died as a result of this one bomb. He gave me a piece of roof tiling which showed the awesome effects of the bomb, and hoped I would place it near my desk when I was writing the Hiroshima chapter. I did.)

Togo, the foreign minister, had the same reaction and requested an immediate audience with Molotov. Before he could greet the foreign commissar, Molotov handed him a message to the Japanese government. It stated that the Russians had accepted the proposal of the Allies, the Potsdam Declaration. Therefore, as of August 9, the Soviet Union would consider itself in a state of war against Japan.

Nagasaki

On the morning of August 9 the second bomb, larger and even more deadly than the first and nicknamed "Fat Man," was dropped on Nagasaki, the most Europeanized and most Christian city in Japan—a harmonious blend of the cultures of East and West with its many Christian churches and schools, hundreds of Western-type houses, and such tourist attractions as the legendary home of Madame Butterfly overlooking the harbor. There were 200,000 residents.

Here we also interviewed many survivors of the bombing. One of these was Shigeyoshi Morimoto, who had, three days earlier, miraculously escaped death in Hiroshima, where he had been at work making antiaircraft kites for the army. He and three assistants had been less than nine hundred yards from ground zero, the point above which the bomb exploded in pinkish light like a cosmic flashbulb which the Japanese described as a *pika* (lightning flash). By some freak, the wreckage of their flimsy workplace had protected them, and Morimoto had taken a freight train to his home, Nagasaki. "I had this strange premonition that the bomb would follow me to my own home, and I had to warn my wife."

It was almost eleven in the morning of the 9th when he entered his shop in the very center of the city and breathlessly started telling his wife that a terrible bomb had been dropped in Hiroshima and he was afraid Nagasaki would be next. At exactly one minute past eleven the bomb dropped. Morimoto was just beginning to describe the *pika:* "First there is a great blue flash—" A blinding blue flash cut off his words. He automatically flung back a trapdoor in the floor and shoved his wife and infant son into their shelter. As he pulled down the heavy lid there was a monstrous tremor, like an earthquake.

Morimoto's shop was the original drop point, but the overhead clouds had changed the point to several hundred yards northeast of the Urakami River, almost exactly between the Mitsubishi Steel and Arms Works and the Mitsubishi Torpedo Factory. By a stroke of fate the Morimotos were saved from certain death.

Hachiro Kosasa had gone into the storehouse of the torpedo factory to get some metal material when he sensed something vaguely odd. "I turned and saw the windows glowing with colored light and figured a gas tank must have exploded. I dropped to the floor just as the ceiling collapsed." Unaware of deep cuts in his head and thigh, he staggered toward the plant's infirmary for help for his fellow workers, but it was gone. "Outside in the darkness I could see people milling around helplessly. My instinct was to escape, try to get home." Weak from loss of blood, Kosasa tied a legging around his thigh as a tourniquet and, driven by fear that his body might not be found by relatives and given a proper funeral, headed south toward the Mitsubishi Steel and Arms Works. "But soon my legs kept crumbling and I had to go on my hands and knees."

Midori Nishida, a messenger girl at the works, had her hair set afire by the *pika.* She tried to escape across a railroad bridge, unaware that she was heading for the center of destruction. The railroad ties had been burned out, and she inched across, balancing on the twisted rails. "I could see bodies in the river below." The buttocks of one woman near the bank were blown up like balloons. Nearby a black-and-white cow, covered with raw spots of pink, was placidly lapping water.

Midori almost fell and called for help from a girl coming the other way. "It was a classmate, but when she saw me she burst into tears and refused to touch me. Resentfully I continued to the east bank past a charred naked man standing like a statue with arms and legs spread apart. He was dead. Then I came to bales of charcoal and realized they were human beings. Their faces were huge and round as if puffed up by gas." There were no buildings— only flat, smoldering rubble. "Then I saw someone else from my class, a boy." But he didn't recognize her until she spoke: "Are you really Nishida-san?"

All around they could hear agonized voices pleading for help. "I felt irresistibly drawn to them," Midori told us. She was in panic and fled back toward the river followed by her new companion. They found a place shallow enough to ford and passed a mother and daughter seated on a scorched futon. The girl was leaning forward, dead, her head drooping in the water. "The mother stared at me blankly and I wondered why she didn't pull her daughter out of the water." Midori was unaware that the soles of her own sneakers were burned through.

Americans put the death toll at 35,000, but officials of Nagasaki assured us it was 74,800, with at least 100,000 more dying later from injuries and radiation poisoning.

The Emperor's Decision

In Tokyo that horrifying evening of August 9, the cabinet was still locked in debate. The spokesman for the militarists, General Korechika Anami, was as adamant as ever, and just before eleven, Prime Minister Suzuki adjourned the meeting. There was only one thing left: to call upon the emperor. Suzuki summoned an immediate imperial conference, and the conferees were brought to the imperial underground complex, the *obonko.*

At ten minutes before midnight the emperor entered. For more than two hours the endless arguments were repeated almost word for word. Then the old prime minister slowly rose. It appeared to Hisatsune Sakomizu, who had been Premier Okada's secretary during the 2/26 Incident and was presently serving as secretary of the cabinet, that Suzuki was at last going to reveal the convictions he had repressed for so long. But what he said would astonish everyone even more: "We have no precedent—and I find it difficult to do—but with the greatest reverence I must now ask the emperor to express his wishes." He turned to his majesty and asked him to decide whether Japan should accept the Potsdam Declaration outright or demand the conditions which the Japanese army wanted. "Unaccountably," Sakomizu told us, "he stepped away from his armchair toward his majesty. We all gasped, and Anami exclaimed, 'Mr. Prime Minister!' "

But Suzuki kept advancing toward his majesty. He stopped at the foot of the emperor's small podium and bowed very low. With an understanding nod, his majesty bade Suzuki to sit down. "The old man," Sakomizu told me, "apparently couldn't catch these words and cupped a hand to his left ear, and the emperor beckoned to him to return to his place. Once he was seated, the emperor got to his feet."

The emperor's voice, usually expressionless, was noticeably strained. "I have given serious thought to the situation prevailing at home and abroad and have concluded that continuing the war means destruction for the nation and a prolonging of bloodshed and cruelty in the world." The others listened with heads bowed. "I cannot bear to see my innocent people suffer any longer. Ending the war is the only way to restore world peace and to relieve the nation from the terrible distress with which it is burdened."

When he paused, Sakomizu glanced up at his majesty. "He was gazing thoughtfully at the ceiling as he wiped his glasses with a white-gloved hand. I felt tears flooding my eyes and noticed that the conferees were no longer sitting stiffly in their chairs but had thrown themselves forward—some with outstretched arms, prostrate on the tables, sobbing unashamedly. By now the emperor had regained his own composure and began speaking in a voice choked with emotion until forced to stop. I wanted to cry out, 'We now all understand his majesty's wishes. Please do not condescend to say another word.' "

"It pains me to think of those who served me so faithfully," continued the emperor, "the soldiers and sailors who have been killed or wounded in far-off battles, the families who have lost all their worldly goods—and often their lives as well—in the air raids at home. It goes without saying that it is unbearable for me to see the brave and loyal fighting men of Japan disarmed. It is equally unbearable that others who have rendered me devoted service should now be punished as instigators of the war. Nevertheless, the time has come when we must bear the unbearable. . . . I swallow my own tears and give my sanction to the proposal to accept the Allied proclamation on the basis outlined by the foreign minister." In other words, they must accept unconditional surrender.

At last Suzuki and the others stood up. "I have respectfully listened to his majesty's gracious words," said Suzuki. The emperor started to reply but instead nodded and slowly, as if burdened by some intolerable weight, left the room.

A Last-Minute Mutiny

At last peace had come, thought Sakomizu. It was obvious that everyone in the room that evening of August 9, 1945, had bowed to the emperor's decision. But he wondered about the idealistic young officers like those who had mutinied in the 2/26 Incident back in 1936, and what their present-day equivalents might do.

On the hot, muggy morning of August 10, Anami met with some fifty officers of the War Ministry at a hastily called conference in an air raid shelter at army headquarters on Ichigaya Heights. When they were informed that those attending the imperial conference had decided to accept the terms of the Potsdam Declaration, the officers were clearly ready to revolt, despite Anami's attempt to overawe them with his personal authority. Secretly wishing that the emperor would change his mind and continue the war, Anami burst in on Marquis Kido during breakfast on August 13 and insisted that there be "a final Decisive Battle." Kido, while acknowledging what a difficult task Anami had to keep the army in line, reminded him of his sacred obligation to accept the emperor's will.

From the many participants I interviewed I was able to piece together a complete account of events in those fateful days. The deeper we got into each story, the more excited each one became, and details began to pour out. One of the ones with whom I spent the most time, Sakomizu, shed his reticence and began giving me more and more detail until both of us were exhausted.

The military did rise in revolt, in a scenario eerily reminiscent of the 2/26 Incident of 1936. Their leader was a Major Kenji Hatanaka, who devoutly believed that unconditional surrender would destroy *Yamato damashi* (the spirit of Japan) and *kokutai* (the national essence). Sure that he could persuade General Anami to join the conspiracy, he and his comrades crowded into the general's house on the eventful night of August 13. To carry out their plans to imprison Kido, Suzuki, Togo, and Yonai, to proclaim martial law and to isolate the Imperial Palace, they would need the support not only of Anami but of Yoshijiro Umezu, commander of the Kwantung Army; Shizuichi Tanaka, army chief of operations; and Takeshi Mori, who commanded the troops defending the Imperial Palace area.

Anami criticized their staffwork and planning; he temporized by agreeing to use his influence with Umezu "first thing in the morning" (though he knew Umezu was firmly committed to supporting the emperor). The plotters were not satisfied, so Anami hinted that he might cooperate. But the following morning he made it clear to them that neither he nor Umezu would support them. They spent the afternoon trying to persuade others to join them, even though senior officers advised them to abandon the attempt.

Those who were present in the Imperial Palace and later at the broadcasting center told me how the Emperor's speech barely made it to actual airing.

During the course of the afternoon of August 14, a crew from NHK, Japan's main broadcasting service, had arrived at the palace to record the emperor's surrender announcement. Only at midnight did the recording go forward—and the resulting disks were locked in a safe in the palace by one of the emperor's chamberlains. During the night of the 14th and early morning of the 15th the conspirators began to surround the palace. Around 11:00 P.M. they had tried to convince General Mori to join them. Impatient with his reluctance, the rebel officers finally lost control of themselves and slaughtered Mori as well as his brother-in-law, Colonel Michinori Shiraishi. With Mori dead, the key division protecting the palace fell under Tanaka's command.

Mori's death momentarily ended serious opposition to the coup within his command, the Konoye Division. (We heard the details, the first Westerners to do so, from a number of Hatanaka's associates who had survived, such as Lieutenant Colonel Masataka Ida and Lieutenant Colonel Masahiko Takeshita, General Anami's brother-in-law.) Early in the morning of August 15, Hatanaka and Ida went by staff car to the headquarters of Eastern District Army. Tanaka was not there, so the rebel officers were attempting to persuade his chief of staff, Tatsuhiko Takashima, to join them when word came from Major Hidemasa Koga, Tojo's son-in-law, that the Konoye Division had just revolted and that the Eastern District Army must join them.

One company from the division, under orders bearing the murdered Mori's seal (which had been affixed by Hatanaka), went to NHK broadcasting center to control what went out on the air; another thousand soldiers sealed off the palace grounds. But the majority of them had no idea they were acting as rebels; they thought they were merely reinforcing existing guard units at the palace. By this time the emperor had finished; the recordings had been locked away. The rebels sent in a search party to seize them.

As Toshiko and I heard from those involved in the imperial household, the rebels were frustrated at every turn. Yoshihiro Tokugawa, an imperial chamberlain whose ancestors had ruled Japan for more than two hundred years under the Shogunate, had prudently locked the peace announcement recordings in a safe because he had expected just such an attempted coup.

Hatanaka had isolated the emperor but failed to capture the recordings. Then came the beginning of the end of the coup—the Eastern District Army would not join in—and once the men in the Konoye Division began to realize that their commander had been killed, Ida and Hatanaka knew, they would refuse to play any further part. Hatanaka decided to try to stop the NHK broadcast. Ida went to Anami's home, where he found the general preparing to die. Anami had decided to set an example and thus put an end to confusion in the army and all plotting and coups. Takeshita and Ida told us, in horrific detail, of how this excruciating suicide took place—not through *seppuku,* which would have possibly implied a blameless death, but through *kappuku,* in which the general thrust a dagger deep into his abdomen, then slashed twice—to the right and then straight up. It was so excruciatingly painful that few could force themselves to do it. And even after this, Takeshita had to deliver the *coup de grâce.*

As macabre as these accounts were, Toshiko and I were getting perhaps the first full story of the events in the palace and in the military and government at the highest levels in these final days, a complete story that was known only in parts by the actual participants. These men, quite understandably, had not been eager to get together in the postwar years and discuss how painful it had been for each of them either to deliver Japan from the nightmare of surrender or to "bear the unbearable" and obey the emperor's will.

Before dawn of August 15, Major Hatanaka and a few rebels were in control of the NHK building. At gunpoint he ordered Morio Tateno, who was about to broadcast the early morning news, to give him the microphone so he could talk to the nation. Tateno told us how he had stalled the rebels. Then Hatanaka intervened. "I have to convey my feelings to the people," he told

Tateno. Then a call for him came through from Eastern District Army. Hatanaka took the phone and listened. He'd gone back on his word to abandon the revolt, and now faced a direct order to desist. He still wanted to make a final explanation to the public, but his request was denied. He hung up. It was all over.

At 7:21 A.M. on the morning of August 15, Tateno made a special announcement to the nation: "At noon today the emperor will broadcast his decree. Let us all listen respectfully to the voice of the emperor."

Although organized opposition to surrender had ended, many intransigent individuals and groups remained ready to give up their lives to prevent it. The palace staff still feared that there would be another attempt to destroy the emperor's recordings. Even getting the disks from the safe on the second floor and through the Imperial Household Ministry was risky, so two separate ways were devised to get the master version and the copy out of the palace. Both arrived at NHK unharmed, and the master copy was locked in a safe.

At 11:20 A.M., Hatanaka fired a bullet into his head with the same pistol he had used to kill General Mori. In his pocket was found a poem:

> *I have nothing to regret*
> *now that dark clouds have disappeared*
> *from the reign of the emperor.*

At almost the same moment the chairman of NHK took the recording marked "Original" out of his safe. The broadcast, even without the presence of his majesty, was ceremonial. At exactly noon, Chokugen Wada, Japan's most popular announcer, said, "This will be a broadcast of the gravest importance. His majesty will now read his imperial message to the people of Japan. We respectfully transmit his voice."

Then the voice that few had ever heard went out to the nation. The strange imperial language, coupled with poor reception, enabled few to understand exactly what he was saying. It was only evident that a surrender, or something equally catastrophic, had occurred. Millions wept—perhaps more people weeping simultaneously than at any other moment in the world's history. Despite the humiliation and sorrow, however, the emperor's words brought an undeniable feeling of relief to his people. At the *obunko* his majesty intently listened to his words on a prewar RCA radio. At the Household Ministry, Kido reacted with mixed emotions: "Despite my sorrow that Japan had been forced to surrender, I felt a secret triumph because what I had been striving for so diligently had finally been achieved."

Tojo's Final Days

When MacArthur arrived and took command of Japan in the fall of 1945, Tojo was confined in his modest home in Setagaya. He sat writing in his small office; on one wall there was a full-length portrait of him in full military regalia. Mrs. Tojo told us that her husband had urged her to leave the house, together with their maid; the children had already been evacuated to Kyushu. "But I was reluctant to leave, fearing he might commit suicide, as so many high officers had already done. Yet I left. There was such a crowd that we had to go through the garden of the house across the street owned by Dr. Suzuki." The doctor had earlier marked Tojo's chest with charcoal to indicate the location of the heart. "I could hear American soldiers shouting threats. Then I heard a muffled shot and the soldiers began breaking into the house. Even where I was, I could hear the sound of splintering wood."

Tojo had shot himself. The bullet had entered almost exactly where Dr. Suzuki had marked his chest. "I did not shoot myself in the head," he told doctors at the hospital in Yokohama, "because I wanted the people to recognize my features and know I was dead." When General Robert Eichelberger, the Eighth Army commander, came to see him, Tojo tried to bow. "I am dying," he said. "I am sorry to have given General Eichelberger so much trouble." He then asked the general to accept his saber. But American doctors saved his life.

He was sentenced to death as a major war criminal after a long trial. In prison he became a changed man. Religion now dominated his life. "I welcome death," he told the prison chaplain, a Buddhist priest. "Now my body will soon become part of the soil of Japan; and my death will be not only an apology to the Japanese but a move toward peace and the rebuilding of Japan." He had even developed a sense of humor. With a grin he held up a Cannon washcloth and said, "Kannon-sama [the Buddhist Goddess of Mercy] has finally appeared." In his final testament he apologized for the atrocities committed by the Japanese military and urged the American military to show compassion and repentance toward the civilians of Japan, who had already suffered from the air attacks and two atomic bombs.

His wife, despite the great distress it caused her, was totally open to us about her husband's final days. He was sentenced to death on November 12, 1948, after a trial in which he insisted that all blame be placed on him, none on the emperor. Just after midnight on December 22, 1948, he mounted the thirteen steps to the gallows and was hanged.

[12]

Endgame

The Emperor

By the beginning of 1967 I was winding up our research. My interview with Emperor Hirohito had been canceled at the last moment because of a book on his majesty published by an Englishman, who, according to the Household Ministry, strayed far from the truth. Marquis Kido had set up the interview, and, as compensation, I was allowed to interview the chamberlains who had served the emperor during the war.

They described him as an unlikely-looking emperor, slouching around the palace in frayed baggy trousers and crooked tie, dreamily peering through glasses as thick as porthole lenses, so oblivious of his appearance that occasionally his jacket would be fastened with the wrong buttons. He disliked buying new clothes on the grounds that he couldn't "afford" them. He was so frugal that he even refrained from buying books he wanted, and he wore down every pencil to a stub. He was completely without vanity, a natural and unaffected man who looked and acted like a village mayor. Yet this small, round-shouldered person, the chamberlains insisted, had some of the qualifications of greatness: he was totally without pride, ambition, or selfishness. He wanted only what was best for the nation.

Theoretically the emperor had plenary power: all state decisions required his action. But according to tradition, once the cabinet and military leaders had agreed on a policy, he could not withhold his approval. He was to remain above politics and transcend all party considerations and feuds, for he represented the entire nation.

A more positive emperor, like his grandfather, the great Meiji, might have consolidated his power; by the Meiji Constitution, Hirohito was commander in chief of the armed forces. But he was a studious man who would rather be a scientist than a monarch. His happiest days were Mondays and Saturdays when he could retire to his modest laboratory and study marine biology. Nor did he have the slightest wish to be a despot. From his trip to

Europe as a crown prince he had brought back a taste for whiskey, Occidental music, and golf—along with an abiding respect for the English version of constitutional monarchy. He could also defy tradition and court pressure when principle was involved. After the Empress Nagako had given birth to four daughters, he refused to take a concubine or two so that he could sire a male heir—and within a few years he was rewarded with two sons by Nagako.

The chamberlains praised him for having the courage to act outside his realm of power, demonstrating this when he read a poem of peace by his grandfather at the imperial conference in 1941, thus forcing the militarists to make another try for peace with America. And in the last days he had saved the nation by taking the burden of surrender on his own shoulders.

An Attempt to Defuse the Vietnam War

One entirely unexpected consequence of my research in Japan was getting personally involved in a complex gambit to end America's role in the Vietnam War. It was just gathering the fatal momentum that would lead to a tragedy for both the Vietnamese and American people, a tragedy that could have been averted in 1966. I had met a man named Asaeda. We had much in common—our views on the Orient were similar.

Major Shigeharu Asaeda had been the assistant to Colonel Masanobu Tsuji, the idol of the most radical officers and *the* mystery man of the Orient. Asaeda told us of Tsuji's machinations in Guadalcanal, Malaya, and the Philippines, as well as Asaeda's version of the inside story of his notorious disappearance when, long after the war, an American senator, John F. Kennedy, had urged Tsuji to go into China and set up a secret meeting between the United States and the leaders of that country. Tsuji left on this mission in the late fifties and was never heard of again.

I said I needed proof, and the next day Asaeda brought a large envelope filled with more than a dozen passports—all with his own picture but each with a different name. He said he had accompanied Tsuji on all of the trips during which Asaeda and Tsuji had been dealing with the leaders of countries in the Middle East, South America, and Asia. Asaeda swore he was still carrying out Tsuji's worldwide schemes and deals and had recently returned from mainland China. The Chinese had learned about the books Toshiko and I had published and asked if we would help set up a secret meeting with President Johnson so the Vietnam War could be settled. Contrary to common belief, Asaeda explained, the Chinese were bitter enemies of Ho Chi Minh. Since Vietnam bordered China, the Vietnamese were regarded as an enemy, but the Chinese had to pretend they were supporting Ho for political reasons. The Chinese believed that if America and China worked together secretly they could defuse the Vietnam conflict. The Chinese suggested they send one of their top officials to Tokyo to meet secretly, "through the back door of the U.S. embassy," with President Johnson.

I took the proposition to John K. Emmerson, one of the few Asian experts to survive the McCarthy-inspired State Department purge. He was now the top assistant to our ambassador to Japan, Professor Edwin O. Reischauer. He conferred with the ambassador, who also approved. I suggested we use, as go-between in Washington, someone I felt would be sympathetic, Averell Harriman. Emmerson approved, since Harriman was now ambassador-at-large. After a long wait we finally got an answer from Washington. The president would see the Chinese representative, but it must be through the *front door* of the embassy. When I informed Asaeda, he was furious. The Chinese could never accept such a stupid proposal! That would immediately bring into the open the Chinese secret opposition to Ho Chi Minh. But Asaeda passed it on, and the answer was: "The Americans are not serious." It would take a president I didn't like to finally astound everyone by meeting with the third most powerful nation in the world.

I left Tokyo alone in early March 1967 to go to Okinawa. Toshiko had many details to clear up, including the job of obtaining a visa for Hiroko, our housekeeper, so that she would join us in Connecticut. I stayed several days in Okinawa giving talks at the universities, trying to answer questions about Vietnam. I told the students what I had learned in the Philippines, adding that a number of Japanese generals had told us they hoped we would not become embroiled in the mainland as they had. Vietnam, they predicted, would develop into even more of a quagmire for us than China had been for them.

On March 15, 1967, Toshiko arrived in Okinawa and we started on our roundabout return home by way of Singapore (a gold mine of information), Kuala Lumpur (the highlight was a two-headed cow), Bangkok (a sightseeing wonder with the most romantic and most filthy river in the world), Tehran (interviewing on the last Big Three meeting), and Greece—where we finally had a memorable vacation, ranging all over the country, guided by a young woman who hated the current regime. Finally we got to Paris and my long-awaited second meeting with Chip Bohlen, who had interpreted for President Roosevelt at the Cairo meeting with Stalin and Churchill in 1943. He was polite, but the openness of our first meeting had vanished.

The Job of Writing

On April 19, 1967, we finally arrived back in Sharon, Connecticut, and by the 1st of May I was ready to outline the book on Japan. Before I married Toshiko I would write ten hours or more a day. She had immediately cut me down to eight hours and then to seven. But during that April I still had not recovered from our long trip, and she insisted that I cut down to six hours. I fixed a daily schedule: "Get up at 7:00 A.M.; exercise and walk, 8:00–8:45 A.M.; start writing, 8:45; lunch, 12:00; resume writing, 12:45; quit, 2:30; exercise, etc., 2:30–4:30; prepare for next day's writing, 4:30–6:00; evening free; bed at 11:00 P.M. (Total writing, 5 hours; total day's work, 6½ hours.)"

People who don't write often take seriously the habits of those presented as writers in the movies. All, of course, have writer's block and can't get going. They type madly, pulling out paper after paper and tossing the sheets into the wastebasket. Anyway, our hero or heroine finally gets an inspiration and you see him or her wildly typing all through the night and—behold! The next morning the writer has a complete novel! Or a play! Or a work of history! All in one night! And of course the book is a big hit and some leave the movie theater hoping to get an inspiration and become a great writer overnight.

Back to my outline. A disciple of Dickens, I revere chronology. Like Dickens, I have a great many incidents to present in detail. For *The Rising Sun* my first task was to sort all of my interviews and documents, putting each in its proper place within the time frame. Then I divided all this material into chapters, with the first dealing with the 2/26 Incident in 1936. Then I continued outlining, chapter by chapter, until I reached the final one dealing with the emperor's radio announcement of the surrender. On the Fourth of July I finished the outline and turned to all the material on the 2/26 Incident, trying to visualize it as it evolved.

As Porter Emerson Browne had instructed me many years before, I then looked down on my characters and let them do what they had to do. In a week I had reconstructed in my mind the entire 2/26 Incident as it had taken place. Then I began to type, and I let the characters tell me what they had to say. That first day I wrote seven pages, and it took me ten days to finish this chapter. I made no corrections but started Chapter 2. (Incidentally, I always made carbon copies of all my drafts. I had vowed after reading *Hedda Gabler* never to let *my* manuscript get burned. I put the carbon copies in our little studio in the backyard in case our house burned down.)

New Arrivals

That summer of 1967 the Matsumaras, Toshiko's parents, who loved America, visited us. We took them to New Hampshire and to our favorite old hotel in Lexington, Massachusetts. One day I asked Orie, Toshiko's mother, if she had meant it when she had said, "You will make Toshiko very happy." She smiled. "I hoped."

Soon after they left, we decided that Sharon was too isolated, and in one day we found a pre-Revolutionary house in the country between Danbury and West Redding. It had been built by a British major in 1714 and by now had received two additions. We bought it and moved on October 24. I lost a week of writing but soon finished the first eight chapters, which took my narrative to the eve of Pearl Harbor.

Soon after we moved in, Toshiko and Hiroko, who was already going to night school in order to learn English, had the house in order and we had joined a nearby golf club. Every day I either played nine holes of golf or jogged down the road and into the woods for two miles. It was the perfect life for a writer, and the following spring, 1968, brought more happiness: Toshiko was pregnant. Her parents joined us and would stay for the rest of the year, through Tamiko's birth. Orie had a green thumb and did wonders to our yard, and Toki, her father, was on hand to help me with the book. He considered me a supremely wealthy man because we had in our backyard a huge rock weighing many tons. I told him that almost everyone in Connecticut was wealthy with rocks, and that was why we had so many stone fences. During that period Hiroko and Toshiko did the Japanese inspired landscaping that, surrounds, our house today, very little altered.

Another guest arrived in the spring of 1968. While jogging in the woods one day, two puppies—obviously mongrels—tagged at my heels. I tried to get rid of them but they knew a sucker when they found one and followed me home. Only a few days earlier, Toshiko had said it would be wonderful if we got our baby a dog. I called to her and said she had her wish. She disappeared and came out a few minutes later to say that a neighbor would take the male dog. We kept the female and gave her the name Butchy. I insisted she be an outdoors dog, allowed in the kitchen only to eat. I put her in the garage and she howled all night. So I announced I was going to build a dog house. Toshiko was convulsed with laughter at the thought of me trying to use a saw and hammer. So I said Butchy could come indoors but must be confined to the kitchen. Within a week she had the run of the house.

By the beginning of December 1968 I was almost finished with the revised version of the first draft. On the 4th I drove Toshiko to the Presbyterian Hospital in New York for an examination. Her doctor thought she might need a cesarean. We returned to the hospital on December 8, Toshiko's birthday, but it was a false alarm and we came back to Danbury. Then at 1:15 A.M. the contractions started and we were back at the hospital by 4:45 A.M. and Tamiko Matsumara Toland was born at 4:52 P.M.—six pounds, ten ounces.

On February 9, 1969, we were hit by a heavy downfall of snow that was three feet deep in the driveway and five feet high at the back of the house, covering half of our rear windows, a snowfall that would cost John Lindsay his job as mayor of New York. We were snowbound. On the 12th we finally managed to get out of the driveway and I headed for New York to start the editing. It had taken us little more than a month to revise *The Last 100 Days,* but *The Rising Sun* would take until May 5—fourteen months. I had to go to New York eighty-four times, and eventually both Bob Loomis and I were worn out.

What Next?

I was already trying to dredge up a new book, and early in the fall of 1970 I woke up with the idea of doing a book on Adolf Hitler. I had written about him in two books, but was never satisfied. This time I would take five or six years and talk with those closest to him. I wrote to Manteuffel, Skorzeny, and others and soon received enthusiastic replies. Otto Skorzeny was sure he and others could get me to many who had known Hitler intimately.

Bob was enthusiastic, and we soon had a contract. When I saw it I blew up. For my other books I had been given 15 percent royalty, but I was now reduced to 12½ percent. Paul Reynolds, my agent, called Bob's boss and protested, but was told that I had taken up so much of Bob's time with editing *The Rising Sun* that I must accept this reduction. I refused; and when the editor insisted, I told Paul to get me another publisher.

I felt sure my agent would have no trouble getting another publisher, but nothing turned up until July 1971, when Paul called to say Sandy Richardson of Doubleday would love to have the book. A contract was drawn with only one change: Doubleday felt the advance I had been offered by Random House was not sufficient and added another $25,000 to make sure I would have enough for thorough research. Doubleday also did not want any movie rights. I accepted and began delving into the life and times of Adolf Hitler.

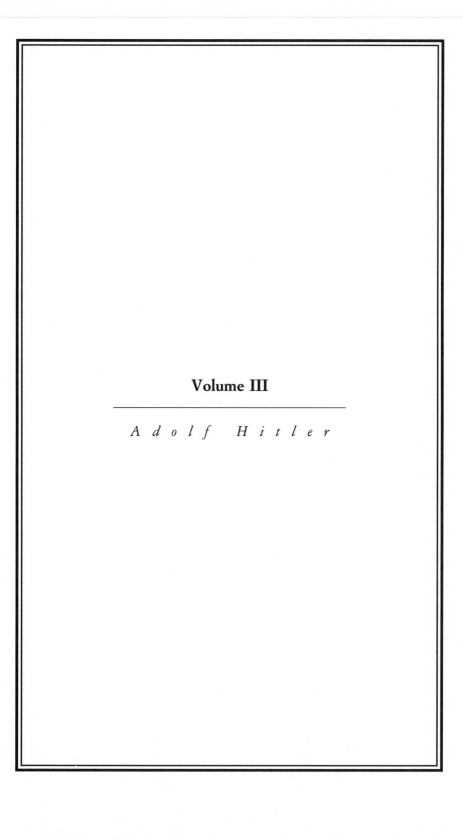

Volume III

A d o l f   H i t l e r

[Part One]

The Quest (1 9 7 0 – 1 9 7 6)

{1}

Off to Germany

Starting My Search for Hitler

My first task in researching *Adolf Hitler* was to learn enough German to conduct my own impromptu interviews. I enrolled at the Westport Berlitz School, began my first class at 9:00 A.M. on July 30, 1970, and was released in a stupor at 1:45 P.M. My next three lessons were the same length, but then I was jumped to eight hours a day with half an hour for lunch.

A fortnight or so later I took a week off to write a book review and take the final revisions of *The Rising Sun* to *Look* and talk to their salesmen. On September 6 I received an advance copy of *Look*'s first installment and saw the magazine had done an excellent job. A few days later, Bob Loomis called to let me know that the Literary Guild had taken *The Rising Sun* as its first choice. Once again it had been an "A" book at the Book-of-the-Month Club but was rejected by the independent judges.

With a renewed passport and a new overcoat, on October 1, 1970, I left for Munich on the first of three extended trips to Europe during the following year. I would conduct more than 150 long interviews with people directly involved in Hitler's private and public life. These would help me portray him, as objectively as possible, as a man, a politician, and a military leader. I hoped to reveal a figure even more frightening than the traditional caricature by giving the demon a human face. I would emerge from my three trips completely exhausted but with a collection of startling details about Hitler's life, until that time generally unknown, which would provide new perspectives on many well-known events by exposing falsehoods and distortions.

I trailed Hitler from his birthplace to all the scenes of his youth, following him to the end by revelations from those who were close to his personal life, and by his military attachés, his dietitians, his party leaders, his doctors, his devoted followers, and his enemies. I learned from those who loved and those who hated him, from those who believed he was the Savior of the World and those who believed him to be the greatest criminal in history.

I learned that he was never a paper hanger nor a house painter but was once a choirboy who loved to read westerns and play cowboys and Indians, that he wrote several plays and the libretto for an opera, that he was plagued by a paranoiac fear of cancer and by a genuine heart condition, that he was a vegetarian, that he could type, barely drive a car, and play the piano indifferently, that he used an exerciser to stay in shape and, like Napoleon, had a photographic memory that overwhelmed his military leaders, that he was the first head of state to promote modern urban planning and antipollution devices in cities, that at least four women attempted suicide because of him and three of them succeeded.

Most important, I learned that the "Jewish Question" was a lifelong obsession which directly or indirectly influenced almost all of his major political and military strategies, that he was the central architect of the Final Solution and that some of its methods were inspired by the U.S. government's subjugation of the American Indian, and that the Nazi laws defining "Jewishness" were carefully drawn to exclude both Jesus Christ and Adolf Hitler himself, who feared that one of his grandparents might have been a Jew.

From the first I found people not only willing but eager to see me. The two most important people I interviewed on my first trip were Luise Jodl, wife of Alfred Jodl, chief of operations of the armed forces, and Albert Speer, the Nazi architect and close associate of Hitler. In my two sessions with Frau Jodl, starting in midmorning and ending in late afternoon, she gave me a vivid picture of her husband—"quiet, reserved, a great lover of nature and his Bavarian home, a great Alpinist, an ardent skier and sportsman." She revealed that he never had personal contact with the Führer but witnessed the terrible fits of temper Hitler displayed during the Stalingrad battle. "Hitler would not shake hands with him for months, nor would he eat with him or Field Marshal Keitel. My husband was admitted to the daily strategy sessions but they never exchanged a word."

Albert Speer was equally affable and helpful. He had heard that I had once sent material back to an interviewee for corrections, and I told him that I did that for everyone regardless of rank or nationality. I stayed for lunch with his family, and by the time I left his home late in the afternoon I knew I had found a marvelously rich source of information, but one, I later learned, who needed watching.

The Rising Sun *Meets the Critics*

In the meantime I received a flood of letters from Toshiko—first news about our infant daughter, Tamiko, who was learning to swim and who had been receiving amorous attentions from an eight-year-old neighbor boy. Then came the tragic news that our dear friend Jean Ennis of Random House had died of a heart attack. She and John Barkham had given me a wonderful send-off luncheon just before I left for Germany, and I remembered the first time she had insisted on taking me to a late meal with James Michener at the Algonquin Hotel. We had met at the time when my very first book, *Ships in the Sky,* had just been published and, to my surprise, was receiving warm reviews. "I am going to get you for Random House," she had of course promised. At her funeral a Jewish spiritual leader had said, "Jean died alone, in solitude and of solitude." She had done so much for me.

Toshiko also wrote that she had received ten copies of *The Rising Sun,* which had been beautifully done except that the jacket picture of Marquis Kido and me, as well as the photo of Admiral Yamamoto with Japanese pilots, had been reversed. And soon after my return I received the first review from a prepublication reviewer. It was devastating, calling my book an insult to all Gold Star mothers. I was reminded of the terrible review of *But Not in Shame* in the daily *New York Times* and wondered if I had gone too far in my effort to be objective.

But this was soon followed by a heartening avalanche of rave reviews. Walter Clemons in the *New York Times* wrote: "Though it is harder reading than . . . *The Last Hundred Days, The Rising Sun* is a better book, deeply sympathetic to the Japanese but therefore scrupulously avoiding scoring easy points off American self-righteousness toward Orientals. . . . *The Rising Sun* is a noble book."

Congratulations from individuals followed. "It illuminates," wrote Pierre Salinger, "more than any other book I have ever read, the Pacific side of World War II and contains within its pages many accurate prophecies of the problems we face now, particularly in Southeast Asia." Walter Lord called it "a book of awesome scope," adding that he was most impressed by "John Toland's humanity. Whatever side he is covering in a war, he is on the side of the people—not just the admirals and generals and statesmen, but the yeomen and corporals and clerks. He feels for them all."

After I returned home, Toshiko and I went to Chicago in late December for three days of publicity for our book. We found a large display at the leading bookstore and spent much of the first day signing autographs. The two best events were an interview with an old friend, Bob Cromie of the *Chicago Tribune,* and the Kupcinet show, at that time probably the most effective talk show for publicizing books in the country. There would be about four guests who would comment on various subjects. Years before, when I had been one of the guests, Kup brought up *The Dillinger Days* and asked me why I had made a hero of Dillinger. I was caught off guard and sputtered a defensive reply that fell flat. This time Toshiko advised me not to join in any discussion until *The Rising Sun* became the topic, and if Kup asked why I had made "heroes" of the Japanese I was to discuss the world situation which lay behind the war.

I prepared myself the night before the show, rereading specific passages in the book. I kept my mouth shut while the other guests talked vociferously. Kup eventually remarked on my silence and brought up my book. Sure enough, he wondered why I had written so favorably about the Japanese, who had started the war. I began as Toshiko had suggested, stating that war with Japan had come through mistakes by both America and Japan. The latter was almost solely responsible for bringing herself along the road to war with America through the seizure of Manchuria, the invasion of China, the atrocities committed against the Chinese people, and the drive to the south. But this course of aggression had been the inevitable result of both the West's efforts to eliminate Japan as an economic rival after World War I and the Great Depression, coinciding with Japan's population explosion and her need to find new resources and markets in order to continue as a first-rate power.

After a few minutes, Kup interrupted, but two of the other guests, Norman Mailer and a Hollywood actor who had spent time in Japan, told him to pipe down. I then explained the unique position of the emperor, the explosive role of *gekojuko* (acting on one's own), and the perceived threat of Communism from both Russia and Mao Tse-tung, which had developed into paranoiac fear among the Japanese. Kup again interrupted but again was told to lay off.

Kup gave up. After talking for more than twenty minutes, I wound up by declaring that the villain was the times. Japan and America would never have come to the brink of war except for the social and economic eruption of Europe after World War I and the rise of two great revolutionary ideologies, Communism and Fascism. When I finished there was loud applause from the lighting and camera crew—and even Kup. From then on we became good friends.

In early February we left for San Francisco and Los Angeles. With us were Tamiko and Hiroko, who were going on to Tokyo with Toshiko while I headed back to Germany. Toshiko and I were kept busy with interviews and luncheons, and in Los Angeles we spent our free moments with my three aunts. Floss was in heaven. To her, Toshiko was my perfect companion.

Back to Germany: Skorzeny

When I landed in Hamburg I went directly to my favorite hotel, the Prem Am der Alster—small, homey, and on the waterfront, where I could take walks. I had come to see Otto Skorzeny. He had been felled by an unusual sickness, and I had heard from his wife, Ilse, that he had come close to death in Madrid. The doctor who specialized in his disease had a hospital on the outskirts of Hamburg, and Otto had come secretly to Germany, where he was still wanted for a second trial. I expected to find him in bed, but he was as lively as ever and insisted we have dinner at his favorite restaurant. I protested. He was a wanted man and would surely end up in prison. He had been warned that some officials wanted to hold him for retrial. But he only laughed at my fears, and we took off with two bright young men who considered themselves his aides.

I had hoped the restaurant would be intimate and quiet, but when we stepped inside there was an instant hubbub, and soon men crowded around Skorzeny—who was as easy to hide as a bass drum in a bathroom. They extended menus to be autographed, and Otto, acting as if he had not a worry in the world, reigned supreme until I could finally drag him to a booth. I had been told that the food was wonderful, but I could only think of getting out of there fast. As we headed for the door there was another rush toward Otto for autographs. On the street Otto extended his arms in ecstasy. "Hamburg!" he roared as I hustled him into a taxi.

He wanted to visit another night spot, but I had an important interview the next afternoon with General Otto Remer, who had been instrumental in rounding up the conspirators in the famous army bomb plot against Hitler. Skorzeny said he had by chance been in Berlin at the time and he was the one who had taken over the headquarters building and arrested the top conspirators. I could see that the two Ottos would not think too much of each other, but when Skorzeny suggested he join us at my hotel for dinner after the interviews, I weakly agreed.

Throughout the meal there was a subterranean contest between the two men, and it was with relief that I set off with Remer in the driving rain. Not only was the rain blinding but Remer was probably the worst driver I'd ever seen. Remer never realized that in the long drive to his home near the Baltic Sea we narrowly escaped complete disaster in the continuous downpour thirty or forty times while he was expounding on his actions in Berlin. It was impossible to tape him or take notes, and by the time we arrived at his home I had only a confused picture. But he kindly offered to repeat everything on tape. Dawn was breaking by the time we had finished.

I spent another day with him, because I wanted his views on Hitler. Then Remer drove me to Lübeck, where Count Bernadotte had held his last meeting with Himmler, and I took a train to Hamburg, arriving just in time for my interview with Admiral Karl Dönitz. Skorzeny, knowing of my schedule, insisted on going along as an interpreter. What happened during the next three hours would have made a wonderful comedy sketch. Unlike my earlier joint interview with Skorzeny and Rudel, this one brought out great color but precious little useful historical data. The two men talked fast and furiously about the entire war while I helplessly tried to make sense out of chaos. Finally I gave up, only wishing I had a camera to film two of the most important figures of World War II reducing it to a Marx Brothers scenario. It was, without a doubt, the worst interview I had ever attempted to conduct. Not a single sentence I heard would ever make the first draft of my book.

Eva Braun

A few days later I moved into my new apartment in the center of Schwabing, the student section of Munich. That, too, could have been used for a Marx Brothers movie—as a setting. It was the only finished apartment in a four-story structure, and I needed a flashlight at night to climb up through the skeleton framework. The agent had promised it would have light and heat before I arrived, but I found neither. Nor had I been told that there was a noisy *Gasthaus* directly underneath which did not close until three in the morning. I already knew there was no bed, only a mattress, two sheets, a table, and two chairs. Other furniture would soon arrive, I was told. It never did, and I slept on the floor for more than three months.

Through Nerin Gun, who had written a biography of Eva Braun, I met Eva's best friend, Herta Schneider. I had an all-day appointment for March 4. When I opened the door of my apartment to go out I was greeted by a blast of sleety snow. The streets were treacherous, and to my dismay I found the windshield wipers of my parked Volkswagen frozen solid. But because of the engineering ingenuity of Hitler, who drew the original design and insisted on an air, rather than water, cooling system, the engine started immediately.

I cleared off the windshield to the accompaniment of shrieks from several Germans who were incensed that a foreigner would park all night in front of their homes. Within a few hundred yards I had to stop, get out, and clean the windshield, and the next three hours were probably the worst in my life. That I survived was a miracle, since I had to stop every ten minutes to clean the ice off the windshield and avoid being crushed by speeding cars driven by people who seemed to think that blinking their lights would make me disappear.

I finally arrived at Garmisch Partenkirchen and stumbled up to the Schneider home. My sodden, woebegone appearance led to a warm welcome from the Schneiders, with much clucking and towels and a pair of Herr Schneider's socks and slippers. Fate again intervened—if I had been at peak form they wouldn't have taken pity on me and treated me like family. Herta Schneider had been very cool on the telephone, but soon she was showing me her personal photographs of Eva, and while she was out of the room looking for letters her husband told me of his harrowing trip on foot from Moscow to Germany as an escaped prisoner of war. It was a dramatic story, and I suggested putting it in the book. But Herr Schneider said it might endanger the many Russians and Poles who hid and fed him on the long trip through enemy country. After that day I had three more invaluable interviews with Herta during the following months. She told about Eva's deep depression in 1935 when Hitler was so busy he neglected her, as well as her recovery when the Führer began treating her like a wife; and how Eva invariably was the central figure in his "family circle." What impressed me most was Herta's revelation that Eva loved Hitler deeply and had, against his orders, left home to be with Hitler in besieged Berlin. "She told me she knew she was going to her death but wanted to be at his side at the end."

Little Tamiko Meets the Japanese

During this second trip to Germany I preserved my sanity largely because of the flow of mail from Tokyo. Toshiko wrote, for example, about our wedding anniversary, when she had invited four aunts for lunch to meet our infant daughter, now three years old. "They were all delighted with Tamiko's Japanese vocabulary and bilingual expressions, as well as her quick, knowing manners." They had all arrived an hour ahead of schedule. "One aunt had cooked all kinds of delicacies and red-bean rice for the occasion, and another had fixed a specialty using grass from her garden. She also brought bean bags for Tamiko which she had made the night before from old pieces of cloth from family kimonos that had once been worn on auspicious occasions. Another aunt came in a dressy kimono that was more than thirty-five years old. Because she was about to become seventy-seven, she was made the guest of honor and we celebrated her seventy-seventh birthday. (This anniversary is given special celebration in Japan because the figure 77 can be spelled into a *kanji* meaning 'joy.')"

In March, Toshiko wrote that her mother had just been on national television. At eighty-one she had been valedictorian of her class at Setagaya Women's College. She and Toshiko's father doted on Tamiko. Her father wrote, "Intelligence is coming to her at full speed," and he marveled not only at her mastery of the Japanese language but also at her adoption of Japanese customs. When he changed clothes she handed him his overcoat; she used the politest form when calling him *Oji-i-chama* (Granddaddy); and when putting on her tiny shoes very slowly, she sternly told herself, *"Hayaku!"* ("Be quick!").

Much of Toshiko's time was spent in preparing *The Rising Sun* for publication in Japanese. The publishers decided to bring it out in five volumes instead of six. "The fact that the number five is considered better [luckier] than six in Japan," she wrote, "greatly influenced the decision." The title *The Rising Sun* in English would be on the cover along with the Japanese title *The Rise and Fall of the Japanese Empire.*

The Pulitzer Prize

Through March and April I endured my spartan apartment, still the only finished one in the building, and on the day I left, the real estate agent arrived to return my two-hundred-mark security payment. "Everything is in order," I told him, pointing at the mattress, the pillow, the two chairs, and the scanty cooking materials I had laid on the table. He was so flustered that he mumbled something incomprehensible and shoved two bills at me. I was so angry that I shoved them in my pocket without even looking at them. It took three trips to pack my belongings into my Volkswagen, and as I was about to take off I pulled out the two bills. To my amazement they were thousand-mark bills. Undoubtedly he had made the mistake in his fluster, but I took off for Hamburg having persuaded myself that his better nature had risen to the surface.

There were even brighter surprises ahead. On my return to the Prem Hotel on May 3, weary after a full day of interviews, the night clerk handed me a cable from Paul Reynolds: *The Rising Sun* had won the 1971 Pulitzer Prize for nonfiction. I was stunned. It was too early to call Toshiko on the other side of the world, but my mother in Red Bank would be awake. I expected her to be excited, but all she calmly said was, "Oh, yes, somebody told me." She asked for no details—only gave me a report on the reactions of her neighbors.

I then called Tokyo. The whole family was already celebrating. A reporter had come to the house to bring the news, and Toshiko's young nephew rushed up and told her, "Uncle John won the Pulitzer Prize!" My reply to Toshiko was, "*We* won the Pulitzer!"

No sooner had I put down the phone than a call came from Red Bank. My mother was bubbling with delight. The editor of the local paper had just called with the news. She had thought I was telling her about the Overseas Press Club award I'd received a month earlier. In the next few days I received cables from Paris, England, and the United States. Scores of letters arrived in Danbury. Our senator, Lowell Weicker, was delighted.

"When I read of your Pulitzer Prize," wrote Walter Lord, "my first reaction was, 'How wonderful for John!' My next was, 'I hope Random House got the message!' Which goes to show I have a little of the old samurai spirit myself."

Theodore White, whom I had never met, offered his heartiest congratulations in a long letter. "If I may trust you—and I know I can—let me add a bit to the story, because what I have to say may greatly please you. There were three judges on the jury for the nonfiction category—Bob Cromie of the *Chicago Tribune,* Herman Cogran of the *Chicago Sun,* and myself. They dumped no less than 150 books on us to read in the fall months—and believe me, if you try to give serious attention to 150 books in a two-month period, it's mind-blowing.

"I dreaded the confrontation with the other two judges, for I was sure that none of us would agree on what could possibly be the best books of those published in 1971. We decided that the only way to begin work was for each one of us independently to list the top five books in rank from 1 to 5 and, after that, we looked forward to the most dismal discussions.

"What happened was quite simple: The Number 1 book on each list unquestionably was Toland's *The Rising Sun.* I don't think that three judges of the Pulitzer Prize ever felt more self-congratulatory or more relieved when they found themselves in such reflex agreement. The other candidates on our lists were so disparate that it seemed as if we had been reading different books of different years in different countries.

"Having read your book and realizing how much you savor such inside stories, I felt you would like to know the inside story on 'The Making of the Pulitzer Prize—1971.'"

In early summer of 1971, exhausted from endless interviewing, I returned home for a period of rest and relaxation. Toshiko and I attended my thirty-fifth class reunion at Williams, and then in June headed off to La Crosse, where chance placed the annual meeting of the Wisconsin State Historical Society, which was presenting its yearly award to me. My delighted cousins took me to the old Toland homestead, my grandfather's house, and friends and family gathered round to celebrate our visit. We then spent some time at Squam Lake in New Hampshire, accompanied by my mother.

My next job was to organize my large carton of tapes. I had made copies, and Toshiko agreed to transcribe them. But they were a complex mixture of German and English, and the German pronunciations and accents were impossible for either of us to decipher. I decided that on my return from my third trip to Germany I would have to find some professional who was fluent enough in German to do the transcribing.

Adolf's Early Years

All summer I had recharged myself for the final long trip to Germany, and I was eager to get back to Munich. This time I had much better lodgings—an apartment lent me by Nerin Gun on the outskirts of Schwabing. At last I had a bed, furniture, and kitchen equipment. Nearby was a large park for walking, and down the street was a quiet restaurant, the Schopenhauer, where I could get good food and read in peace. Two days after arrival I set off with my assistant, Wolfgang Glaser, to follow the trail of Hitler from his birthplace to his seminal days in Vienna.

On the top floor of the Pommer Hotel in Braunau, a German town just across the River Inn dividing Austria and Germany, we found two old women who remembered the baby Adolf. No, they had never before been interviewed. They told of the complicated Hitler household. I learned that young Adolf was sickly and his mother, Klara, nursed him until he was almost five years old. Then the customs service reassigned his father to Linz. Klara and Adolf stayed in Passau. It was then, recollected my informant, that Frau Hitler had just had another baby and Adolf enjoyed a carefree life.

We located his next home, a farmhouse some thirty miles southwest of Linz. Before long another child was born. His father, now retired, drank heavily and made life miserable for Adolf, often beating both Adolf and his older half brother, Alois Jr., with a whip. Alois Jr. ran away at fourteen, leaving Adolf the main victim of his father's bad temper.

A few months later they moved to the town of Lambach, six miles away, and I was shown their apartment on the third floor of the Gasthof Leingartner. Several people still remembered the unhappy family. Adolf did well at school and also attended the choir school at the monastery. On the way to

the monastery he had to pass by a stone arch inwhich was carved the monastery's coat of arms, featuring a swastika.

Hitler idolized the abbot, Padre Bernhard Groner, and the story was that
he hoped to take holy orders in the Catholic Church. I had already interviewed Ernst "Putzi" Hanfstaengl and his wife, Helene, many times. They
had been close friends of Hitler in 1922, and Putzi later became the Führer's
press secretary. Helene told me that as a small boy Hitler's "most ardent
wish was to become a priest. He often borrowed the large kitchen apron of
the maid, draped it about his shoulders in vestment fashion, climbed on a
kitchen chair, and delivered long and fervent sermons."

The restless Alois moved two years later to Leonding, a village on the
outskirts of Linz. The small house was still standing across from the cemetery
wall. I found three men at the Gasthaus Stiefler who had vivid memories of
the elder Hitler; one of them had been present when he died of pleural
hemorrhage at the table for regular patrons. I took a picture of his gravestone,
which could be seen from the Hitler house.

Until the day he died, Alois had daily thrashed and harassed Adolf. Helene
Hanfstaengl, whom Hitler had adored, had told me of the time Adolf decided
to run away from home. Somehow Alois learned of these plans and locked
the boy in an upstairs room. During the night Adolf had tried to squeeze
through the barred window. When he couldn't quite make it, he took off
his clothes. Just as he was wriggling his way to freedom, Adolf heard his
father's footsteps on the stairs and hastily withdrew, draping his nakedness
with a tablecloth. This time Alois did not whip him but burst out laughing,
shouting to his wife to come up and look at the "toga boy." Ridicule hurt
worse than any switch, and Hitler told Frau Hanfstaengl it took him "a long
time to get over the episode."

By this time he was eligible to enroll either in a *Gymnasium,* which placed
emphasis on classical education and prepared a student for a university, or a
Realschule, which was more technical and scientific. The nearest *Realschule*
was in the city of Linz, and Hitler made the more than three miles on foot.

I got a tip that there were several prospects for interviews living in Urfahr,
a suburb of Linz just across the Danube. This was where the family had
moved after his mother's operation for cancer. I found their rooms on
the second floor of an attractive stone building at Blutengasse 9. The occu-
pant knew nothing about Hitler but thought her landlord, who lived down
the street, had known him. In a few minutes I was talking with Josef Keplinger. Yes, he had known Hitler well. They had been close school friends,
and that was why he had bought the stone building down the street. He
brought out several pictures Hitler had painted, and we talked all afternoon.

As I left him wondered why no one else had ever tried to interview him.

"We all liked him at desk and at play. He had 'guts.' He exhibited two extremes of character which are not often seen in unison: he was a *quiet* fanatic." After school, Adolf was their leader. "He had learned to throw a lasso, and we played cowboys and Indians down by the Danube meadows." Hitler also held sway at recess, lecturing his group on the Boer War and passing out sketches he had made of gallant Boers. He even talked of enlisting in the army. The war helped arouse in young Hitler a yearning for German nationalism, a feeling shared by most of the boys. "Bismarck was for us a national hero," recalled Keplinger. "The Bismarck song and lots more German hymns and songs of the same character were forbidden to be sung." It was a crime even to possess a sketch of Bismarck. "Although privately our teachers felt that we boys were in the right, they had to punish us severely for singing these songs and brandishing our German loyalties."

But Adolf took his Germanism far more seriously than the other boys. "Perhaps it was rebellion against his father, who was a stout advocate of the Hapsburg regime." Keplinger had once accompanied Adolf part of the way home, up the steep Kapuzinerstrasse. At the top of the hill, Hitler stopped before a small chapel. "You are not a *Germane* [old German]," he bluntly told Keplinger. "You have dark hair and dark eyes." His own, he noted proudly, were blue and his hair (at that time, according to Keplinger) was light brown.

I had read that Hitler, while he was in Linz, spent several summers with relatives in Spital, near the border of Czechoslovakia. The town was so tiny that Glaser and I had trouble locating the small road leading up a hill to it. We were soon inside the former home of Anton Schmidt, Klara's brother-in-law, where we saw the room Adolf shared with his mother. We learned that he played with the Schmidt children, once making them a colorful dragon kite, yet often paced up and down or drew pictures and would get angry if the children interrupted him.

Our next stop was Vienna. I wanted to explore his failed attempts to enroll in the Academy of Fine Arts. He was turned down three times. His drawings were so lowly regarded on his second attempt that he wasn't even allowed to take the test. The third time he returned with a large portfolio of paintings. Although the professor in charge admitted they showed remarkable architectural precision, Hitler was again turned down. I had read how finally, without funds and unwilling to work, he had wandered for three months as a tramp, sleeping in parks and doorways. In rain he took refuge under the arches of the rotunda of the Prater, the famed amusement center. Winter came early, and he was forced to enter cheap flophouses or a laborers' barracks, a dirty refuge that had to be shared with other homeless. All this reminded me of the depression and the life of bindle stiffs. I knew that he finally found refuge in the Asyl für Obdachlose, a shelter for the destitute. The place still existed, and I was allowed to investigate and ask questions. The officials told me Hitler had spent little time here and I should go to his next refuge, the Mannerheim, about a half mile down the Danube.

This turned out to be a large building at Meldermannstrasse 25-27 which could accommodate five hundred men. But at first I was turned away. No reporters allowed. Our good friend Otto Zundricht was now in the United States, but a friend of his wangled a permit and I spent the next two days in the place. I talked to several old inmates who said they knew Hitler and showed me the tiny cubicle he had occupied. It was about five feet wide and seven feet deep, with just enough space for a small table, a clothes rack, a mirror, and a narrow cot. It was messy, but one man explained that in Hitler's day everything was tidy. Today's occupants reminded me of the frequenters of the Bowery and other American skid rows. The showers, so much appreciated by Hitler, were now dismantled, since they were not being used. The standards of cleanliness and neatness, explained the manager, had deteriorated since Hitler's day despite efforts of the present administration to maintain them.

My two untidy guides agreed. "You should have seen it then," one said. In Hitler's day there were clean reading and game rooms. There was a library and a "writing" room where a dozen men could carry on private business. They took me to the corner of one room where Hitler used to paint diligently. His comrades respected him because of his artistic airs. Invariably polite, he never stooped to familiarity, though he was always ready to help or advise a fellow worker. But if politics ever came up, he would toss aside his brush and start shouting and gesturing, his long hair flying. The real Adolf Hitler was starting to manifest himself.

Hans Hitler

On October 5, 1971, Toshiko and Tamiko arrived in Munich. Tamiko was delighted with my apartment and the nearby park, where we walked every day. I had promised Frau Schneider I would bring them for a visit, and the Schneiders were entranced by Toshiko.

We then visited Vienna, one of Toshiko's favorite cities. We attended a symphony performance directed by a young Japanese, Seiji Ozawa, whom I'd never heard of. In the middle of the performance the music suddenly stopped and Ozawa solemnly announced that Pope John had died and they were going to play something in his memory. I had never before been in an audience which responded instantly as one person: all of us, foreigners and natives alike, were deeply moved.

In mid-November the girls left for America, and I worked overtime, making three long trips to the north in order to finish my research. When I was halfway back to Munich, my faithful Volkswagen suddenly collapsed. I was towed to a garage and learned that the engine, like the one-horse shay, had totally collapsed. I sold the remains for a hundred marks and a ride to Munich with my baggage. I then flew to Hamburg for a possible interview with one of Hitler's relatives. I'd heard a rumor that some of the Hitler family still lived in Hamburg, and Hein Ruck, Skorzeny's assistant there, who had struck me as a man who could overcome obstacles, reported that he had found one of them.

It was pouring on the morning we were to meet at Hein's home. The bell finally rang and Hein bounded to the door shouting a hearty "Heil Hitler!" I was not amused. He then led in Hans Hitler, the Führer's second cousin. He had a briefcase, and as I watched pop-eyed he drew out picture after picture of the family—pictures I'd never seen before. There was Hitler's father with Alois Jr. on his lap; Hitler's half sister, Angela, and her son Leo; and Angela and Alois Jr. with Granny. He also had a Christmas card from Hitler as well as other family documents including a letter in Angela's writing to Alois Jr. about her visit to Adolf in prison after the Beer Hall Putsch. That letter put an end to the myth that his family did not enthusiastically support his political career. "His spirit and soul," she wrote, "were again at a high level. . . . the goal and victory is only a question of time. God grant it be soon."

Hans Hitler talked openly until noon. He admitted that Angela, Hitler's half sister, *had* insisted on making public appearances despite her stepbrother's disapproval. "She liked to make herself important . . . and Hitler could not tolerate that." Another relative on his mother's side, Fritz Pauli, was more of an embarrassment to the Hitler family. He not only married a Jewish woman but, having a peculiar sense of humor, delighted in publicizing it. He printed up postcards of the Hitler family tree with his wife's name, Rosenthal, as the bottom branch, then passed them out with the remark that this was the Jewish side of Adolf Hitler.

As Hans showed me the documents and pictures, he revealed that both he and Heinz Hitler (son of Alois Jr.) had fought in Russia and been captured. "I escaped to Germany," he said. But Heinz died in captivity. I knew all this was valuable material and asked if I could borrow it for a few moments. "Yah!" exclaimed Hein before Hans Hitler could object. I handed the material I wanted to my interpreter and told her to get Xeroxes. Hein passed around drinks while she was gone. Within the hour my interpreter returned with the originals and copies, and I could at last breathe normally.

After this extraordinary find, I felt confident that I had gathered enough material in Germany to make a useful book. I headed home, stopping off in London to interview Sir Oswald Mosley and his wife, Lady Diana Mosley. One of the famous Mitford sisters, she had spent the war imprisoned with her husband, and had endured the infatuation of her sister, Unity, with Hitler. Known as "Hitler's English girlfriend," this one of Lord Redesdale's five daughters had attempted suicide over Hitler and survived with a bullet in her head; the bullet could not be removed and would, after years of invalidism, kill her.

This interview seemed to round things off. I landed at Kennedy airport determined to "find out what I knew by writing it all down."

{2}

The Beer Hall Putsch

Once back in Danbury I began mulling over the mass of material I had collected and started a rough outline. I had uncovered new details, particularly from Putzi Hanfstaengl, his wife, Helene, and their son Egon.

By the politically precarious year 1923, a time when the infant Weimar Republic had already revealed that its foundations were anything but sturdy, Adolf Hitler, then living in Munich, had surrounded himself with a diverse group of adherents from every class, all of whom shared his intense nationalism and fear of Marxism. Among them was a German-American patrician, Ernst Hanfstaengl, whose mother came from a distinguished New England family and whose father's family were well-known patrons of the arts who owned an art-publishing business in Munich. A graduate of Harvard, Ernst was an accomplished pianist. Very tall, he was nicknamed Putzi ("Little Fellow"). Hunched over a piano keyboard, he was a familiar sight on social occasions in the homes of well-to-do Bavarians.

Putzi and Helene Hanfstaengl befriended Hitler during his early years of political struggle; he became a frequent guest in their home, and for many years Putzi served as Hitler's foreign press secretary, until Nazi officials decided that he was dangerous and tried unsuccessfully to arrange for his death. I wanted very much to talk with Putzi, Helene, and Egon, for they could reveal much about the inner workings of Hitler's government and for several years all of them were intimately familiar with Hitler's household entourage.

With the death of Putzi and Helene, her candid memories can now be revealed here in full. Helene had requested that much of this material remain private until after her death.

At the time I first interviewed her in 1963—a rare event as she never gave them—she not only spoke at length but lent us her unpublished memoirs.

Despite an astrological warning against taking action in 1923, Hitler insisted on leading a march on Berlin that November to take over the government, having drawn almost 25,000 new members into the Nazi Party since January. At noon on November 10 the march began at the Bürgerbräukeller, half a mile from the center of Munich. But once Hitler's motley collection of Putschists—some in full uniform or parts of tattered World War uniforms—reached the Odeonsplatz, they were blocked by state police. When the police opened fire, the Putschists replied but were immediately overwhelmed. Hitler had been dragged to the ground by his bodyguard so sharply that his left arm was dislocated.

Hitler managed to escape with several comrades and fled by car to the Hanfstaengl country place in Uffing. Putzi was still in Munich at their cramped apartment, but Helene was in Uffing with Egon. The maid reported that someone was knocking softly at the door. "I went downstairs," Helene recalled, "and without opening asked who was there. To my amazement I recognized the unmistakable voice of Hitler. Quickly I opened the door. There he stood, ghastly pale, hatless, his face and clothing covered with mud, the left arm hanging down from a strangely slanting shoulder."

She told us how she had taken him in and cared for him, helping him endure a restless first night with a fever and pain caused by his dislocated arm, wrapping him tightly in a traveling rug to ease the pain. The wanted man stayed in hiding for several days, while plans were concocted for getting him out of the state of Bavaria and into Austria. She told me how Hitler had surrendered to panic and depression, once taking his gun out and preparing to shoot himself rather than suffer the ignominy of capture.

But after only a few days had passed, with the police searching nearby houses, it became clear that there could be no escape for Hitler. Helene Hanfstaengl's worries about harboring Hitler were compounded by the necessity of keeping a close watch on her little son for fear he might tell someone that "Uncle Dolf" was visiting. When the police finally arrived in force, it was rather an anticlimactic moment.

There was a sudden rumble of powerful motors, commands, and the startling bark of police dogs. "We waited. The minutes dragged on. I told Hitler that when they demanded entrance, I would go answer myself. I went downstairs and told the maids to stay quietly in the kitchen and to keep Egon with them, so as not to startle the child too much. I walked to one of the windows on the ground floor and peered out between the shutters. Imagine my surprise when I saw a soldier stationed there with a bayonet at charge, holding a police dog on the leash. The man was so startled at my sudden and silent appearance that he jumped and of course jerked the leash. The dog began to bark furiously, giving the signal to all his companions to do likewise. A veritable pandemonium broke loose."

Then came a knock. On opening the door, Helene saw a young, very diffident army lieutenant accompanied by two police officers. The lieutenant introduced himself—his name was Braun—and apologetically stated that he was ordered to search the house. Helene invited him in. "Follow me," she said and proceeded up the stairs silently. She noticed Braun and the two police looking furtively behind them. The silence of the house was distinctly uncanny to the three men. She silently opened a door. There stood Hitler.

"The unexpected apparition so startled the three men they inadvertently stepped back for a moment. I motioned them in, and when the door was closed, Hitler, who had finally regained his composure, broke forth in a tirade against the government and the officials, raising his voice more and more, particularly when Lieutenant Braun, in a distinctly apologetic tone, said he must arrest Hitler for high treason." This triggered a defiant outburst from Hitler, denying this charge vociferously. But he soon realized he would have to submit and curtly asked Braun to waste no time, demanding to know where he was being taken. The lieutenant said he would spend the night in Weilheim, the nearest town.

It was bitterly cold, but Hitler refused any of Putzi's suits that Helene offered him. He was led away hatless, clad only in the blue bathrobe with his own coat draped over his shoulders.

Egon had heard the men coming down the stairs, and he broke away from the maids. He ran into the hall calling, "What are the bad, bad men doing to my Uncle Dolf?" This almost broke Hitler's composure. He patted the boy's cheek, then silently shook hands with Helene and the maids. He turned quickly and went out the door. Helene caught a last glimpse of his deathly pale face as the car turned on the road to Weilheim. "In less than ten minutes all was as quiet as though the events of the past hours had been but a bad dream."

She told me that she frequently reflected on her actions when Hitler had threatened to commit suicide. "I have since often thought that I might have changed the current of history, had I only known what Hitler would accomplish in the years to come. On the other hand, I have since been convinced that the attempt to shoot himself was only one of his many melodramatic gestures."

Christmas Eve 1924

Nonetheless, Hitler was alive and well. After arriving at Weilheim about 9:00 P.M., he was formally arraigned at the district office and then hustled to the prison at Landsberg, some forty miles west of Munich. When he was finally released from prison in late December 1924, Hitler was, so lonely that he didn't know what to do with himself. He realized it would take time to regain "contact with reality" and decided to remain quiet for several weeks before undertaking the huge task of reconciling dissident members of his own party.

He needed a respite, and sought it on that snowy Christmas Eve at the new home of the Hanfstaengls in Munich, where I later spent so many hours interviewing Putzi. In 1924, they had moved from their cramped apartment to this spacious house across the Isar River. It was a pleasant area, then boasting such prestigious neighbors as Thomas Mann and Hjalmar Schacht, the new Reich commissioner for national currency.

I interviewed the Hanfstaengls many times. I first encountered Putzi when researching for *The Last 100 Days* at his luxurious home on the outskirts of Munich. It was a tall, imposing structure, and the man who answered the door was also tall and imposing but friendly. In good English Putzi greeted me and then escorted me into his large living room, which looked like a storehouse.

"This," he said proudly, "is where I entertained the Führer so many times." He showed no remorse or regret. He climbed with agile clumsiness over piles of books, stuffed cartons, and heaps of clothing to a piano. He sat down as if that moment were the beginning of a performance at the Met and began to play as if I were Hitler.

This was the first of numerous lengthy meetings, over an eight-year period, each one different. I usually arrived at 9:00 A.M. and left late in the afternoon, but several times I stayed until 10:00 P.M. Occasionally we sat on the landing of the stairway leading upstairs and had lunch with people who had known Göring and Hitler. When I left each time, I would be far more exhausted than Putzi despite his constant pacing, playing the piano, and plowing through the clutter to find papers and pictures.

A month or so after our first meeting in 1963 when I was researching *The Last 100 Days,* he introduced me to his son, Egon, who appeared temperamentally to be the opposite of his father. Although also musical, he was quiet and composed as he calmly described in detail his meetings with "Uncle Dolf," who would romp with him on the floor. Egon ultimately persuaded his mother—long divorced from Putzi—to see Toshiko and me during the second German research trip in 1971. I expected to find Helene reticent and close-mouthed, but she answered all my questions fully. Her memory for details was extraordinary. I believe it was the presence of Toshiko which made her so open. She had also been reassured by her son that everything I wrote about her would be shown to her for correction. As we were leaving, she handed me her unpublished memoirs, written in English, which I have donated to the Franklin D. Roosevelt Library, and whose contents I can now discuss here.

The house in Munich was dominated by a spacious studio whose furnishings included a strikingly handsome antique cupboard dating back to the time of Martin Luther, a curious table with spiral legs on which rested a delicate Chinese cabinet brought from Canton in 1865 by Putzi's father, and a Steinway grand piano on which stood a life-size bust of Benjamin Franklin. Bookshelves lined the room, containing masses of historical works, an entire shelf of music literature, and copies of *Punch*. On the walls hung two woodcuts by Franz Masercel, an etching by Cadimir, and a painting of three children. There were ornamental pieces from China, Italy, America, France, and England. It was a room that would be a cultural oasis for Hitler. For here was art, literature, and music—and the pervading presence of Helene Hanfstaengl, a handsome, welcoming woman of culture who was also blessed with a quiet sense of humor.

Daylight was fading when the newly released Hitler arrived. Egon, who then would be four in two months, later remembered hearing a front doorbell ring, then his father's booming voice in the hall and someone stamping to knock the snow off his boots. "Finally came the resonant voice that had made such an impression on me. I ran up to Hitler, shouting, 'You're here again, Uncle Dolf!'" Hitler picked Egon up and told him with a grin what a big, fine boy he had grown to be. Hitler looked around nervously, then said, almost pleadingly, "Hanfstaengl, play me the 'Liebestod.'"

"So down I sat," recalled Putzi, "and hammered out this tremendous thing from *Tristan und Isolde,* with Lisztian embellishments, and it seemed to do the trick." Hitler began to relax.

Helene entered with her new daughter, Herta. Hitler crooned over the baby and apologized for all the trouble he had caused Helene when he sought refuge in their home after the Beer Hall Putsch. He surveyed the studio. "You are the most feudal acquaintance I have," he finally said to her. Suddenly, in midsentence, he darted a glance over his shoulder. "'I'm sorry,' he explained to Helene. 'That's what jail does to you. There is always some damn jailer standing behind, watching you.'"

"As we sat down for dinner at a table lit by candles," recalled Helene, "Hitler pointed to Putzi's massive chair with a lion's head carved at the end of each armrest. 'Ah! That's the naughty chair, that wicked chair we had to punish so!'" He smiled at Egon and, seeing the boy had no idea what he was talking about, explained how he had once slapped the chair when Egon had bumped into it and hurt his head.

Finally the time came for *Bescherung,* the presentation of gifts that Christmas Eve. The parents excused themselves while Hitler and Egon waited in the dining room. The two walked over to a window, staring out silently for some moments. Then the cook led them toward the studio. "As we approached it," explained Egon, "I saw my mother's head disappear behind the quickly closing door. Then Father began to play 'Stille Nacht, Heilige Nacht' on the Steinway inside, and we all sang—that is, the cook and the maid and I—and Hitler just listened."

Once Helene opened the door, Egon rushed in to see a Christmas tree glistening with lights and surrounded by a mountain of presents. "The two gifts I'd asked for were there—a saber and a cooking stove!"

Gone was Hitler's inner tension. He began striding up and down the room like a soldier, hands clasped behind his back, as he recounted scenes from the Great War. A little later he abruptly launched into a political tirade that made Putzi feel almost physically sick. "To my horror he spouted a still further distilled essence of all the nonsense that Hess and Rosenberg were concocting." It was a drastic change in Hitler, a new sense of direction—a sinister development. His anti-Semitism seemed even more virulent.

Before he left, Hitler managed to have a few moments of privacy with Helene in the studio. "I was seated on a large brown sofa and all at once he dropped to his knees, put his head in my lap, and said, 'If only I had someone to take care of me!' "

"Look, this won't do!" She asked him why he didn't get married.

"I can never marry because my life is dedicated to my country." Germany was his bride.

"I thought he was acting like a little boy—not a lover—and perhaps he was." Seventeen years ago, almost to the day, his beloved mother had died in agony. "It would have been awful if someone had come in," recalled Helene. "Humiliating to him. He was taking a chance, he really was! That was the end of it and I passed it off as if it simply had not happened."

[3]

The Family Circle

Adolf Hitler's Daily Life

The most fascinating phenomenon facing me when I started my research had been the existence of two inner circles that revolved around Hitler. One was composed of top associates and public officials like Goebbels, Göring, and Hess and their wives. The other, a more intimate group known as the Family Circle, included Eva Braun and her best friend, Herta Schneider; Hitler's two youngest secretaries, Gerda Christian and Gertraud Junge; his chauffeur, Erich Kempka; his pilot, Hans Baur; his valets, Heinz Linge and Karl Krause; and some of the younger adjutants (SS Colonel Richard Schulze, SS Major Otto Günsche), Navy Lieutenant Karl-Jesko von Puttkamer, and the representative of the Luftwaffe, Nikolaus von Below. A few belonged to both circles, most notably Martin Bormann, who had once served as Hess's secretary. Although unknown to most Germans, the indefatigable Bormann became Hitler's shadow, remaining at his elbow most of the day to jot down the Führer's slightest whim on cuff or notebook. It was he who ordered his secretary adjutant and art adviser to the Führer, Heinrich Heim, to copy down surreptitiously Hitler's "Table Talk."

Occasional members of the Family Circle included Putzi Hanfstaengl and his wife, Helene; three of his architects, Speer, Giesler, and Frau Troost; his two favorite warriors, Skorzeny and Rudel; and the Belgian Nazi leader Léon Degrelle, whom Hitler treated as a son.

All of the above who survived into the 1960s and 1970s I had interviewed by 1971 except Gertraud Junge, commonly called Traudl. Although I had learned much about Hitler from his two older secretaries and Gerda Christian, it had taken me months to persuade his youngest secretary to meet me. I had located her in Munich and taken her to dinner several times, but it was not until I was finally invited to her home to meet her sister that I made progress. After explaining that I was only looking for facts, and that I sent back to those I interviewed all material for corrections, her sister made a comment: "Why don't you give it to him?" I had no idea what she meant, and held my breath. Traudl then left the room and returned with a bulky package—an unpublished manuscript about her relations with Hitler.

With this new information I felt I could adequately portray the Family Circle. Traudl had been one of the nine young women brought to Hitler's headquarters in East Prussia in late 1942 to be tested as a replacement for Gerda Daranowsky, who had left a job with Elizabeth Arden to work for Hitler and later resigned to marry General Eckhard Christian. Gerda, attractive and vivacious, had brought liveliness into the Family Circle, and it was apparent that Hitler missed her. When Traudl, a naive, impressionable twenty-two-year-old, found herself alone with Hitler, she could not hide her agitation. He reassured her: " 'You don't have to get excited,' he told me, as if dealing with a child. 'I myself will make far more mistakes during the dictation than you will.' "

Her trembling hands made it difficult for her to hit the typewriter keys. "Even so, I thought I had done well. If I was chosen, Mother would be unhappy, for she disliked Hitler. After the First World War, Father had joined the Bund Overland and become a follower of Hitler." Her mother, feeling rejected, had taken Traudl and her sister to live with her parents. The morning after the test-interview, Traudl learned that she had been chosen and moved into the main headquarters bunker with the other two secretaries. "For four weeks I didn't see the Führer and wondered if this was another test." Then on January 30, 1943, Traudl was summoned to see him. Was she supposed to take an oath of loyalty? "Do you want to stay on the job?" he asked.

" 'Yes,' I said without hesitation."

Later she learned that Hitler had chosen her because all the other candidates were Prussian and he preferred girls from Munich. He was also impressed by her father's being a war veteran and a member of the Nazi Party.

While at lunch she was called to take dictation. It was a speech celebrating the tenth anniversary of the party's coming to power. His valet at the time, Hans Junge, escorted her to Hitler's office. The Führer's first words were "Are you sure you're not too cold, my dear? It's icy in here."

" 'I'm quite all right,' I said, immediately regretting it."

He paced back and forth as he dictated, never referring to notes. Fearing she might have missed something, she extended toward him what she had written. But he only smiled and shook her hand. "Don't worry. I'm sure it's all perfectly right." By the time she left, her feet were frozen. Junge explained later that the Führer liked to work in a very low temperature. She was soon at home in this strange new world and learned from his valet, Heinz Linge, who knew his peculiarities, how to recognize when the Führer was in a good enough mood to approach with bad news. "The only other permanent dweller of the bunker in the Wolfsschanze was Julius Schaub, his personal adjutant, and it amazed me why Hitler kept him around, limping after his master as a result of wounds in the First World War while cupping his ears to catch any words from his beloved Führer. Moreover, he was not too bright and no one but the Führer took him seriously."

Almost every evening she would attend a movie in a barracks. Almost everyone went except Hitler. Here she became acquainted with members of the Family Circle like Dr. Brandt and Dr. Theo Morell, a skin specialist who had cured Hitler's stomach cramps back in 1936 when all other doctors had failed. "He was fat, swarthy, and peered nearsightedly through thick glasses. The other doctors were shocked when he would occasionally inject two patients with the same needle. He also had dirty nails. The man I instantly disliked was Martin Bormann, whose crude horselaughs often exploded during a movie."

Late in March 1943 the daily routine changed when Hitler decided to transfer the entire general staff to his mountain retreat, the Eagle's Nest on the Obersalzberg. Traudl and the two middle-aged secretaries packed up two ordinary typewriters, two that were equipped only with capital letters, and one with extra-large type which Hitler could read without his glasses.

Everything worked like clockwork, and the Führer's train, the *Amerika,* left at precisely the scheduled time. "My own compartment was luxurious compared to my quarters at Wolfsschanze. There was hot and cold running water, a telephone, and the floor was covered with a plush carpet."

She was startled when invited the next day to have dinner with the Führer. "It was like a family gathering with the Führer as the genial father." She was also impressed to see that every time the train stopped he would personally make sure that his dog Blondi was led out to the platform. When Traudl retired to her comfortable room she watched other trains pass in the night, trains which had none of the comforts of the *Amerika*—no heat, no food.

By the time they approached Munich she had become very friendly with Lieutenant Hans Junge. The valet told her that Eva Braun was the mistress of Hitler's home, the Berghof, and was treated as such by all—all, that is, but the wives of Ribbentrop, Göring, and Goebbels, who openly snubbed her. The office staff would all stay there as Hitler's houseguests, and she would meet the rest of the Family Circle.

"Life at the Berghof was welcome after the grim surroundings of the Wolfsschanze, but even so I was disappointed." In these halls were great paintings and exquisite pieces of sculpture. It was all inspiring and beautiful, but cold and impersonal. "I was ill at ease and felt not like a guest but an employee."

The entire Berghof was like a tomb throughout the morning, but near noon, cars roared up to deposit officers for the daily briefing session, and in minutes the great hall, designed for peaceful conversation, was alive with arguments as life-and-death decisions were made. When the briefing was over, the guests waiting patiently in their rooms were informed that the last officer had left and lunch would soon be served. "It was after 3:00 P.M. by the time Eva appeared with her two dogs. Hitler first kissed her hand and then began to greet his guests one by one, while Eva greeted other guests."

Once all the guests were greeted, Hitler began teasing Eva about her dogs—which he called "hearth-brushes." She retorted by saying Blondi was more calf than dog. It was astonishing to Traudl to see someone emerge from a serious and often stormy briefing and suddenly become a good-natured host entertaining friends at his country home. The transformation was not only unexpected but even a bit ludicrous. Eventually Linge approached Dr. Brandt's wife, informing her that the Führer would escort her to lunch. Other guests received seating assignments from an orderly. Hitler led the way with Frau Brandt, and Traudl soon learned that Bormann and Eva were always the second couple. She also learned that Bormann was even more flagrant in his extramarital affairs than Goebbels, and had kept his wife almost permanently pregnant with nine children. He explained to his wife that these affairs had been consummated in the name of National Socialism, and she had suggested in a recent letter that he bring his latest mistress, M., to their home so that "one year M. has a child, and the next year I, so that you will always have a wife that is mobile."

After lunch Hitler set out for a round stone building which resembled a silo, camouflaged in the nearby woods. This was his "escape"—a tea house where he sipped apple-peel tea and listed to Eva's gossip until he fell asleep and took a nap. At 7:00 P.M. he spent two hours in a nonmilitary conference, then led his guests into the dining room.

The military would arrive after the evening meal for the evening conference. The guests were to remain in the dining room; Hitler didn't want the women to mix with the military. It was nearly midnight by the time he returned to sip his tea and eat apple cake while regaling the company with stories of the old days. This went on until the air raid reports came in at about 4:00 A.M. and the Führer was assured that all enemy planes had left Germany. Then, and only then, could he go to bed.

What most disturbed Traudl about the meals was the way Hitler ate—

gulping down the food as if there would never be another meal. He himself was disturbed because Traudl ate so little. "You're too thin. Men don't think a girl should look like a boy."

Hitler was amused—and not at all offended—whenever Dr. Morell dozed off after drinking a glass of wine, his fat arms folded over his great stomach, his eyes closed tight, his thick glasses magnifying them—a sight which Traudl found frightening. On one occasion Colonel von Below, the Luftwaffe adjutant, nudged Morell, who abruptly woke up, assumed the Führer had told a joke, and broke into a big smile.

"Are you tired?" asked Hitler.

"No, my Führer, I was just daydreaming."

One evening when Hitler was talking about the life he imagined for his retirement after the war, Traudl forced herself to ask, "When will this war be over?"

"As soon as we win it," he replied. But his friendly expression had instantly turned cold. The Reich *would* win, he declared emphatically, because Germany was fighting for an idea, not for Jewish capitalism like the enemy. Russia was the only dangerous ally, because the Russians were just as fanatic as the Germans. *"But right will conquer!"* This outburst startled Traudl, because he rarely spoke to the Family Circle about the world or politics.

On Good Friday 1943, Traudl also saw him change from benevolent host to intense fanatic when Hoffmann's daughter, Henriette von Schirach, arrived at the Berghof. She had just endured a horrifying experience in Holland. One night she had seen several hundred Jewish women being forcibly moved across a bridge. A voice shouted, "Aryans remain behind!" A friend told her about the atrocities being committed against the Jews, and she promised to inform Hitler, who supposedly didn't know what was going on.

At the gathering of the Family Circle that evening, Henriette told Hitler what she had seen with her own eyes. At first he seemed baffled and said nothing. The others in the room remained silent and avoided looking at her. Then Hitler, seated, turned slowly toward her, and she was startled to see his face drawn. His skin and eyes seemed colorless. "The demons are devouring him," she thought as he stared at her. Then he rose slowly and struggled to retain his self-control, but suddenly shouted, "You are a sentimentalist! What business is it of yours? The Jewesses are none of your business!" To Hitler this display of sympathy was sheer sentimentality—tittle-tattle about humanity!

Terrified, she ran up the wide marble stairs, his furious voice pursuing her. An adjutant followed. "Why did you have to do this?" he gasped. "You have made him very angry! Please leave at once!" She located her husband in the canteen, and they drove past the guards. According to her story it was 5:00 A.M.

Two of Hitler's most intimate, but radically different, associates in the Family Circle were Albert Speer and Martin Bormann. Speer was always a welcome visitor, and Traudl liked him as a competent professional who could speak frankly to the Führer. When they disagreed, Hitler often bowed to Speer's arguments. Speer felt completely at home in the Family Circle except when Bormann, whom he detested and feared, was present. It was obvious that Bormann wanted to make himself so essential to Hitler that he could control all those close to the Führer. He had helped turn Hitler against Baldur von Schirach, now the Gauleiter of Vienna, with disparaging anecdotes from Austria.

Erich Kempka, Hitler's chauffeur, told us that he was also one of Bormann's targets. "But Bormann had to be subtle, since it was obvious the Führer treated me almost like a son." Kempka admired Bormann's devotion to Hitler, but detested his cruelty to those who stood in his way. He would give someone a present one day and the next day knife him in the back. Bormann was a sadist. Kempka's detestation was shared by Bormann's own father-in-law, Reichsleiter Walther Buch, who would leave the Obersalzberg immediately if he learned that his son-in-law was coming. And Bormann still refused to speak directly to his own brother, Albert, even though Albert had obligingly divorced his part-Jewish wife.

The circle had noticed Traudl's burgeoning romance with the handsome young Hans Junge, a particular favorite of Hitler's, but as yet the Führer knew nothing about it. They finally told an adjutant to pass on the news to Hitler, who looked at her with a knowing smile. She was so embarrassed that she wanted to disappear, for she had told the Family Circle a few months earlier that she had no interest in men.

That evening, as they gathered in front of the fire, Hitler announced with a great sigh, "I really have such bad luck with my staff! First Christian married Dara and took my best secretary, then I found a satisfactory replacement, and now Traudl Humps is going to leave me—and take with her my best servant!"

She and Hans had already decided to postpone their engagement when he had finally been given permission to fight on the Russian front, but in May, when Hitler called her in for dictation, he startled her by suggesting she and Junge get married immediately—before Junge left for the front. Traudl was astounded.

She didn't argue, and assumed the Führer would forget the matter, but he kept urging them until they finally got married in June 1943. Upon her return to the Wolfsschanze the excitement of being at headquarters in East Prussia had worn off, and she was beginning to understand the danger of living in a world that was completely dominated by the Führer.

"I realized at last that everyone else at Wolfsschanze had exactly the same thoughts and even used the same words." Having a vague fear that such close contact with Hitler kept her from having thoughts of her own, she started a diary in the hope of retaining her objectivity.

Now that she was regularly eating lunch with the Führer, she had lost her bashfulness and they conversed freely. He talked so incessantly of Eva Braun's wonderful qualities that Traudl asked why he had never married. He would not be a good family man, he replied, since he wouldn't have time for his wife and children. "Besides, I don't want children. The children of a genius have a hard time in the world. People expect such a child to be a replica of his famous father and don't forgive him for being average. Besides, it's common for them to be mentally deficient." Never before had she glimpsed his megalomania. "I was shocked to hear him in all seriousness call himself a genius."

Putzi Hanfstaengl's Last-Minute Escape

When I was writing *Adolf Hitler* I was given access to Helene Hanfstaengl's private memories but was allowed to use very little. Now, since her death, her son Egon has given me permission to tell the story in full and publish the only picture of the entire family, one never previously reproduced.

Although the Hanfstaengls never felt they were a part of the Family Circle, they probably knew Hitler better than did any of its members. Hitler was not only enamored of Helene but liked her son, Egon. Soon after he was made chancellor in 1933 he had invited them to his summer retreat at Haus Wachenfeld on the Obersalzberg. Putzi was too busy but proposed that Helene and Egon go.

Egon and his mother were the only guests in Haus Wachenfeld, but there were many Nazis living in nearby inns or boardinghouses who converged on Haus Wachenfeld during the day. Göring was constantly around, and Egon noticed how he and Hitler often conferred confidentially in the garden—with Göring doing most of the talking. One day Egon and Helene were shocked to hear Göring say, "I have just signed twenty death warrants." Both of them were surprised "at this grim glimpse behind the scenes of glorious statecraft."

One evening Egon was disillusioned to see Baldur von Schirach, recently made leader of the Hitler Youth, under the influence of liquor and looking like "a bowl of Jell-O" when he walked—or rather "oozed along." "And that was supposed to be my leader in the Hitler Youth! I wondered why Hitler stood it."

Despite disillusionment with his leader, Egon's faith in the whole movement was quickly restored by Hitler's winning ways. "One day I found him on the veranda, looking over toward Salzburg and pensively biting the skin around his fingernails all the while. You could just see some houses and what appeared to be the castle." Hitler stood there a long time without uttering a sound. Then he said, "Look, boy, that's Austria over there."

"You were born there, Herr Hitler, weren't you?"

"Yes," he said quietly, "in Braunau on the Inn. It's really a beautiful country."

"Why don't we drive over and visit it? It's only a short way."

Hitler smiled, but not happily. "We will someday. It's really a shame that they don't belong to us. But they'll come home into the Reich someday."

By 1936, Martin Bormann had gained increased influence over the Führer. Still the assistant to Hess, he had wormed his way into Hitler's good graces by sedulously taking charge of small as well as major matters. This meant that confidants like Hanfstaengl were being reduced to minor roles. For some time the Führer had been annoyed because Putzi called him "Herr Hitler" instead of "Mein Führer" and talked to him as though he were an equal.

Hanfstaengl knew he was on dangerous ground, and while he and Egon, now fifteen, were sailing on Lake Starnberg, he said to his son, "Things are not well. We all believed in the movement, didn't we? I am still trying to believe in it." But he had found foul corruption everywhere. "There are many despicable individuals, criminals and perverts, to whom Herr Hitler listens." And war was coming with England and America. "It's dangerous for Germany and for the world. That's not all. The country is in a foul state internally. I ascribe that mainly to the blackguards who are sitting firmly entrenched behind official desks in Berlin and elsewhere. I've tried, God knows, to get at Hitler and warn him. . . . But Hitler refuses to hear me. He refuses to face the sad facts. That's one way of looking at it, and let's hope it's the right way. Yet it looks as though Hitler himself has become corrupt. It's no use saying that he just doesn't know what goes on. He must know. And if he knows, he must be held responsible. . . . I've unearthed many a reeking scandal in the lives of men who wield great power. Today I know things about them that they don't care to have known. They fear the truth, and . . . I'm irksome to them, and they're not going to suffer it. . . . So far they've tried to ruin me with a framed embezzlement scandal. . . . Well, they failed. . . . But they're not through. I expect worse. Yes, I expect to be fighting for life itself before long. They're almost certain to get around to liquidating me outright sooner or later. I can't say now when it'll come."

Egon wasn't really surprised. "Well, Father, if you know they'll try to wipe you out, why don't we flee now, while there's time?"

Hanfstaengl smiled. "It isn't that easy. I helped to bring the party into power." He had saved Hitler several times from physical and political danger, shielding him with his own good name. He didn't want to quit. "We're all responsible. The foundations, ninety-five percent of the original aims, are good. There is still a chance."

Egon fully believed his father when he said that his chances for being rubbed out were excellent. Then Putzi began to give Egon instructions for getting out. "You can see now that a wholly successful escape on my part would be rendered null and void by seizure of your person. That is why you also must make good your escape when the time comes—and let's hope we're both lucky."

Egon's secret preparations for escape had to be so exact and careful that everything would click precisely.

A breeze had sprung up, and their boat, the *Perhaps,* started to dance over the ripples. Hanfstaengl gave his son time to let these things sink into his mind as he outlined his detailed plan. "I was amazed at its simplicity," recalled Egon. "We agreed on a few code words whereby he would tip me off." A sentence beginning with name of their boat, *Perhaps,* would be the signal for Egon to pack and "get moving to one of the prearranged points to be designated at that time." By the time the *Perhaps* returned to the Royal Bavarian Yacht Club, Egon had learned everything "by heart, exactly and indelibly."

Hitler did not act until Putzi's birthday, February 11, 1937, when Putzi was ordered to fly to Spain and protect the interests of German correspondents in Franco's country. Soon after takeoff the pilot revealed that once they were over the area between Barcelona and Madrid, Hanfstaengl would be forced to parachute into the Red lines.

"That will be a death sentence!" exclaimed Putzi.

"I was given orders signed by Göring just before takeoff," said the pilot. He was sympathetic, but what could he do? He said nothing more, but soon one of the engines began sputtering. "Something wrong," he called back to Putzi, adding with a meaningful look, "We're going to have to land at a small airfield."

Once on the ground, Putzi said he was going to call Berlin for instructions. Instead he phoned his secretary, telling her that his orders had suddenly been changed and he was going to spend his fiftieth birthday with his family in Bavaria. Then he informed the pilot that the Führer had ordered him to return to Uffing. Instead he took a night train to Munich and a morning train to Zürich, then sent Egon the one-word message, in code: "Perhaps."

Egon packed a few clothes and an autographed picture of Hitler, slipped an automatic into an overcoat pocket, boarded the Zürich train, and hid in a toilet for several hours. Just before midnight he was reunited with his father.

Putzi and Egon in London

Two years later, Hanfstaengl was still in London with Egon who was attending St. Paul's School. Putzi was living on damages from a libel case he had won against the *Daily Express* four years earlier, as well as on money from English friends. He learned that Hitler had urged his old friend Hermann Esser to visit England and persuade Putzi to return: "Give him my word of honor," said the Führer, "that he can return in complete safety." Putzi's former treatment from the Nazis had been only "a joke, and he didn't have to run away."

Years later, Esser revealed to me at a luncheon in Putzi's home that Hanfstaengl had refused to go back to Germany. Even so, Karl Bodenschatz visited Putzi once more to assure him that he could return to his old position. "Tell Herr Hitler for me," Putzi had said, "that I would consider returning if he sent me a personal letter of apology and offered me a post as his personal adviser on foreign affairs that was not merely fictitious."

No letter arrived from Hitler, but one did come from Hitler's shadow, Bormann, who promised that any punitive measures would be canceled and the cost of his stay in London refunded. Putzi refused, and the persistent Bodenschatz returned once more, this time with the husband of Hanfstaengl's former secretary, a man who was employed by Goebbels. They brought a letter of appeasement from the propaganda minister. When Putzi again refused, Bodenschatz threatened: "If you don't come back, there are other means to silence you."

Putzi retorted that he had already written his memoirs, and copies were locked in three different cities in Europe. "If I die a natural death, they are to be destroyed." If not, they would be published.

"That is pure blackmail," Bodenschatz angrily replied.

"Since when have corpses blackmailed the living?"

Putzi sent Egon to America by way of Canada on September 2, 1939, the day after Hitler's forces invaded Poland. That evening the doorbell rang at his London flat in West Kensington. Two plainclothes detectives were standing at the door. "Mr. Hanfstaengl?" asked one. "We have orders to arrest you as an enemy alien. You don't need to take much with you, as this is only a formality which will last for a few days." Actually it would last for a very long time.

The news of war was revealed to the passengers on Egon's ship soon after Parliament declared war on Germany on September 3. Then he remembered his Hitler Youth uniform. "Why carry the thing any further now?" he asked himself. "The customs official in Quebec might not understand. Beside, I was going home, and I wanted to do it right." That night he unpacked his uniform, carried it on deck, and took a last look at it—the swastika armband, the shoulder pieces with the insignia BANN 325—GEFOLGSCHAFT 13.

"Down it went, and I watched it fall into the wake. Then the cap. I spun it, and it was carried by a breeze far to the side. I watched it get smaller and smaller until it finally hit the water."

Putzi's Service to the United States

Several years later, Putzi was able to be of service to Hitler's formidable enemy, the United States. In the spring of 1943, General William "Wild Bill" Donovan, head of the Office of Strategic Services, America's intelligence service, addressed a question to Dr. Walter Langer, a prominent analyst who had set up a Psychoanalytical Field Unit for the OSS: "What do you make of Hitler?"

This question had fascinated the psychiatric world for many years, and a variety of answers had been proposed. Freud, before his death in London in 1939, had labeled him as simply insane; and Jung, who had once personally observed the Führer, wrote that he resembled a robot: "He seemed as if he might be a double of a real person; Hitler the man might perhaps be hiding inside like an appendix, and deliberately so hiding in order not to disturb the mechanism." Other answers abounded, most of them offered by those who knew little or nothing about Hitler's private life.

Langer had some firsthand knowledge of Nazi Germany. Having been a daily visitor at the home of Freud, he had helped persuade the eighty-two-year-old psychoanalyst to leave Austria because Hitler hated Jews and analysts with equal fervor. He accompanied Freud and his family to the border, where his intervention, as an American citizen, kept storm troopers from detaining Freud and his family.

Dr. Langer told me he had searched the United States and Canada for people who knew Hitler personally, and his best source turned out to be Putzi Hanfstaengl, who had been rescued a year earlier from a prison camp in Canada by his Harvard friend Franklin Roosevelt. Putzi had persuaded a Hearst correspondent visiting his camp to deliver a letter to the president offering his services as a military and political adviser in the fight against Hitler. Roosevelt immediately dispatched John Franklin Carter, one of his advisers, to Canada. "The president accepts your proposal," Carter told Putzi, and several months later an American agent arrived to escort him to the United States. "I have to disappoint you, Dr. Hanfstaengl," said the agent, "for I cannot give you your complete freedom. We have borrowed you, so to speak, from the British, who insist that you remain in custody."

Putzi was taken to Carter's home in Washington, where his host said, "I must first introduce you to the guard appointed by the president in accordance with the agreement with the British government."

This had the effect of a cold shower on Putzi until, pushed into the adjoining room, he saw before him his son, Sergeant Egon Hanfstaengl of the U.S. Army. They hugged each other for the first time in three years.

Eventually Putzi was taken to a stately home in Virginia, Bush Hill, where he wrote about Hitler, his probable reaction to crises, his strengths, his weaknesses, his personal peculiarities. Although its conclusions were flavored by the prejudices and assumptions of Hitler's erstwhile court jester, there were few individuals in the world, let alone Americans, who had observed the Führer so long or so intimately.

{4}

The Final Solution

Hitler's Personal Responsibility

One of the most difficult problems I faced early in 1971 was how to get at the truth about the Final Solution. A number of high-ranking Germans were convinced either that the stories of the killings were gross exaggerations or that Hitler was not personally responsible for the killings. But Toshiko and I had seen Auschwitz and other camps, and my own research had already verified the horrendous magnitude of the Final Solution, and that it *was* the brainchild of Hitler. I had found ample proof of the Final Solution as Hitler's idea in his second book, which he had refused to publish; it was finally published in 1961 as *Hitler's Secret Book. Mein Kampf* had been a great success, since it was a combination of a Horatio Alger novel and a political tract, but the second book—which had no title—was a venture far removed from his earlier success. He hoped it would express his *Weltanschauung,* his philosophy of life, and would unite his private beliefs with his political mission.

"History itself," he wrote in this second book, "is the presentation of a people's struggle for existence . . . just as life itself is an external struggle against death." Mankind's basic need is not only self-preservation but *Lebensraum*—living space. He also discussed the importance of the "blood value" of a people, a concept which he used to support his hatred of Jews. In *Mein Kampf* he had merely called the Jews enemies of the world and, in addition, advocated a drive to the east to attain living space for the German people. But in this unpublished book, for the first time, he demonstrated that his two most urgent convictions—danger of pollution from Jewish blood and Germany's desperate need for sufficient living space—were irrevocably entwined. If the Reich failed to acquire essential living space it would perish, and the only choice was a war of conquest. And if the Jewish menace was not wiped out there could be no struggle for *Lebensraum,* no racial purity, and the nation would decay. He now had a dual mission—seizure of living space in the east and total destruction of the Jews. Each depended on the other. Earlier he had envisioned these two courses as separate but parallel; now he saw them as a single course. He also realized that Luther and other anti-Semites had only *talked* of wiping out the Jews. He, Adolf Hitler, had a blueprint for *action:* a genuine Final Solution.

Hitler's call for mass extermination of the Jews was clear. Perhaps that was why Hitler forbade publication of what became *Hitler's Secret Book.* Perhaps he feared that the hard truth behind his words—mass murder—would be impossible for many Germans to swallow. Several passages in this book offer clues to his motivation for genocide. In two passages his charges of Jewish poisoning and corruption revealed personal obsessions. The first was a reference to Matthias Erzberger, who as a representative of Friedrich Ebert's government signed the 1918 armistice, as "the bastard son of a servant-girl and a Jewish employer." Was he also reminded of his own father? Since childhood Hitler had heard rumors that his paternal grandmother had worked as a servant in a Jewish household of a family in Graz and returned home impregnated by the Jewish son in that home. Hitler finally ordered his lawyer, Hans Frank, to make a thorough but confidential investigation of this possibility. Frank returned, after probing "all possible sources," with a report that stunned Hitler. I learned this from the American psychiatrist who interrogated Frank after the war and persuaded him to write the full account of his experience. It stated that Hitler's father, Alois Schickelgruber, was probably "the illegitimate child of a cook named Maria Anna Schickelgruber who worked for a Jewish family named Frankenberger when she gave birth to her son. And Frankenberger—this happened in the late 1830s—had paid a paternity allowance on behalf of his nineteen-year-old son from the birth of the Schickelgruber woman's son until the boy was fourteen." In 1876 he was legitimized as Alois Hitler, named after the man who had brought him up after the death of his mother: Johan Nepomuk Hiedler, the brother of the man she had married when Alois was almost five.

And could Hitler have been thinking of his own mother, who had died of cancer, when he wrote in his unpublished book, "If a man appears to have cancer and is unconditionally doomed to die, it would be senseless to refuse an operation, because the percentage of the possibility of success is slight"? Fear that his father may have been part Jewish had been haunting him for years, as had his mother's painful death from cancer.

I had already learned from the German historian Ernst Deuerlein that it could not have been a coincidence that, after finishing this secret book, Hitler had gone to a psychiatrist, a party member, Dr. Alfred Schwenninger of Munich, to allay a "fear of cancer." There is no record of his treatment, but Dr. Schwenninger failed to relieve his patient's fear, which he diagnosed as only imaginary. That fear, along with his obsession to eliminate all Jews, would persist to the last day of his life, nor was it surprising that he later confided to Putzi Hanfstaengl that the Jews were "the cancer of the world." I was determined to uncover that Hitler was *the* architect of the Final Solution and I sought out witnesses and documents which amply supported this. The "revisionist" historians in Germany and elsewhere, have attempted to minimize or even deny Hitler's full awareness and responsibility. Such assertions must not remain unchallenged.

A week after the nationwide *Kristallnacht* atrocities against the Jews in November of 1938, Hitler issued the First Regulation in the Reich Citizenship Law, which supplemented the earlier Nuremberg Laws on racial matters. This separated non-Aryans into definite categories. For the first time Hitler defined exactly what a Jew was: a person with at least three Jewish grandparents, or someone with only two Jewish grandparents but who was married to a Jew or who had accepted the Jewish religion. This was followed by a category previously unmentioned: the *Mischlinge,* half-breeds—those with only one Jewish grandparent, as well as those with two Jewish grandparents but who were not married to a Jew or practicing the Jewish religion. These *Mischlinge* were no longer subject to repressive measures. With one bureaucratic stroke Hitler made it possible for a substantial number of his detested enemies to escape the Final Solution. Could it have been that he still feared he himself had a Jewish grandparent and was saving himself?

Except for the few who knew of the Führer's secret fear that he was part Jewish, all were bewildered by the new regulation. Did it mean that his anti-Semitic program was no longer politically necessary now that he was dictator of Germany? Or did it mean that the furious denunciations from the West were to be stilled by an abandonment of his call for Jewish destruction? There was also the possibility that he was just as devoted to the Final Solution as ever, but the time for action had not yet arrived.

The answer came on January 21, 1939, when the Führer told the Czech foreign minister he could not give any guarantee to a nation that did not eliminate its Jews. "The vermin must be destroyed. The Jews are our sworn enemies, and at the end of this year there will not be a Jew left in Germany." They would pay for betraying Germany in November 1918. "The day of reckoning has come." Several days later a circular declaring outright war on Jews was sent to all diplomatic missions and consulates. "The ultimate aim of Germany's Jewish policy," it stated, "is the emigration of all Jews living on German territories." "Emigration" turned out to be a euphemism for "murder." Hitler was taking a bold step, calling for all anti-Semites in the world to back his holy mission to eliminate the Jews. For he was sure that behind polite screens, the other great nations of the world were also in favor of the Final Solution so long as they didn't have to do the dirty work.

In a speech to the Reichstag in 1939, on the sixth anniversary of the Nazi rise to power, Hitler publicly revealed his new policy in even more explicit terms. He personally declared war on world Jewry in the name of peace. England, France, and America, he charged, would shortly realize that Germany wanted peace and the assertion that she intended attacking their neighbors was a Jewish lie. Hitler was publicly lifting the veil of his Final Solution; his private and public worlds were openly merging. "In the course of my life, I have often been a prophet, and have usually been ridiculed for it," he exclaimed. "I will once more be a prophet: If the International Jewish financiers in and outside Europe should succeed in plunging the nations once more into a world war, then the result will not be the Bolshevization of the earth, and thus the victory of Jewry, but the annihilation of the Jewish race in Europe!"

All this evidence demonstrated clearly that Hitler was indeed personally responsible for both the idea of the Final Solution and the decision to put this idea into practice by exterminating the Jews. But I also had to deal with the conviction of many high-ranking Germans that the figure of six million victims was a gross exaggeration invented to serve the needs of Jewish propaganda.

Often those in less exalted positions would furnish details on not only the Holocaust but the strange environment in which Hitler lived and worked. It was these lesser figures who told me how, on January 23, 1942, Hitler announced at lunch, on one of the rare occasions when Himmler was present, "One must act radically. When one pulls out a tooth, one does it with a single tug and the pain quickly goes away. The Jews must clear out of Europe. It's the Jew who prevents everything. When I think about it, I realize that I'm extraordinarily humane." After all, he was merely asking them to go away. "But if they refuse to go voluntarily, I see no other solution but extermination." Never before had he revealed such inner thoughts to his Family Circle; perhaps the appearance of Himmler had inspired him.

Hitler's plans for the Final Solution were on schedule. By spring 1942, there were six killing centers in Poland. Jews were gassed by engine-exhaust fumes in four camps. The two installations near Auschwitz were using Zyklon B, hydrogen cyanide. Atrocities in occupied Russia also continued, despite repeated pleas from Alfred Rosenberg to treat these people as allies, not enemies. He urged Werner Koeppen, Rosenberg's liaison man with Hitler's headquarters in the east, to somehow get the message across that these people were really anti-Stalin.

Two invaluable sources were Koeppen and Heinrich Heim, Bormann's man. Each had been surreptitiously recording Hitler's informal "Table Talk," Koeppen for Rosenberg and Heim for Bormann. I had tracked both men down by contacting people known to have been friendly with them during the war. Finally I located both men. Heim, hearing that I was looking for him, came to me and poured out details about Bormann and Hitler. Heim didn't know it, but Koeppen was living a few blocks away from him, and I actually reunited them.

Before the Hess flight, Koeppen had been able to deal directly with the Führer, but later everything had to go through Bormann, who had put up a stone wall. And Koeppen's sad observation was, "Therein lay the fateful development which, in my opinion, cost us victory in the east."

Judge Morgen Stands Up to Hitler

A most important witness of the atrocities was a thirty-four-year-old German lawyer who worked for Himmler. Konrad Morgen had been brought up with the ethics of law from student days and became an SS judge. I had been told by several interviewees that he had done the most of any man to stop the atrocities. With the help of another SS judge I finally, after several efforts, induced Judge Morgen to talk. I first had to promise never to reveal where he presently lived and practiced law under a pseudonym, since he feared assassination not only by Nazis but by U.S. security agents. At his instruction I took a roundabout trip to his city. I expected to find him suspicious and reluctant to talk, but to my surprise he was open and cordial. "I have been assured I can trust you," he said, and made me promise never to reveal where and how I got his story. After his death I could reveal all the details but still must protect his family's whereabouts. He reminded me of a lawyer friend of mine who had risen from the bottom. Both were calm and assured and spoke quietly with few adjectives or adverbs. I felt at home with both. Morgen was familiar with my work and said that was why he was now willing to talk about his past. He spoke evenly, almost as if he were an observer of his perilous deeds, not a participant.

He allowed me to tape him in his office until well after dark. He told me that even as a law student and as an assistant SS judge he had been outspoken in his disapproval of illegality no matter who committed it. "I based my judgments strictly on the evidence." He smiled wryly. "I exasperated my superiors so much that I was posted to a front-line SS division as punishment." But his reputation was so outstanding that he was transferred in

1943 to the SD (Sicherheitsdienst, the security service headed by Heydrich) Financial Crimes Office. "It was with the understanding that I wasn't to deal with political cases. Early that summer I was given a routine investigative mission to clear up a long-standing corruption case at the Buchenwald concentration camp." Karl Koch, the commandant, had been suspected of hiring out camp laborers to civilian employers. He was also racketeering in food supplies and, in general, running the camp for his own personal profit. But Morgen's initial investigation had failed to bring conviction. "A parade of witnesses insisted he was innocent."

Morgen had encountered exactly the corruption in the Nazi hierarchy that Putzi Hanfstaengl had warned against. He refused to take the line of least resistance and continued to investigate. Buchenwald, even in 1943, had a certain cosmetic coverage of its true nature and functioning—but Morgen quickly broke through this and found out what had happened after the massive influx of Jews following *Kristallnacht,* when the profiteering had increased exponentially. Prisoners who could have served as witnesses had been murdered—so Morgen tracked down the paper trail of bank records that showed how Koch had embezzled 100,000 marks out of money and valuables confiscated from Jewish inmates. His chief, when confronted with this evidence, bucked him up the chain of command until he finally found himself pressing his case to Himmler himself—and to the astonishment of everyone was given the Reichsführer's authorization to proceed.

Morgen returned to Buchenwald, uncovered the network of corruption, and then broke down Koch in interrogation. He confessed, was found guilty, and was hanged. But Morgen did not stop there—he followed the trail of corruption to Auschwitz in Poland and other death camps nearby—and thus he began to focus on the mass murder that was taking place. This time the bureaucracy kept Morgen from reaching Himmler, so Morgen resolved to do whatever was in his power to end such criminality. "I could not do this with regard to the killings ordered by the head of state, but I could do it for killings *outside* of this order, or *against* this order, or for other serious charges." He began expanding his investigations to institute proceedings against as many key officials as possible and thereby undermine the whole extermination system. Even in a totalitarian state run by men who were gangsters and worse, he could use the distorted Nazi penal code against them. Nicknamed "the Bloodhound Judge" by those inside the SS, he brought some eight hundred cases of corruption and murder to trial and obtained two hundred convictions. By the spring of 1945, Himmler ordered Morgen to suspend all investigations—one of his targets being a rather low-ranking SD officer named Eichmann.

From the moment he began to operate within the system by using the system against the system, Morgen was in danger—and this remained true after the war. He received rather brutal treatment from the Allies because he refused to produce evidence, affidavits, and testimony that were, by his code of judicial ethics, not substantiated or admissible. A sympathetic black American soldier allowed him to escape just before he was due to be turned over to the Soviets, and, except for a brief appearance at the Nuremberg trials, he remained in hiding—not only from former Nazis but from Americans as well—until I found and interviewed him.

I drove toward Munich still in a daze. This was one of the few high-ranking Nazis who had stood up against Hitler and the Final Solution—and survived. I would never forget this day. I had heard proof beyond doubt that there had been a Final Solution. When I'd asked Judge Morgen what he thought of the figure of six million dead Jews, he'd thought briefly, then said, "That's about right."

The Bomb Plot Against Hitler

The attempt by high-ranking officers and officials to kill Hitler by setting off a bomb during a conference in his eastern headquarters at Rastenburg on July 20, 1944, failed, along with the attempted seizure of power in Berlin—an attempt vividly described by Remer and Skorzeny, who played key roles in stopping the coup—but left Hitler shaken, prematurely aged, and partly deafened. General Adolf Heusinger, who was standing next to Hitler, told me he saw Stauffenberg plant the briefcase containing the bomb under the table. I could have found no better eyewitness. He confirmed how dramatically Hitler changed after the assassination attempt.

Both Traudl Junge and Gerda Christian listened to the speech Hitler made to the German people after the bomb attempt on his life. It was brief, for his only purpose was to reassure the people that he was invincible. He owed it all, he said, to his destiny. They all returned to the bunker, where Dr. Morell again took Hitler's pulse. It was normal, and Traudl could see that it made the Führer proud. "He needed to be convinced of his invulnerability once more."

The next morning Hitler could still hear nothing with his right ear, and his eyes kept flickering. Dr. Brandt advised him to rest for a few days, but he insisted on visiting the officers who had been wounded when the bomb exploded. Four were dead or dying, and Hitler's chief adjutant, faithful Schmundt, was in critical condition. When he saw him lying as if dead, the Führer wept. "I'm sorry the innocent had to suffer," he told the injured Admiral Karl-Jesko Puttkamer. (He, like other survivors, gave me exact details on the explosion and what followed.) "These gentlemen had me, and only me, in mind." How many times he himself had escaped assassination! "Don't you agree that I should consider it a sign of Fate that it intends to preserve me for my assigned task?" This last attempt, he added, "only confirms my conviction that Almighty God has called me to lead the German people—not to final defeat but to victory!"

Hitler's chauffeur, Kempka, who had driven all night from Berlin, was relieved to find him as calm as ever. "It could have been worse," the Führer said with a smile. But the pain in his ear became so unbearable that Dr. Morell sought help from an eye-ear-nose-and-throat specialist, Dr. Karl van Eicken. He was unavailable, and Dr. Erwin Giesing, who had worked in Dr. Eicken's clinic, was located in a nearby field hospital.

Giesing was the key to all the medical details. He gave me a vivid picture of the other doctors, but it was his wife who persuaded him to give me documents he had that no one had even seen. This was so often the case—wives or sisters or family members would persuade their relative to trust me. Following a lead from one of Hitler's secretaries, I had taken a chance and driven about 150 kilometers to locate him. This is an example of how the detective work in research pays off.

Hitler's Medical Problems

On my second trip to Germany in 1971 I finally located Dr. Giesing in a town near Düsseldorf, and in three long interviews he told of his remarkable meetings with Hitler. He had never before been interviewed extensively. On the last day he even let me see his precious diary. He also lent me letters and documents confirming his exploits. During the war years, Dr. Giesing was youthful, self-confident, and accustomed to making split-second decisions; he looked more like a front-line commander than a doctor. Even so, he recalled that in his first encounter with the Führer he had a strange, uneasy feeling when Dr. Brandt, Hitler's longtime official physician, asked him to treat Hitler's ears. "The feeling became intense during the time I had to wait in a small room of Hitler's bunker for the appearance of this 'tremendous, mystical superman.' " That was how the Führer had earlier been described. Giesing would have preferred their first encounter to take place in a large room so Hitler would have to walk a few steps toward him and Giesing would have a chance to observe him before being introduced. Still, he was the doctor and Hitler only the patient. His uneasiness was dispelled by the Führer, who first gazed at him silently and then managed to express confidence in his new doctor. Somehow Hitler had managed to bridge the great gap in rank and importance with no words. After an examination Giesing assured him that although the eardrum was badly ruptured and the inner ear damaged, there was nothing serious so long as there was no infection of the inner ear.

"My first impression of Hitler was not of a powerful and feared man with a fascinating, hypnotic personality. He seemed to me, from my first observation, an aged, almost exhausted man who had to use sparingly the remainder of his strength. I did not find his eyes soul-penetrating nor his nature tyrannical, as they had been described to me by the press, the radio, and the accounts of other men."

Three days later, Dr. van Eicken arrived to examine Hitler, who described his symptoms in great detail. By now Dr. Giesing had made it a practice to record, as unobtrusively as Heim, everything Hitler said. "I jotted notes in a yellow pocket manual, using a code composed of Latin and personal symbols." After Professor van Eicken confirmed Giesing's diagnosis, he urged Hitler to rest in bed for a week or longer. But Hitler good-humoredly refused. "You have all conspired among you to make a sick man out of me!" But later in the day he asked Giesing to cauterize his left ear again, because it was still bleeding. "I don't feel any pain," he said, adding hastily, "Pain is meant to make a man hard."

Dr. Giesing soon became a welcome member of the Family Circle because of his straightforward, unsycophantic manner with the Führer. Consequently Hitler took him aside for long talks on everything from vegetarianism to ears. After one medical examination he became so fascinated with the workings of the inner ear that he stuck an otoscope into the ear of his hapless aide Linge and explored it with the same attention to detail that he would give to situation maps. Then to Giesing's amusement he took all the tuning forks in hand and began experimenting with the whole set on the patient Linge. After timing Linge's responses with a stopwatch, he said, "You know, doctor, when I was young I always wanted to be a doctor." His voice was almost timid. "But my other career came along and I realized what my true mission was." He then asked Giesing to get him Professor Knich's textbook on otology. Later Linge told Dr. Giesing that on that same evening Dr. Hitler examined the ears of Linge and two orderlies.

By the end of August, Dr. Giesing had already heard Hitler say several times that he had only two or three years to live, and during a visit from Professor van Eicken, he overheard the Führer ask the professor how old he was. "Seventy, my Führer, and I'm going on seventy-one."

"Well," replied Hitler, "I guess I won't become that old. I'm eaten up by worry, sorrow, and bother, and I haven't more than two or three years to live." Hitler stilled van Eicken's protests. "My dear professor, I shall be able to last out the two or three years I yet have to live and work for my people. Then the others will have to find the way to carry on the work."

"Such talk convinced me," recalled Giesing, "that the Führer was certainly a highly psychopathic person, a man who could not be convinced, even when all facts spoke against him. From Hitler's constitutional psychopathy, and from his firm conviction that he knew and was able to do everything better than others, originated a strong neuropathy."

Giesing was so concerned about Hitler's health that he urged him to have X-rays taken of his head. Hitler refused. "I was alarmed. The Führer kept joking to his Family Circle about his right hand, which shook so much he could no longer shave himself, yet still complained to me not only of an incessant ache but of stomach pains." These pains concerned Giesing most of all, and he urged Hitler to stop taking the great number of pills Dr. Morell was feeding him. "Take a ten-percent cocaine solution," urged Giesing. "That will relieve the sinus pain." Hitler obligingly crouched for hours over an inhalator and got such relief that he resumed his intimate conversations. They went from the evils of smoking to the future of Germany. As usual, Giesing took his detailed coded notes. He also subtly undertook secret psychological tests which he described in his diary as "rather primitive." He concluded that his patient was "a neurotic with Caesar-mania."

Professor van Eicken returned again early that September to learn, to his shock, of the injections and numerous pills that Dr. Morell was still giving Hitler. Meeting secretly with Giesing, Brandt, and Hasselbach, he rejected the suggestion that he should warn Hitler directly. Dr. Morell, said van Eicken, still had the Führer's complete confidence.

Within a week, Hitler complained he was kept awake all night with stomach spasms, and the left side of his head ached constantly. When Giesing gave him the cocaine treatment on September 12, he muttered, "Everything is going black!" He was so dizzy he had to grip a table to keep from falling. His pulse was rapid, and Giesing feared it could be a coronary, but in ninety seconds his pulse was again normal. Two days later he had similar pains, and three injections from Morell gave him temporary relief, but on September 16 there was a third mild attack. This time he agreed to do what Giesing had been urging for a month: undergo head X-rays.

That same day Hitler invited Keitel, Jodl, and Chief of Staff Guderian into the conference room, where Jodl summed up their position. There was a respite in the east, where the Soviet summer offensive seemed to have run its course. "But in the west we are getting a real test in the Ardennes," Jodl reported. This was the hilly area in Belgium and Luxembourg that had been a highway to German victory in the Great War and again in 1940.

At the word "Ardennes," Hitler abruptly came to life. Raising his hand, he exclaimed: "Stop!" There was a dead pause. Finally Hitler spoke: "I have made a momentous decision. I am taking the offensive. Here—out of the Ardennes."

Again he could envisage victory, and this resurgence of spirit induced him to keep his promise to Dr. Giesing. On September 19 he went to the Rastenburg field hospital to have his head X-rayed. The next day, Giesing and Morell checked the results, and daily examinations by Giesing continued. Hitler again complained of stomach pains and insisted on taking six of Dr. Morell's black pills. "I was so concerned," remembered Giesing, "I asked Linge to show me the pill container. The label read 'Antigas Pills' and they contained 'Extract nux vomica 0.04 and Extract belladonna 0.04.' " Giesing was stunned. These were two poisons: strychnine and atropine! That could explain his heart attacks, his hoarse throat, and a strange reddish tinge of his skin. But even Dr. Morell's pills brought little relief to Hitler. "The cramps are so severe," he told Giesing, "that sometimes I could scream out loud."

His condition grew worse, and on September 25, Giesing noticed the Führer's skin was not red in sunlight but yellow. The following morning, Hitler, having been awake all night with agonizing pain, could not get out of bed. The Family Circle was horrified. He refused to see anyone and would touch no food. But he finally got up for his daily examination by Giesing. Against opposition by Giesing he insisted on taking the mild cocaine treatment. "No, dear brother," he said wearily, "I think my physical weakness the past few days is due to the poor functioning of my intestines, and cramps." Just before leaving Hitler's room, the doctor secretly snatched a box of Morell's pills and showed the label to Dr. Hasselbach. Horrified on seeing that they contained strychnine and atropine, he advised Giesing to do nothing until Dr. Brandt returned to the Wolfsschanze.

Thus began a bizarre struggle between Morell, who must have sensed what was going on, and the other doctors, who were now forbidden to see the Führer. In despair they turned to the worst possible man, Bormann, who secretly hated Dr. Brandt, to convince Hitler of the dangerous nature of the antigas medication that Morell had been giving him for so long. Bormann promptly rushed to Hitler and accused the doctors of conspiring against Morell for their own personal gain.

But two days later, Giesing was summoned to deal with Hitler's terrible headache, and when Hitler saw him he asked bluntly: "Doctor, how did you

come upon the story of the antigas pills?" After Giesing explained, he said
with a frown, "Why didn't you come directly to me? Didn't you know that
I have great confidence in you?"

"I was not allowed to come in," said Giesing. Neither were Drs. Hasselbach and Brandt.

Hitler changed the subject, claiming that he'd had similar attacks before,
if not as serious. "It is the constant worry and irritation that give me no rest;
and I must work and think of the German people day and night." With a
smile, he sat up straighter. "I feel better already. I'm sure I'll be able to get
out of bed in a few days."

"While I was examining him," explained Giesing, "he said, 'Doctor,
something just occurred to me. This strychnine business can't be too bad
after all; my countrymen in Styria eat it too and feel fine after eating it. They
form a habit, starting from early youth, and after they have been taking it
in increasing amounts for a while, they are able to stand quite a large dose.
I've been told that the amount they take would kill a person who isn't used
to it.' "

"Those people in Styria didn't eat strychnine but arsenic," I corrected.
"They were called arsenic-eaters."

Hitler did not take offense. "I always thought they ate strychnine to stay
alive, but I guess you're right. I am surprised that you know all these things.
If you hadn't told me otherwise, I would have believed that they eat strychnine."

That, replied Giesing, was not particularly expert knowledge but part of
the knowledge of every doctor. "Well, my dear doctor," was the affable reply,
"you are well versed in everything. I am really very grateful to you for what
you have already done for me."

"For the first time I was able to give the Führer a complete physical. After
examining every part of his body I was now aware that the stories about
Hitler's 'one testicle' were lies."

Hitler became talkative. "You see, doctor, aside from this nervous hyper-
activity, I have a very healthy nervous system and I hope that soon all will
be well again." He kept thanking Giesing for all he had done to relieve his
pain. "And now Fate has sent you again to ferret out this antigas story and
you have saved me from further damage, because I would have kept on taking
these pills after I recovered." It was as if he couldn't control his tongue. "My
dear doctor, it was Providence that led you to make this examination and
discover what no other doctor would have noticed. I am, in any event, very
grateful to you for everything and will remain loyal to you—even if you *did*
attack Morell—and I thank you again for everything." He grasped both of

the doctor's hands and squeezed them. "Now may I have more of that cocaine stuff?"

Giesing gave him a small dose. Hitler felt wonderful. "I'll soon be well enough to get up," he said, but his next words were blurred and his face became a deathly white. "My Führer, are you all right?" asked the startled Giesing. Hitler was unconscious. "I turned to summon Linge, but he was answering a knock at the door. Then I realized that Hitler, the tyrant, was at my mercy! 'At that moment,' I wrote in my diary, 'I did not want such a man to exist and exercise the power of life and death in his purely subjective manner.' I thrust a swab stick into the cocaine bottle and hurriedly brushed the interior of the Führer's nose with the cocaine substance, knowing a second dose could be fatal."

To his shock he heard Linge say, "How much longer will the treatment take?"

"Almost finished," he managed to say.

Hitler suddenly drew up his legs as if in pain. "The Führer is having another one of his intestinal cramps," said Linge. "Let him rest."

Hiding his panic, Giesing bicycled back to the field hospital as fast as he could. "Had I killed the Führer? I telephoned Hasselbach about what had happened. I was going to tell everyone that I was returning to my Berlin office, which had recently been bombed." Upon learning that Hitler was still alive, Dr. Giesing returned to the Wolfsschanze to find the Führer friendly but determined to end the furor over the antigas pills. "I still have faith in Morell," he said, and added that he was going to see Brandt in the afternoon to settle the matter personally.

It was settled Hitler-style. He dismissed both Hasselbach and Brandt. Giesing was instructed to see Bormann at once. "I was sure this was the end for me when Bormann seemed amused at my nervousness. It was well known that Bormann enjoyed teasing his victims. 'There's no need for you to take the whole matter so tragically. We have nothing against you. On the contrary, the Führer asked me to give you this letter.' "

Inside was a check for ten thousand marks and profuse thanks. He put the check on the table. "If you refuse to take it," said Bormann, "the Führer will be insulted."

"The next time I reported to the Führer, he held out his hand. 'You will understand, doctor, that this antigas-pill business has to be cleared up once and for all. I know that you yourself acted only out of idealism and purely professional motives.' " Then he did more than profusely thank Giesing: he promoted this man who had tried to kill him.

Dr. Giesing was the kind of informant I would go to any lengths to track down. When you interview someone with this kind of depth and persistence, giving no thought to how much time is passing, he seems to appreciate the effort you've made, particularly if he has never before been sought out. Giesing felt, I believe, a kind of relief in telling me all this not only in the first interview but in two additional long interviews.

It took three separate trips to Germany to do much of this kind of follow-up. After such a trip I would be exhausted and more than ready to go home, reflect on what I had learned, and spend time with Toshiko and Tamiko. They accompanied me on my third trip. Their very presence helped me; people responded with an even greater openness, in part, I think, because so few Germans had ever met any of the former Japanese allies.

The Writing Process

On returning to Danbury in December 1971 I found a letter from Miss Ann Thomas, who had read about my book. She had lived in Germany through the Hitler days as a girl, and she offered to help me. In the past twenty years many readers had offered their services, but I was stunned when she offered to transcribe my tapes. This was a colossal task, and she refused to take any pay. She said it was her duty as a German.

In the next several months I reassembled my voluminous mass of material into chronological order, and in late September 1972, I began typing. The going was complicated, and I only wrote four and a half pages that day, but by the end of the week I had punched out thirty more. I sent every chapter to Ann Thomas, who had moved from Florida to take a job in New York City as a legal secretary, and she would reply—relentlessly picking to pieces my inconsistencies. Every few months she would come to Danbury for several days to work. Her lengthy letters and comments can be found among my papers at the Franklin D. Roosevelt Library. (In 1975 we would receive word that Ann Thomas had died alone in her apartment. Ann had done so much for *Adolf Hitler,* and she wouldn't even get to see the published copy.)

I was also getting help from Bradley Smith, author of an excellent book on the young Hitler. He introduced me to Dr. Rudolph Binion, an expert in German history, who was writing a psychiatric book on the Führer. In my last trip to the National Archives, John Taylor, who had already helped me (as well as many other historians) uncover new material, had suggested I visit a room containing a collection of assorted material in the OSS files. He guessed they might contain some gems. The room was packed with cartons, and I began snooping. Within an hour I had found a restricted U.S. Navy intelligence report entitled "A Psychiatric Study of Hitler." It had been written in 1943 by Dr. Karl Kronor, a former Viennese nerve specialist, apparently present at the original medical examination of Hitler in 1918 at the military hospital in Pasewalk. Hitler had been brought there when blinded by gas. Kronor reported the findings of Dr. Edmund Forster, chief of the Berlin University Nerve Clinic. Little was known about mustard gas, and Hitler's inexplicable initial recovery confirmed Dr. Forster's diagnosis of the blindness as hysteria.

I passed on this report to Dr. Binion, who flew to Germany, located Dr. Forster's family, and found information which shed new light on Hitler's recurrence of blindness upon learning of Germany's surrender. In *Mein Kampf,* Hitler had revealed how he had experienced a "supernatural vision." Like St. Joan, he said he had heard voices summoning him to save his country. All at once "a miracle came to pass"—the darkness encompassing Hitler evaporated. He could see again! He solemnly vowed, as promised, that he would "become a politician and devote his energies to carrying out the command he had received."

Forster had written in his original report that the lack of any medical reason for Hitler's second blindness reinforced his initial conclusion that his patient was definitely "a psychopath with hysterical symptoms." The possibility that Dr. Forster induced Hitler's hallucination that he had received a command from voices was given credence by a novel about Hitler and Forster written by the latter's friend Ernst Weiss, a medical doctor turned playwright and novelist. In this book, *The Eyewitness,* "A.H." arrives at Pasewalk military hospital in 1918 claiming to have been poisoned by gas. A psychiatrist, the narrator, diagnoses the case as hysterical blindness and induces a hallucination through hypnosis.

Early in 1973 I received shocking news: money we had invested with a friend in Washington was almost wiped out. Our wealthy friend Michael Erlanger's lawyer in New York, Peter Repetti, heard about this and asked what I was planning to do. I said we were selling our car and cutting down on everything. And I could write a few articles to keep us afloat. "Ridiculous!" he said, and asked how much I needed until I got the next advance from Doubleday. I told him, and Repetti sent me a check. Years later I asked him why he did it. "I like your books," he said. "Besides, you came from no money and worked your way up. So did I."

By 1974 I was finishing the first draft, and Paul Reynolds arranged a luncheon with Ken McCormick and Carolyn Blakemore, who would edit the book. Paul hoped I would accept Carolyn along with Ken. Paul had known her when she was a literary agent and believed she could be a great help. Ken and I were very familiar with the military, but she didn't even know the terminology and would insist that I explain everything in full and thus make the book accessible to women readers. That night I wrote in my calendar book, "Very good! No problem."

On December 13, 1974, I wrote, *"Der Tag!"* I had finished the monstrosity. I sent the huge manuscript to Doubleday, and on February 3, 1975, I went to New York for the first editorial conference. I told Toshiko I'd be in town three days so we could, with luck, finish the first three chapters.

In the conference room, Ken and Carolyn sat behind their foot-high copies. I felt uneasy even though Ken had written, "I'm totally absorbed with the book and it's a really overwhelming experience." To my amazement, we ripped through the first chapter in twenty minutes. Instead of going through the manuscript page by page, they presented me with written queries and suggestions. By early afternoon we had gone through nine chapters, and I phoned Toshiko that I'd be home that night.

We had only five more meetings, and on May 9, 1975, we finished. In between meetings I had been making cuts and corrections, and without any more meetings, we finished the second draft in three months. While working on the third draft, Carolyn asked me what had happened to Skorzeny's men after they rescued Mussolini on the mountain top. Skorzeny and Mussolini had flown off in a tiny plane. I wrote Otto, and he explained that his men had commandeered cars and driven down the mountain. No one else, he added, had ever asked him that question. The day I received this historic letter, I read that he had died in Madrid. His letter may have been the last thing he ever wrote.

I finished the third draft on October 7, 1975, and felt as if a tremendous weight had dropped off my shoulders. Yet strangely I was not at all exhausted, and the next day I set out for Washington to start work on my next book, *No Man's Land,* on the final days of the Great War.

On my return I got a call from Egon Hanfstaengl. Putzi was dying in a hospital and wanted to speak to Toshiko and me. Our words made him laugh. That evening Egon called us again. "John! He's come back to life!" We called Putzi several more times, but he died a month later on October 6.

By now I had been chosen to serve on the National Archives Advisory Council. There were about ten of us. John Eisenhower and I were the only ones who weren't prestigious professors. I had known John for some time. He had come down to Red Bank to examine my Battle of the Bulge papers, since he was writing a book on the subject, *The Bitter Woods.* He stayed with us several days and completely conquered my mother. She was a super-ardent Democrat, but after he left she said, "If I'd known John I would have voted for his father."

That December, Paul called to say that *Adolf Hitler* was the Literary Guild Selection for next August. Again the Book-of-the-Month Club made it an "A" book but the judges had, as usual, turned it down.

Adolf Hitler was published on September 17, 1976, and most of the reviews were favorable. *Adolf Hitler* was the first book that anyone who wanted to learn about Hitler or the war in Europe must read, said *Newsweek*. "Much that is new or little known . . . a marvel of fact."

The *New York Times Book Review* called it "a marvelously absorbing popular history . . . must be ranked as one of the most complete pictures of Hitler we have yet read."

I plugged the book in major cities from Boston to Los Angeles, and by early October it was number six on the *Times* best-seller list.

No sooner had I arrived back in Danbury than I got a phone call from Carolyn Blakemore. *Adolf Hitler* was being auctioned for paperback, and the offers were far above anything we had expected. She called three more times, and the final offer, late that afternoon, ironically came from Ballantine, a division of Random House. A little later I learned that Germany, England, the Netherlands, and Japan were buying foreign rights. And by the end of the year, sales had climbed above 150,000. Our financial situation had eased.

To celebrate the success of the book, Doubleday had a luncheon for us at their suite above the Fifth Avenue Doubleday Book Store. Sitting next to me was the president of Random House, Bob Bernstein. "How did we lose you, John?" he asked.

"Just a case of two percent," I said, and apparently he had no idea what I meant.

[Part Two]

From Fact to Fiction (1977–1986)

[6]

No Man's Land

An Artist at the Front

In March 1977 I took off for London to finish my researches for *No Man's Land,* a history of World War I that would focus on the men who fought, not the generals. I wanted to do this book to show what the men I had known when I was a boy had endured. Almost none of them returned. I felt I owed them this book. I also had to devote eleven days to publicizing the British edition of *Adolf Hitler.*

After my publicity tour of northern England and Scotland, where I was warmly welcomed, even by academics, I began interviewing the principal characters in my new book. Through a friend I located Paul Maze, a well-known artist and teacher of Churchill, who called him "unique and undefinable." A Frenchman who had attended an English public school, Maze had been determined to serve with the British. Son of a well-to-do merchant, he had been taught to paint by Pissaro, Dufy, and other noted artists who were well fed by Madame Maze at her home in Paris. General Gough, a friend, agreed to put Maze on his staff if he would first get a commission in the French army. Maze, a tall, handsome man in his late twenties, returned a few weeks later in a resplendent uniform (designed by himself) and a huge sword. "I also had given myself a title that was resounding to English ears: *maréchal de logis.* In French it merely meant that I was a sergeant major." He laughed, and I knew I had found another great character. "I was commissioned to roam Fifth Army on my own initiative, making sketches of trenches, emplacements, and strategic terrain features."

At the start of the great German attack in March 1918, he was up front when five thousand heavy guns simultaneously pounded the British Third and Fifth Armies. In the chaos, Sergeant Maze, on his own initiative, set off by motorcycle to see what was going on at Fifth Army's junction with Third Army. In the next few days he was in constant motion as word spread that this battle would decide the outcome of the war. The French and British units were separating and leaving a gap between them; moreover, the French had all of the big guns belonging to the British XVIII Corps and were ignoring orders to return them. Maze told me the unforgettable story of how he was sent to face down a French general and get the British guns released. He succeeded, in part because when a French officer ignored the written order Maze carried from the commanding general, Maze drew himself up. "I am the *maréchal de logis,*" he said with authority. "The guns must come back!"

Maze laughed. "The French officer heard only the *maréchal* of my lowly title and was flustered. The stylish cut of my uniform, though battle-stained, was obviously that of a high-ranking officer." And so was his imperious manner. The guns were returned. And the lines held.

A Victorious Cavalry Charge

Incredibly it was the British cavalry which stopped the Germans a few days later. I got this story from an infantryman, Frank Rees, and the papers of Brigadier Jack Seely, commander of the Canadian Cavalry Brigade, at the Imperial War Museum. Seely saw the situation was desperate. If the enemy was not stopped, the main line from Amiens to Paris would be broken and the French and British forces compelled to fall back. "I knew that moment to be the supreme event of my life," revealed Seely. "I believed that if nothing were done the retreat would continue and the war would be lost."

He decided to take a key ridge with the force at his disposal, rode through his own front lines, and hurled his cavalry at the Germans. Other mounted units, including Lord Strathcona's Horse, followed.

An infantryman in the shallow trenches, Frank Rees, told me he would never forget that moment. "I could not believe my eyes when I saw a jingling, jangling troop of cavalry canter up and turn into line behind me."

The cost of the charge was horrendous: in minutes, 70 percent of the leading squadron of Strathcona's Horse, commanded by Lieutenant G. M. Flowerdew, were dead from rifle and machine-gun fire. The enemy broke and ran. Flowerdew himself was on the ground with bullets in both thighs and two in his chest. "Carry on, boys!" he shouted, then uttered his last words: "We have won!"

Shrapnel and Machine Guns Everywhere

I found Private H. Howard Cooper through the Imperial War Museum. A month after the great German attack in March he had been with fresh troops sent from England to man the Bassee Canal Defense Line in Belgium. A year earlier the nineteen-year-old had been called up from the sixth form of a school near Liverpool. He was, in a sense, a replacement for his older brother, who had almost been killed a few weeks earlier in the bitter fighting at Peronne. It is impossible to describe in this space the horror, courage and endurance—on both sides—that Cooper told me about, an account I presented virtually in its entirety in *No Man's Land.*

By the time Cooper told me about his experiences in two other battles, we were friends. For years we corresponded, and several times Toshiko and I visited his home. He never changed. I can still hear his calm, still somewhat youthful voice. He never became an old man.

Cooper and men like him, including the Americans who entered the war in its last stages, haunt me to this day.

Deleting One Hundred Pages

The past two years, 1977 and 1978, had been busy with speeches, research, and writing the first two drafts of *No Man's Land.* In the first draft I had become so fascinated by the original material, located at the State Historical Society of Wisconsin, on Raymond Robins, chief of the American Red Cross in Russia and a close friend of Lenin's, that I devoted more than a hundred pages to the dealings between Americans and Russians in early 1918. But Carolyn Blakemore and Ken McCormick of Doubleday, as well as Carl Brandt, my agent after the retirement of Paul Reynolds, agreed that this was fascinating but unnecessary. I knew they were right and began the book where I should have—with the great German attack of March 1918. But I have never regretted spending the time on those deleted pages, since they had given me a close-up view of the revolution.

I finished the final draft on July 10, 1979, and found that it ran about 225,000 words. It was the first selection of the Literary Guild and the Military Book Club, and brought my fifth Overseas Press Club award. Most of the reviews were favorable, although several critics chastised me for stating that although the U.S. entry into the war in 1917 had tipped the scales, the people mainly responsible for victory were the stubborn British. I was commended as a military strategist and the book was praised as "scrupulously accurate," "absorbing," and "another blockbuster," but it never got onto the *Times* best-seller list.

I made the usual publicity tour but was relieved to get back to the next book, which I had started a year earlier. This one would appear on the best-seller list, but would also bring me stinging attacks from almost every respectable newspaper and academic historian in America. The *Washington Post* would lead the assault and declare that it meant the end of my career. It was called *Infamy*.

Infamy

"The Dirtiest Frame-up"

While I was writing the last draft of *No Man's Land* in 1979, I received a call from Admiral Kemp Tolley, who had written *Cruise of the "Lanakai."* When he was a lieutenant at Asiatic Fleet headquarters in Manila just before the attack on Pearl Harbor, he had been personally instructed by President Roosevelt to set out on a mysterious mission. He was to arm the windjammer *Lanakai,* a two-masted interisland schooner, with a cannon and a machine gun, provision her for a two-week cruise, and be ready to sail in twenty-four hours. Tolley was aware that his was but one of three small ships on a joint mission, and he was to relieve the *Isabel,* commanded by another lieutenant, John Walker Payne, Jr., which was already on her way to the Indochina coast.

Admiral Tolley, whose ship was about to set sail when the bombs fell on Pearl Harbor, told me he was convinced his mission was a trick to incite war with Japan, and the lieutenant who was to command the second little ship shared the opinion that they were to be bait for the Japanese. Tolley said he had other information indicating that Roosevelt knew the Japanese carriers were coming and suggested I write a book on the subject.

I thanked Admiral Tolley but wanted to get back to *No Man's Land.* Nevertheless, he persisted in sending me additional information. This disturbed me deeply, since I had categorically stated in *The Rising Sun* that the president had no knowledge that a Japanese strike force was approaching Pearl Harbor. Even so, many aspects of Pearl Harbor had troubled me. The various investigations of the raid on Pearl Harbor after the war had left too many crucial questions unanswered.

Had there truly been a "winds" execute message in late November or early December 1941 indicating the attack was coming? In late November 1941, the Japanese Foreign Office advised its representatives abroad that in case diplomatic relations were about to be severed with the United States, Great

Britain, or Russia, a signal in the form of a false weather report would be broadcast and all code papers were then to be destroyed. If the signal was *Kitano kaze kumori* ("North wind, cloudy"), that meant a break with Russia; *Nishi no kaze hare* ("West wind, clear"), a break with Britain; and *Higashi no kaze ame* ("East wind, rain"), a break with the United States.

Had the nine investigations been an elaborate cover-up to place the blame primarily on the two commanders in Hawaii, Admiral Husband E. Kimmel and General Walter Short, while whitewashing those in Washington? Had some of our military and civilian leaders lied under oath? Had these good men been persuaded or threatened into perjuring themselves? *Was* it possible that Roosevelt had engineered a conspiracy among his top brass and advisers to get America into the war with Hitler by the back door?

I was so disturbed I told Toshiko I had to find out. She warned me that there could be trouble, but I assured her that the truth would be welcomed. I telephoned my agent and Doubleday. With everyone's approval, once I had finished the final draft of *No Man's Land,* I dove into the murky depths of Pearl Harbor.

Tolley was delighted and we soon became friends. He introduced me to two sons of Admiral Kimmel. A third son, Captain Manning Kimmel, had gone down with his submarine when it hit a mine off a small island in the Philippines. Both Ned and Tom Kimmel had been navy officers, and they promised to give me all their information. Soon my mind was far from the battlefields of Belgium and France. Neither Kimmel nor Short had been given Purple intercepts—the information decoded by Washington from the Japanese Purple Code, the secret system used to transmit information between Tokyo and her foreign embassies. Thirteen parts of a fourteen-part message were decrypted in Washington on December 6, 1941, and these made it obvious that the Japanese were completely dissatisfied with the American reply to their final offer in the long ongoing negotiations between the two countries. Once the president read these thirteen parts that evening, he turned to Harry Hopkins, his chief adviser, and said, "This means war."

But no warning was sent to Hawaii. In fact, no Purple intercepts had ever been sent to Admiral Kimmel. The following morning, December 7, General George C. Marshall arrived at his office, unaware—so he claimed—of the decrypted message until 1:00 P.M. He telephoned Admiral Harold R. Stark, who offered to send the warning through the navy's rapid-transmission facilities. "No thanks, Betty [Stark's nickname]. I feel I can get it through quickly enough." He sent it by Western Union. I always thought that had been ridiculous, but I had accepted the general view that Marshall feared a phone call might be tapped. The message was delivered hours after the last Japanese planes had left behind a devastated Pearl Harbor.

I learned from Kimmel's sons that on December 7 their father was watching the attacks on Battleship Row at an open window when a .50-caliber bullet struck the left breast of his white uniform. It smacked into his glasses case and fell to the floor. His picked it up, put it in his pocket, and said, "I wish it had killed me." His career was over, for he was convinced that he should somehow have prevented what was happening. Nevertheless, looking cool, the austere Kimmel strode into an inner room. When he emerged a few minutes later, a yeoman noticed that his four-star shoulder boards had been replaced with two-star boards. He had demoted himself from his temporary rank of full admiral to the permanent rank of rear admiral.

"Oh, no, admiral," a young aide said.

"Hell, yes, son."

In February 1942, Kimmel was retired by letter. Kimmel protested the wording by Admiral Stark, of his retirement: "Make over your own world. Let courage be your architect. . . . Pending something definite, there is no reason why you should not settle yourself in a quiet nook somewhere and let Old Father Time help this entire situation, which I feel he will—if for no other reason than that he always has."

Kimmel replied: "I stand ready at any time to accept the consequences of my acts. I do not wish to embarrass the government in the conduct of the war. I do feel, however, that my crucifixion before the public has about reached the limit. I am in daily receipt of letters from irresponsible people over the country taking me to task and even threatening to kill me. . . . I have kept my mouth shut and propose to do so long as it is humanly possible."

Incidentally, I had interviewed Admiral Stark three times for *But Not in Shame* and he'd still been indignant at the "cavalier" way he himself had been sent out of Washington—after writing this letter to Kimmel—to a relatively minor post in England where he had little clout.

Pearl Harbor had been arguably the greatest collective national trauma in our history. The blame had to be placed somewhere—and the obvious targets were Admiral Kimmel and General Short, the two senior commanders in Hawaii. A series of no less than nine investigative hearings were conducted by the military and the Congress—and Secretary of War Henry Stimson even conducted an inquiry of his own, the results of which were made available to one of the later congressional hearings.

Unresolved open questions about what happened in the months and days just prior to Pearl Harbor—who in the U.S. military knew what and when they knew it—remain matters of contention to this very day. At the heart of the ongoing controversy lies the greatest secret of the United States in World War II—the breaking of first the Japanese diplomatic code and later, when the war was on, other Japanese codes, including the naval code JN-25. A very small number of U.S. Army and U.S. Navy personnel were allowed to handle the decoding, processing, and dissemination of intercepts snatched out of the air from far-flung intercept facilities in the Pacific and elsewhere. Further reinforcing the need for absolute secrecy was the fact that America and Great Britain shared codebreaking information derived from intercepts of German, Italian, and Japanese encoded radio transmissions processed at their respective facilities. This priceless information, through which the Allies could know, often well in advance, the inmost secrets of Axis strategy and operations, was made available to an even smaller number of people, such as President Roosevelt and Prime Minister Churchill, General Marshall and his counterpart in Britain, and commanders in the field like Eisenhower, MacArthur, and Montgomery. But it was a highly select list—and often the handling of intercepts and their decoding resulted in less than timely deliveries to "customers" like Churchill and Roosevelt, although as the war went on this became less of a problem.

In order to protect this great secret (one that was almost blown by Colonel McCormick's *Chicago Tribune* in the middle of the war), men like Marshall and others who knew of the scope and importance of these decodes had to use every means to protect them. This became a rather complex matter when Kimmel and Short pressed to have these decoded intercepts made part of the record in various hearings.

A fascinating cast of characters were caught up in the drama that unfolded after December 7, 1941. *Infamy* not only recapitulated the events in that drama, it asked questions and presented evidence that a great many people in the military and civilian establishments of the day were still unwilling to consider. I can only advise readers who are interested in following up on the full story to read *Infamy* and make up their minds. What I did not, could not, know when it was published was how many minds in high places were already made up. Powerful and influential people were not prepared to pay attention to the previously unheard witnesses (including military personnel ranging from admirals and generals down to enisted men from the United States as well as from other services in Allied countries like Holland and England) that I dug up as I proceeded through a labyrinthine investigation that went quite a way toward answering some long-standing open questions—and opened up more than a few new ones.

Once again, I attempted to pursue a course of "nonideological" history and let the participants speak out. But I had no conception of how deep the attachment to official and accepted versions ran—nor of the virulence of the reaction against someone who attempted to question it.

Shortly after I had finished writing *Infamy*, I visited my mother on her ninety-third birthday at High Ridge, a Christian Scientist home near New York City. I had never seen her so calm. My daughter Diana had recently come to see her, along with her husband and two children, and Mother was grateful that she had finally met her two great-grandchildren. I told her several stories from *Infamy*; after listening to them, she told me that she thought this would be one of my best books. Two days later, while interviewing an American POW who had survived the Nagasaki bomb, I got a call from Toshiko. My mother had died peacefully in her sleep. It was a terrible blow. She had protected me and encouraged me since I was a boy while my father saw me as a failure. I owe my success to my mother and her family.

I Take a Beating

After collecting all this material I was persuaded that President Roosevelt had indications that Japanese carriers were about to attack Pearl Harbor. It is not clear why the Army and Navy Departments deprived Kimmel and Short of vital messages from the summer of 1941 up to late in November. It may have been because of Marshall's fear that the Japanese would discover that the United States had broken their Purple Code; or the natural tendency of intelligence officers to guard new information almost obsessively; or interservice and interdepartmental rivalries.

Although both Marshall and Stark approved waging war with Hitler and Mussolini, both had vigorously opposed inciting Japan to battle, since neither the army nor the navy was yet ready for a two-front war. At first, Roosevelt agreed, but then he was faced with the most momentous decision of his life when a number of reports to Washington indicated that the missing Japanese task force, *Kido Butai,* was heading eastward toward Hawaii.

From my research it appeared apparent that by December 4 a small group of advisers, including Secretary of War Henry L. Stimson, Secretary of the Navy Frank Knox, and General Marshall, were faced with three options. To Japan and the world they could announce word of the approaching *Kido Butai;* this would indubitably have forced the Japanese to turn back. Second, they could inform Kimmel and Short that Japanese carriers were northwest of Hawaii and order them to send every available long-range patrol plane to discover this force; and again *Kido Butai,* still out of range of Pearl Harbor, would have turned back.

The third option was to keep Kimmel and Short and all but a select few in ignorance so that the Japanese could continue to their launching point unaware that they had been discovered. This would ensure that the Japanese would launch their attack. If Kimmel and Short were made privy to the secret, they might possibly react in such a way as to reveal to the Japanese that their attack plan was known.

This course would be a calculated risk, but Roosevelt, like Churchill, could take a gamble. Nor did risk at that moment seem so great. In May 1941 the president had received a memorandum from Marshall describing Oahu as the strongest fortress in the world, with assurance that any enemy naval force would be destroyed before it neared Pearl Harbor. Long a navy man, Roosevelt believed in the navy's power. He had also been receiving reports on the low efficiency of Japanese pilots, whose planes were second-rate. Most Americans shared this feeling, and cartoonists ridiculed Japanese attackers as small, buck-toothed, and wearing glasses. Consequently the Pacific Fleet would not only stem any Japanese attack with little loss to U.S. shipping but would easily wipe out the invader. After all, the reports sent to Roosevelt mentioned only *two* carriers. In fact, there were six. Had he known that six carriers were en route he probably would not have taken this gamble.

But if the United States responded to the attack and destroyed the two carriers, it would have been catastrophic to the Japanese militarists and perhaps eliminated Japan as a menace in the Pacific in a single blow. Moreover, Kimmel's two available carriers would be out of Pearl Harbor and the remaining warships were in no real danger of being sunk. Aerial bombs were not much of a threat, and the waters of Pearl Harbor were thought to be too shallow for a torpedo attack.

I had heard a story that this third option was carried out secretly by the militarists, but Marshall and Stark could never have plotted this alone, since both regarded themselves as under the direct command of Roosevelt. And both were honorable men. When I asked navy personnel if they thought Admiral Theodore Wilkinson, who had informed Captain Johan Ranneft, a Dutch naval attaché, of the tracking of two carriers, would keep this information from the president, they all protested that this would be impossible. He too was an honorable man, and what would he gain from such a stupid plot?

I had no doubt that Roosevelt knew about the approaching carriers but believed there were only two. Personally I had admired the President ever since I had first seen him at Williams College. He was a remarkable leader and had pulled us out of the Depression. But I believe that, following the maxim of world leaders, he must have been convinced that the ends justified the means, and so truth was suppressed. The greater tragedy was the attempt to put all the blame for Pearl Harbor on Kimmel and Short.

I started writing *Infamy* on June 26, 1980. It moved along quickly and was soon sent off to the publisher.

Doubleday's publicity department sent bound galley proofs to a number of well-known historians for possible quotations to be used in advertising. Only John Eisenhower responded: "John Toland has been fearless in his pursuit of the truth. . . . *Infamy* is not only readable and suspenseful; it is probably his most controversial book to date." By early 1982, Doubleday had distributed advance copies, and the hoopla began. On February 4 a TV team from Japan arrived in Danbury. A month later NBC, CBS, and CBC appeared in order to film me. Four days afterward a Canadian TV crew arrived. Then the reviews started coming in. The editor of the *Washington Post* "Sunday Book Section" called me. I had done a number of reviews for her and she thought I should know I was getting a terrible review. For the first time a book had been taken away from her and given to the editorial department. The editors attacked *Infamy,* claiming it was full of blatant errors and conclusions. They were not impressed by any of my so-called revelations and were particularly sarcastic about a key informant's story, apparently forgetting their own "Deep Throat."

Infamy, predicted a number of critics, meant the end of my career. One of the few favorable reviews came from the *New York Times Book Review:* "Mr. Toland has written a thriller. He recounts the attack dramatically and then reviews the investigation in a way that raises doubts and questions." The other favorable reviews came from the right, with the *Los Angeles Times* calling it a "shocking account of judgments distorted by politics and career hunger and racism. . . . fascinating reading." Despite all this bad press, I was overwhelmed with call-in radio shows. In one week I had fourteen, most of them interested only in the new material, but when I started my tour in Washington in late April I was met with outright hostility. On the second day in the capital I didn't have time to get lunch or dinner before appearing in the evening at the National Archives. The hall was filled, and I could feel that most of those attending were with me. After speaking for about an hour I came to the question-and-answer period, but the man who had introduced me had wisely disappeared and I had to handle it alone.

The first question came from a booming voice proclaiming me a liar. It was from an Englishman named Costello who had come uninvited to our home several weeks previously and insisted I join him in "sinking" the author of another book on Pearl Harbor that was on the best-seller list. Costello had also written a book on the subject. While I was telling him I never attacked a fellow author, Toshiko had taken me aside and quietly said, "Get that man out of the house." I did, after lending him some material he needed.

One example of the way accounts from key witnesses were disregarded or treated with outright contempt by Costello and other critics was that of a distinguished Dutch naval officer, a former attaché in Washington, retired Admiral Johan E. M. Ranneft, who was living in Houston at the time I was researching *Infamy*. In 1941 the Dutch army had intercepted a message from Tokyo to the Japanese ambassador in Bangkok, encoded in Purple, which the Dutch had also successfully broken. This intercept and decode was made available to British and then American army and navy officers, who made sure that it reached Washington—sent in U.S. Navy code to the War Department through the Navy Communications Center. And this was followed up with two subsequent warnings to Washington.

When I flew to Houston and met with Ranneft, in the presence of his son, who had been a student in the United States during the war, the admiral stated flatly: "I was the one who knew about the attack on Pearl Harbor." I taped this interview, one of the most important ones for the entire book. Later it was charged that I had interviewed Ranneft when he was alone, dying, and hallucinating in a hospital oxygen tent. The tape of this interview is available at the FDR Library among my papers and other tapes. On it his voice is strong and his words clear and certain.

He started by saying he and his son thought it was time to reveal the facts about Pearl Harbor. On December, 2, 1941 he was a captain and the naval attaché of the Netherlands in Washington, and he paid a visit to the Office of Naval Intelligence, where he queried Rear Admiral Theodore Wilkinson, chief of the Intelligence Division, Office of Naval Intelligence, and other intelligence officers. As usual they were most frank with Captain Ranneft, since he had done the U.S. Navy a great service. On witnessing a demonstration of the 40mm Bofors gun on a Dutch ship in the Caribbean, Captain W.P.H. Blandy, chief of ordnance, found it so far superior to all other antiaircraft guns that he was determined to get it for the U.S. Navy. But there were complications. The weapon had been developed jointly by the Netherlands navy and two private companies, Hazemeyer-Signaal and the Swedish firm of Bofors. Blandy realized how difficult it would be to get Swedish approval, so he asked his good friend Captain Ranneft for the blueprints. "Without consulting my superiors in exile in London," explained Admiral Ranneft, "I managed to procure a set of blueprints from Batavia and turned them over to Blandy." Hours later a perturbed Swedish naval attaché protested this violation of patent rights. "I assured him that the decision had been made by the Dutch government in London and any complaints should be lodged there." (After the war, former Dutch secretary of defense Dekkers told Admiral Ranneft it was lucky he hadn't asked the

Dutch government for the blueprints. "We should have been obliged to answer no," he said. Eventually the U.S. government did pay large sums to both Bofors and Hazemeyer Signaal.)

"I was startled on December 2 when one of the American naval intelligence officers pointed to a map on the wall and said, 'This is the Japanese task force proceeding east.' " The position was halfway between Japan and Hawaii. "I said nothing, only wondered how the Americans had managed to track the missing carriers."

This corroborated another key informant's story. The admiral went on to relate that he cabled Dutch naval quarters in London and also reported the information in person to Netherlands Minister Alexander Loudon. Then he wrote in his official diary, "Conference at Navy Department, ONI. They show me on the map the position of two Japanese carriers. They left Japan on easterly course."

On the afternoon of December 6, Ranneft arrived at the Office of Naval Intelligence, where he found Admiral Wilkinson and his assistants. "After they told me of the Japanese movements towards the Kra peninsula, I asked about the two Japanese carriers heading eastward. 'Where are those fellows?' "

One of the officers put a finger on the wall chart four hundred miles or so north of Honolulu. "I asked what the devil were they doing there. Someone said vaguely that the Japanese were perhaps interested in 'eventual American intentions.' This made little sense to me, but I said nothing. And no one mentioned anything about a possible attack on Pearl Harbor; but I wrote in my official diary, 'I myself do not think about it because I believe that everyone in Honolulu is 100 percent on the alert, just as everyone here at ONI is.' I returned to my embassy, went to Minister Loudon's office, told him what I'd heard, and cabled my superiors in London."

That same evening, Captain Ranneft was summoned after dinner to the home of Minister Loudon in Washington, where he also found the military attaché, Colonel F.G.L. Weijerman. "The minister told us he'd just returned from the White House and that Roosevelt had told him he had sent a message to the emperor. If there was no immediate answer, said the president, war would probably break out on Monday."

I asked if his government had ever censured him for turning over the plans of the Bofors gun. Ranneft only said, "They made me an admiral." And in 1946, Admiral Chester Nimitz personally presented him the Legion of Merit Degree of Commander. His citation read: ". . . Discharging his responsibilities with great skill and initiative, Rear Admiral Ranneft rendered invaluable assistance in prosecuting the war against a common enemy. . . . his contribution to the development of Naval ordnance was of inestimable aid to ships of Allied Navies carrying out defensive and offensive measures against the enemy."

Then Admiral Ranneft told how he had casually mentioned to an old friend, Admiral Samuel Robinson, who had initiated the largest shipbuilding program in American history, that he was amazed to keep reading that the Americans were taken by complete surprise at Pearl harbor. How was this possible when ONI officers had shown him a chart that the Japanese task force was only some four hundred miles from Honolulu on December 6? "Robinson was stunned. He knew nothing about it and suggested I ask Admiral Stark [chief of naval operations] how this was possible. Later in the afternoon Robinson called me back with a terse message: it was not necessary for me to see Stark; Robinson had just called Stark, who refused to comment on the matter."

I told the admiral that I needed confirmation of his visits to the ONI from his official diary. Unfortunately, he said, there had been a fire and much of his diary was burned. He had sent the remnants to the Historical Department of the Netherlands Ministry of Defense. A week later I got a packet from Holland. Fortunately all of the diary for December 1941 remained intact and I had proof. I did find one differing piece of information. Ranneft had told me the Japanese carriers were four hundred miles *north* of Hawaii and his diary stated *"westerlicht."* I phoned Ranneft, and he said he was now sure it was north and asked me to keep it that way, but I included a photograph of the diary excerpt in my book.

Now Costello was shouting that I had lied about the Ranneft material. There was such a hubbub that evening in the hall in the National Archives I couldn't understand what he was saying, and several U.S. Marine officers quieted him down. By that time I was feeling a bit woozy but continued for another half hour until Costello again leaped up and charged that the official diary excerpt which I had reproduced in my book stated the carriers were four hundred miles *westerly,* not north, thereby invalidating the *entire* report. This charge was later repeated by others time and again. I continued another ten minutes or so and suddenly felt as if I were going to vomit. The next thing I knew I was lying on my back surrounded by women.

A good navy friend, Earl W. Gallaher, whose squadron sank two carriers at Midway, was in the front row with his wife and a nurse. He later told me that I had suddenly toppled stiffly to the right, landing on my right shoulder. His nurse had leaped onto the stage to give me mouth-to-mouth resuscitation. Then another woman leaped up and began pulling the nurse away. While they were struggling, Earl saw Toshiko sailing onto the stage to separate the contestants.

When I came to, I was appalled to find myself surrounded. Jill Merrill, the publicist for the National Archives, another good friend, said jokingly, "John, we don't need this kind of publicity. What happened?"

"I think I'm pregnant."

I was loaded on a stretcher, and as I left the National Archives, Costello loomed over me. "Did I cause this?" he asked.

"Not at all," I replied.

I was examined at the nearest hospital and was advised to stay all night, but I refused. It was merely a combination of not having eaten all day and then suffering my own personal "Pearl Harbor" when Costello attacked me. Carolyn Blakemore, who was supposed to have dinner with us that evening, suggested I postpone the publicity tour starting two days later in Chicago. I refused, but was persuaded to cancel my appearance the next night at the American Book Awards as one of the judges for history.

Originally Toshiko was to remain home during the tour to take care of Tamiko, but she insisted on accompanying me to Chicago. I needed her help while there to get out of bed and get dressed, and it was suggested that I go back to Danbury. But the Irish driver assigned to us was so helpful in getting me around that I persuaded Toshiko to go home instead of continuing to Dallas. So the national tour continued.

I finally arrived in San Francisco, where I had always gotten along well. But I was greeted with the announcement that the Press Club Book and Author Luncheon, where I was to speak the next day, had been canceled, with no reason given. Several hastily arranged appearances were set up, but my reception was cool and occasionally hostile. A cartoon in a West Coast newspaper pictured me in a Japanese plane dropping a copy of *Infamy* on the grave of Roosevelt. The caption read not "TORA, TORA, TORA!" but "TOLAND, TOLAND, TOLAND!"

I headed back to Cincinnati (fairly friendly) and Cleveland (not so friendly). On the same series of TV appearances and book-and-author luncheons in Pittsburgh was a Catholic priest, Father Andrew M. Greeley, who wrote very popular novels about the church. He could see what I was going through and said he had been enduring such hostility ever since his first book. He had survived by convincing himself that the bitter criticism was really a form of high praise. I laughed and headed for Boston, the last stop. Toshiko drove up to take me home. Two mornings later a crew from the leading Japanese TV company, planning a two-hour special on Pearl Harbor Day, arrived at 9:00 A.M. They left at 9:00 P.M.

I was dazed. What had happened in the past few months completely puzzled me. I had thought the factual, documented revelations in *Infamy* would interest almost everyone, particularly the academics—or at least be given a fair hearing. Just before publication the heads of the Asian departments at both Yale and Princeton had urged me to speak at their universities. I had agreed and sent them autographed copies of *Infamy*. Neither professor answered. Reviews by history professors were almost universally savage.

Toshiko's observation was, "John, you're so naive!" But I knew I would never change. There was only one thing to do: get moving with my next project—this one a novelization of *The Rising Sun*, with the fictional characters involved with historical people. It would be the saga of two families, one American and the other Japanese, bound by friendship and marriage, caught in the political and personal crossfire of the war neither of them wanted or made. For the time being, anyway, the hell with history.

[8]

Gods of War and Occupation

After years of writing history, I was now in a position to return to my first love—the creation of characters and their lives in my imagination. My desire to be a playwright gradually evolved into a hunger to explore history through fiction. The hundred or so short stories and several novels I had written over the years remained unpublished. But I resolved to take a period in history that I knew well and recast it as fiction.

The Heroism of a Maryknoll Priest

By late November 1981 I had completed a rough outline for *Gods of War.* My fictional American family, the McGlynns, would consist of the widowed father, a college history professor who is also an adviser to Roosevelt; his elder son, Will, a POW; the younger son, Mark, a Marine Corps runner in the island-by-island advance; the younger daughter, Maggie, a war correspondent, based on my friend Dickey Chapelle; and the older daughter, Floss, married to a Japanese diplomat, Tadoshi Toda. Tadoshi's family would include his father, Akira, a steel executive, based on Toshiko's father; his mother, Emi, "a modern girl," based on Toshiko's mother; two brothers; and a teen-age sister, based on Toshiko.

I had selected the 1st Battalion, 6th Marines, as young Mark's unit, and its commander, Lieutenant Colonel (later Lieutenant General) William K. Jones, spent hours with me at his home, where we re-created specific scenes between Willie K., as he was generally known, and Mark. We would tape for hours until both of us were satisfied. General Jones recommended that I work with his former top sergeant, Lewis "Mickey" Michelony, Jr., a former navy boxing champion who had won silver stars at Tarawa, Saipan, and Okinawa. Lew became fascinated with the book and interviewed more than seventy former officers and men of the battalion. In turn I had interviewed Mickey many times, and I felt I had a grip on the battalion's engagements.

What especially concerned me was Mark's reaction to the battle for Guadalcanal. He had been nauseated and depressed by the savagery and deaths,
whereas Lew and the other Catholics were better able to recover. So he decided to become a Catholic. I had no idea of the procedure involved in
conversion, and Willie K. advised me to see the battalion chaplain, Msgr.
Joseph Gallagher, and Bishop John J. O'Connor, head of the Military Vic-
arate in New York City. The bishop was enormously generous and helpful,
not only explaining how a person converts to Catholicism but offering in-
cisive comments on man's frailties, especially the power of sexual urges. He
later became a cardinal, and we are still good friends.

A third priest, Father Robert Emmett Sheridan, helped with this problem
and also recounted his personal experiences in the Philippines. When the
Japanese invaded he had left his post and walked all the way to Bataan to
serve in a hospital. He also told me of the heroism of his close friend Father
William Cummings, another Maryknoll priest, showing me the notes and
material on Cummings in the Maryknoll Library. He had been one of the
1,619 prisoners of war aboard the *Enoura-Maru* bound for Formosa. The hold
was seventy feet wide and ninety feet long. Halfway up one side of the vast
chamber stretched a balcony where the sick were segregated. Human waste
dripped down from the balcony onto those below. There was little food or
water. It was literally a hell ship. Father Cummings selflessly kept hope alive
in the most appalling circumstances.

As they neared Formosa the prisoners heard the drone of planes, and panic
swept the hold as men scattered for safety. A young captain shouted, urging
them to stay put: "You are as safe in one place as another." The ship was
under deadly attack by American aircraft. Many prisoners were killed in the
charnelhouse of the hold.

Then once more came the distant whine of planes. The Americans were
coming back. Father Cummings shouted for quiet in a commanding voice.
The cries and moans ceased. He raised his eyes and looked upward. "Lord,"
he said as if talking on a direct channel, "I do not understand all your ways.
You have permitted us to go through a terrible ordeal. We are just hanging
on to life, and if you leave us to our own devices we will die in the next air
attack. Lord, I ask you to intercede. Guide these pilots to other targets. Spare
us from further punishment!"

The planes swept over, but no bombs fell on the *Enoura-Maru*. When the
ship landed in Takao, Formosa, of the 1,619 men who had left Manila, fewer
than nine hundred remained alive. On the trip from Formosa to Japan, more
died of the bitter cold. The mournful shout of "Roll out your dead!" reminded one survivor of the grim stories of the London plague. Selfishness

was rampant, and one man commented that prison life either corrupted you or ennobled you. Another man said, "Both."

These survivors recalled that the best examples of humanity were the chaplains. The most devoted were a Lutheran, another Protestant, and the indomitable Father Cummings. Every night at nine o'clock, Cummings would cheerfully announce, "Chaplain calling, boys!"—and then start with the Lord's Prayer and continue with a special prayer for those who had died and those who were dying. This would be followed by a short talk urging—demanding—the men to keep up their hope and faith. "Just one more day!" he would plead each day, and ask the men to forgive their enemies.

But Cummings was also wilting under the incredible hardship. It was obvious that he would not last much longer unless he got more water. That night he was fed several spoonfuls but refused to take any more. "Share it with the boys," he said and passed out. The next day he found it difficult to go on his daily round, and at the evening devotional he collapsed. "I'll be all right, boys," he told those who carried him back to his sleeping space. He tried in vain to crawl out the next morning. His lips were parched and cracked, and his voice was weak. But that evening he insisted that someone hold him erect and he managed to say the Lord's Prayer weakly.

"You are going to make it," he said to a man named Mosher. "We came this far." Mosher got some water from snow which another man had sneaked from the deck at great risk, and brought it to the padre.

"I am very cold," said Cummings.

Mosher found a straw mat and, with the help of another man, wrapped it around his own shoulders and then over the priest, hoping his own body heat would warm him.

"I feel all right," said Cummings. Fifteen minutes later, Mosher felt his hand. There was no pulse. "Father Cummings is dead," he announced. Silently they wrapped the priest in the mat, and the next morning they placed him on top of a pile of dead. After ropes were lowered into the hold, a boatswain tied a running bowline around Father Cummings's feet and a half hitch around his neck. "All right, take him away!" he called.

All watched as the emaciated body slowly rose against the winter sky. As Father Cummings emerged from the hold he was illuminated by a ray of sunlight.

I decided to put Will McGlynn, the POW, on this ship and make him part of this ordeal. Father Cummings became a central force in the book. He was real—but fiction allowed me to show how his grace and courage touched and sustained others. There are some truths that only fiction can tell. The writer's version of any imagined character builds on all the reality he can find. Cummings was an excellent subject, for there were still people alive who remembered him.

Help from a Japanese Doctor

By early January 1982, I had almost finished the novel, but I needed to do more research in Japan, and on January 7 all three of us left Danbury. In Tokyo we immediately settled in a pleasant apartment in Motoazabu, lent to us by friends who were in the States. It was on a small hill overlooking a famous Buddhist shrine. We rested for a week in Hakone, and then I started to interview. Because of pain in my right shoulder from my fall at the National Archives, I had some trouble getting up from our Japanese bed-on-the-floor in the morning, but once I had soaked in the small, deep Japanese tub I was set for the day. We put Tamiko into the American School at Tachikawa. Unlike in New York City, here it was safe for her to travel to and from school by herself.

By early December I was finding it much more difficult to get out of bed. Toshiko and her sisters did their utmost to cure me. Her brother-in-law, a well-known psychiatrist, arranged several tests, which indicated nothing wrong, even though my right shoulder was almost useless.

I was finally taken to a doctor who claimed his magic shot could cure such complaints. His office occupied almost the entire floor of a building, and we found some fifty or sixty patients, some half dressed, waiting for treatment. When the doctor heard I had written *The Rising Sun,* he put me at the head of the line despite grumbling from those waiting. As I sat on a table, he spent some time telling us of the famous people—including a Mideast potentate—he had cured, and he had pictures to prove it. Then he tested the strength of my left hand. It was low. Then my right hand registered almost zero. He warned me that the shot might hurt and jabbed my right arm. The pain was indescribable, and Toshiko later told me my face turned blue. Suddenly, however, the pain stopped. The doctor tested my right-hand grip, and it was normal. For the first time since our arrival I slept the whole night and got up with no difficulty. When I returned the next morning, a shot to my left arm was painless and the strength in my left hand returned to normal.

On January 21, 1983, I returned home—alone, so that Tamiko could complete her school year. Toshiko insisted, despite my protests, that I take along a huge electric device that she thought would keep me in shape. I assumed that the airline would never take it aboard, but Toshiko knew one of the senior officers and the gadget was allowed on the plane. I was warned that there might be trouble at JFK with U.S. Customs. When a JAL man wheeled the monstrous object up to the U.S. inspector, he gaped. Then he said, "Are you John Toland the writer?" I said I used to be, and he summoned a baggage handler to take the machine and my baggage. Waiting outside was my daughter Marcia and her daughter. She had heard I needed help, and she drove me to Danbury.

Marcia and Heidi left after four days, and I continued work on the novel. When Toshiko and Tamiko returned in June, I was having trouble hitting the keys of my old portable, so I was persuaded to get an electric typewriter. It lasted two days. Even music could not overwhelm its infernal buzzing. Tamiko suggested I get an electronic machine. It lasted less than a week, since I had never learned how to typewrite properly and made a lot of mistakes, which infuriated the machine. I returned to my battered Royal manual typewriter, and by early November I had finished the final draft of *Gods of War.*

When the book was published in 1985, I got a glowing tribute from Leon Uris and praise from the *New York Times,* but many reviews were mixed and some hostile. It did well, however, in Japan, and the Franklin Library selected it for its Signet First Edition Society.

A Chinese Professor

I was too involved with the sequel, which would cover the occupation of Japan, to publicize *Gods of War* by traveling. I centered the second novel on the same two families, dealing with the period from October 1945 through April 1949, when MacArthur was the American shogun during the long and arduous trials of Japanese war criminals. While Professor McGlynn and his twins, Maggie and Mark, are busily involved in the Occupation, son Will, a former POW and now a civilian lawyer, returns to Tokyo to join the prosecution team for the trials. I wanted to portray both the U.S. and Japanese points of view during the years of hardship when the conquered people were trying to rebuild their nation from rubble, and I wanted to offer glimpses into a modern Japan waiting to be born.

In early 1985 I received a request from the U.S. Information Agency to lecture in China and then proceed to the Philippines, where the end of the war was being commemorated. I immediately accepted. In the special message included in the Franklin Library edition of *Gods of War* I had stated why I had written three books on the war with Japan. "I chose the Pacific War, convinced that Asia would be *the* continent of the twenty-first century and that the peace of the world depended on the closer relationship between that continent and the West."

For years I had been eager to see China, and I also had to get to the Philippines to see the Aquinos, who had suffered a terrible loss: Benigno Aquino, Jr., the opposition leader, had been assassinated in 1983. Earlier I had been among those who wrote President Marcos to allow the imprisoned Benigno to receive proper medical attention in Boston. Marcos allowed Benigno to leave, but after recovery he had returned to Manila despite the warning of Tony, his older half brother, that it was a trap.

I flew to Tokyo on January 25, 1985, and picked up Toshiko, and we set off for Beijing. In a wild three days from the 29th to the 30th I addressed a dozen university audiences in the capital and Shanghai. To my surprise I found that I was well known. *The Rising Sun* and several other books had been pirated, and *Adolf Hitler* was being prepared for publication. I was fascinated to find China fulfilling my predictions. The advent of foreign trade, particularly with the United States, had apparently started the country on the road to a market economy.

When we returned to the lobby of our Beijing hotel after our first day of talking, we were approached by an energetic Chinese, Hua Qingzhao, a professor of history. He said he had met a friend of mine in Europe and heard I would be in China. "I will show you the real Beijing" he said as he maneuvered us out of the hotel. We were soon eating in a restaurant that was all-Chinese and listening to his dream of writing a true history of Harry Truman "through Chinese eyes." He told us about the great changes in his country and intimated that few Americans ever saw the real China. For instance, how many knew there was a subway in Beijing? So he took us to a subway and later loaded us into a bus which was jam-full. A young man got up and offered his seat. When I started to help Toshiko into the seat, the young man insisted I take it. "We revere old people," explained Hua.

The next day he took us on a strenuous tour of the Forbidden City, assuming we wanted to see everything. We were exhausted by the time we got back to the hotel and learned there was about to be a dinner in our honor. I asked if Professor Hua could join us. Hua sat on my right, and a man from the embassy in charge of Fulbright Fellows was on my left. "You two should get to know each other," I said, explaining that Hua needed a grant so he could write about Truman. He got the grant, and for the next two years Hua and I would meet in Danbury, Washington, and the Truman Library to exchange material on Truman and the Korean War.

A Close Call in the Philippines

I continued on to Manila alone on February 4, since six hotels had been burned down in political protests in the previous four months. Expecting a nostalgic celebration of the historical triumph brought about by the joint efforts of Americans and Filipinos, I was surprised at my first lecture to encounter strident opponents who, in the question-and-answer period, insisted that the real World War II enemies of the Philippines were not the Japanese but the Americans. These protesters, I discovered, were from the radical left, and though they were greatly in the minority, they would continue to dominate my appearances throughout the islands. They charged that MacArthur stormed into Manila only to rescue American and Allied prisoners and that he was therefore guilty of the massacre of some 100,000 civilians in the Philippine capital by a desperate, bloodthirsty Japanese naval detachment.

Since I had also come to do research for the sequel to *Gods of War,* I sought an interview with President Marcos, who had won medals for bravery on Bataan and was an able guerrilla leader. The embassy informed me that he was reportedly very sick and would see no one, but to my surprise a young officer appeared the day after my arrival and told me the president would be happy to see me. I arrived at Malacañang, the presidential palace, to find the president in good spirits. He had no objections to my taping him in the presence of half a dozen officers. Although I'd been told I'd be lucky to get ten minutes, I stayed for more than an hour, and he answered my questions promptly and in detail. His mind was clear, although the journalists who had been unable to see him the past few months had assured me he was dying.

While shaking hands with him I noticed a four-star general behind him, smiling. "Don't you remember me, John?" he asked.

It was Major Ramos, who had set up my trip through the islands in 1960 and was now head of the army. He quietly set up a private appointment in which he described, off the record, the situation in the Philippines and revealed that he was going to support Corazon Aquino, whom I had also met long ago, for president.

As I was leaving the palace in a hurry to reach a hotel where I was scheduled to be one of the speakers at a meeting, a young officer said Imelda Marcos wanted to see me. Mrs. Marcos was gracious and expressed the hope that Toshiko and I would visit her soon at her town in Cebu. I saw through the charm; she was a very devious woman who would try to use me to help her get favorable publicity. The meeting at the hotel was under way by the time I arrived, and as I started talking I heard mutterings—word had gone around that I had just seen Marcos. I was asked if he really was dying. I said he appeared in good health to me; his diction was clear and his mind was sharp.

The next day I had dinner with Tony Aquino, and the following morning we drove north to the family homestead in Tarlac. After a sentimental tour of the old house where I had first met the young governor and his attractive wife, soon to become president, we drove to Tony's pleasant retreat in a shady grove where thirty-nine members of his wartime guerrilla group were gathered for a reunion. Stretched between a pole and a tree was a ten-by-three-foot banner:

WELCOME
JOHN TOLAND
TARLAC GUERRILLA CHAPTER

We spent the afternoon talking about the old days, and I was asked many questions—but none suggesting any shortcomings of MacArthur as a liberator.

After a week I left my papers and valuables in my safety-deposit box at the Regent of Manila Hotel and left for the four southern islands. The first stop was Cebu, where I had interviewed President Osmeña long ago. As in Manila, my lectures were marred by anti-American, anti-MacArthur diatribes. It was the same on the island of Panay. In my final lecture in Ilo Ilo City to students of Central Philippine University, I spoke not only of the considerable contributions to victory made by Filipinos but of my own theory of "living history" based on interviews with individuals who were present at crucial events. I also elaborated on the theme I had propounded earlier—that the twenty-first century would be the Century of Asia. Years of research in the Orient had convinced me that the Middle Kingdom—China—would be the geopolitical centrum of the world, and that the superior work ethic and expert workmanship, not only in Japan but throughout the region, would shift world leadership from the West. My conviction had been strengthened, I concluded, by my recent trip to China, where I found all groups receptive and eager for more contact with Americans and Europeans.

My lecture was enthusiastically received by these students, and I hoped they would take over the question-and-answer period. But the radical leftists launched their attack on America and MacArthur.

In exasperation I finally broke in, "I am tired of hearing such nonsense!" I warned the students that these were but a few discordant voices corrupting history with politics, and they should listen to their parents and grandparents to find the truth about the liberation of the Philippines.

For years, I said, American historians had been writing frankly about MacArthur's mistakes and egotism, as well as his truly great achievements. That, I said, was the American way. I concluded with a question: "How many of you students would like a visa to the Soviet Union?"

Not a hand went up.

The next morning, February 14, I was awakened by a friend. The Regent of Manila Hotel was in flames! It had been torched simultaneously on the second and ninth floors. My room was on the sixth. A group calling itself "the Angels" had done it as a "protest against the U.S.–Japan support" of the Marcos regime. The fire alarm had been knocked out, as were all the lights. The death toll so far was thirty but there were still people inside. I felt sadness for those who died and fortunate to be spared.

After several tries I got a phone connection to Toshiko in Tokyo. I told her I was on Negros Island and all I'd lost were my papers and valuables, including my passport. A little later she also got a call from the U.S. embassy in Manila. A report had gone out that I was missing and feared dead. She said she'd just heard from me and I was safe in Ilo Ilo. She appreciated their concern.

The hotel was still smoldering when I returned. I asked if the safety-deposit boxes had survived, and I was told it was too soon to tell. I was taken to another hotel and given a huge apartment. Several days later I was finally allowed to pick my way over boards to the waterlogged remains. All my papers were safe.

After our return to Danbury on February 17, I wrote—at a request from UPI News Features—a long account of my experiences in the Philippines. "I am still convinced," I concluded, "that the twenty-first century will be the Century of Asia. And that this will be the century in which men and nations finally learn the secret of each other's differences and live in lasting and just peace. If not, I doubt if there will be a twenty-second century."

By mid-March, *Gods of War* was doing well, and in April 1985 we set off on a publicity trip for the book. We returned in early May and I resumed work on *Occupation.* By December I had made such good progress that I began thinking about the third novel, which would deal with the Korean War. I heard from Mickey Michelony, who had been helping me on *Occupation,* that there was to be a Korean War Reunion of Marines in San Diego. This would be invaluable. In early December I spent three days listening agape to the experiences of officers and enlisted men. Their stories, told baldly without embroidery, stirred me so much that on the trip home I decided that this book should not be a novel but another work of history. Mickey, who had been highly decorated for heroism in this forgotten war, agreed to be my full-time assistant and take care of interviews west of the Mississippi as well as at all U.S. Army and U.S. Marine reunions.

My daughter Tamiko was doing well at the Choate School, but going her own way. I had advised her not to take a course in Russian, since it was such a difficult language, but she soon became so involved in all things Russian that she went with a student group to the Soviet Union for twelve days, returning with such enthusiasm that I knew she, like her father, had become hooked on this strange country.

The Phony Hitler Diary

In May 1985 I was appalled to see a blurb on the cover of *Life* about a Hitler diary. It took only a few minutes to recognize this as just another hoax from East Germany. Hitler's observations on such important events as Hess's flight to England were ridiculous, as was all the frank talk about his love life. My phone soon began to ring. I told newspaper and TV stations that this was a clumsy fraud like all the others—even if a million or more dollars had already been paid for it. Hitler could not possibly have written the sections that took place soon after the July 20 bombing, since Albert Speer had assured me that he had, at the time, asked the Führer to autograph a copy of *Mein Kampf* for a friend and Hitler refused because his right hand was still partially paralyzed.

I was cautioned to keep quiet because some prominent American historians had authenticated the diary. Then I got a call from Professor Brad Smith, an expert in this field who was in London doing research for a book on intelligence. Trevor-Roper had just stated in the *London Times* that the diary *was* genuine. I was upset because I admired the man. I told Brad I was convinced the document was a fraud and I was staking my reputation on my conviction.

. Then came a call from a TV show. I believe it was called *Frontline.* That night there was to be a special one-hour TV show on the diaries from both Washington and New York, and the producers wanted me to appear in New York. I agreed without hesitation. There were others on the show: a man from *Life* and a handwriting expert. As we were waiting I told the *Life* man that his magazine should be ashamed of itself for putting such nonsense on the front cover.

On the air, when asked for my opinion, I bluntly declared that it was not only a fraud but a poor one. Hitler's signature on the document, for example, was an obvious fake. I owned an original, and the *f* in his signature had a bar across going downward, whereas the bar in the fake went upward. After listing other blunders I concluded that whoever had paid the large sum for the fraud need only to have taken a sheet of the paper to the Koblenz Archives for testing its age.

After the handwriting expert agreed with me, a call from Germany cut in and my old nemesis David Irving was saying, "I agree with John Toland." The next day, to my amazement, Irving flip-flopped and said the diary *was* genuine. I must have been still laughing when the announcement soon arrived that the paper *had* finally been tested. It was made long after Hitler's death.

I Learn I Am Not a Novelist

In June 1985, Tamiko graduated from Choate with varsity letters in archery and riflery. She had been accepted at Michigan, Columbia, and Cornell and chose the last because it had the best Russian department. When I mildly suggested she apply at Williams, her reply was, "It's too dinky!" Of course it was. That was why I liked it.

In mid-July we were invited to help celebrate the Russian "Peace Cruise" of the *Delta Queen* down the Mississippi with a scheduled stopover in La Crosse. I was to make several speeches, but when we arrived I was requested *not* to welcome the Russians. I was disappointed, because I had hoped Tamiko would have a chance to talk with them. Apparently our hosts had just discovered that all my books were banned in the Soviet Union, where I had been branded a capitalist liar.

While the Russians were landing we were taken to the local library, where I was to make a speech. Our Chinese friend Hua Qingzhao, who had been doing research for his book at the Truman Library, suddenly appeared. He pretended to be a Japanese relative who was coming to the library for a reception, since he didn't want the Russians to know he was Chinese. As I was starting my speech, the Russian delegation poured in. I had a difficult time keeping a straight face.

As soon as I finished the final draft of *Occupation* in 1986 I began work on the Korean War history. My agent, Carl Brandt, was delighted with the project and got me a generous advance from Doubleday in February 1987. The reviews of *Occupation,* published in 1987, were again mixed. Typical was one in the *Milwaukee Journal* with the headline "Toland's Fiction Improves a Bit." The reviewer did like the "dramatic, surprising finish in the final chapters." Unfortunately the good points were "more than overcome by Toland's too lengthy historical renderings of the trials, a clear sign that he is still overly dependent on letting more description carry the moment when his characters have nothing to say or do."

I felt this reviewer had made some good points. So did Mike Hinkemeyer in *Rave Reviews*. "It is as if Toland first wrote an excellent history of the postwar period—Tojo, in particular, is portrayed in fascinating detail—but then someone said, 'John, if you dumped a lot of characters in this thing, it could be a novel.' Unfortunately, characters do not a novel make, and flat characters who stand around playing straight men to historical personages devalue both the novel form and a book of legitimate history."

I knew Hinkemeyer was right. I was not a novelist, and I thanked God I was already back in my proper niche. My imagination was always held back by the weight of reality. The discipline of recording history was in conflict with my powers of invention—such as they were. But I had finally done what I wanted to do for so much of my life.

[Part Three]

In Mortal Combat (1 9 8 7 –)

[9]

"One Good Man Can Work Wonders"

I felt a personal commitment to explore that "forgotten war" in Korea. It was a turning point for the United States in Asia and would result in today's economically booming South Korea facing a closed and hostile North Korea.

To create a suitable framework I spent the first five months of 1987 doing interviews and archival work in the United States. The research task was formidable; Mickey Michelony, a key real character in *Gods of War,* became an invaluable assistant to me. We interviewed over two hundred people in the United States alone, ranging from General Matthew Ridgway, one of my favorite commanders, to Colonel Robert Taplett, commander of the 3rd Battalion, 5th Marines, as well as eight of Taplett's enlisted men, two of his officers, and a dozen U.S. Marine associates. In Korea, where Mickey had preceded me to set things up, my first interviewee in September 1987 was General Paik Sun-yup, the first South Korean four-star general, who escorted me to the "Bowling Alley" near Seoul where he had helped to stem the North Korean breakthrough. Through Paik I conducted the first interview in depth given by General Chung-Il-kwon, the ROK (Republic of Korea— i.e., South Korea) chief of staff early in the war, and was introduced to many civilians who had gone through hell, including Father Philip Crosbie, a survivor of the infamous Death March in North Korea.

In Taiwan we met with more than fifty Chinese soldiers who had fought against the Allied troops but had later refused repatriation after being held as prisoners of war. And in China I not only gained access to their counterparts who had opted to go home but was permitted to be the first Westerner to see material on the Korean War from the archives of the Academy of Military Science, People's Liberation Army.

News Reporters Caught in Seoul

In the United States in early 1987 I had located six former war correspondents who vividly described the first harrowing days of the unexpected North

Korean attack. The ill-armed ROK army was collapsing, and the capital, Seoul, had been abandoned by Syngman Rhee and his government. The North Koreans, spearheaded by Russian-made tanks, appeared unstoppable.

At about 6:00 P.M. on June 27, 1950, a plane approached Kimpo Airfield, a few miles west of Seoul. Four correspondents—Keyes Beech of the *Chicago Daily News,* Burton Crane of the *New York Times,* Frank Gibney of *Time,* and Marguerite Higgins of the *New York Herald Tribune*—could see Americans below frantically waving bedsheets and pillowcases, signals that Kimpo was still in friendly hands. After landing they were all driven across the Han River bridge. They found Seoul apparently peaceful and rushed into KMAG (Korean Military Advisory Group) headquarters. "I suggested we stay all night at KMAG," recalled Beech. Late that night someone shouted that the North Koreans were in the city. The correspondents hastily dressed and collected their typewriters and bags as an American major told them enemy tanks were approaching the Han River bridge. "If I were you," he advised, "I would head there too. If you hurry, you'll still have time to make it."

In today's world of satellite links and live video coverage of wars from every troubled part of the post–Cold War world, it is hard to imagine the primitive conditions under which these intrepid reporters had to cover the desperate defense at Seoul and then its collapse. They were in the thick of the battle, some wounded, none immune to or protected from the dangers that threatened the lives of South Korean soldiers and civilians caught up in the maelstrom. As I described their stories in my book, I wondered at their many close escapes from death and was amazed at their admirable persistence in "getting the story out" when that meant filing by whatever cable or radio link a reporter could find—when and if he or she could find one at all.

Two figures from the American military, General Walton Walker, commander of the combined and beleaguered American–South Korean forces, and Army Private Frank Myers, exemplified the courage and endurance of our outnumbered and hard-pressed men in the first days of what became, with ultimate UN support, a "police action" that was to cost more American lives than Vietnam.

I got General Walker's story from those who served with this tenacious and inspiring commander. In a number of accounts of the war, Walker had been severely criticized, but when I met people like Mike Lynch, then a captain and the general's private pilot, I discovered quite a different story. Lynch recalls occasions when he and the general flew so low that Walker could actually shout orders and encouragement to his men below. After a series of terrible battles in which Walker and his outnumbered men fought, and retreated, and fought again, in September of 1950 Walker's lines finally held and General Douglas MacArthur, the supreme commander, launched an amphibious landing at Inchon, a move that would be hailed as a military stroke of genius. But as Mike Lynch explained to me, the situation had changed dramatically between the time he chose Inchon and the actual landing. Walker opposed Inchon, because recent radio intercepts suggested that Kim Il-sung, the Communist leader of North Korea, planned to commit everything to capturing Pusan before UN forces could get in place and stop him. That would place the bulk of the North Korean forces south of the Taejon-Taegu axis—that is, halfway between Inchon and the tip of the Korean peninsula—on the date of the proposed Inchon landing. While much of the NK tactical and logistical reinforcement could bypass Seoul whether traveling north or south, it *had* to pass through Taejon in order to influence the battle. Therefore Taejon, not Seoul, was the key to a successful development. It would be much less heavily defended than Inchon, and the landing force could reach Taejon on the second day. It would take at least a week and perhaps more for the landing element to reach Seoul, which would be formidably defended.

Moreover, the bulk of the North Korean forces trying to drive Walker into the sea would be trapped and could be wiped out by air and artillery with relatively few losses. Once the NK forces had been eliminated, the U.S. and ROK forces would meet little resistance in a drive to the 38th parallel, the line dividing North and South Korea. At this point the ROK forces could take over and the U.S. units sent to the rear to handle future threats while the UN resolved the political issues.

But MacArthur insisted on Inchon. The massive U.S. Marine landing went ahead, making a magnificent spectacle. The opposition was desultory. MacArthur was praised as a military genius—despite the indications that the enemy was little discomfited by his success. (In fact, Mao and Chou En-lai had correctly deduced that Inchon would be the target.) Only twenty marines had been killed and 179 wounded. But the road from Inchon to Seoul would be another matter. By the time, twelve days later, that U.S. Marines tore down the North Korean flag flying next to the Capitol Building in Seoul, U.S. casualties were staggering—and, as General Walker had predicted, the North Korean army had escaped to the north to fight another day. And to have some new allies along with them.

I could sense Mike Lynch's frustration as we talked for many hours about the lack of appreciation of Walker's accomplishments. He told me, in a bitter tone of voice, that he found himself at the point where he "hated everyone above Walker and everyone below. But that's what you get, I thought, when you take a bunch of administrative guys and give them a command in peace-time so they can get promoted."

Unfortunately, General Walker could not speak for himself. Leading his Eighth Army, supported by ROK troops, he smashed the North Korean army that was near Seoul. After Walker had crossed the 38th parallel and taken Pyongyang, MacArthur ordered him to head for the Yalu River. Walker feared this would force the Chinese to cross the Yalu to protect their borders. He was proved correct in late November 1950 when massive Chinese forces crossed the Yalu and initially threatened to annihilate Walker's army and marine forces, which had been instructed by MacArthur to race north and link up with Walker at the Yalu.

The Marines would undergo the virtually indescribable ordeal of retreat from the Chosin Reservoir. Walker managed to stall the Chinese attack and had withdrawn his Eighth Army south of the 38th parallel, setting up a defensive position some thirty miles north of Seoul. On the morning of December 23, 1950, Walker's jeep was involved in an accident on an icy road, and Walker died in the same fashion as his mentor, George Patton. He had been on his way to the front lines to award his son, Sam, a second Silver Star.

General Matthew Ridgway replaced Walker. It was through him that I initially learned about Mike Lynch, whom he had inherited from Walker as his private pilot. Ridgway told me, "I believe he knows more about the Korean War than anyone else." With these men I relived some of their more hair-raising experiences in the air and some of the nearly impossible landings, particularly one on a dike that was not much wider than the plane's landing gear and all of three hundred feet long. They barely made it and then began taking small-arms and mortar fire. As he had in Normandy, Ridgway believed in being with the troops and seeing what was going on firsthand. The real miracle of the day was Lynch's being able to get the plane turned around so that they were able to take off—during a lull in the increasingly heavy mortar fire.

By the end of July 1950, Army Private Frank Myers proved himself just the kind of soldier that Walker relied on. When his unit was trapped in the area of Hadong, an important road junction near the tip of Korea, he and the remnants of decimated American troops managed to break out and make their way back to friendly lines, despite the enemy's fifteen-to-one advantage. Myers was also precisely the sort of witness to history that I searched for: as Ridgway had led me to Lynch and thus a very different picture of General Walker, the human chain of informants led me to Myers.

While the battle of Hadong was raging, MacArthur flew from Japan to

Korea and declared there would be no evacuation of American forces. Walker, too, was determined that there would be no more withdrawals. Myers, after two days of rest, learned the enemy was breaking through U.S. lines. He found himself thrust into a leadership role and placed in charge of 125 men by a captain who thought Myers had both guts and brains.

They slowly withdrew under heavy, continuous attacks, finally getting some air and artillery cover that ripped into the North Koreans. After a day's rest and treatment for a sore ankle at a dispensary, Myers found himself in another heavy North Korean attack, then another. GIs all around him were pulling back to what remained of a front line. Hobbling on his now virtually disabled ankle, he somehow made it to safety and was taken to another dispensary. His ankle was greatly swollen, but he had no sooner lain down than someone ran in yelling, "Gooks are surrounding the place!" Myers sprang up, seized a rifle, and limped into the street. "I was so surprised to see half a dozen NKs that I lost my balance and fell." One Korean slashed at him with a bayonet, but it only scraped the side of his leg. He fired from a sitting position, forcing the NKs to take cover, then hobbled to the train station, where wounded were being loaded. No sooner had Myers piled into the train than he saw enemy troops running toward him. He and other wounded began firing out the windows. "I figured I alone must have hit seven enemy before the train finally pulled out."

The next thing he remembered was an ambush, and he again began shooting out of the train window. He passed out, and when he came to he was on a stretcher and a nurse was trying to take the rifle out of his hand while he mumbled something about getting back to his unit. Next he heard a loud, strange sound and jerked upright. He was in a clean white room between fresh clean sheets. The sun was bright. He saw a pretty lady in a white dress. "Where are Mom and Dad?" he asked. "Where am I? In heaven?" Once he realized that he was alive, Myers wondered if he was still an officer after what he thought had been a temporary battlefield commission. But, of course, he was still a buck private and nobody was writing up any decoration for bravery.

{10}

In Dubious Battle

Lieutenant Colonel Robert Taplett, commander of the 3rd Battalion, 5th Marines, was tall and lean, a thirty-two-year-old native of South Dakota— and a perfect example of General Walker's belief that one good man could do wonders. Because of the combat he would see and the force of his character, I knew he would be one of the best people to represent the marines' experience in this stage of the war. The surgeon in his battalion remembered thinking, "What an enlistment poster he'd have made. He spoke in a staccato way with no warmth, and seemed hard as nails." While that was one aspect of Taplett, I was to discover many others, all of which combined to make him a superb leader in combat.

On September 3, 1950, and in the days that followed he would be caught up in a struggle for the Obongi-ni Ridge, just east of the Naktong Ridge, the area in which Walker finally stabilized his lines and stopped the North Koreans from taking Pusan. That afternoon he had come across a GI bivouac area on the ridgeline; dead bodies littered the ground or had been killed as they slept. Taplett and his men dug in. Just before dawn of the following day the regimental commander, Colonel Murray, told him to contact the army combat team that was supposed to be on his right. Taplett radioed back: "There isn't anybody out there except North Koreans." In the days of confused fighting that followed, the North Koreans took incredible casualties, and yet they kept coming. From the accounts of the battle that I heard from those involved, it was a perfect example of the "friction of war." Coordination with army units was difficult, the weather, as so often in Korea, would make air support impossible, U.S. Marine and North Korean T-34 (Russian-made) tanks went head to head, and at the most desperate point of the struggle to take the objective, Obongi-ni Ridge, which blocked the route to the Naktong River, the North Koreans were so close to one unit that the marines were lobbing grenades at them almost nonstop.

Ultimately relieved by Army units, Taplett and his marines would soon play a key part in the Inchon landing. And then they would survive the results of MacArthur's military genius—the harrowing retreat from what the marines would forever call "Frozen Chosin."

My views of MacArthur were substantially revised as I got deeper into the war and as I talked to those who had fought it. I began to question not only his military genius but his geopolitical insight as well, at least with respect to Korea and China.

Freezing and Fighting at the Chosin Reservoir

After placing Syngman Rhee back in power in late September 1950, Mac-Arthur had been instructed by the Joint Chiefs that his next military objective was the destruction of the North Korean armed forces, but under no circumstances were his troops to cross Manchurian or Soviet borders. Mac-Arthur had replied that Walker's Eighth Army would attack across the 38th parallel with the objective of seizing Pyongyang, the capital of North Korea. To the east his chief of staff, Major General Edward Almond, would make an amphibious landing on the eastern coast with X Corps and then drive westward across the peninsula to help Walker take the capital.

But MacArthur's vision took him far beyond Pyongyang. He wanted all of Korea. At the peak of his military fame, MacArthur was confident that he held the upper hand. Almond was instructed to send the marines up the west side of the Chosin Reservoir, 150 miles northeast of Pyongyang, then turn northwest and join Walker's army. Together they would race to the Yalu and end the war. But the elements of Walker's army that were supposed to meet Almond's marines were already retreating. A huge Chinese army had secretly crossed the Yalu during the nights. Mao had set a trap, and Walker, who had objected to penetrating so deeply, was driven back before Almond's forces could reach him.

Almond, unaware of this disaster, set out to join Walker's army as scheduled, on November 27, 1950, but almost immediately ran into massive Chinese forces. More Chinese reinforcements arrived, and the marines were forced to fall back. At this point, Colonel Taplett's battalion had been assigned the mission of seizing the commanding ground on both sides of the road to the rear. As he began occupying these two high-ground positions he was ordered by Murray to report to the marine CP. Plans had changed. Instead of occupying the high ground, Taplett was instead ordered to lead a breakout. This meant that he would have to clear the way to the rear—and safety.

Late that evening his Item Company took the first objective on Hill 1520, a big spur. "I'm going to attack across the plateau to another spur ahead of me," he then radioed Item's commander, Captain Schrier. But about midnight, Schrier called from the hill, "I'm running into a buzzsaw up here. It's going to be a disaster."

"Okay," said Taplett. "Pull back to the first position and set up for the night." Then came another message from regimental headquarters: resume the attack to the rear. "I am not going to resume any attack at night," replied Taplett. "Not over terrain I know nothing about." He was again ordered to resume the attack and reluctantly called Schrier. "I've got pressure from the two combined commanders. Can you attack again?"

"I'll try," said Schrier, but soon ran into another buzzsaw. The earth was so frozen that foxholes were barely below ground level and gave little protection from the shower of mortar rounds, grenades, and small-arms fire. Veterans of World War II in Item Company thought it was worse than Iwo Jima. After taking heavy casualties, Schrier called Taplett: "We're under very heavy attack, Tap. From the front and both sides."

During the night, Taplett received reports of heavy fighting and realized the situation was desperate. Again and again he tried in vain to reach Item Company, and after several hours he found Schrier at the aid station. He had been shot in the throat and all he could say was, "Impossible. Everybody killed." Only about twenty men had come through alive.

"I called Murray: 'Christ! Item Company has been chewed up! We're in a hell of a mess up here!' " At this point he had only headquarters and supply people on the road.

"We're going to renew the attack," said Murray, and promised to send help.

But only one tank arrived. "When I emerged from the aid tent, I saw Colonel Murray walking toward me. He asked what was happening. 'We already filled you in on the radio.' "

"Well," said Murray, "we're going to continue the attack."

"Then I'm going to need some additional people," Taplett replied. "I've just got two companies now, and one company is down. How Company has only about sixty people and G Company about eighty. Item Company is gone." He had to have somebody on the road. There were roadblocks ahead, all of them protected by enemy fire. "I've been on the point up the road and it's pretty touchy. I'd like to get somebody out in front."

Murray said he would send up one tank. "And we're going to form a composite company out of the remnants from the 7th Marines and artillery and engineers."

Taplett sighed. It was going to be more of the same for at least another day and night. The next day, December 2, he was still leading the way to the pass which led to safety despite the terrible casualties. They had to fight for every yard. By noon, George Company along Hill 1520 had secured its objective, but the composite company of Dog and Easy, called "Damnation," which was to clear roadblocks, was stalled near a demolished bridge. After calling in Corsairs, which efficiently cleared the Chinese from the ravine, Taplett ordered How Company to move through the high ground south of a bend in the road, but How's people were soon pinned down while trying to cross a stream.

Taplett was walking down the road with Swede Swenson, his radio operator, followed by the radio jeep, when machine-gun fire chattered from the right. "I realized it was coming from high ground above How Company. I heard a strange, gaspy sound but kept going and then, when more fire came in, I hit the deck."

He turned and couldn't see the radioman. He found Swede in the snow at the side of the road. "What the hell's the matter with you?" Taplett asked. Swenson was indispensable, and always at his best in a crisis.

"I'm in bad shape," he mumbled. A round had gone through the radio on his back and into his lungs. Taplett looked for the jeep driver, who had been right behind him. He too was bleeding. "I called for litters and medics." It was getting dark as the engineers ahead finished constructing a bypass around the blown bridge. Taplett sent his single tank forward. Minutes later he learned that it had slid off the road. "Get some people in the motor platoon," he radioed, "and see what you can do about getting this damn thing moving."

Eventually the tank was in place and the advance continued. But George Company was in trouble, its commander wounded. Spirits were sagging throughout the battalion, and the will to fight was fading. Taplett started up the road with a new radio operator and found the tank sitting near the ditch. Lolling nearby were several marines. "Where's the Dog-Easy's company commander?" Taplett asked.

"In the tank."

Machine-gun fire came from the hill on the right, and bullets spattered in the snow. Taplett wiggled on his stomach to the far side of the tank and got on the phone at the back. Angrily he yelled at the commander.

"I'm not coming out," was the muted reply.

"If you don't, I'm going to get you court-martialed," Taplett shouted. There was no answer. "Okay, you lousy son of a bitch! You stay in the tank!" As he turned to go back, his helmet flew off, creased by a bullet from the hill. Then he heard someone calling, "Taplett! Taplett!" He turned and saw a man coming through the snow.

"I'm Lieutenant Eddy!" he called. "I've got a message from Colonel Murray."

"You can tell him that he can wait and give it to me himself." Eddy explained that after reaching the Toktong Pass, Taplett was to turn over the attack to the 1st Battalion of the 7th Marines. Colonel Litzenberg, commander of the 7th Marines, wanted Taplett to continue his attack immediately. "Ray Davis and his people on Toktong Hill are attacking toward you and driving the Chinese right into your arms."

"Tell Colonel Litzenberg he's full of shit! We're chasing a lot of Chinese in front of us, but there's none running into our arms. If he doesn't believe it, he and Murray can come up here themselves."

No one came, and Taplett reorganized his headquarters and supply people, then pulled George Company down off the hill on the left. When Taplett got a secondhand message from his own regimental commander, he told the informant, "You tell Ray Murray that as far as I'm concerned, I want to continue the attack into Hagaru-ri." This was their goal. "I don't want to stop. My men's feet are going to freeze up if they stop. I think we've broken through all resistance. We'll be able to walk all the way to Hagaru-ri without a shot fired."

By the dawn of the following day, December 3, six inches of new snow covered the ground. Taplett's last mission was to break through the Chinese that were blocking the pass so the marines could reach Hagaru-ri. George Company led the way with a tank. Then came Taplett's engineers. Forty-eight had started two days earlier; now there were seventeen. Taplett was up front with them. How Company, which had been fighting all night on the heights, was doing its best to keep pace.

His men were doing so well that Taplett again asked Murray for permission to keep going rather than have someone else take over at Toktong Pass. But his plea was denied and Taplett stayed behind to herd the entire straggling column of marines through the pass.

Three weeks later on Christmas Day of 1950 the exhausted marines were recuperating at the marine brigade bivouac near the end of the peninsula. There was little peace, however, for Taplett. He and other officers of his battalion had decided to send someone to Tokyo for liquor to enliven a celebration open to all ranks. An officer named Hap volunteered to go, and returned with several cases. The next morning, Murray, learning that Hap had gone to Tokyo for liquor, called Taplett and stated that Hap had been absent without leave.

"No, he wasn't," retorted Taplett. "I knew he was there."

"Someone should be court-martialed for this."

"You can do any goddam thing you want, Ray. But if it wasn't for this battalion you wouldn't be here today, and neither would any of the rest of us. What I did, I did with the concurrence of all my officers and NCOs. I don't see anything wrong in sending Hap over. There wasn't anybody that made any money on it, and nobody made off with the major share of the booze. It was shared by the entire battalion as a Christmas present—and a reward for the job they did up at the reservoir."

The matter was dropped. And Bob Taplett, although one of the most remarkable marine officers—according to several subordinate officers who later became generals—never got to be a general.

"AHH, NO!"

I was able to find many of the men who had survived Chosin, but perhaps the most extraordinary and heroic story was that of one man in the 7th Division, Private Ed Reeves of the 3rd Battalion, 31st Infantry Regiment, who had been sent with his unit to the east side of the reservoir. When the Chinese suddenly attacked the battalion, he had been tossed in the air by a mortar explosion. He watched blood flowing from many holes in his arms and feet as he was pulled into a farmhouse with other wounded. By then the bitter cold had frozen the blood of his wounds. He was sure his left foot was gone, but his right foot might make it.

While Taplett was clearing the way to the rear on the other side of the reservoir, Reeves was in a truck heading south. All along the road, incoming fire killed some of those riding with him and wounded others. Then the motor went dead and the wounded were told to walk across the reservoir ice to marines on the other side who would help them.

Reeves couldn't go. Once he moved his legs, he passed out from the pain. Those who were able to do so left—some crawling, some dragging others, some leaning together for support. They apologized for not being able to help Reeves and the others who couldn't move, and then headed across the fields toward the reservoir.

After a while a group of Chinese walked up to the truck. Shouting and poking the GIs with bayonet points, they motioned for them to get up and go with them. Sleeping bags were unzipped and wounds shown to the Chinese, who didn't want badly wounded prisoners. The Chicoms (Chinese Communists) moved on.

Later a Chinese officer appeared at the tailgate of Reeves's truck. "He was obviously important," Reeves told me, "since he traveled alone without a political watchdog. He wore polished leather boots and a clean, long great-coat and said, with a British accent, 'Good day, gentlemen.' "

The wounded men reminded him of the Geneva Convention rules for POW treatment: shelter, doctors, food. "I am sorry I can give you none of those things," he replied regretfully. "If I am heard talking to you like this I'll be shot. I stopped to say, God bless you, the Lord be with you." He turned and walked away. The other wounded were angry that this Chinese officer had not helped, but Reeves felt that God was assuring him, "You're not alone. I know all about this."

North Korean families of old men, women, and children came past in truck formation. Pausing, they would peer in at the wounded GIs, then bow slightly. "I felt honored that they'd do this right in front of the Chicoms who might chop their heads off." He felt the ache and helplessness of being a POW.

"Needing help and hope, I took out my pocket Bible, turned to the Twenty-third Psalm, and read it aloud." His comrades listened quietly.

"Hey, driver," Reeves called to a badly wounded man up front, "where's that smoke coming from?" A dark cloud was rising above the road. The driver called back that the trucks ahead were being burned with the wounded inside. "I'd expected death many times, but not being burned alive. I prayed that God would take this terrible fear away and let me die like a man. Then I told Jesus I'd see him soon." Amazed at the peace that followed, he sat up and watched, waiting to die and thinking about seeing Jesus.

The gas in Reeves's truck had drained through bullet holes in the back. When three Chinese couldn't set fire to the vehicle, they divided their job. One started shooting the wounded who had rolled under the truck for shelter. Another shot into the truck from the tailgate. The third Chinese climbed up on the side of the truck, leaned over, and started killing the GIs, one shot in each head. He worked toward the front, where Reeves sat. "The man next to me went into eternity and the rifle barrel moved toward me. I said, 'Jesus, here I come.' "

The muzzle blast knocked him flat. Opening his eyes, he looked at the Chicom, amazed that he wasn't dead. You don't miss at four feet! The amazed Chinese looked back, then climbed down from the truck. Once all the Chicoms had left, Reeves slid into his sleeping bag, zipped it up, then checked his head. Only a scalp wound!

"I was the only one in the truck to survive, and I lay among the dead with my eyes shut. When I could hear no enemy I tried to get up off the truck." Each time he'd start to faint, slide back into the sleeping bag, then pass out. He thought, "God, why am I alive when everyone else is dead? If

you want me off this truck, *you* do it. I can't." During the night, Chicoms
would climb into the truck searching for combat boots. Reeves would watch
them feel the GI's feet through the sleeping bags. If they found boots, they
hauled the body out, took the boots, and put them on. "Each time they felt
my feet, I held myself stiff, like a frozen body." They wanted leather combat
boots and he had only shoepacks. They would eventually leave, and he'd try
to get off the truck again. Then pray.

When dawn finally came, the Chinese were moving boldly along the road.
"I knew help must now be far away. I peeked out and watched them loot
GI bodies, then pile them on the road behind the truck." After looting and
stacking the bodies from the truck, they unzipped Reeves's bag. Holding
stiff, he played dead while one searched his pockets. A fist hit his face. The
Chicom had felt the warmth of a live body. They beat him, then threw him
off the truck. "My prayer to God was answered! At last I was on the ground!
But I couldn't stand up, no matter how much the Chinese ordered, kicked,
and hit. Finally two lifted me by the hair and held me against the tailgate
while a third searched my pockets." After pitching him onto the pile of
corpses, they picked up their rifles. "I said, 'Jesus, here I come.' They
pounded my head with rifle butts. I tried to protect my head with my hands,
but my broken fingers hurt too much. A Chinese lifted my head by the hair
and looked into my face. I told myself, 'Don't blink or breathe. Just stare
up the road." The Chinese let go his hair, then left with the other Chicoms
and their loot.

Reeves crawled from the corpse pile to a tree beside the road. Grasping
the tree, he worked himself up to his feet and tried to walk. Three times he
fell flat. Sitting against the tree, looking at the far shore of the reservoir, he
prayed aloud in anger, "Lord, if the mortar didn't kill me, the shooting
didn't kill me, and the beating didn't kill me, you must want me out of
here!" An answer came to mind: "You must crawl before you can walk."

He crept on elbows and wounded knees through snow-covered fields toward the reservoir. Chinese on the hills watched him but didn't shoot or try
to stop him. Why? he wondered. He crossed railroad tracks and more fields.
Smooth hardness under the snow caused him to stop and clear away snow
with an elbow. Thick ice! He was on the reservoir. He began to sing. Over
and over he repeated, "Yes, Jesus loves me!" By now it was dark. He started
crawling across the ice and doggedly kept moving until his strength was
almost gone. His elbows and knees kept slipping out, dropping him to the
ice. Each time it took longer to force his limbs back into position for crawling. Needing rest, he rolled into a ball with his hands under his armpits
inside the open jacket. Just starting to doze, he heard the squeak of feet in

the snow. He rolled to his back to see, forty feet away, a Chinese with a submachine gun moving cautiously toward him. After all the pain and effort to escape, this Chinese would loose one burst and it would all be over. In disgust he threw out his hands and shouted, "AHH, NO!" The startled Chinese turned and ran away. "I watched in amazement until the enemy disappeared into the night. The Chinese had a gun. I had no weapon, yet the Chinese had run. Why?" Wide awake now, he rolled over and crawled on. Cadence-count didn't help keep him moving, so he softly sang songs of boyhood faith over and over. "Yes, Jesus loves me, the Bible tells me so," and "Jesus loves the little children, all the children of the world. Red and yellow, black and white, all are precious in his sight . . ." Another mile of ice was covered.

Overwhelming exhaustion and numbing cold kept him from feeling much pain. He willed his limbs to move. They responded, one limb at a time. He didn't know when dawn came on December 5. He'd covered about three miles and was moving southwest toward the shore when something green moved in the shore's underbrush. He called, "Hey, GI, come here!" A wounded GI came out on the ice and walked to him. As he stood looking down at Reeves, three marine Corsairs made a circling stack above them. The lowest plane dove, flew past them, and fired at the enemy in the rear. "I shouted for the GI to write 'Help' in the snow. The GI started writing by dragging a foot. As the planes zipped past, the GI and I waved to get attention. A plane roared past and turned back." With lowered flaps, the plane circled them just above the ice. The pilot was signaling "O.K." The three planes dropped low to fly a circle of protection.

A little later a marine jeep, driven by PFC Ralph Milton, stopped beside them. He and Lieutenant Colonel Olin Beall surveyed the area, fearing a trap. They knew the Chinese would sometimes shove wounded GIs onto the ice, then wait to ambush the rescuers. Milton eased the jeep up beside the two wounded men. The colonel climbed down and helped the GI into the jeep, then squatted next to Reeves. "Where do you hurt, son?" he asked.

"Please watch the legs, sir."

Beall picked up Reeves and gently placed him in the jeep. His field pants had come undone in the long crawl; the colonel tucked them under Reeves's feet, then took off his own parka and wrapped it around Reeves. As they sat side by side, Reeves looked up at Beall's silver-gray hair. "Colonel, sir," said Reeves, "you sure look like Santa Claus to me."

Soon Reeves was in a C-47. As the plane vibrated in the air, Reeves thought, "He answered. Every time I asked God, He answered." The prayers had not always been answered the way he expected, but they had been answered.

At Yonpo Field he got his first meal in nine days at an aid tent. It was delicious—hot C-ration soup. He was given another shot and put on another plane, which gently rocked him to sleep. He was unconscious as he was loaded onto still another plane and taken to a rear area, where he was eventually aroused by terrible pains in his head and feet. "It hurts! Knock it off!" he yelled at his stretcher bearers. But they trotted on, bouncing him up and down while the front pair of legs banged against his head and the rear pair kept hitting his feet. A sergeant ran up beside them screaming, "Put him down!" They kept trotting, and Reeves kept yelling. The sergeant grabbed one of the bearers, pulled him to a stop, and forced them both to lower the stretcher. The sergeant chewed out the bearers. They weren't impressed until he pulled out his .45 automatic and stuck it under the nose of the lead man. "If I ever see you treat a wounded man like that again," he growled, "I'll blow your brains out!"

At Tokyo General Hospital, whenever he woke up and groaned, he was given another shot. His food trays sat next to his bed untouched. At one point he awoke to hear doctors nearby saying that a Private Reeves was dying. "Don't waste time on him. There are too many others in the room to be treated." Reeves needed to show them he wasn't dying and called the nurse for food. To the amazement of the nurse he ate everything and asked for more. "I was moved to another room and told that if I lived for three more days I'd be put on a plane to the States. I did, and they sent me home."

After the war, he told me, he and his wife (who had seven children with him) served as voluntary missionaries in North, South, and Central America. "We have seen thousands make the decision to receive Christ as Savior. Thousands of believers have dedicated their feet to Christ's service and Christ declares these feet beautiful—Romans 10:15–16."

{11}

Captives and Heroes

During March and April of 1951, Ridgway's troops pushed back the Chinese, and the situation grew so critical that Mao's troops surrendered in unprecedented numbers. And by May 26, a Communist party committee of one division conceded that there was only one thing to do—disperse the division and try to get back across the Yalu River. Near the end of May, Mao ordered the troops to turn the war into one of sheer endurance, forcing the Americans to join in positional warfare in which bloody fights were waged with little exchange of land, as in World War I. So began the long rocky road—not to end until August 1953—to an uneasy peace. Many of the men who had endured the huge losses and gains of territory in the past see-saw year were gone. Those like Taplett and Mike Lynch, who had fought so desperately in the Pusan Perimeter, on the drive north, and in the desperate days of winter, were no longer present.

Meanwhile an even more bitter war was raging in the prison camps. Many of those in the UN prison camps attacked their guards and took possession of their quarters. Such revolts would have been simply wiped out in the North Korean and Chinese prisons, although a few hardy souls did attempt to escape. In my book I told the story of a former helicopter pilot, Chief Petty Officer Duane Thorin. In a North Korean camp not far from the Yalu River, he decided he would take a partner and selected a rugged private, John Shaw, a truck driver. Shaw had picked up some Korean and was in good physical condition. He, in turn, insisted on taking along another private. Thorin did not have a compass but could use the north star to guide them.

In pitch darkness, Thorin and his companions began their arduous march to the Yalu. Discovered by a Korean woman, they were captured and brought back to camp.

Thorin endured unspeakably brutal treatment and pressure to "confess" for month after month but never broke, for he knew that the North Koreans were using prisoners as pawns in propaganda games. Some were finally pressured to write confessions of things they never did. When an uneasy truce finally came in August 1953, Thorin was in the last car of a train carrying UN POWs for exchange.

Thorin wrote a book about his experiences. He insisted that I tell in detail about the courageous fliers who had refused to confess they had dropped germ bombs. No prisoner had shown more obstinacy than Captain Theodore Harris, the pilot of a B-29. His steadfast refusal to cooperate for more than ten months had led to frequent beatings—which only made Harris more stubborn. He was finally put before a firing squad and offered a blindfold, which he refused. "This," he was told, "is only a sample of what you can expect if you don't confess."

In late January 1953 he was blindfolded, shoved into a truck, and taken to Mukden, China. But the Chinese were no more successful than the North Koreans. Harris would endure mental and physical torture that was as horrific as American POWs experienced in Vietnam. He was threatened with death on countless occasions and finally told he had been found guilty as a war criminal and would be punished. Finally, on September 1, four days before the cease-fire, Harris—who was temporarily paralyzed from the waist down—was transferred to a train, where, for the first time, he met his five crewmen. They were all taken to a tent in Kaesong. A document was read in Korean and then in English stating that Harris and his B-29 crew admitted their guilt in waging biological warfare. He refused to be repatriated until the Communists gave him a copy of the document in English showing that the paragraph in which he admitted that other USAF units had waged germ warfare was stricken. It took half a dozen soldiers to cart him off to Freedom Village, handcuffed but still protesting—one of the last American prisoners to find freedom, and one the Communists must have been extremely relieved to get rid of.

The war that was not a war but—in President Truman's words—a "police action" was over, and a peace that was not a peace finally descended on Korea. The war ended in almost the same place it had started, at the cost of more than two million Korean civilians, and another two million Chinese, North Korean, South Korean, and American and other United Nations soldiers killed in battle.

Death March

I knew that noncombatants had been caught up in the war, so in my research trip to South Korea, Mickey Michelony and I constantly looked for such people. One of the most memorable was an Australian priest, Father Philip Crosbie, who had been captured near the 38th parallel. He was among the eighty-seven civilians of various nationalities imprisoned near the Yalu River. These included an Englishman, Herbert Lord, lieutenant commissioner of the Salvation Army; three men from the British legation in Seoul; a dozen captured Tatar businessmen and their families; many Roman Catholic sisters and priests, headed by Bishop Patrick Byrne; and six men and women from the Methodist Mission in Kaesong. In late October 1950 they were marched through rain for three days. "You are now under strict military discipline," they were then told by a North Korean major. "We are going to march to Chunggang-jin." This was more than a hundred miles distant.

For the story of this incredible journey in that bitterly cold November I interviewed more than a dozen civilians and GIs in 1987 and 1988. As they moved eastward, Father Crosbie saw a large group of American military prisoners lining up in preparation for joining the march. The civilians fell in behind the POWs, and they were told they had to march sixteen miles the first day. The grueling pace was hard on everyone, particularly the emaciated young soldiers, who kept falling out from exhaustion, only to be rousted and pushed forward.

As the march ground on, military prisoners who faltered or fell behind were shot out of hand—or their officers were held responsible for allowing dying men to lag behind and be shot. Mother Béatrix, a seventy-six-year-old nun who, with her companion Mother Eugénie, had spent fifty years caring for the poor and orphans of Korea, was shot and her body casually rolled down the steep slope of a hill. As they went beyond the boundaries of endurance, they still tried to help each other—Salvation Army Commissioner Lord literally towing a Russian widow, Madame Funderat, with a rope, the younger priests supporting the eighty-two-year-old Father Villemot. The North Korean major in charge, known to his captives as "the Tiger," was unpredictable—sometimes giving prisoners a brief ride on a passing vehicle.

Then came the snow and with it the deliberate executions of the POWs. All of the clergymen attempted to give what spiritual comfort they could to the men—now feeble, tottering skeletons—knowing that the murders would continue and that they were helpless to prevent them. Father Crosbie said, "If there had been any hint of humanity the day before, it came to end that horrifying day, November 4, 1950." During that ghastly morning, twenty-one POWs were murdered, and Crosbie realized for the first time what had happened to Mother Béatrix and the eighteen soldiers who had fallen out the day before.

The march finally ended on November 8 at the town of Chunggang-jin. The prisoners, including the exhausted Mother Eugénie, had completed a journey of more than a hundred miles over rugged terrain in the bitter cold and snow, leaving almost a hundred dead along the way. The long trek now had a name: the Death March.

I have kept in touch with Father Crosbie, who is still at his lonesome parish near the border of North Korea. I can still see him and his fellows on the gruelling march—helping others as I hope I would have done if I had been there.

{12}

Journey's End

Inside Communist China

When we left Taiwan in November 1987, we were still hoping to get permission to do research in China, though we knew North Korea was closed to us. But the government officials, although polite, remained vague. Apparently no one wanted to take the responsibility for turning us loose among the veterans of the war.

Finally, in the spring of 1989, our friend Professor Hua Qingzhao persuaded China's World History Institute to invite me to Beijing as guest lecturer in history. We were in the midst of sending Tamiko off to Leningrad, where she would study for a semester, but were able to leave on April 27, 1989, for what I hoped would be the wind-up of my book. I had to hear the Chinese side of the war.

We found Hua and his assistant in a state of excitement. Something unheard-of was going on not only in Beijing but in the other large cities. The young people in the universities, led by the graduate students, were vocally attacking the corruption in high places. Surprisingly, ordinary citizens were backing their demands for action. There was even talk of holding a mass protest in Tiananmen Square.

I realized that we couldn't have arrived at a more opportune moment. It was like my initial exploration of Japan—the time was ripe. After my first lecture at the World History Institute, a young officer offered to give us information if we didn't use his name. The next morning he talked at length about Mao's tactics in the war and how he had taken charge personally, going over the heads of the general staff. It was an intriguing interview but of little use without documentary backup. We took a break for lunch and, while driving up a narrow street, were suddenly engulfed by a seemingly endless crowd of cheering students. They had just held their first mass meeting in Tiananmen Square, and when they saw Toshiko taking pictures they cheered and waved at us.

Our interviewee was overwhelmed. It was a miracle. The students were actually doing what they promised to do. He was so excited that he promised to bring his superior, Colonel Yao Xu, who during the war had been deputy chief secretary of the Political Department, Chinese Volunteers. Commissar Yao had worked closely with Chairman Mao on tactical matters.

The next morning appeared a huge officer dressed in the old traditional black garb. Colonel Yao had read *The Rising Sun* and was soon pouring out what I had been looking for, and he promised to provide documents. In late August 1950, after studying disturbing intelligence reports, Mao had made an intense study of the unusual movements and operations for some sort of U.S. Marine offense in the Pusan Perimeter. After mulling over the situation with his young assistants and reexamining MacArthur's past victories, Mao and Chou En-lai concluded that it would be an amphibious landing. Logic dictated that it would come on the west coast at one of five possible ports. Inchon, he decided, had to be the target, since it was closest to Seoul, the heart of Korea. And because of the exceptional tides and weather, the most likely date for the "surprise" assault would be September 15.

The prediction was passed on to Kim Il-sung, premier of North Korea, and several days later, North Korean intelligence agreed with Mao. Any doubt had ended after the September 10 napalm attack on Wolmi-do, the island just off the coast near Inchon, by marine planes. Aware that MacArthur was about to land, Kim Il-sung composed a message to his troops: "Protect and defend all liberated areas! Defend with your blood and life every mountain and every river!" In fact, however, no enemy artillery blasted the American fleet, and the marines did not encounter stiff resistance along the beaches. Twenty-one marines were killed and 179 wounded, including Gene Jones, a cameraman for NBC-TV, who had told me of the numerous escapes he and his twin brother, Charlie, had made during the war.

The token resistance at Inchon came because Kim, ignoring advice from his subordinates, had insisted on using his troops to launch, on September 1, an all-out assault on the Pusan Perimeter in the south, expecting to destroy Walker's Eighth Army, end the war, and receive worldwide acclaim as a military leader. Because of exhausted troops, lack of ammunition and fuel, and UN air attacks that wrecked road and rail communications, Kim's ambitious operation was a miserable failure.

Commissar Yao confirmed his subordinate's story about Mao running the war from a little house just outside the Forbidden City walls. Here he lived with his wife, and every day two young officers he trusted would help him work out the day-by-day strategy and then send orders directly to Peng Teh-huai, commander of the Chinese Volunteers, who became his strategic partner throughout the war.

The next day we learned that the students were still at Tiananmen Square and, to everyone's surprise, men had walked out carrying a huge banner stating that the Chinese Communist press backed the students. With every day, public support grew in Beijing, Shanghai, and the large cities.

When I lectured at the Academy of Military Science in 1989 I sat next to the director, Major General Wang Daopang, and I wondered what his reaction would be when the interpreter announced that my topic was "Non-ideological History." After about an hour I stopped for questions. The queries were always to the point, and I was surprised my audience knew so much about my books. Later, the general nudged me. "We've all read your books, and we think nonideological history is what we should have in the People's Republic."

When I asked if we could have our picture taken with him, he was as affable as Commissar Yao had been. While Toshiko was readying her camera outside the headquarters building, he suggested we walk over to the gate which identified this place as the Academy of Military Science, People's Liberation Army. He suggested that Toshiko be in the picture. I stood between the general and Toshiko, clutching the plastic shopping bag containing my materials. Later he assured us we could get copies of official military reports on the Korean War.

By now enthusiasm for the students had spread to the military, and there were many TV shots of the older students lecturing young soldiers and giving them candy bars. According to our friends, all was peaceful despite pleas to the students, from international TV people, for "action."

Although I had been warned that the Chinese would never let me interview former POWs who had been lured back to the homeland only to be imprisoned, we found officials in Beijing very helpful. These men now felt free to talk openly of how they had been taken to a concentration camp in Manchuria for "reeducation," on the premise that anyone who had dealt with the West—even in prison—could not be trusted. After several years, these men, who had fought so doggedly not only in the battlefield but in the Allied prison camps, were sent home, where they were shunned by their own families as traitors. They returned to their places of work only to be given minor jobs. Zhang Zeshi, a former high school principal, was demoted to teacher. "Almost every day I had to stand on a table and confess my sins." After a year of this, he was demoted further, to janitor. "I complained," said Zhang, now the successful proprietor of a restaurant, "and was sentenced to ten years in prison."

Another POW, Ding Shang-wing, revealed that when he got home his wife was forced to divorce him. One daughter died for lack of medical treatment, and the other was so scorned as "a traitor's daughter" that she disappeared. "I was imprisoned several times for a total of twelve years," Ding revealed, "and wasn't released until 1983."

We also learned that Peng, the commander of the Chinese Volunteers, who had fought so loyally for Mao in the Korean War, was ousted from his post as defense minister in 1959 and a decade later was tortured to death during the Cultural Revolution. The officer who provided this information told me that "if these true believers had been discredited and punished, one can imagine what would have happened to former Kuomintang soldiers who had been assured in one of the 'Explainer' tents that they would be treated well in the People's Republic of China!"

Shanghai

In early May of 1989 we left for Shanghai, where I gave another lecture on nonideological history to university students. Then we took the new material I had received from the military and headed inland to the pleasant city of Yangzau, where Marco Polo served as governor. Here we met Hua, who had rented a minivan and took us on trips inland, but we spent most of our time studying the new material and deciding which pages should be translated.

When we returned by rail to Shanghai a week later we learned that the city was in turmoil. Students had taken over the central city, and only one taxi driver was willing to take us from the railroad station across the river to our hotel. About a mile from our destination we were stopped by students. They were polite but insisted we walk the rest of the way, and several helped carry our luggage. That night the continuous roar outside reminded me of the rowdy night football rallies of a large Midwestern university. The next day Gorbachev was due to arrive from Beijing. We were warned to get up early so we could get through the lines and reach the airport on time. As I was waiting next morning in the lobby I could hear an officious U.S. Navy officer giving instructions to correspondents on Gorbachev's trip to the Navy that afternoon. I later learned he had canceled the navy trip and headed back to Moscow.

The airport was jammed with foreigners trying to get out of China. Our plane was delayed for an hour or so. Loaded as I was with tapes and papers, I prayed we could get out before they were confiscated. Things had heated up at Beijing. By now international TV was helping turn the student protest against official corruption into a circus, but there was as yet no violence.

When we finally took off I felt relieved, and after a week of research and shows in Tokyo we left for home, arriving in Danbury on May 22, 1989. By telephone we kept in touch with Hua, and he told us that the military force at Tiananmen Square had been replaced by units far from Beijing that had never seen the capital. He feared something might spark real trouble. Some dissidents not connected with the students had damaged railroad property, but the students were being blamed. Finally came the incident of a young man single-handedly stopping a tank. Our friends in Beijing felt sure this had been inspired by TV.

A few days later, on June 3, I wrote in my calendar book, "Bad end in Beijing." We called Hua over and over, but kept getting a busy signal. We were finally told that the lines to China were out, but five days later we got through and learned that all of our friends were safe.

Curious Days on the Publishing Scene

On November 30, 1989, I finished the first draft of *In Mortal Combat,* and in mid-December I took the second half of my manuscript to Doubleday. By now the company was owned by a German company, Bertelsmann, and most of those I had worked with had gone. Carolyn Blakemore had left and was already doing well on her own. About the only friendly face was that of Ken McCormick. The new editor, Herman Gollob, a man with an imposing record, talked with me only briefly, but when I got home I wrote in my calendar book: "Curious. Curious." On January 26, 1990, Carl Brandt informed me that Doubleday had turned down the book. It wasn't like other histories of the Korean War. Five days later we received offers from Morrow and Harper. We settled on Morrow. My new editor, Harvey Ginsberg, called. He was enthusiastic and only asked that I cut the manuscript to 225,000 words. I said that was no problem, since I always cut my final version. A month later I met Mr. Ginsberg and confided to my calendar book: "Very good! No problems!"

Carolyn edited the book and Carl made his usual excellent suggestions. The prepublication review from *Publishers Weekly* was encouraging. "In a book full of impressive features, the most noteworthy is this: Toland has gathered previously inaccessible material enabling him to describe Mao Zedong's direct role in the war as well as that of his field commander, Peng Teh-huai. The 'forgotten war,' in which four million people perished, has never before been described more interestingly."

A week later a friend from the *New York Times,* William Honan, called to tell me that we had a full-page "rave" in the Sunday edition. "Unlike so much on Korean history, his narrative is not only well informed but free of partisan baggage. Great struggles raise both practical and moral issues. 'Was the Korean War worth waging?' Mr. Toland asks. His response is worth repeating. 'It was a war of cruelty, stupidity, error, misjudgment, racism, prejudice, and atrocities on both sides. . . . Yet recent events in both Asia and Europe call a negative view of the Korean War into question. The forgotten war may eventually turn out to have been the decisive conflict that started the collapse of communism. In any case, those who fought and died in that war did not fight and die in vain.' "

The *Washington Post,* which had predicted my demise after *Infamy,* both chided and praised me. "At times, his exhaustively detailed accounts of battlefield tactics will try the patience of all but the most devoted military buffs. But at its least, as in the chapter on Douglas MacArthur's '5,000-to-1 gamble' in the amphibious landing at Inchon, Toland's writing conveys the tensions, terror and confusion of a long, bloody struggle. . . ."

Several reviewers spoke patronizingly of the book as mere "popular history," and others, like Robert Elegant in the *National Review,* had mixed feelings. "*In Mortal Combat* is a triumphant vindication of the often derided technique of re-creating history by the paper-and-ink of brief film clips with voice-overs by hundreds of participants in a great event." But he was irritated by what he regarded as my obsessive dislike for MacArthur, "who is attacked not only for his political and intelligence failures, but for his strategic triumphs. Nonetheless," he concludes, "this is a memorable achievement."

But my favorite comments were made by my former editor at Doubleday:

> Crow isn't the most popular dish in our company cafeteria, and hell, it ain't even kosher. But what the devil, I'll take a great big bite anyway and say, Congratulations on that rave in the *TBR.* You and Carl and Carolyn must have worked your asses off on the re-write, and I salute your professionalism.
> As Harold Ross once said, Goddamit, God bless you.
> Best, Herman

Looking Back

I once ran across an entry on my writing career in *Contemporary Authors,* Vol. 6, which presented a revealing summary of critics' evaluations of my work in a section called "Sidelights." The opening paragraph of this entry defines the kind of history I have endeavored to write: "For each of his books, Toland interviews the actual participants in an historic event, sometimes several hundred of them, in order to get all sides of a story from those people who know it best. He relates these interviews as objectively as possible. 'I believe it's my duty,' he says, 'to tell you everything and let you draw your own conclusions. I keep my opinions to a minimum.' "

I have never been upset by negative criticism, though I remember how much it pained Trollope toward the end of his career and how it forced Hardy to abandon fiction and turn to poetry after the hostile reception of *Jude the Obscure.*

In my naiveté I had poured out *Infamy,* expecting that my friends in Washington and in academia would welcome my revelations, and it almost overwhelmed me to receive letters from good friends proclaiming that I had made a terrible mistake. *Infamy* had destructive physical and emotional impacts on me, but now I am glad that I bearded the tiger (or whatever one beards). In all my books I tried to tell what I thought to be the truth, no matter whom it aroused. I remembered those great lines from St. Jerome: "If an offense come out of the truth, better it is that the offense come than that the truth be concealed." I would like those lines engraved on my gravestone.

I had been asked to write a history of the Vietnam War but refused. To me it was not a war but a tragic mess for all concerned. I had no stomach for it. Instead I began this autobiography, which I had always imagined would be my final work.

I started writing the first eight chapters of "Growing Pains" in the third person, striving to distance myself from my own experience. But something kept digging at me to do another "living history" on the last days of the war with Japan, based on new material. But I was not young enough for the rigorous research needed and instead began working on Hitler's private life, buttressed by new material I had unearthed. After finishing the first draft, however, I learned there would be difficulties with Doubleday, since it was bringing out a new quality paperback edition of my *Adolf Hitler.*

So I returned to the autobiography, changing to a first-person narrative, and after having brought it to the present I realized that I had not tried to explain why I had spent almost thirty-five years of my life writing about war. Why had I so enthusiastically accepted the U.S. Army's suggestion that I write about the Battle of the Bulge? And why had I become so engrossed with telling the story on all levels and from all sides?

Had I been engrossed in battle stories because of the action I had personally missed? My most dangerous moment during World War II was the day a B-24 bomber roared past our office in New York and smashed into the

Empire State Building, and I suspect that I was drawn to this subject because of a secret shame that I had not served at the front.

I now believe that the main reason I wrote about war was that basically I hate it. In my books the enemy is war, not those we fought. After all these years I finally realize that this hatred of war started when I was at the Jefferson Elementary School and heard one of the great heroes of World War I speak about his company, which had been surrounded by the Germans but held out against tremendous odds. Instead of talking about heroics he began telling us about all those who had died—of those who had dropped at his feet calling for Mama and home. To our great embarrassment, he began to weep and had to be led away. Everyone was disappointed and some thought he was a weakling. A few days later we learned he had committed suicide. (See *No Man's Land* for the story of his part in World War I.)

At the time I was an avid reader of *Wings* and the never-ending tales of courage in the air. But never a tear. I did keep reading *Wings* and was thrilled to meet an ace; but later I read *All Quiet on the Western Front* and, like so many of my contemporaries, I saw the horror of war. Forgotten were the heroes of the Boy Allies series and *Wings.* This was real life, and though I was not at all political, I became permanently inoculated with peace. When I became a Communist I chose to join the American Peace Mobilization. I picketed for peace in front of the White House. And yet, like so many of my comrades in APM, I tried to enlist the day after Pearl Harbor. Later I opposed the Korean War and publicly decried the Vietnam and Gulf wars.

When I made my instant decision to write about the Battle of the Bulge, I now believe I was primarily drawn to this subject by my yearning for enduring, universal peace. I believe that is why, in my books, I have made war the enemy, not its participants. And perhaps that is why I have been able to put myself in the skin of a German or a Japanese as easily as that of an American or one of our allies. I have shown heroism and cowardice on both sides. I hope I have followed Porter Emerson Browne's advice to let my characters do what they had to do and say what they had to say.

What I wanted to show was the insanity of war. I leave that to younger historians.

It took many years to get where I am, but I was always a slow learner. Yet every work I wrote—including plays, short stories, and novels—had been my university. As Toshiko told me, "They were steps to success." At Williams I never took a course in history and so had to write a history of a kind which I labeled "living history." Soon I was winning prizes and then the ultimate Pulitzer for *The Rising Sun.*

The Boy Scout of twelve who told an endless story to other Boy Scouts confined to a tent by pouring rain was already on his way. Porter Emerson Browne warned me that I had to write at least a million words before I sold one. But he must have seen the zeal and determination burning in me that was even more important than talent. I hope my long journey to success will encourage other young writers to persevere, no matter what.

Index

Index

Index

Index

Index

Index

Index

Index